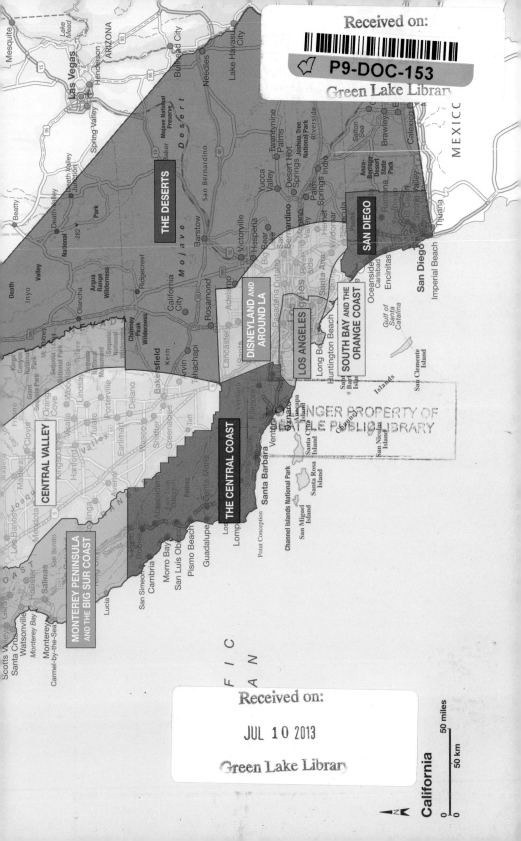

THE DESERTS

SAN DIEGO

DISNEYLAND AND AROUND LA

LOS ANGELES

SOUTH BAY AND THE ORANGE COAST

CENTRAL VALLEY

THE CENTRAL COAST

MONTEREY PENINSULA AND THE BIG SUR COAST

MEXICO

California

50 miles

50 km

INSIGHT GUIDES
CALIFORNIA

APA PUBLICATIONS **L**

Part of the Langenscheidt Publishing Group

The first Insight Guide pioneered the use of creative full-color photography in travel guides in 1970. Since then, we have expanded our range to cater for our readers' need not only for reliable information about their chosen destination but also for a real understanding of the culture and workings of that destination.

Now, when the internet can supply inexhaustible (but not always reliable) facts, our books marry text and pictures to provide those much more elusive qualities: knowledge and discernment. To achieve this, they rely heavily on the authority of locally based writers and photographers.

How to use this book

Insight Guides have been structured to convey an understanding of a region and its culture, and to guide readers through its best sights and activities:

The **Best of California** section at the front of the guide helps you to prioritize what you want to do.

The **Features** section, indicated by a yellow bar at the top of each page, covers the natural and cultural history of California and includes illuminating essays on California cuisine, the fabulous wines, the movie industry, and all the many sporting and outdoor activities you can get up to.

The main **Places** section, indicated by a blue bar, is broken down into Northern and Southern California and forms a complete guide to all the sights and areas worth visiting. Places of special interest are coordinated by number with the maps.

The **Travel Tips** listings section provides full information on transportation, accommodations, eating out, activities, and an A–Z section of essential practical information.

The photographs are chosen not only to illustrate the beauty and glamour of California, but also to convey its cultural diversity. Visitors instinctively understand the word "Eureka," California's state motto, when they first discover this rich region. The word means: "I have found it" in Greek. With its mountains, redwood forests, beaches, cosmopolitan cities, and varied lifestyles, California is one of the world's most exciting travel destinations.

The contributors

This, the eighth edition of Insight Guide California, was commissioned by **Sian Lezard** and edited by **Naomi Peck**. It builds on the work of American-born commissioning editor **Martha Ellen Zenfell**.

The guide was updated by **Barbara Rockwell**, a writer, editor, and life-long California resident. From backpacking in Yosemite's high country and houseboating on Lake Shasta to discovering hidden staircases in San Francisco and little-known wines in Napa, she never tires of getting to know the state better. She regularly contributes to California guidebooks and is the author of *San Francisco Step by Step*.

The photos were taken by **David Dunai**. **John King** proofread the book, and it was indexed by **Penny Phenix**.

Contents

THE BEST OF CALIFORNIA: TOP ATTRACTIONS

From sun-kissed beaches and ancient redwoods to iconic Hollywood sights and the splendid Golden Gate Bridge, here is a rundown of California's top ten attractions.

△ **Yosemite National Park.** From the sheer granite cliffs of El Capitan to waterfalls and green meadows, the crown jewel of America's national parks is heaven for adventurous types. See page 209.

△ **Redwood Forests.** Awe-inspiring ancient redwoods tower over visitors in old-growth state parks. Some of these majestic giants, 1,000 years old and reaching 300ft (90 meters), are the largest living things on earth. See page 185.

◁ **Golden Gate Bridge.** San Francisco's famous bridge opened in 1937, four years after construction began. Painted not gold but "international orange," the bridge is one of the world's favorite icons. See page 126.

▽ **Wine Country.** The emerald vineyards, lush red wines, warm sunshine, and fresh California cuisine of Napa and Sonoma counties make them ideal for a road trip. Or for the best views, take a hot-air balloon ride. See pages 153 and 157.

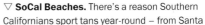

△ **California Cuisine.** Alice Waters changed the restaurant industry forever when she got local farmers to supply her with the freshest seasonal ingredients for her daily changing menus. See page 73.

◁ **Monterey.** Coastal Monterey offers something for everyone: Steinbeck's Cannery Row, the Monterey Bay Aquarium (arguably the world's finest), plus diving in kelp forests and swimming with sea otters. See page 166.

△ **Hollywood.** Synonymous with the movie industry, Hollywood today pays homage to its cinematic history with attractions like the Hollywood Walk of Fame and opulent old movie houses. See page 253.

△ **Death Valley.** The lowest point on the North American continent, Death Valley can be insanely hot in summer, but is awash with colorful desert wildflowers and cactus blooms in spring. See page 309.

▽ **SoCal Beaches.** There's a reason Southern Californians sport tans year-round – from Santa Barbara to Santa Monica, and Huntington Beach to San Diego, the state's southern coast is packed with miles of sunny beaches. See page 264.

△ **PCH.** In the Los Angeles area, Highway 1 is also known as the Pacific Coast Highway, or the PCH. The road twists and turns along SoCal's breathtaking coast, offering gorgeous views of both land and sea. See page 287.

THE BEST OF CALIFORNIA: EDITOR'S CHOICE

Spectacular scenery, wine tours, architectural landmarks, kid-friendly activities, and unique experiences... here, at a glance, are our top recommendations for making the most of your visit.

The notorious Alcatraz.

ONLY IN CALIFORNIA

Alcatraz. Haunting yet fascinating, "the Rock" is a former high-security prison on an island in the San Francisco Bay that once housed some of America's most notorious criminals. See page 115.
Cable cars. Wonderfully old-fashioned cable cars creakily lumber up and roll down San Francisco's hills, ringing their bells as passengers hang out the sides. See page 119.
Grauman's Chinese Theatre. This 1920s-era LA movie palace in Hollywood has a forecourt of illustrious hand and footprints. See page 253.
La Brea Tar Pits. One of the world's most famous fossil locations, these bubbling pools of asphalt have

been revealing prehistoric remains since the 1900s. See page 258.
Santa Catalina Island. With two-thirds of its interior protected land, beautiful Catalina is calm, practically car free, and ideal for a day trip. See page 289.
Hollywood Walk of Fame. One of Los Angeles' most famous attractions, where over 2,400 star-shaped plaques are emblazoned with celebrities' names. See page 254.
Zazzle Bay to Breakers. A crazy annual footrace involving thousands of people in outrageous costumes – or nothing at all – filling the streets of San Francisco. See page 359.

Exhibit in San Jose Museum of Art.

Getty Center. This stunning LA cliff-top complex combines art, architecture, and delightful gardens, all of which you can explore for free. See page 268.
Hollywood Bowl. Instantly recognizable by its dome shape, this classic performance amphitheatre in Los Angeles attracts music lovers who come to hear classical music and jazz concerts. See page 254.
San Diego Museum of Contemporary Art. A world-class modern art museum in two locations, one in downtown San Diego, and the other in a fabulous ocean-front setting in La Jolla. See page 319.
San Jose Museum of Art. Nearly 1,500 works of art are housed here, including glittering blown-glass sculptures by Dale Chihuly. See page 148.
SF MoMA. Housing Northern California's premier art collection, the distinctive San Francisco Museum of Modern Art was designed by Swiss architect Mario Botta and features a five-story glass

roofed staircase. See page 121.
Civic Center. San Francisco's Asian Art Museum, Main Library, War Memorial Opera House, and Davies Symphony Hall are all clustered together near City Hall. See page 123.

The Getty Villa in Malibu.

Cable car in San Francisco.

Lake Tahoe and the Sierra Nevada.

BEST FOR KIDS

Disneyland. Mickey Mouse isn't the only attraction: families flock here for Space Mountain, the Fantasmic! fireworks show, and the rides at California Adventure. See page 280.

Universal Studios. Attractions based on Back to the Future, Jurassic Park, and Shrek are winners for kids – and adults too. See page 276.

San Diego Zoo. Looking for giant pandas? Visit lush Balboa Park for one of the world's most impressive zoos, with a more natural setting that uses moats instead of cages. See page 321.

SeaWorld. Watch irresistible dolphins, "killer" whales, sea lions, and a vast array of fish, then hit the rides at this over-the-top San Diego water park. See page 318.

Pier 39 Fisherman's Wharf's. Pier 39 has an aquarium, street performers, sea lions, and a wax museum. Ice cream sundaes at Ghirardelli Square aren't far away. See page 114.

Monterey Bay Aquarium. Don't miss feeding time at this spectacular seaside sanctuary with over 350,000 specimens. See page 167.

Knott's Berry Farm. America's first theme park delights with gunfights, Camp Snoopy musicals, and fried chicken dinners. See page 283.

Calico Ghost Town. Not far from the Mojave Desert, an 1880s silver-mining town is now a theme park. See page 306.

Exploratorium. Kids and science come together for a day of fun in San Francisco's Palace of Fine Arts, with hands-on exhibits involving light, color, sounds, and other sensory thrills. See page 126.

MOST SPECTACULAR SCENERY

Avenue of the Giants. Surrounded by Humboldt Redwoods State Park, this 31-mile (50km) stretch of highway offers a jaw-dropping display of giant redwoods. See page 184.

Big Sur. Hugging the rugged coast in a series of switchbacks, Highway 1 south of San Francisco through the Monterey Peninsula to Big Sur may be the most spectacular route in America. See page 171.

Lake Tahoe. The sparkling blue lake is stunning in summer as well as winter, when skiers come to tackle surrounding mountains. Nearby is Devils Postpile National Monument, the gigantic, geometrically fractured core of an ancient volcano. See page 207.

Joshua Tree National Park. Joshua Tree is a strange, other-worldly place, with huge sandstone boulders the color of sunsets and rust, interspersed with oddly shaped and often very old Joshua and yucca trees. See page 302.

Yosemite Valley. Look in awe upon the giant Half Dome, sheer-faced El Capitan, and gushing waterfalls. It's not surprising that millions visit each year. See page 209.

The High North. A remote and stunning domain of mountains, valleys, volcanoes, rivers, canyons, and basins. See page 221.

Theme park ride at Knott's Berry Farm.

Stinson Beach in Marin County.

BEST BEACHES

Huntington Beach. Ever wonder where "Surf City USA" is? You just found it. See page 291.

Cabrillo Beach. Cabrillo has windsurfing, scuba diving, whale watching, a good aquarium, and views of Santa Catalina Island. See page 288.

Malibu's Zuma and Surfrider beaches. Popular with surfers, sunbathers, and bird-watchers, Malibu's beaches have wetlands, flower gardens, tide pools, and terrific bird-watching perches. You can spot celeb houses too. See page 263.

Venice Beach. There's terrific people-watching

potential here, from hippie artists to muscle-bound men. See page 266.

Santa Cruz. This stylish town has three beaches: Main Beach has the boardwalk, Cowell Beach is for learner surfers, and Steamer Lane is for experts and their boards. See page 165.

Santa Monica Beach. The soft white sand flanking Santa Monica Pier is a wonderful place to enjoy Pacific sunsets. See page 264.

Stinson Beach. Despite the chilly water, Stinson is the most popular beach in the San Francisco Bay Area. See page 142.

Ferris wheel on Santa Monica Pier.

Walt Disney Concert Hall.

ARCHITECTURAL HIGHLIGHTS

Academy of Sciences. The award-winning Renzo Piano-designed eco-house in San Francisco's Golden Gate Park has a living roof. See page 130.

Balboa Park. Ornate Spanish Colonial Revival-style buildings fill San Diego's museum-filled park. See page 320.

California State Capitol Building. The state's capitol building (gorgeous from the inside too) has dominated the Sacramento cityscape since 1869. See page 193.

Hearst Castle. This castle in the sky was built by William Randolph Hearst, the media magnate who was the subject of Orson Welles's *Citizen Kane*. See page 176.

Mission Dolores. The only mission chapel that is still intact, Mission Dolores is also the oldest building in San Francisco. Immortalized in Hitchcock's *Vertigo*, a

serene cemetery holds the remains of some of the city's first leaders. See page 127.

Painted ladies. These tall, stately Victorian homes can be found all over San Francisco, but some of most vibrant and colorful border Alamo Square. See page 129.

Transamerica Pyramid. Likened to an upside-down ice-cream cone, the 48-floor building built in 1970 by William L. Pereira is now one of San Francisco's favorite icons. See page 121.

Walt Disney Concert Hall. The home of the LA Philharmonic is a gleaming modern design by noted architect Frank Gehry. See page 251.

Winchester Mystery House. Full of staircases that lead nowhere and doors that open into walls, this is a building like no other. See page 148.

OUTDOOR FUN

Diving in Monterey. Explore thick kelp forests in Monterey Bay, a popular place to get scuba certified in Northern California. See page 91.

Hiking Half Dome. Brave souls make the steep climb up Half Dome (the last part with cables to hold onto) for magnificent Yosemite views. Make reservations in advance. See page 210.

Hiking in Muir Woods. San Francisco in the morning; redwoods in the afternoon. Take a stroll under grand trees and stop at the Pelican Inn at Muir Beach for a spot of tea or a cold mug of mead. See page 141.

River rafting. Complete beginners take float trips through Coloma Valley, while experienced rafters can tackle Class IV rapids south of Sacramento. See page 367.

Winter weekends in Lake Tahoe. Hit the slopes for skiing or snowboarding, cross-country skiing or snowshoeing, in the lovely setting of the Sierra Nevada mountain range. See page 96.

Bumpass Hell in Mount Lassen Volcanic National Park.

ICONIC HOTELS

Mission Inn Hotel and Spa. Utterly breathtaking architecture – from intricate spiral staircases to flower-topped balconies – and grand vistas make this riverside hotel one of the most beautiful in the state. See page 346.

The Ahwahnee Hotel. The grande dame of Yosemite's hotels, this elegant historic lodge built in the 1920s is the most luxurious way to enjoy Yosemite Valley. See page 343.

Hotel del Coronado. Built in 1888, the Coronado's red turrets and Victorian style make it unmissable on the San Diego beachfront. It's unforgettable, too. See page 347.

The Beverly Hills Hotel. Affectionately known as the "Pink Palace," this old celeb haunt has counted John F. Kennedy, Elizabeth Taylor and Richard Burton, Charlie Chaplin, Spencer Tracy, Marilyn Monroe, John Wayne, and the Duke of Windsor among its guests. See page 260.

The Palace Hotel. A fine tea or lunch in San Francisco's first hotel is an utterly opulent reminder of the city's past. See page 340.

Madonna Inn. With imaginative interiors and bizarre themed rooms, this landmark hotel is pure kitsch to some, and a creative wonder to others. See page 344.

WINE COUNTRY HIGHLIGHTS

Calistoga spas. With thermal hot springs feeding warm pools, and volcanic mud treatments. See page 157.

Hot-air ballooning. Get a bird's eye view of this pretty region. See page 157.

Dining with a view. Auberge du Soleil's terrace is one of the prettiest outdoor dining spots in the Wine Country. See page 351.

Napa Valley Wine Train. Take a tour of Napa Valley in lavishly restored 1915 Pullman dining and lounge cars. See page 155.

Oxbow Public Market. Taste everything from oysters to organic ice cream. See page 155.

Relaxed wine tasting. Follow a picnic lunch at Martini's with tastings at Paraduxx or Frog's Leap. See pages 156 and 155.

MONEY-SAVING TIPS

National Parks Pass Frequent visitors to California's national parks should buy an "America the Beautiful" pass ($80) which covers entrance fees for the holder, a vehicle, plus any passengers at more than 2,000 federal recreation sites in the country. www.nps.gov/findapark/passes.htm

Passes CityPass offers visitor cards for San Francisco or Southern California that provide discounts to major attractions, and cut down on waiting in lines. Go to CityPass.com. Alternatively, try the Go Cards (www.smart destinations.com), which offer access to a long list of key attractions. Or you can customize your pass based on a more limited set of sites you plan to visit.

Groupon If you're planning your trip at least a month in advance, register at sites like www.groupon.com, www.living social.com, or www.bloomspot.com to receive emails with steeply discounted coupons for restaurants, bars, spas, and activities for the cities or regions you select.

Free museums Many museums in major cities have a free day once a month, or during evening hours. Call or visit individual websites for details. For always-free museums, visit the Getty Center, Getty Villa, and Griffith Observatory in Los Angeles, and the Cable Car Museum and the Musee Mechanique in San Francisco.

Joshua Tree National Park.

Rodeo Drive in Beverly Hills.

THE REAL 'GOLDEN STATE'

While it's nicknamed the Golden State, California is actually an incredibly diverse range of destinations, each with its own beautiful natural wonders, impressive cultural attractions, and engaging personality.

Los Angeles.

California is often thought of in north and south halves. In general, the upper half conjures up images of foggy San Francisco, Silicon Valley tech nerds, great wine, a cold and rugged coast, redwood forests,Tahoe for skiers, and Yosemite for backpackers. The south is about sunshine and warmth, with blonde surfers catching waves along its coast, celebs and image-obsessed wannabes flocking to Los Angeles, families enjoying Disneyland, and chic Palm Springs, the gateway to miles and miles of inland desert.

Of course the reality is a much more complex picture. In the north, liberal San Francisco boasts cultural landmarks like the Golden Gate Bridge and historic cable cars, plus world-class museums and an innovative food scene. Just an hour and a half away is Napa Valley, where you can sip Cabernet while gazing at miles of lush vineyards, followed by the meal of a lifetime at French Laundry.

A breathtaking drive south for a few hours along the rugged coast brings you to Big Sur for great hiking, while a drive north connects to the Marin Headlands and Muir Woods, then quiet coastal towns like Mendocino. Head inland and you're taken back to Gold Rush days in Old Town Sacramento.

Head further into nature to find Northern California's 3,000-year-old redwood trees in old-growth state parks and Yosemite National Park's stunning granite peaks and water-

Casino in Avalon, Santa Catalina Island.

falls. The South can hold its own in the nature department: inland are massive deserts, Anza-Borrego Desert State Park's wildflowers, and Joshua Tree National Park's twisted trees. The coastline south of Big Sur leads to Pismo Beach's giant sand dunes and clouds of Monarch butterflies. Further along are Paso Robles vineyards, the Channel Islands, and white-sand beaches perfect for surfing and sunbathing.

Chic Santa Barbara, known as the "American Riviera," is quietly upscale, while San Diego draws surfers to the beaches and families to the the zoo. Sprawling Los Angeles has something for everyone: celebrity-spotting and TV tapings, the Getty Center and LA Museum of Contemporary Art, food trucks and trendy bars, lovely beaches and watery Venice. And, of course, Disneyland.

Celebrating the Hispanic Cinco de Mayo festival in Pasadena.

CULTURAL DIVERSITY

Throughout its history, California has seen waves of immigrants attracted by opportunities the state had to offer, with the newcomers bringing new values. California's changing ethnic mix has significant political, social, and artistic implications.

California is the third-largest state in America and ranks highest in number of inhabitants, but perhaps what is less appreciated is that no other part of America can claim such ethnic diversity. From the onset of the industrialized era, the state's population has been melded by boom cycles of immigration: Mexicans, Europeans, the Chinese and Japanese, African-Americans from the South, Russians, Armenians, Asian Indians, Koreans, Salvadoreans, Iranians, Filipinos, Samoans, Vietnamese. Almost 60 years ago, the well-known historian Carey McWilliams was already referring to Southern California as an "archipelago of social and ethnic islands, economically inter-related but culturally disparate." Today, the students of the Los Angeles Unified School District (LAUSD) alone speak more than 90 different languages.

Theme park ride at Knott's Berry Farm.

When Los Angeles was founded in 1781, more than half of the settlers were of mixed black, American Indian and Spanish blood. To this day, a large percentage of the Latino population resides in Southern California.

Tides of immigration

When California joined the Union in 1850, it was considered to be the final frontier, a land promising spiritual and social riches. Boosters furiously sold the fable of the Golden State to the rest of the Union, and pioneers armed with little more than faith came in search of sunshine, fertile soil, and freedom from oppression.

The blending of cultures had begun long before, over two centuries ago when Spanish Franciscan monks arrived to set up missions throughout the state and spread Catholicism to indigenous peoples. Before the end of the 19th century, though, the American Indian population had been decimated and their mestizo (mixed-heritage) descendents found themselves pushed southward by an influx of miners flooding the foothills of the Sierra Nevada mountain range.

The development and growth of California's industries throughout the 19th century brought new tides of immigration. The Chinese initially came as railroad workers

Beverly Hills was once called Rancho Rodeo de Las Aguas. It was owned by Maria Rita Valdez, the granddaughter of black founding settlers.

on the Central Pacific construction gangs, before branching into agriculture and fishing. African-Americans also came as railroad employees, in smaller numbers at first and then, during World War II, to fill manufacturing and service jobs.

saturated Southern California with visions of manifest destiny.

In the 20th century, the most significant influx occurred in the 1980s, when hundreds of thousands of Mexicans and Central Americans fleeing civil strife and political persecution immigrated, both legally and illegally, to California.

Failures in multiculturalism

For much of the 20th century, California was hardly a model of open-mindedness. During the depression in the 1930s, the county of LA

Marijuana, for sale on Venice Beach boardwalk, has been legalized for medical purposes.

Japanese and Anglo-American immigrants

And towards the turn of the 20th century, Japanese immigrants arrived in search of opportunities in the emerging produce industry, which they eventually came to dominate very successfully, from packing and shipping the fruit to setting up small stands and bigger enterprises to sell it.

Nothing, however, compared to the tidal wave of Anglo-Americans who arrived from the Midwest during the 1880s (and then again – fleeing the parched dustbowl farms of the prairies – in the 1920s). Already having established major colonies around the San Francisco and Sacramento areas, they

"repatriated" thousands of Mexicans on relief, loading them like cattle onto trains. When the need for cheap labor beckoned, Mexicans once more became a necessary commodity in the burgeoning economy.

Early in World War II, the notorious Executive Order 9066 authorized the internment of all Japanese on the West Coast – most of whom lost everything they owned. During the same decade, African-Americans who escaped the repression of the Deep South were barred from living in certain neighborhoods by restrictive housing covenants.

As a result of such practices, clusters of ethnic communities formed where people could feel protected and cultures preserved. San

In California's metropolitan areas, churches often served as the nexus of a community – spiritually, socially, and politically. The first was the African Methodist Episcopal Church in south central Los Angeles, the city's first African-American church.

Francisco's Chinatown is one such example, developing out of necessity as a refuge from abuse: Until the 1960s, when immigration laws changed, the Chinese had been subjected to severe and continual harassment, and discriminatory legislation had deprived them of eligibility for citizenship, ensuring that they had no legal recourse.

Later, as the job market plummeted in recession-hit California in the 1990s, tensions between ethnic groups amplified. The eruption of civil unrest in Los Angeles in 1992 was a wake-up call to the entire US, an indication that the ethnic stew was boiling over.

The artistic face of multiculturalism

It is perhaps the necessity of asserting one's identity in this Babel-like sea of cultures that has made California the state in which more trends and artistic movements seem to take flight than any other. The hippy movement being one example, while rap music has been linked to the malaise that occurred after the Watts rebellion in 1965.

Assembled from the shards of the uprising, the Watts art renaissance delivered up a number of visionaries. Theirs was the poetry of frustration, self-assertion and, unlike some contemporary rap, hope. Bold, bright graffiti art also arrived hard on the heels of disenfranchisement. "Tagging" (initialing) property provided inner-city teens – primarily Latino – with a voice that the larger culture refused to hear. Today, rap's impact on the media and advertising has been palpable.

California also adopted customs of Asian immigrants. Health-conscious Californians submit to strenuous programs of yoga and meditation, and feed on Pad Thai, sushi, and *pho*. Beat Generation writers, who tumbled around San Francisco in the 1950s, derived much of their inspiration from Buddhism, and Japanese and Chinese poetry.

The experience of facing society as "other" in California has produced some of America's finest writers and artists since the 1940s, including playwright William Saroyan, who grew up in an Armenian enclave of grape growers and farmers in Fresno; poet and novelist Alice Walker, best known for *The Color Purple*; essayist Richard Rodriguez, who writes about gay and Latino assimilation and the politics of multi-culturalism; Filipino-born artist Manuel Ocampo, whose paintings often depict symbols of racism and the brutish imperialism of the colonials; theater artist

Mexican farmworker in San Joaquin Valley.

LATINO COMMUNITY ACTIVISM

Although Latinos in California are heavily involved in community activism, they are generally under-represented in the political arena. One reason is that the number of Latinos who are citizens – and therefore capable of voting – is much smaller than the actual population. Although it has since changed, for many years the only notable Latino leader was the late Cesar Chavez, the widely admired president of the United Farm Workers of America. Chavez gained fame during the early 1970s for his battle to secure decent working conditions for the mostly Mexican farm laborers.

By 2013 it is thought that, much to the displeasure of conservative white people, the number of people of Latino or Hispanic descent will outnumber non-Hispanic Caucasians in California.

Anna Deavere Smith, whose performance piece *Twilight: Los Angeles, 1992* concerned the riots that devastated the city, told through the voices of the people who experienced it; and novelist Amy Tan, who found the characters

While many California towns and suburbs are relatively homogeneous, others are home to diverse pockets of cultures that border one another, highlighting differences in religions and customs.

California is hip-hop and cha-cha-cha wrapped in a dazzling gold-flecked sari. And now, more than any time in the history of the state, multiculturalism is thankfully reflected in the offices of elected and appointed officials: mayors and congressional representatives, city council members, and police chiefs.

Ukulele players in San Diego.

of her widely acclaimed *Joy Luck Club* in the Chinatown (San Francisco) of her childhood.

Multi-ethnic style

California epitomizes the best and worst of what being a truly multi-ethnic society can mean. There are some who believe that the obsession with tribalism is a leading factor in causing the sometimes bitter divisiveness throughout the state. Others say recognizing California's many ethnic groups is the first step towards peaceful coexistence. What has become more and more evident, though, is that the people of California have slowly absorbed each other's habits and styles, tastes, and mannerisms.

FESTIVALS

There are celebrations up and down the state that reflect California's multi-ethnic population. San Francisco's Chinese New Year celebration is one of the biggest in America, while Vietnamese New Year has devotees in San Jose. Oakland has a Greek cultural festival in May and San Diego a Pacific Islander's festival in summer. Cinco de Mayo, the Mexican holiday, is celebrated in all major cities, while Brazilians, Scots, Irish, and Germans all have their own street parties. For a list of monthly festivities, consult the "Calendar" section of the *LA Times* or check the *San Francisco Chronicle*.

BREAK JOB FRT. $59.95
BREAK JOB RR. $69.95
CLUTCH JOB $119.95 +PARTS
TIMING BELT $119.95

MOST CARS

419

Directing Los Angeles' notorious traffic.

Annual Blessing of the Animals ceremony in Los Angeles.

One of the murals on the Great Wall of Los Angeles, depicting Californian history.

BOARDING SCHOOL

ASIANS GAIN CITIZEN

HIP & PROPERTY

DECISIVE DATES

Exhibits at Columbia State Historic Park, a restored Gold Rush town.

Pre-1500s
The Miwok, Ohlone, and Wituk tribes occupy much of the land now known as Northern California.

1579
Sir Francis Drake lands at Point Reyes, reporting to Europe that California is an island.

1770s
The Spanish found a *presidio* and mission near San Francisco Bay.

1781
Don Felipe de Neve founds what will become Los Angeles.

1769–1823
Spanish padres found 21 missions between San Diego and Sonoma.

1846
The US declares war on Mexico and captures California.

1848
Gold is discovered in the Sierra foothills.

1850s
Native Americans sign away up to 90 percent of their lands in treaties.

1858
The Butterfield Stage Line delivers Los Angeles' first overland mail.

1859
The Comstock Lode discovery turns San Francisco into a prosperous metropolis.

1869
The transcontinental railroad is completed, terminating at Oakland.

1873
The world's first cable car runs in San Francisco.

1876
The Southern Pacific Railway arrives in Los Angeles.

1886
Harvey H. Wilcox opens a sub-division of LA his wife names Hollywood. He wants it to be "free of vices such as alcohol".

1892
Oil is struck near what is now Los Angeles' MacArthur Park.

1905
Abbott Kinney opens his Venetian-style resort near Santa Monica.

1906
A massive earthquake (8.25 on the Richter scale) rocks San Francisco.

1932
LA's Coliseum, then the world's largest stadium, hosts the Olympics.

1933
A Los Angeles earthquake (6.3 on the Richter scale) kills 120 people.

1937
The Golden Gate Bridge is opened to an uproarious reception.

1939
LA's Union Station, the last of the great railroad terminals, opens.

1945
The United Nations Organization is born in San Francisco.

1947
California passes a law against smog.

1950s
The "Beats," a bohemian literary group, start hanging out in San Francisco's North Beach.

1955
Disneyland opens in Anaheim.

1960s
Hippies flock to San Francisco's Haight-Ashbury district, celebrating the Summer of Love in 1967.

1965
Rioting in Los Angeles' Watts area kills 34 people.

1968
Presidential candidate Robert F. Kennedy is shot and killed in Los Angeles.

1971
An earthquake (6.6 on the Richter scale) kills 64 Southern Californians.

1974
Oil tycoon J. Paul Getty donates his Los Angeles home as a museum. BART (Bay Area Rapid Transit System) starts a regular transportation service.

1978
San Francisco mayor George Moscone and supervisor Harvey Milk are assassinated by a former Supervisor.

1980
Former governor of California Ronald Reagan becomes the 39th US president.

San Francisco's Golden Gate Bridge.

1980s
The computer industry's phenomenal growth puts Silicon Valley on the map.

1989
An earthquake collapses a freeway and causes destruction in the San Francisco Bay Area.

1991
Berkeley Hills fire destroys over 3,000 homes.

1992
LA police officers are acquitted of beating a black motorist, starting riots that kill 50 people.

1995
The new Museum of Modern Art in San Francisco's SoMa district spearheads a downtown building boom.

1995–97
The murder trial of football star O.J. Simpson grips the nation.

2003
Movie star Arnold Schwarzenegger becomes California's governor in an historic recall election.

2005
George Lucas moves his movie studio to San Francisco's Presidio.

2006
The first Amgen Tour bicycling race, from San Francisco to LA.

2007
Wildfires from Santa Barbara to San Diego kill 12 people and destroy 1,500 buildings.

2008
The Writers Guild of America goes on strike.

2012
Barack Obama, America's first black president, is re-elected for a second term, beating Mitt Romney. Construction begins on a high-speed rail line connecting San Francisco and Sacramento to Los Angeles and San Diego.

See Greek, Roman, and Etruscan antiquities at the Getty Villa in Malibu.

NATIVE TRIBES AND EUROPEANS

For 10,000 years, a network of California tribes
thrived and prospered, harvesting the riches from
land, lakes, and sea. Then the white man brought
disease and religion, decimating and subjugating the
Native American population.

The first tenants of the rich land that became California were the prehistoric tribes that, through the centuries, crossed the land bridge of the Bering Strait and slowly filtered down into the North American continent. By the time the Europeans arrived, it is thought that some 230,000 Native Americans were living in the northern region of the continent. However, so many native people died soon after Europeans arrived that anthropologists have had to rely on patchy mission records to estimate the population's size.

Map of California and Mexico dating from 1676.

The early tribes

Customs, talents, and preoccupations varied from tribe to tribe, each with separate identities and distinct languages. The Miwoks and Ohlones around what is now San Francisco Bay were nomads, sometimes trekking from coastal shell mounds up to the oak groves on what are now the Berkeley Hills, or to meadowland and its rich harvest of deer and elk. It is thought the two tribes socialized a little, but warily.

> California has the largest Native American population in the US. The temperate climate and easy access to food sources meant that around one third of all indigenous peoples lived in California.

The land around the bay probably supported more humans than any other California locale, but the area where the city of San Francisco now stands was not much frequented. It was a sandy, windy, desolate place compared to the lushness of the Berkeley Hills, the mild slopes of Mount Tamalpais, or the woods of the southern peninsula. In fact, San Francisco today has more trees and wildlife than at any other time in its history.

In the south, the Chumash tribe, living in what is now Santa Barbara, were adept fishermen who used seashell hooks, basket traps, nets, and vegetable poisons, even catching fish with their bare hands. The tons of shellfish eaten over centuries have left us with mounds of discarded shells that can now reach 20ft (7 meters) deep.

The Chumash in particular were expert boat builders. Canoes were made with easily worked timbers such as red cedar and redwood, and were distinguished by their symmetry, neatness of finish, and frequent decoration. All of this was achieved with limited tools, the principal ones being chisels, curved knives, abrasive stones, wedges, and sharkskin. One of their elegant vessels can be admired today at the Santa Barbara Museum of Natural History.

The California tribes' lifestyle prospered for 10,000 years with few major changes and, by our standards, few possessions. The arrival of white people bewildered them and radically changed the culture of all Native Americans.

peninsula (known today as Baja California) which stretched down between the sea and a gulf, he believed he'd found a long-lost fabled island, and he named it "California." But the discovery of the state of California is officially credited to Juan Rodríguez Cabrillo, the Portuguese commander of two Spanish caravels, who is thought to have embarked from the Mexican port of Navidad in June 1542. He explored most of California's coast, entering San Diego's "enclosed and very good" harbor in September 1542.

Sir Francis Drake, sailing around the world in 1579 in the Golden Hind, passed by the

Members of a native tribe dancing near the San Francisco Mission, 1822.

Their acquisition of manufactured articles such as guns, metal utensils, axes, knives, blankets, and cloth led inevitably to a decline in native arts and crafts. With the encroachment of white settlements, warfare became a unifying force and tribes that had been enemies united against the intruders. But even this did not save them: They had survived regular earthquakes and droughts, but the white man proved too strong for them.

The age of exploration

Hernando Cortés, the Spaniard who conquered Mexico, sailed up the west coast of North America in 1534. Stumbling upon a

entrance to the bay of San Francisco without noticing an opening. His log shows that he anchored just north and sent several landing parties ashore.

Then, 23 years later, Sebastian Vizcaíno arrived in the south, searching for suitable ports of call for his Manila galleon on its annual return to the Philippines, which was part of the Spanish Empire at the time. What Spain most needed was a safe haven from marauding Dutch and British pirates for the treasure ships en route to Spain, which were laden with riches from across its empire. But the pirates weren't the only people the Spanish needed protection from. The canny and ambitious Spanish king,

> For over 65 years it was believed that one of Drake's landing parties may have left behind a small brass plate that was discovered in 1936 near Drake's Bay. But in 2003 it was declared an elaborate hoax.

Charles III, was also keenly aware that Russian fur traders from the north posed a risk to Spain's land claims, as the traders were increasingly hunting farther and farther south, even

Oil painting of Hernando Cortés.

coming down as far south as Bodega Bay.

Vizcaíno gave lasting names to several California sites, such as San Clemente Island, San Diego, and Santa Catalina Island. Of more importance was his glowing report on the virtues of the California coast, which urged Spain to colonize the state.

Converting the native peoples

What followed was another 150 years of lassitude until the overland arrival in 1769 of Gaspar de Portolá from Baja. Crossing the Santa Ana river and exchanging gifts with friendly tribes, de Portolá's band passed by the bubbling tar pits of La Brea, through the mountains at Sepulveda Pass to Lake Encino,

and headed northwards to open up the route to Monterey.

"The three diarists in the party agree that the practical discovery of most significance was the advantageous site on the Los Angeles river," noted John Caughey in a volume published by the California Historical Society to mark the city's bicentennial. "Equally important were the numerous able-bodied, alert, and amiable Indians because Spanish policy looked towards preserving, Christianizing, hispanizing, and engrossing the natives as a major element in the Spanish colony now

Engraving of Sir Francis Drake, published in 1628.

to be established." Over the centuries, Spain had developed a standard method for settling new territory: using the sword to cut down any opposition from the native peoples, and pacifying the area with the introduction of Christianity. This was the approach used in California, where between 1769 and early in the following century a chain of 21 Franciscan missions was established between San Diego and Sonoma. These missions enslaved hundreds of coastal Indians into an endless round of work and prayer.

Mission life

As early as 1775 the native peoples rebelled: In an uprising at the San Diego mission one of the Franciscans was killed. But abolishing age-old tribal customs and introducing a complex religious structure centered on endless work eventually converted the native Americans into obedient servants.

The object of every mission was to become self-sufficient, to which end the Indian men became farmers, blacksmiths, tanners, home builders, vintners, and other types of useful laborers. Meanwhile the Indian women focused on cooking, sewing, and laundering.

"White" diseases such as measles and chicken pox killed thousands of Native

ask for as many as 50,000 acres (20,200 hectares). In practice, of course, the acts were barely observed: tribes were driven out into the world of poverty and helplessness, ill-equipped to deal with white men's laws.

Some people returned to the hills, others indentured themselves as ranch hands or turned to drinking and gambling. Meanwhile, the orange groves and the productive gardens were cleared or ploughed under, and the missions – the so-called "string of pearls" – were transformed into a patchwork quilt of profitable ranches.

Mission Basilica San Diego de Alcala.

Americans and as a result they developed a mortal fear of mission life. Nevertheless, benevolent despotism kept thousands in the missions and it was their labor that made the system successful.

Not until the Mexican government's secularization decrees of 1834 (following its independence from Spain and acquisition of the province of Alta California in 1821) were the native people freed – only to exchange their status for that of underpaid peons on the vast ranches.

In theory, the Secularization Act of 1834 gave lay administrators and Native Americans the right to ownership of the missions and their property; a potential ranchero could

NATIVE AMERICAN CUSTOMS

California tribes led a simple life, their igloo-shaped homes of reed providing breezy shelter in summer, while deer-skin roofs afforded protection during the rainy season. When it grew cool, open fires were built in the homes, with holes in the roof allowing the smoke to escape. In warm weather, the men and children were naked except for ornamental jewelry such as necklaces, earrings, bracelets, and anklets. They kept warm when needed with robes of yellow cedar bark or crudely tanned pelts. Some groups practiced tattooing. The women wore two-piece aprons made of deer skins or reeds.

THE MISSIONS OF OLD CALIFORNIA

The 21 historic Franciscan missions spread out along California's coast offer a fascinating insight into California's Spanish Colonial period.

California's chain of Spanish missions that runs from San Diego to Sonoma marks a significant chapter in the state's history. Under pressure in the mid-18th century to establish a presence in its Alta California territories, Spain charged Father Junípero Serra and his Franciscan missionaries with the task of establishing a network of missions to be situated along the coast, following the success of those that Spain had built in its colony of Mexico.

The first settlement was in San Diego, where Father Serra raised a flag in 1769. Over the next 54 years, another 20 missions would be established roughly a day's journey apart along the El Camino Real ("The Royal Road").

At each of the timber and adobe missions – which all feature the thick walls, small windows, and elegant bell towers usually associated with Mexican churches – the Europeans introduced livestock, grains, agriculture, industry, and the Catholic religion to Native Americans. The missions were also the repository of some of the state's most treasured murals and art.

Following the Secularization Act of 1834, the missions fell into disuse and were abandoned until interest in them was sparked again in the 1880s by Helen Hunt Jackson's magazine articles that brought attention to the plight of former mission Indians. Now, despite the ravages of time, revolt, and neglect, most of the missions still operate as active Catholic parishes.

For more information, see the relevant chapter: ie, San Francisco (see page 127), Santa Barbara (see page 242), San Juan Capistrano (see page 293), and San Diego (see page 318).

Mission San Gabriel Arcángel.

Mission Santa Clara de Asís was founded in 1777. Although ruined and rebuilt six times, the settlement was never abandoned.

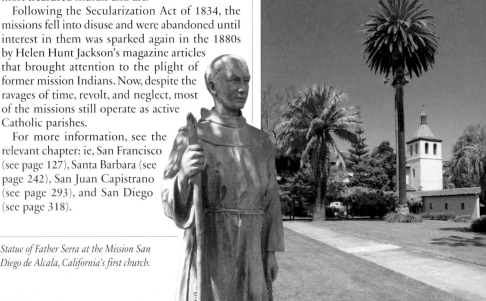

Statue of Father Serra at the Mission San Diego de Alcala, California's first church.

Inside Mission San Juan Capistrano, in Orange County, which has extensive grounds containing gardens, fountains, and adobe buildings.

THE MISSION OF SAN JUAN CAPISTRANO

Orange County's Mission San Juan Capistrano has several interesting legends associated with it. The first is very much tied to reality: for at least two centuries, cliff swallows have been visiting the church each spring, building their nests out of mud in the tiled roof. They arrived each year on or around March 19 – St Joseph's Day – flying north from their winter vacation in Argentina. Legend says the influx began back in the mists of time when the original brood took refuge in the mission's eaves after a local innkeeper destroyed their nests. More recently, the swallows have been finding other places to nest, but the mission continues to try to woo them back.

Another legend that is associated with the mission – described as "an American Acropolis" – is that of a woman named Magdalena whose penance was to walk up and down the church aisle with a lighted candle, to atone for disobeying her father by courting a man of whom he disapproved. On occasion, it is said, her candle can still be seen shining among the ruins of the cruciform Great Stone Church in which the poor unfortunate perished during an earthquake. The Great Stone Church, one of the oldest sections of the mission still standing, has recently been restored to its former glory.

For more information on Mission San Juan Capistrano, see page 293.

The beautiful Old Mission Santa Barbara, known as the "Queen of the Missions," was established in 1786 and is fronted by attractive gardens.

Nests at Mission San Juan Capistrano.

PULL AWAY CHEERILY!
(THE GOLD DIGGER'S SONG.)

Pull Away Cheerily: The Gold Digger's Song, by composer Henry Russell, was about the Australian and Californian gold rushes.

WRITTEN AND SUNG BY **HARRY LEE CARTER,** IN HIS ENTERTAINMENT OF
"The Two Lands of Gold."
ALSO SUNG BY
GEORGE HENRY RUSSELL,
IN MR PAYNE'S POPULAR ENTERTAINMENT,
"A Night in the Lands of Gold."
MUSIC COMPOSED BY
HENRY RUSSELL.

LONDON: MUSICAL BOUQUET OFFICE, 192, HIGH HOLBORN;
& J. ALLEN, 20, WARWICK LANE, PATERNOSTER ROW.

N^{OS} 691 & 692. MUSICAL BOUQUET.   COPYRIGHT.

FROM RANCHOS TO STATEHOOD

It started as a war with Mexico over territory that Americans thought should be theirs. But it ended by transforming a wild and savage wilderness into the 31st state of the Union.

After three centuries of Spanish rule, Mexico finally broke away and declared itself a republic on September 27, 1821. Coincidentally, secularization of the missions was then sought by Spanish-Mexican settlers, known as Californios, who complained that the Catholic Church owned too much of the land. Eight million acres (3.2 million hectares) of mission land were fragmented into 800 privately owned ranches, with some governors handing out land to their cronies for only a few pennies per acre.

Life under the Californios

Orange orchards were cleared for firewood, herds were given to private hands, and the predominant lifestyle quickly changed to that of an untamed frontier-style cattle range. Cattle ranching in this part of the world, however, made few demands upon its owners. With no line fences to patrol and repair on the open range, and no need for vigilance because of branded stock, the *vaquero* had little to do but practice feats of horsemanship to prove his masculinity and impress the *señoritas*.

An 1842 portrait of Richard Henry Dana, author of the influential Two Years Before the Mast.

The vaquero's sports were violent, including calf branding, wild-horse roundups, bear hunts, and cock- and bullfights. His entertainment included dances, and at his fiestas he was bedecked in gold-braided clothes dripping with silver.

Author Richard Henry Dana, who visited the state in 1835, called the Californians "an idle thriftless people," an observation lent considerable weight by the lifestyle of so many of the rancheros, who found it a simple matter to maintain and increase their wealth. The sudden influx of prospectors to the north created an immense demand for beef, which the southerners were readily able to supply.

Yankee trading ships plied up and down the coast, operating like floating department stores offering mahogany furniture, gleaming copperware, framed mirrors, Irish linen, silver candlesticks, and cashmere shawls. These trading ships were the first opportunity for many native-born Spanish settlers to obtain jewelry, furniture, and other goods from the old world. Sometimes the trading ships, which had survived the precarious Straits of Magellan, would stay an entire year.

A genteel contraband soon developed. To reduce import taxes, ships worked in pairs to transfer cargo from one to the other on the open seas. The partially emptied ship would then make port and submit to customs inspection. With duties paid, it would rejoin its consort and reverse the transfer. Sometimes the Yankee traders used lonely coves to unload their cargoes, which were eventually smuggled ashore. The weather remained temperate except for the occasional hot, dry, gale-force

meanwhile, fell into ruins: restoration of the missions began only in the 20th century after they were declared historical landmarks.

In 1834, Governor Figueroa issued the first of the Secularization Acts, which in theory gave lay administrators and Indian neophytes the right to ownership of the missions and their property. Having been first introduced to the "civilized" world and then enslaved, the native peoples were disoriented. At the height of the mission era, as many as 20,000 Indians had been tied to the system as unpaid laborers, and were now psychologically ill-prepared to cope with freedom.

After the Battle of Monterey, Mexican General de Ampudia surrenders to American General Taylor during the Mexican-American War of 1846–8.

Soldiers who'd finished in the army often stayed in California rather than return to Spain or Mexico. Under Mexican law, a ranchero could ask for up to 50,000 acres (20,200 hectares); native slave labor became part of the plunder.

wind the Native Americans called "wind of the evil spirits." The Spaniards called them *santanas*, a name which today has become corrupted to Santa Ana winds. Now and again an earthquake rumbled down the San Andreas fault. The rancheros spent their energy rebuilding damaged haciendas, made from red-tile roofing set on white-painted adobe brick walls. The missions,

The Mexican–American War

Official Washington soon became aware of this land of milk and honey on the Pacific coast. President Andrew Jackson sent an emissary to Mexico City in the 1830s to buy California for the sum of $500,000. The plan failed.

When James K. Polk took office in 1845, he pledged to acquire California by any means. Pressured by English financial interests that plotted to exchange $26 million of defaulted Mexican bonds for the rich land of California, he declared war on Mexico on May 13, 1846.

News of the war had not yet reached California, however, when a group of settlers stormed General Mariano Vallejo's Sonoma estate. Vallejo soothed the men with brandy

> *In addition to being denied legality and having their labor exploited and their culture destroyed, the Native Americans had been fatally exposed to alcoholism and all manner of foreign diseases.*

and watched as they raised their hastily sewn Bear Flag over Sonoma. The Bear Flag Revolt is sanctified in California history – the flag now being the official state flag – but for all its drama, it was immaterial. Within a few weeks Commodore John Sloat arrived to usher California into the Union.

Most of the fighting took place in the south. The war in the north effectively ended on July 9, 1846, when 70 hearty sailors and marines from the ship *Portsmouth* marched ashore in Yerba Buena village and raised the American flag in the village's central plaza, now Portsmouth Square in San Francisco.

The bloodiest battle on California soil took place in the Valley of San Pasqual, near Escondido. The Army of the West, commanded by General Stephen W. Kearney, fought a brief battle during which 18 Americans were killed.

Kearney's troops skirmished with Mexican–Californians at Paso de Bartolo on the San Gabriel River. The Californios, however, soon capitulated to the Americans, and California's participation in the Mexican–American War finally ended with the Treaty of Cahuenga, signed by John Fremont and General Pico.

The treaty came into force on July 4 (US Independence Day), 1848, and made California a territory of the USA. Only through fierce negotiation was San Diego placed on the north side of the Mexico–California border.

For three decades after America had acquired Alta California in 1848, Los Angeles remained a predominantly Mexican city infused with a Latino culture and traditions. But the arrival of the Southern Pacific Railroad triggered a series of land booms with the subsequent influx of Anglo-American, Asian, and European immigrants eventually outnumbering Mexicans 10 to 1.

Meanwhile the Native American population continued to suffer. From 1850 onwards the Federal government signed treaties (never ratified by the Senate) under which more than 7 million acres (2.8 million hectares) of tribal land dwindled to less that 10 percent of that total. Next to suffer from marginalization and

racist attitudes were the Chinese, thousands of whom had poured into Northern California from the gold fields and, later, into Los Angeles after the railroads had been completed.

California was rushed into the Union on September 9, 1850, as the 31st state, only 10 months after convening a formal government. But it had already drafted a constitution that guaranteed the right to "enjoying and defending life and liberty, acquiring, possessing and protecting property, and pursuing and obtaining happiness," with hindsight a typically Californian mix of the sublime and the practical.

The California flag.

THE PONY EXPRESS

When California gained statehood in 1850, mail from the East took six months to deliver. Overland stagecoaches cut this to less than a month, but in 1860, the sinewy riders of the Pony Express brought San Francisco much closer to the rest of the nation. Mail travelled over hostile territory from St Joseph, Missouri, to the young city of San Francisco in only 10 days. Riders had just a revolver, water sack, and a mail pouch, the most famous of them being 15-year-old William "Buffalo Bill" Cody. Just as quickly, though, came the Transcontinental Telegraph, and on October 26, 1861, the Pony Express closed its doors.

THE CALIFORNIA GOLD RUSH

Gold and silver were the stuff of dreams, making millionaires out of ordinary men and, sometimes, paupers out of millionaires. Gold fever grabbed the nation and California's population exploded.

Gold was discovered in California's Placeritas Canyon, north of Mission San Fernando, in 1842. Francisco Lopez, rounding up stray horses, stopped to rest beneath an oak tree. He opened his knife to uproot some wild onions, and their roots came out attached to something gleaming bright in the sun – a nugget of gold. Six years later, gold was discovered in quantity at Sutter's Mill, near Sacramento. Word quickly spread east and the stampede began. Soon a torrent of gold-dazzled prospectors gushed west through the Sierras to California.

Gold is discovered

The first big discovery of gold took place in the Sierra Nevada foothills, at a sawmill beside the American River. The mill belonged to John Augustus Sutter – a man, one contemporary wrote, with a disastrous "mania for undertaking too much." Born in Switzerland in 1803, Sutter arrived in San Francisco in 1839. Despite a disorderly career as a Swiss Army officer and dry-goods merchant, he somehow impressed Alta California's authorities enough to receive a Central Valley land grant of nearly 50,000 acres (about 20,000 hectares). Naming his land "New Helvetia" and using Native Americans as serf labor, Sutter set out to create his own semi-independent barony.

Sutter's Fort, at what is now Sacramento, was often the first stop for bedraggled pioneers after their harrowing Sierra crossing. Sutter gloried in providing comfort and goods (at a price) to California's new settlers. He planted wheat and fruit orchards, bought out the Russians at Fort Ross, and, in 1847, decided to build the sawmill that was his ultimate undoing.

Pony Express Rider Leaving Station, artist unknown.

James Marshall, who had been hired to oversee the mill's construction, peered into the millrace on January 24, 1848, and noticed a bit of shiny material. It was, of course, one of the millions of smithereens of gold that had been tumbling down the streams of the Sierra for millennia.

After applying "every test of their ingenuity and the *American Encyclopaedia*," and deciding that it was indeed gold, Marshall and Sutter raced back to the sawmill and found quite a bit more.

Realizing his New Helvetia would be overrun if word of the discovery leaked out prematurely, Sutter swore his mill hands to secrecy.

But nuggets kept popping up in bars and stores all over the region. Soon shopkeeper Sam Brannan would break the news in San Francisco, and the secret would be well and truly out.

Gold fever takes hold

When Sam Brannan ambled down Montgomery Street with a vial of recently prospected gold, San Francisco's population numbered less than 1,000. By early 1850, when the madness was in full swing, the population topped 30,000.

California's mission towns and farms joined in the scramble.

Gold fever worked its way to the states of Utah and Oregon, where two-thirds of the able-bodied men were on their way to the dig-gings. Entire caravans of covered wagons made their way west. Ships in the Pacific spread the word to Peru, Chile, Hawaii, and Australia. Lieutenant L. Loeser carried a "small chest... containing $3,000-worth of gold in lumps and scales" back to Washington, DC, where it was exhibited at the War Office, increasing greed in the capital. On December 2 1848, President

The Monitor, by Henry Sandham, published in 1883, shows hydraulic mining for gold.

"As a lumber enterprise, the mill was a fail-ure, but as a gold discovery, it was a grand success," said a later report of Sutter's Mill.

The word quickly spread all over California: stores closed, city officials left their offices, soldiers deserted, sailors jumped ship, and the exasperated editor of the *Californian* announced the suspension of his daily news-paper because the staff had walked out. San Francisco was left nearly deserted, its shops stripped of axes, pans, tents, beans, soda crack-ers, picks, and whatever else might conceivably be of use. Monterey, San Jose, all of Northern

Polk told Congress that the "extraordinary accounts" were true. A few days later, the *New York Herald* summed it up: "The El Dorado of the old Spaniards is discovered at last."

How claims were staked

Hundreds of thousands of reveries were fixed on the fabled Mother Lode region, which ran for 120 miles (190 km) from north of Sutter's Mill to Mariposa in the south. Forty-niners (as the Gold Rush min-ers were known) first worked the streams of the Klamath Mountains in the far north: later, the southern deserts had their share of boom towns. But the Mother Lode's wooded hills and deep valleys were the great centers of the raucous, short-lived argonaut civilization.

Gold Rush mining, especially in the early days before the streams were panned out, was a simple affair. The Mother Lode was owned by

> "The whole country," wrote the Californian editor, "resounds with the sordid cry of gold! gold! gold! – while the field is left half-planted, the house half-built, and everything neglected but the manufacture of shovels and pickaxes."

Prospectors with shovels and pickaxes.

the federal government, and claims were limited to the ground a man and his fellows could work. Stockpiling claims was impossible and hiring a workforce was unlikely. There was scant reason to make another man rich when one's own wealth-spouting claim was so easily achieved.

There was money to be wrung out of those hills. The problem lay in keeping it. In 1849, $10 million of gold was mined in California; the next year, four times that amount. In 1852, at the pinnacle of the Gold Rush, $80 million wound up in prospectors' pockets.

The Sierra streams did much of the miner's work for him. The rushing waters eroded the hillsides and sent placer gold (from dust to nugget size) rushing downstream. A miner crouched by the streambank scooped up a panful of gravel, shifting and turning his pan as the debris washed out and the gold sank to the bottom. Later, sluices were built and holes were dug. Finally hydraulic mining took over, although this was banned in 1884 after causing dramatic ecological damage to the foothills.

Water rights

The endless disputes over water rights, which continue to this day, mostly date to the days of the gold prospectors when miners, whose claims were far from stream beds, collaborated to build ditches funnelling water from sources whose "riparian rights" (that is, owning the adjoining land) were in conflict with "appropriation rights." The introduction of hydraulic mining, bringing streams of water to bear on hillsides, intensified the problem. The extensive network of canals and flumes which eventually brought water a long way from its original source came to be worth more than the claims it served, but the conflicting arguments over who had a prior right to the water were never entirely solved. (However, as the mines petered out, the agribusinesses of the state's central valleys gained the lions' share.)

As easy as it was to find, the Mother Lode's gold was easier to lose – to rapacious traders, in the gambling halls and bawdy-houses, and to the simple foolishness of young men. But for most prospectors it was a grand adventure. Many returned home sheepishly, but full of stories for their grandchildren.

San Francisco in the Gold Rush

California as It Is and as It May Be, Or, A Guide to the Goldfields was the title of the first book to be published in San Francisco (in 1849). In it, the author F.B. Wierzbicki wrote that the city looked like it had been built to endure for only a day, so fast had been its growth and so flimsy its construction.

"The town has led the van in growth… there is nothing like it on record. From eight to 10 thousand may be afloat on the streets and hundreds arrive daily; many live in shanties, many in tents, and many the best way they can… The freaks of fortune are equally as remarkable in this place as everything else connected with it; some men who two years ago had not a cent in their pockets, count by thousands now…"

Truly, nowhere was the Gold Rush's magic more powerful than in San Francisco. Bayard Taylor, a reporter for the *New York Tribune*, described the atmosphere as a "perpetual carnival." What he found when he returned from four months at the diggings was not the town of "tents and canvas houses with a show of frame buildings" that he had left but "an actual metropolis, displaying street after street of well-built edifices… lofty hotels, gaudy with verandas and balconies… finished with home luxury and aristocratic restaurants presenting daily their long bills of fare, rich with the choicest

Gold was first found on John Sutter's property.

technicalities of Parisian cuisine."

For most of the '49ers, the city was rough and expensive. Eggs from the Farallone Islands sold for $1 apiece. Real-estate speculation was epidemic. Each boatload of '49ers represented another batch of customers. As the city burst from the boundaries of Yerba Buena Cove, "water lots" sold for crazy prices on the expectation they could be made habitable with landfill, and, indeed, much of today's downtown San Francisco is built on landfill.

Most of California's new tenants had little desire to lay the foundation for the orderly society that would surely follow the Gold Rush. The popular conception was that the foothills were crammed with gold. "Ages will

not exhaust the supply," Bayard Taylor wrote. In the end, the winners in the great money-scramble were those who took the time to sink roots by establishing businesses and buying land, taking advantage of the '49ers' disdain for tomorrow. In 1853, the Gold Rush began to wind down. Real-estate values fell 20 to 30 percent. Immigration slowed to a trickle, and merchants were cornered by massive oversupplies ordered during the heady days. The men who started the Gold Rush, John Sutter and James Marshall, were only two of the many losers in the great game.

> None of California's new towns, much less San Francisco, was built with much care or foresight. Pre-Gold Rush street plans were expanded out from flat Yerba Buena Cove without paying attention to the city's hills.

Marshall ended his days in 1885 near the site of his discovery, broken-down, weepy, shaking his fist at fate. Sutter, whose barony was overrun just as he'd feared, kept a brave front for some years. But history had swept him aside, too, and he died in 1880 after years of futile petitions to Congress for restitution.

The Silver Rush

Whatever chance California had of becoming placid was swept away in 1859 by yet another flood of riches flowing down the Sierra slope. This time it was silver, not gold, that geared up the rush. One of the most comfortless outposts of the Gold Rush had been centered around Nevada's Sun Mountain, on the dry eastern slope of the Sierra near Lake Tahoe. There was a little gold up in the Virginia Range, but eking a living out of the area's irritating bluish clay was wicked work. In June 1859, a sample of that "blue stuff" found its way to Melville Atwood, an assayer in Grass Valley. Examining it closely, Atwood found an astounding $3,876 worth of silver in that sample of ore.

At first it appeared that the Silver Rush would mimic the Gold Rush of a decade earlier. "Our towns are near depleted," wrote one spectator. "They look as languid as a consumptive girl. What has become of our sinewy and athletic fellow citizens? They are coursing through ravines and over mountaintops" looking for silver.

One of the athletic young men who rushed up to the Virginia Range was Mark Twain. In his marvelous book, *Roughing It*, he describes how he and his fellow almost-millionaires "expected to find masses of silver lying all about the ground." The problem for Twain and the thousands like him was that the silver was in, not on, the steep and rugged mountains, and getting it out was no simple matter of poking and panning.

The Silver Rush, it turned out, was a game for capitalists, men who possessed the money to dig tunnels, purchase claims, and install the expensive machinery and mills that transformed the "blue stuff" into cash. They were men like William Ralston of the Bank of California in San Francisco, and the four legendary "Bonanza Kings" – James Flood and William O'Brien, former saloon-keepers; and James Fair and John W. Mackay, old miners whose Consolidated Virginia Mining Company regularly disgorged $6 million a month.

The treasures of the Comstock Lode flowed from the boomtown of Virginia City to San Francisco. By 1863, $40 million of silver had been wrestled out of the tunnels, and 2,000 mining companies traded shares in San Francisco. At one time, more speculative money was wrapped up in Comstock mining shares than actually existed on the whole Pacific Coast.

The Comstock Lode lasted until the 1880s, plumping up California's economy with the $400 million that the Virginia Range yielded. In San Francisco, Billy Ralston, the Comstock's

greatest mine owner, had taken over from Sam Brannan as the city's top booster. (Brannan was going broke trying to make his Calistoga resort "the Saratoga of the West," and died without a dollar to his name in 1889.)

Ralston rebuilt America's largest city hotel; he bought sugar refineries, lumber, and water companies; and as the 1860s drew to a close, he happily made confident preparations for what he and his fellow plutocrats thought would be the capstone to the state's greatness – the long-awaited completion of the Transcontinental Railroad in 1869.

Entrance to the Golden Rule Mine in Tuolumne County.

VIGILANTE JUSTICE

In San Francisco, hoodlums (a word coined in late-19th-century San Francisco) had organized themselves into gangs like the Sydney Ducks and the Hounds. In addition to setting some of the city's fires, these gangs were known for routine robberies, beatings, and generally ugly behavior. In 1851, the forces of social stability asserted their constitutional right to "acquire, possess and defend property" by warring against the criminal elements in the community.

The robbery and beating in early 1851 of a merchant named C.J. Jensen inflamed the righteous, especially Sam Brannan – a man who, according to historian Josiah Royce, was "always in love with

shedding the blood of the wicked." Newspapers like the *Alta* brought up the specter of lynch law, and Brannan shouted that the time had come to bypass "the quibbles of the law, the insecurity of the prisons, and the laxity of those who pretend to administer justice."

A Committee of Vigilance was formed; soon a member of the Sydney Ducks (a gang of criminals from Australia) named John Jenkins was hanged for stealing a safe. Within two weeks Sacramento also had its vigilante corps and other California towns followed its lead. California's first bout of vigilantism put a damper on crime only for a while.

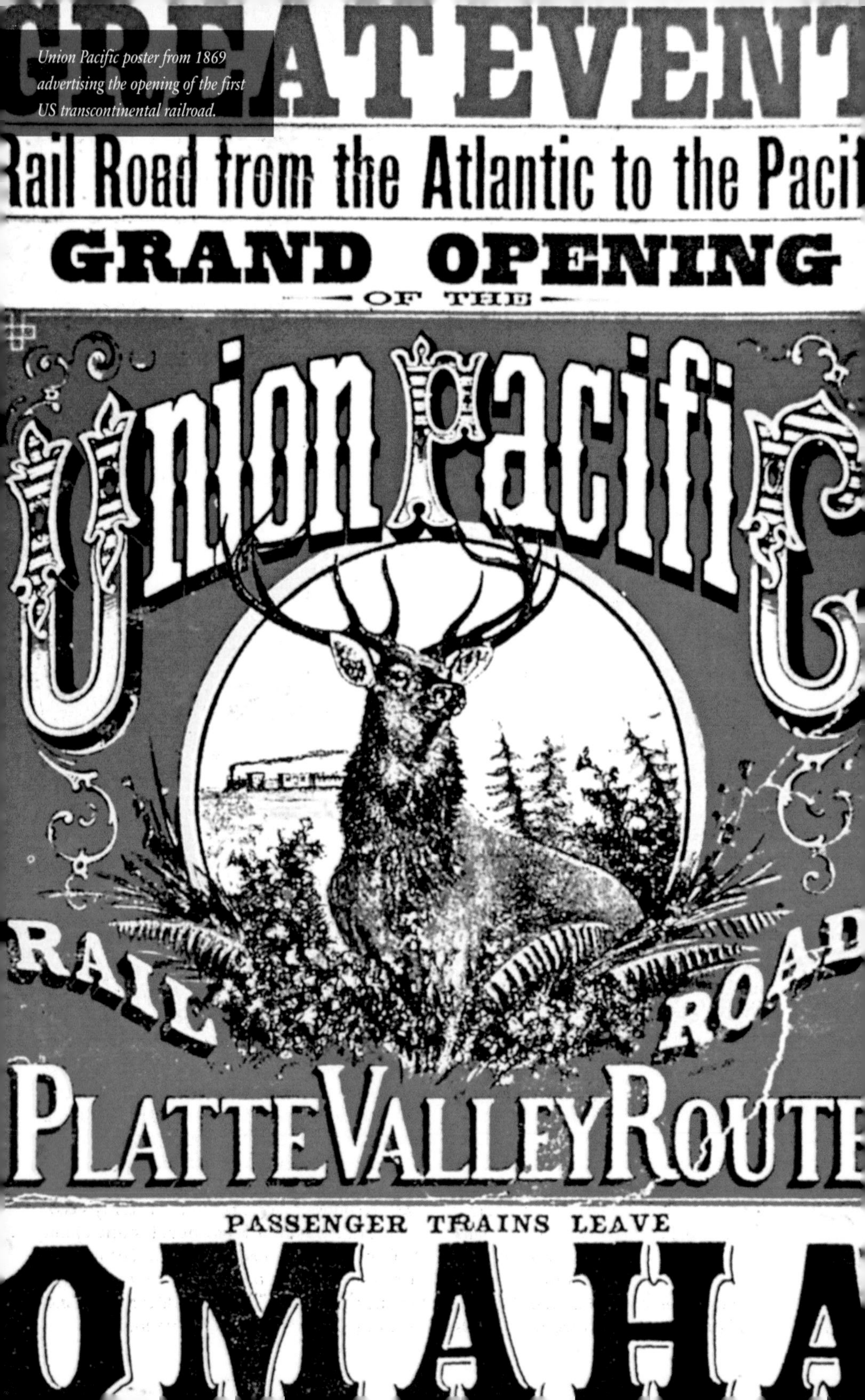

Union Pacific poster from 1869 advertising the opening of the first US transcontinental railroad.

BOOM AND BUST YEARS

After enjoying immense wealth from the discovery of gold and silver, the state was hit by massive unemployment. But California was too rich to suffer for long, thanks especially to the agricultural industry and oil production in the south.

Plans for a railroad linking the coasts had been floating around for many years. When the American Civil War broke out, Congress, intent upon securing California's place in the Union, at last stirred itself. In the winter of 1862, the Pacific Railroad Act granted vast tracts of land out west, low-interest financing, and outright subsidies to two companies – the Central Pacific, building from Sacramento, and the Union Pacific, building from Omaha, Nebraska, in the Midwest. As it happened, the Civil War largely bypassed California, but it nonetheless prompted the building of a railroad that brought unexpected havoc to the residents of the state.

In his regarded and widely read book, *Progress and Poverty*, Henry George, a journeyman printer and passionate theorist, had warned that the increasing dominance of the railroads would prove to be a mixed blessing. He predicted that California's immature factories

Officials and workers drive in the last spike of the Pacific Railroad, linking it with the Central Pacific Railroad at Promontory Point, Utah, 1869.

> When Frank Norris wrote The Octopus in 1901, no one had to guess at the reference: the Southern Pacific (as it was renamed in 1884) had its greedy tentacles in every corner of the state.

would be undersold by the eastern manufacturing colossus and that the Central Pacific's ownership of vast parcels of land along its right of way would drive prices of agricultural land shamefully high. George even foresaw the racial tensions that would result from the railroad's importation of thousands of Chinese laborers, who flooded the state's job market in the 1870s.

Problems with the railroads

George's prophecies began arriving with the first train. In San Francisco, real-estate dealing of $3.5 million a month fell to $1.5 million a month within a year. "California's initial enthusiasm soon gave way to distrust and dislike… an echo of the national conviction that the railroads were responsible for most of the country's economic ills," was the assessment of historian John W. Caughey in his book *California*. "The railroad became a monster, the Octopus. It was a target for criticisms by all those made discontented and bitter by the hard times of the Seventies."

The genius of the Central Pacific was a young engineer named Theodore Dehone Judah who had built California's first railroad, the 22-mile (35-km) Sacramento Valley line, in 1856. He spent years crafting the crucial route across the Sierra at Donner Pass. Unfortunately for Judah, the Central Pacific's other partners were uncommonly cunning and grabby men.

Charles Crocker, Mark Hopkins, Collis Huntington, and Leland Stanford, who became known as "The Big Four," had been lured west by the Gold Rush. They were Sacramento shop-keepers when they invested in Judah's scheme.

dictator of California politics for years. Between them, the railroad barons raised private invest-ment, earned government subsidies, acquired bargain-priced land, imported cheap labor from China and by their exploitative and monopolist practices made themselves multi-millionaires.

As the biggest landowners and biggest employ-ers, the immensely rich railroad barons were able to manipulate freight rates, control water sup-plies, keep hundreds of thousands of productive land acres for themselves, and subvert politicians and municipalities. It was years before state regu-lation of the railroads became the norm.

Gold seekers en route to California to join the Gold Rush, 1849 or 1850.

With few Americans willing to take part in the hard labor of building the Central Pacific (and the high cost of those who did), Charles Crocker hired cheaper Chinese labor: hard-working, they were sometimes derisively called "Crocker's Pets."

Shortly after Congress dumped its largesse in their laps, they forced Judah out of the Central Pacific. He died, aged 37, in 1863, still trying to wrest back control from his former partners.

The Central Pacific made the Big Four insanely rich. The government's haste to get the railroad built, and Stanford's political maneu-vering, made the Central Pacific the virtual

In the beginning, at least, carping at the Big Four's use of the railroad's treasury as a kind of private money preserve was a game for mal-contents and socialists. In the mahogany board-rooms of San Francisco's banks, on the editorial pages of its newspapers, in the overheated stock exchange, up and down Montgomery Street, the verdict was the same: the railroad would bring a firm and fabulous prosperity to California.

In April 1868, five years after construction of the First Transcontinental Railroad had begun on Sacramento's Front Street, the first Central Pacific train breached the Sierra at Donner Pass. On May 12, 1869, the ceremonial Golden Spike was driven at Promontory Point, Utah, and the coasts were finally and irrevocably linked. "San

Francisco Annexes the Union" read one San Francisco headline. But the rush of prosperity failed utterly to materialize. Only a few deep thinkers – none of them ensconced in boardrooms – had understood the financial calamity the railroad would bring. In the winter of 1869–70, a severe drought crippled the state's agriculture. Between 1873 and 1875 more than a quarter of a million immigrants came to California. Many were factory workers and few could find work. The "Terrible '70s" had arrived, which certainly for William Chapman Ralston were a calamity. As head of San Francisco's Bank of California, he had presided over the boom mentality that was a legacy of the Gold Rush.

The mid-1870s saw the depression at its deepest. On "Black Friday," April 26, 1875, a run on the Bank of California forced it to slam shut its huge oak doors at Sansome and California streets. Driven into debt by Comstock mining losses and by the failure of the railroad to bring prosperity, Bill Ralston drowned while taking his customary morning swim in the Bay.

Ralston's death signalled the end of California's booming affluence. Those hurt most by the great shrinkage of capital in the 1870s were the state's working people. During the Gold and Silver rushes, California's laborers had enjoyed a rare freedom to move easily from job to job and to dictate working conditions. Now, however, with massive unemployment, unionization began to take hold. For the next 60 years California suffered recurrent bouts of labor strife.

Agricultural growth

The depression was slow to disappear, but California was too rich to suffer permanently. In the next few decades, it slowly built its economic strength up to the point where it could compete with America's prosperous East Coast.

After decades of depending on the land to deliver riches in the form of gold or silver or minerals, the state developed its agricultural lands as never before. In the Central Valley, wheat, rice, and cotton became major cash crops. In the late 1870s, the fertile Napa Valley began to produce fine wines in earnest.

Sometime between 1873 and 1875, two or three orange trees were sent from the Department of Agriculture in Washington to Eliza and Luther Tibbetts in Riverside, not far from San Diego. The young trees had been budded from a seedless orange whose origin was

Bahia, Brazil. The Tibbetts planted the trees, little knowing that a decade later navel oranges would dramatically alter the agricultural, economic, and social patterns of the entire region. The Washington navel orange, as the seedless and sweet fruit was officially known, became (in the words of Charles F. Lummis, editor of the Los Angeles Times) "not only a fruit but a romance."

Durable enough to survive long-distance shipping, this citrus fruit hit its prime in 1889 when more than 13,000 acres (5,300 hectares) of land in the six southern counties were devoted to its cultivation.

Tropical fruit became an early industry in sunny southern California.

Growers formed a marketing cooperative, the California Fruit Growers Exchange, famed for its ubiquitous trademark, Sunkist. In a mere 18 months, New York Tribune editor Horace Greeley's "Go west, young man" philosophy became a reality. Many boomtowns took root and soon the population of the south equalled that of the north.

This vast semi-tropical, often desert-like land reached its potential. Thousands of acres of good farmland sold by the railroads at low prices were planted with wheat, oranges, grapes, cotton, tea, tobacco, and coffee. Irrigation converted vast tracts of this arid waste to fertile land bearing fruit and field crops.

Agriculture, crucially boosted by rail transportation, became the backbone of Southern California's economy. Well before the new century began, the enterprising Edwin Tobias Earl made a fortune from his invention of the refrigerated railroad car.

The rise of the south

Los Angeles, too, was now growing fast: in every decade from 1870 onwards it doubled its population. Before the end of the 19th century, the *Los Angeles Times*, whose editor Charles Lummis had hitchhiked across country from the Midwest, was proclaiming that it was no place for "dudes, loafers, paupers... cheap politicians, business scrubs, impecunious clerks, lawyers and doctors."

dig this *Zanja Madre* or Mother Ditch, paying him off with land instead of scarce city funds.

The land, a tract bordered by today's 6th & Main streets and Pico Boulevard and Figueroa Street, eventually made Childs so prosperous that, in 1884, he spent $50,000 to build a 1,800-seat opera house. At the ocean, frontage at Santa Monica owned by Southern Pacific Railroad magnate Collis P. Huntington almost became the Port of Los Angeles, but intensive lobbying by rival Santa Fe railroad chiefs won out and San Pedro was chosen instead. Already the region was annually producing almost 5 million barrels of

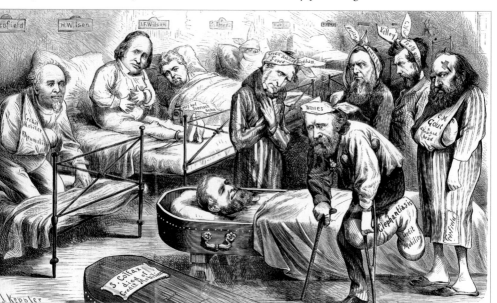

Cartoon on the scandal of 1872–3, when Credit Mobilier, a company formed by Union Pacific Railroad stockholders, was a lucrative but corrupt source of income for congressmen and railroad builders.

It is hard to imagine what they had against the last-mentioned category, especially in a city growing so sophisticated that by 1897 it boasted the first orchestra to be established west of the Rockies. Eight years later, Abbott Kinney's ambitious reconstruction of Venice on coastal marshland added an international touch, although his initial high-minded attractions soon gave way to motor racing and carnival events.

The pueblo of Los Angeles had become a prosperous community, facing its perennial problem: a shortage of water. To assure a steady water supply, the city fathers made plans for a lengthy trench running from the river and hired a Vermont-born shopkeeper, Ozro W. Childs, to

oil, the exporting of which was greatly facilitated by the subsequent opening of the Panama Canal.

California's bounty

Southern California's growing reputation as a health resort was responsible for the next big wave of newcomers, enticed by the climate, the abundance of thermal and mineral springs, and the boosterism of such communities as Pasadena, Riverside, Ojai, and Palm Springs. The state was already first in honey production; and vineyards, citrus, and walnut groves blossomed over thousands of acres. "Buy Land in Los Angeles and Wear Diamonds" was typical of the slogans that lured newcomers into the area, where they were met straight from the train with bands, barbecues, and fast-talking salesmen.

In Califiornia's vast deserts and verdant valleys, figs, rice, vegetables, and cotton became profitable crops. The balmy climate encouraged dairy farming, livestock, and poultry raising. And, from the turn of the century, in this already bountiful land, oil production became the most profitable of all.

Due to early huckstering by the big railroads, whose salesmen had gone to such lengths as spiking thorny trees with oranges to sell worthless land, real estate had long been big business. In 1886, Harvey H. Wilcox named his new sub-divi-

Since 1854, California's capital had been Sacramento, but it was San Francisco that ruled a rapidly coalescing state.

Agriculture in the Central Valley had grown in response to the needs of the exploding population; in the decade of the 1850s, California's cattle herds grew from 262,000 to more than 3 million. Towns like Stockton and Monterey were thriving as '49ers set up shops and sank roots. The Gilded Age, with its extravagance and corruption, continued right up to one fateful morning in 1906, after which nothing was the same again.

One of the earliest maps of Hollywood, from 1887.

sion Hollywood. After Wilcox's death, his widow sold a plot of land on Cahuenga to a French flower painter named Paul DeLongpre and it was his palatial house and floral gardens that became the area's first major tourist attraction.

A rapidly coalescing state

That same year, ground was broken at Hollywood and Highland for the soon-to-be-famous Hollywood Hotel and for Whitley Heights, an elegant hillside community that became for early movie stars what Beverly Hills would be in later years. Planned as a completely separate community, Hollywood was obliged in 1903 to join the city of Los Angeles, along with many neighboring communities, to obtain an adequate water supply.

THE GILDED AGE

While San Francisco's boomtown mentality may have taken a beating, as the 19th century wore on the city's historic predilection for high living remained. During the Gilded Age at the end of that century, Rudyard Kipling visited San Francisco (his first visit to America) and called it "a mad city, inhabited for the most part by perfectly insane people whose women are of a remarkable beauty." San Francisco's society had "a captivating rush and whirl. Recklessness is in the air." Kipling also famously noted that "San Francisco has only one drawback. 'Tis hard to leave."

Poster showing the port of Los Angeles, 1899.

THE EARLY 20TH CENTURY

The Great Earthquake of 1906 had immediate, devastating consequences for San Francisco. LA was now in the spotlight, gaining wealth from oil production, and renown from Hollywood's movie industry and advertisements proclaiming it "the land of perpetual summer".

The beginning of the 20th century was a hugely transformative period for California's major cities. Propelled by oil discoveries, new water sources, and a new extensive network of electric trains, Los Angeles tripled its population to 300,000 within a decade. Meanwhile, San Francisco struggled to recover and rebuild after a terrible earthquake and fire devastated the city in 1906. Within a decade, however, its Downtown had received a complete makeover, and the city jubilantly hosted a world's fair, the 1915 Panama Pacific International Exposition.

By the 1930s, "California became that legendary land of perpetual summer," enthused a writer in the Federal Writers Project guide to the state, "of orange groves in sight of snowy peaks, of oil wells spouting wealth, of real-estate promising fortunes, of cinema stars and bathing beauties. It seemed to promise a new start, a kinder providence, a rebirth of soul and body."

Postcard c.1900 depicting Broadway, Los Angeles.

The US government funded the Federal Writers' Project (FWP) in 1935 to help support historians, teachers, writers, and librarians during the Great Depression. The goal was to produce guide books that would promote tourism.

The growth of the south

Spurred by the discovery of oil in 1892 in what is now the Westlake area, Southern California mushroomed from an agricultural community to an industrial complex. Realizing it was sitting on a fat reservoir of wealth, Los Angeles developed the "Salt Lake Field," followed by fields in Huntington Beach, Santa Fe Springs, and Signal Hill. Oil derricks sprouted from the hills to the sea.

The initial unparalleled growth of Southern California was due in large part to the Owens Valley scandal, and additional water brought in by Los Angeles' Water Bureau Superintendent William Mulholland. Today, these aqueducts supply 525 million gallons (nearly 2 billion liters) of water a day. As water problems slowed to a trickle, the flood of newcomers to Southern California continued at an astonishing rate.

Trains and trolley cars

Although downtown LA was linked to Pasadena and Santa Fe by an urban railway, the

Southern Pacific's Collis P. Huntington devised in 1901 a vast interurban network of electric trains to connect the entire area.

"The whole area within a radius of 70 miles of the city took on a new life," wrote Huntington's biographer, Isaac Marcosson, in 1914. "Villages became towns; towns blossomed into miniature cities." When the author Henry James came by on a lecture tour in 1905, he said he'd never seen such an efficient transit system in all his worldwide travels.

Within five years, however, traffic had become problematic. When Los Angeles held

Collis P. Huntington.

its second annual motor show in 1909, it had more cars on its streets than any other city in the world, and the population was still soaring.

Movie madness

It was the film industry that really shot Los Angeles to fame and, unwittingly, it was Leland Stanford whose wager about a galloping horse helped launch it. With its origins in the nickelodeon, the movie industry began to emerge around the turn of the 20th century and headed west partly to escape the stranglehold patents held by the New York-based Edison company and partly because of California's superb climate, which made outdoor filming cheaper and easier.

Within a dozen years, the streets of Harvey Wilcox's sedate town of Hollywood were filled with intruders bearing cameras and megaphones, roping off streets, crashing cars, and staging pretend shoot-outs. Some prolific directors were turning out one-reel Westerns or comedies almost daily. The locals didn't like it at all. "They thought we were tramps," recalled screenwriter Anita Loos. "They saw themselves as being invaded and supplanted as elegant ladies and gentlemen so they ganged up on us."

> *Los Angeles, said Collis P. Huntington, was "destined to become the most important city in the country, if not in the world. It can extend in any direction, as far as you like." Within a decade his trolley cars stretched everywhere.*

From 1926, the Pickford-Fairbanks Studio immortalized such luminaries as actor Charlie Chaplin and directors D.W. Griffith and Cecil B. de Mille. Comedy became king. Mack Sennett's Keystone Kops had the whole nation laughing. Before long, studios sprang up in Culver City and Universal City, as well as in Hollywood. The latter name had by now become more or less synonymous with the word "movies."

Silent movies accompanied by organ music gave way to the "talkies." Hundreds of movie houses sprang up, and instant fortunes came to stars, directors, and producers, while novelists earned more from film rights than from their

WEALTH BY STEALTH

An infamous plot hatched in 1904 to steal water from the Owens Valley via a 250-mile (400km) pipeline over the Tehachapi Mountains to Los Angeles made fortunes for a private syndicate and allowed LA to grow to unprecedented levels. One of the syndicate's members was General Moses H. Sherman, whose advance knowledge of what land was about to be enriched came from serving on Los Angeles' Board of Water Commissioners. This scandal, which left the Owens Valley dry, formed part of the storyline for Roman Polanski's 1974 film, Chinatown.

original novels. Studios wielded great power, starting instant fads, and shaping tastes and ideas the world over.

In the summer of 1920, the population of Los Angeles reached 576,000, for the first time surpassing that of San Francisco, and LA became the 10th most populous city in the country. The southern portion of the state was "the world's closest approach to bedlam and babel," sneered journalist and politician, George Creel, with columnist Westbrook Pegler urging that the same territory "be declared incompetent and placed in charge of a guardian."

The San Francisco earthquake

While LA spent much of the early 20th century expanding, San Francisco spent it rebuilding: an earthquake measuring 8.25 on the Richter scale shook Northern Californians from their beds at 5.12am on April 18, 1906. When the deadly San Andreas fault lurched that morning, it sent terrifying jolts through an area 210 miles (338km) long and 30 miles (48km) wide, from San Juan Bautista in the south to Fort Bragg in the north. Other towns, like San Jose and Point Reyes Station near Drake's Bay, suffered more from the initial shock than San Francisco. Church bells jan-

> The 1906 earthquake – measuring 8.25 on the Richter scale – and subsequent fire in San Francisco killed more than 300 people and destroyed 500 square blocks and 28,000 buildings.

gled chaotically, dishes fell, windows shattered, dogs barked, Enrico Caruso (appearing locally in the opera *Carmen*) was scared voiceless, and San Francisco's new City Hall crumbled. In just 48 seconds, it was all over, but the city lay in ruins.

The subsequent fire destroyed 28,000 buildings over an area of more than 4 sq miles (10 sq km). It killed 315 people; the bodies of 352 more were never found. The city had experienced many earthquakes before, but none on this scale, and in a city that hosted more than 40 percent of the state's population (compared with around 3 percent today), the effect was cataclysmic. Although the awareness of the mighty San Andreas fault extended back a

dozen years, there had been no prior warning of, or preparations for, this major upheaval. Only an unearthly low rumble preceded fissures opening up and spreading wavelike across the city.

With its alarm system destroyed, the Fire Department lacked coordination, and the commandant of the Presidio, Brigadier General Frederick Funston, leaped in unauthorized to fill the gap in authority. When the brigades did arrive, they found mangled mains lacking any water supply. Hundreds were dead or still trapped in smoking ruins, 500 city

The Hollywood Bowl, c.1920.

AIRBORNE LOS ANGELES

Six years after the Wright brothers made their pioneering 59-second flight in North Carolina in 1903, Los Angeles hosted America's first international air show. A half million visitors came to watch Glenn Curtis set a 55mph (88kmh) speed record, including Glenn Martin, who promptly set up a plant that turned out one plane a day by the time World War I was declared. His employee Donald Douglas started his own company; within a few years, Douglas's DC3 was carrying 95 percent of US air traffic. Goodyear began blimp services to Catalina. Western Air Express carried cross-country mail. In 1920, scheduled flights began from Los Angeles to San Francisco.

blocks were leveled, and a handful of people had been shot or bayoneted by Funston's inexperienced militia who had poured into the streets to keep order and prevent looting. Golden Gate Park became the home of as many as 300,000 people for at least the next few weeks. Cooking inside the tents was banned, sanitation was rudimentary, water was in very short supply, and rats (and therefore the threat of the bubonic plague) were a dark, lingering menace.

But there was a strong will to recover. A Committee of Forty on the Reconstruction

The bank behind the regeneration of San Francisco's small business after the 1906 earthquake and subsequent fire later become the Bank of America, the nation's largest.

'On this site will be erected a six-story office building to be ready for occupancy in the fall.' San Francisco's renaissance was inevitable. The new, improved, taller buildings of Montgomery Street, the Wall Street of the west, were needed to process all the money churned out by the

Aftermath of the San Francisco earthquake of 1906, around Bush Street and Kearny Street.

of San Francisco was formed to define the tasks to be undertaken and A.P. Giannini's tiny Bank of Italy, making loans to small businesses intent on rebuilding, was at the forefront of those determined to revive the city's fortunes.

Aid poured in from all over the world, $8 million worth within the first few weeks. Even the much-reviled Southern Pacific Railroad pitched in generously, freighting in supplies without charge, offering free passage out of the city, and putting heavy equipment and cranes to work on the enormous task of clearing the debris.

The photographer Arnold Genthe wrote, "While the ruins were still smoking, on top of a heap of collapsed walls, a sign would announce:

state's industries, farms, and banks. The Port of San Francisco was still one of the world's busiest harbors. San Francisco's historic business of making business was unstoppable.

In 1911, San Francisco elected a new mayor, James "Sunny Jim" Rolph, a purveyor of goodwill whose reign encompassed some of San Francisco's giddiest times. The 1915 Panama Pacific International Exposition, which occupied 600 acres (240 hectares) of reclaimed land in what is now the Marina, is still considered one of the greatest of the world's fairs. Today, only one vestige of the flamboyant celebration remains: the Palace of Fine Arts Theatre. It was saved from gradual decay by civic benefactors in the 1960s.

MODERN TIMES

Beatnik bards and happy hippies flocked to find fulfillment in the state where experimentation was encouraged; this ethos went on to pave the way for technological advances in Silicon Valley and the movie industry.

The last half-century saw California's population boom, its movie industry lead the way in modern cinema, its political events impact the nation, and its Silicon Valley produce companies like Facebook and Apple that have not only impacted the state but also become household names around the world.

Population boom

In 1940, the population of Los Angeles numbered 1.3 million, of which about 9 percent was Mexican, 3 percent Asian, and 3 percent African-American. By 1950, the City of Angels' 2 million population made it the fourth-largest city in the United States.

The war had plunged California into a frenzy of activity. Twenty-three million tons of war supplies and 1.5 million men and women passed through the Golden Gate during the war's 46 months. The ports of San Francisco, Sausalito, Oakland, Vallejo, and Alameda were busy around the clock building and repairing ships, and loading supplies for the war machine.

In the Bay Area alone, the federal government spent $3 billion on shipbuilding. A new wave of immigration swept into the region as new factories needed new workers – 100,000 at the Kaiser Yards in Richmond, 90,000 more at Sausalito. Within two years of America's entry into the war in December 1941, the number of wage-earners in San Francisco almost tripled. The federal government doled out $83 million in contracts to the California Institute of Technology (Cal Tech) alone.

Even though 750,000 Californians left for military service, the state's wage-earners increased by nearly a million in the first half of the 1940s. After the war, the great suburban

1946 poster advertising The Big Sleep, starring Humphrey Bogart and Lauren Bacall.

sprawl got under way as war workers and their families settled down to post-war prosperity.

World War II gave a tremendous boost to California's aircraft industry, which increased statewide from fewer than 10,000 employees to more than 300,000. When the war was over, a gradual shift in the industry's workers from mainly blue-collar laborers to scientists and technicians meant, as historian Bruce Henstell wrote, that "aeronautics was replaced by something called aerospace."

The anti-conformists

As a new, almost instant society, California has always felt free to experiment. Many of its

The San Francisco Giants made history in 2010 by defeating the Texas Rangers to win the baseball World Series. The city exploded in Giants pride for their team, who were considered underdogs going into the series.

newcomers, from the "Anglo hordes" of the 1840s to Gold Rush adventurers, to present-day arrivals, have come to the state to escape the burdens of conformity elsewhere. The great majority of Californians have always been set-

for the nation's press who ogled at their rambling poetry readings, sniffed at the light marijuana breezes drifting out of the North Beach coffee houses, and wondered if civilization could stand such a limpid assault. The beatniks, it seems, mostly wanted America to go away. But it wouldn't, and before long "beat" had become a fashion and North Beach a tourist attraction.

The beat generation

The beats, however, had struck a nerve of dissatisfaction and alienation in America.

Beat writer Jack Kerouac.

Beat poet Allen Ginsberg in 1956.

tled and to one degree or another, God-fearing. But the anti-conformists – the colorful, free-thinking minority – have given California its name for verve and drive.

In the 1950s and 1960s, according to author Mike Davis, Los Angeles became "the capital of youth," but it was in San Francisco that the first stirrings of post-war protest and florid eccentricity were felt. While the American nation settled into a prosperous torpor, the city's historically Italian North Beach area became the haunt of a loosely defined group of poets, writers, declaimers, and sidewalk philosophers – the beatniks.

In the 1950s, they seemed titillating and somehow significant, a tempting combination

Though it was never a coherent movement, it produced juice-stirring literary works like Allen Ginsberg's *Howl* and Jack Kerouac's *On the Road*. That inspired alienation gave rise to two parallel, dissimilar, but oddly congruent movements: the angry politics of the New Left and the woozy love fest of the hippies. The first significant protest of the great, protest-rich 1960s took place in San Francisco in the decade's first year. In mid-May, the House Un-American Activities Committee opened a series of hearings in City Hall. When hundreds of demonstrators met the committee in the rotunda, the police reacted furiously, turning water hoses and billy clubs on the crowds. Dozens of protesters were carted off to jail, but the angry shouts in City Hall were heard around the world.

The locus of dissent was the University of California at Berkeley. There the Free Speech Movement kept up a steady assault against racism, materialism, and the stifling "multiversity" itself. As the horrors of the war in Vietnam grew more apparent, the New Left spread across America and the world, tilting at governments, bombing, marching, and changing the way America looked at itself. The hippies, though, attacked their target with gentler weapons. While the New Left ranted at the evils of

apogee in the massive Be-In assemblage, and the celebrated Summer of Love.

At first, San Francisco was amused by the hippies. But as altogether too many sons and daughters of wealthy, respected citizens took to marijuana-induced meandering, and as the LSD hysteria took full flight, public sympathy for the nomads gradually began to evaporate.

Tensions and rioting

By the mid-1960s, the African-American population in LA had multiplied tenfold and were

The riots in 1992 over the acquittal of Rodney King's arresting officers left over 50 people dead.

an affluent and smug, hypocritical society, the hippies tried to undermine that society with glimmering love and peace, and wearing far-fetched clothes.

The hippies of Haight-Ashbury

In the mid-1960s, San Francisco became the mecca of the hippie revolution. It was a natural refuge for spacey idealists, having been created by youthful myth-chasers. Former beatniks slid easily into the free-and-easy hippie style centered around the Haight-Ashbury neighborhood, with its funky, cheap Victorian houses, and Golden Gate Park handily nearby for roaming. By 1967, the Haight was thronged with long-haired young men and women, the movement reaching its

fed up with discriminatory employment and "unwritten" housing restrictions. On one hot summer evening in 1965, the palm-shaded ghetto of Watts exploded. For six days, the inner city boiled until the National Guard restored order. Almost 30 years later, in April 1992, with conditions in the black and Chicano areas largely unchanged, violence erupted again. The acquittal of four police officers recorded on video beating a African-American man, Rodney King, sparked the worst racial violence in California's history.

By the time the dawn-to-dusk curfew was lifted, there were over 50 dead and 2,500 injured, and 5,200 fires had occurred. South Central LA was devastated. The Rodney King case provided the spark for already existing tension, setting off the intricately connected time bomb of race, poverty, and the state of the inner city. The seemingly never-ending explosion of gang violence in Los Angeles, for example, has focused national attention on the problem of urban poverty.

Scandals and celebrity thrills

Barely a year goes by without major California events making headlines the world over. From 1994 to 1997, TV viewers were glued to their screens by the arrest and trials in

Occupy Wall Street protestors in 2012.

Los Angeles of former football hero O.J. Simpson. There was the much publicized 2003 recall of Governor Gray Davis and the election of mega movie star Arnold Schwarzenegger in his place, plus all the trials and legal woes of Michael Jackson, and starlets like Paris Hilton and Lindsay Lohan.

In a crime and trial that sparked mass demonstrations in Oakland, BART Police Officer Johannes Mehserle was sentenced to two years in prison for fatally shooting Oscar Grant on New Year's Day in 2009 – a shooting that was variously labeled involuntary manslaughter and a summary execution.

In 2011 and 2012, the focus shifted from televised trials to live protests, as Occupy Wall Street protesters filled streets and parks in major cities, from Oakland and San Francisco to Los Angeles.

Dot-com and beyond

At the start of the millennium, the future looked bright in San Francisco. Nearby Silicon Valley invigorated established industries and spurred thousands of start-up companies. Venture capitalists threw money at shiny ideas, stock prices soared, and the housing market hit new heights. Recent college graduates earned more money than they could count, but much of the prosperity owed more to innovative book-keeping than real business acumen.

The bubble burst on October 9, 2002, and many of these new millionaires were forced to return home to their parents. Today, California's tech fortunes are on the upswing; in 2012

THE FILM INDUSTRY

Hollywood's film industry eventually shook down into the major studios that dominate the industry today and are household names internationally. The "Big Six" are 20th Century Fox, Paramount, Warner Brothers, Columbia, Universal, and Disney. The Hollywood area is still host to a few smaller, independent production companies such as Lionsgate, DreamWorks, and the Weinstein Company. It is also home to all kinds of ancillary businesses and services such as recording studios, prop houses and talent agencies, lighting equipment companies, and equipment rentals.

The entertainment industry is one of the most highly unionized industries in California, with the Screen Actors Guild and American Federation of Television and Radio Artists (SAG-AFTRA) claiming more than 160,000 members nationwide, most of them in Los Angeles. The Directors Guild of America and the Writers Guild of America account for most of the rest of the talent, in addition to all the behind-the-camera workers such as grips, gaffers, film editors, carpenters, plasterers, publicists, costumers, art directors, sound people, and cinematographers, who are represented by the International Alliance of Theatrical Stage Employers (IATSE) and the American Federation of Musicians (AFM). Studio drivers are in the Teamsters.

Facebook went public, and Twitter moved to bigger digs in downtown San Francisco. One of the results of so many well-paid young professionals is that the rental prices in the city are very much on the rise.

Whether it's the dramatic rise and fall of the dot-com economy, scandals, or the thrill of celebrity, California will always be on the radar. Over 37 million people live in the state and speak over 90 different languages. Many Californians deeply identify with and prefer one half of the state to the other, inspiring a rivalry – sometimes friendly, sometimes less so. Compared to Southern California's trendy celebrity culture, Northern California considers itself laid-back and authentic. In the North, there are liberal and eclectic San Franciscans, redwood forests, and the Lake Tahoe ski slopes. In the south are beautiful beaches and balmy weather, spray-tanned blondes, and celebrity culture.

There will always be much excitement in a place with such diverse communities and a high concentration of artists, entrepreneurs, scientists, and trendsetters, who love the fact that California is home.

The pier at Santa Monica.

SAME-SEX MARRIAGE

In 2004, San Francisco's Mayor Newsom authorized the city to begin issuing marriage licenses to same-sex couples, inciting a 29-day wedding frenzy during which some 4,000 couples married. A month later licenses were halted by order of the California Supreme Court and the marriages already made were declared invalid.

The city's gay population and their supporters were undeterred, and filed a lawsuit contending that the revoked legislation violated California's constitutional guarantee for equal treatment. The appeal went to the state Supreme Court in 2006 after the ban against same-sex marriage was upheld. In May 2008 the court overturned the ban, but that victory was short-lived. In November 2008, the Proposition 8 ballot measure passed, defining marriage as a union only between a man and a woman. A year later, the state Supreme Court upheld the proposition but ruled that the unions of same-sex couples previously married were to be considered valid. In 2010, a federal court declared the ban unconstitutional, a decision which was upheld in 2012 by the US Court of Appeals for the ninth circuit. At the time of publishing, there are still further appeals in the works, and same-sex marriages are not available. However, with California leading the way, same-sex marriages are now legal in several other states.

Blessing of the Animals ceremony, Los Angeles.

Cottonwood Canyon Ranch, in the Morongo Valley.

CALIFORNIA CUISINE

California's menu is as varied as the people who live there. From sun-dried tomatoes to sushi, tandoori to tacos, the state is a food-lover's fantasy, bursting with color and flavor.

What are you hungry for? One of California's most quintessential experiences is its food. A multitude of influences and trends have converged in this state, making it an adventure destination for foodies from around the world. Walk just a few blocks in most sizeable cities and you will have a choice to whet even the most cosmopolitan of appetites: tacos and burritos, tandoori and curries, noodles and sushi, Mongolian barbecue, pasta and pizza, falafel and bagels, piroshki and baklava, and on through the global menu. It's not only the diversity of food that sets California apart; it's also the innovativeness and quality of food across the board.

Fresh, seasonal ingredients

The words "California Cuisine" have a dual meaning. Intuitively, they describe the general food of the state, but the term has also come to encapsulate a food movement begun by chef Alice Waters at Chez Panisse in Berkeley that emphasizes using local, in-season ingredients.

The Napa Valley Barrel Auction draws international wine lovers to bid for (and taste) Napa Valley wines.

Alice Waters opened Chez Panisse in 1971. Waters set out with no formal training, just a year spent abroad eating her way round Europe. To Waters, freshness was the cardinal virtue and foods were cooked simply so as to bring out their natural flavors.

Chez Panisse opened as a typical French bistro. Frustrated by an inability to get the quality goods that she found in France, Waters began encouraging local purveyors to bring produce to her door. Farmers grew special vegetables to complement a specific dish and hand-reared livestock and poultry to meticulous specifications. Small-time fishermen sold her their catch and, for the first time in years, local oysters were farmed.

Armed with local ingredients, the Chez Panisse kitchen went to work. The result? The strictly French food became less French, and the menu suddenly offered dishes such as ravioli made like gnocchi from potato starch and garlic, and the very English jugged hare.

Waters-trained chefs began to branch out on their own, and the Chez Panisse philosophy spread to other restaurants and other states. The fervor for freshness chimed with the Californian ethos, and in a few short years some chefs have been elevated to celebrity status.

An organic and sustainable approach

With the California Cuisine movement and Californians' generally eco-friendly leanings, consuming organic foods and promoting sustainability in food production have become extremely popular in the state. Restaurant menus credit their suppliers by name – whether by ranch, farm, or cheesemaker. Residents and companies sign up for organic produce boxes to be delivered to their homes or offices, full of

A pumpkin festival is held in Half Moon Bay every fall.

fresh, seasonal fruits and vegetables grown in nearby farms or urban gardens.

Urbanites also buy fresh produce directly from local growers at outdoor farmers markets, a staple in many communities. There you'll find everything from ripe fruits and seasonal vegetables to sustainably raised beef to cheese, jams, honey, nuts, and herbs.

In San Francisco, the Ferry Building Farmers Market has become one of the city's most popular tourist attractions. Large, popular farmers markets are also found in Napa, San Luis Obispo, Santa Monica, and San Diego, along with the Original Farmers Market in Los Angeles.

Of course, it is easy to shop local in California, whether you're looking for almonds, artichokes, olives, or tomatoes: the state's agricultural industry is the largest in the world, producing more than half of the state's fruits and vegetables.

The focus on produce seen in the state's countless farmers markets is also in line with Californians' generally health-focused attitude: it perhaps comes as no surprise that most restaurants include vegetarian – and often vegan – options predominantly on the menu rather than as a back-up. In major cities, you can expect to find several entirely vegetarian restaurants.

Diverse menus

California's overall menu is hardly restrictive, however. You name it, it's here – Peruvian, Mexican, Vietnamese, Ethiopian, Thai, Italian, French, Creole, Chinese. And it's good! To understand what makes this incredible array possible, it helps to consider California's geographic and cultural orientation: the influence of Mexican neighbors to the south and Asian neighbors to the west; the vast tracts of rich soil that make it one of the most fertile and productive places on earth; a climate friendly to growing just about every kind of crop all year round; and local waters that yield a bounty of fish and seafood.

Traditional European fare, especially Italian and French, has long been available in California, particularly prominent among the more expensive restaurants. Today, these upscale restaurants have also become highly regionalized, reflecting Californians' passion for European travel and an increased familiarity with specific regional dishes from, for example, Tuscany and Provence.

But more than these factors, the many people who call themselves Californians define the local food. The vast majority came from other parts of the world (many recently, others a generation or two ago), bringing native regional cuisine with them. Particularly in California's large cities, sizeable ethnic communities support their own specialty food shops and produce markets, as well as an often remarkable number of restaurants (Los Angeles, for example, claims to have around 500 Korean eateries). This results in a vitality, availability, and diversity that, for the curious diner, can make for a fascinating food experience.

Local specialties

California hasn't imported everything, though. In addition to huge amounts of produce, the state is famous for more specific local specialties. In San Francisco you can pair tangy sourdough bread with fresh Dungeness crab. Or warm up with a toasty Irish coffee, which was supposedly invented at the Buena Vista Café near Fisherman's Wharf. In Los Angeles, Koreatown is a foodie hotspot for ethnic authenticity, and East LA is the place for tacos

Chefs fear him and owners schmooze him. Michael Bauer, San Francisco Chronicle food critc, can make or break a restaurant. Go to: www.sfgate.com and search blogs for "bauer."

al pastor (spicy grilled pork and pineapple). Meanwhile San Diego is famous for fish tacos; Drakes Bay near San Francisco delivers deliciously fresh oysters; the Coachella Valley southeast of Palm Springs farms 95 percent of the world's dates; the state's Sierras yield honey, wild blackberries, and ollallieberries, chanterelle mushrooms, and venison; while sustainably farmed abalone comes from the North Coast.

Wine, beer, and coffee

No discussion of California eating pleasures would be complete without mentioning its

world-famous wines, of which locals are justifiably proud. California vintages from the Napa and Sonoma valleys northeast of San Francisco first achieved world-class status in the 1970s, and along the way have been joined by ever better wines from other parts of the state.

According to the Brewer's Association, California has far more breweries than any other state; popular ones include Sierra Nevada (Chico), Anchor Steam (San Francisco), Anderson Valley Brewery (Mendocino), and Bear Republic (Healdsburg).

In terms of other beverages, California is

Sushi in a San Francisco restaurant.

serious about coffee too, and offers plenty of alternatives to the worldwide chains. In fact, you can't walk a block in the downtown areas without passing people scurrying along clutching a to-go cup. Coffee has evolved into an art form here. In San Francisco's North Beach are popular family-run establishments like Caffé Trieste; Peet's Coffee & Tea (where the founders of Starbucks used to buy beans) originated across the bay in Berkeley. Meanwhile Blue Bottle Coffee Co. and Ritual Coffee Roasters approach coffee brewing in much the same way winemakers approach wine. Blue Bottle calls their process "artisan micro-roasting" and uses organic, shade-grown beans.

FOOD TRUCKS

One of the most interesting food trends in recent years has been the popularization of food trucks. Serving everything from Korean tacos to gourmet grilled cheese, curries, and cupcakes, these small restaurants on wheels are literally large catering trucks with kitchens. Roving around town, they often broadcast their location for that day's lunch hour on Twitter or their company website. The trend first picked up speed in LA – which now has well over 200 trucks including the popular Kogi BBQ truck – and then spread to San Francisco and major cities around the country. Want to try one? Bring cash and be prepared for a 15-minute wait.

FINE WINES OF CALIFORNIA

California's 2,000-plus wineries produce 90 percent of the country's wine, and they continue to win awards and worldwide critical acclaim.

In the 18th century, when the Franciscan fathers began winemaking, the grapes were dumped into troughs, trampled into pulp, and hung in cow skins to ferment before leaking into casks. "In those days the flavor was not described with enthusiasm," wrote the Napa Historical Society's Meredie Porterfield, "but that is what passed for wine in early LA."

California wine has come a long way since then, both in terms of quality and quantity. Today, the state accounts for 90 percent of the total US wine production. The reliably warm weather allows wineries to use very ripe fruit which makes for a fruitier wine, rather than the more earthy flavors of Europe It also means higher alcohol levels, with some Californian wines having over 13.5 per cent.

Napa and Sonoma get the lion's share of publicity, although they produce less than a quarter of the wine. Many more millions of gallons emanate from the San Joaquin Valley, the so-called "jug wines" which are mass-produced and low-priced. Other major wine areas are around Paso Robles, the Santa Ynez Valley near Santa Barbara, and, in the far south, the emerging vineyards of Temecula.

Despite increasing sophistication in bottling and manufacturing, basic winemaking has changed very little over the centuries. Wine is, after all, just fermented grape juice, not manufactured but generated by living yeast cells that ferment grape sugars into grape alcohol.

Wine tasting at the annual Napa Valley Barrel Auction.

The Napa Valley Wine Train is a smart restaurant serving regional cuisine in a collection of early-20th-century rail cars that convey passengers around the Napa Valley.

For more about wine and the Wine Country, see pages 79 and 153.

Detail on the Napa Valley Wine Train. A round-trip journey takes three hours.

The Napa Valley Barrel Auction brings together vintners and wine lovers to taste and bid for Napa Valley wines.

SUSTAINABLE WINEGROWING

Sustainable winegrowing and winemaking practices are a quickly growing trend in California. Many California wines are now labelled organic, meaning they have no added sulphites to prolong shelf-life, no synthetic pesticides or nonorganic chemicals were used, and natural alternatives were used for soil enrichment, pests, weeds, and vine disease management.

Additionally, vintners and growers who represent one-quarter of the state's wine acreage and 40 percent of the annual wine case production currently participate in the voluntary Code of Sustainable Wine Growing program. Introduced in 2002, the code aims to establish environmental standards and practices from ground to glass, including methods minimizing pesticide use, reducing water and energy use, building healthy soil, protecting air and water quality, recycling natural resources, and maintaining surrounding habitats.

Examples of such sustainable winemaking practices include using sheep and beneficial birds to control weeds and pests, using drip irrigation and process ponds to conserve water, and composting and recycling in an effort to minimize waste.

In 2012, the California Sustainable Winegrowing Alliance (CCSW) developed a third-party certification program related to the California Sustainable Winegrowing Program (SWP) – essentially like a LEED (Leadership in Energy and Environmental Design) certification program for wineries.

Napa contains a greater acreage of Cabernet Sauvignon grapes than any other California county.

n a tour or tasting class to gain access to the wine cellars.

ringer Winery was established in Napa Valley in 1876 by German Beringer brothers. The estate's Rhine House was ilt to recreate the family home on Germany's Rhine River, d is on the National Register of Historic Places.

Hot-air balloons drift over Napa Valley's vineyards.

CALIFORNIA WINE

California wines are world-class, but its winemakers are approachable; from Sonoma to San Luis Obispo, the state's wine regions happily welcome 21 million visitors each year to their wineries.

From breathtaking Napa and Sonoma valleys' concentrated selection of world-class wineries to the quiet vineyards of the Santa Barbara region in the south, California wineries are set up to welcome visitors and dazzle with their offerings. At tucked-away wineries in Monterey and Mendocino you feel like the only guest, while at talked-about vineyards in the Napa Valley you'll feel like you're in on the latest Wine Country buzz.

California's wine history

The first winemakers in California were 18th-century Spanish missionaries who used wine in religious ceremonies. Large-scale vineyards were established around the Los Angeles area in the 1830s by Jean-Louis Vignes, a French vintner. But the real birthplace of California wine is arguably Sonoma County.

Wine grapes were first planted in Sonoma County around 1812 in Fort Ross. Father

Numerous wineries offer wine tastings and tours of their facilities.

Father Junípero Serra, who founded many of the state's missions, had no taste for California's indigenous wild grapes and instead imported quality vines from his native Spain.

Jose Altimira, founder of the Mission San Francisco de Solano at Sonoma, and General Vallejo, who colonized Sonoma and Napa counties by granting land to his relatives and friends, were the first northerners to dabble in winemaking. Then Count Agoston Haraszthy, a flamboyant Hungarian political

refugee, pushed the Sonoma region into wine stardom. He began in 1857 at Buena Vista, Northern California's oldest winery, accumulating wine-grape cuttings for California's growers on journeys to Europe. After he died, his protégé Charles Krug, a German political exile, opened Napa Valley's first commercial winery in 1861, and by the 1880s, valley wines were winning medals in Europe.

Prohibition nearly decimated the industry, but following its repeal in 1933, Beaulieu Vineyard's Georges de Latour, the Mondavi family, and others began resurrecting the industry. In the 1960s, a wine boom began as large corporations marketed vintage-dated varietal wines at reasonable prices, and small, privately owned wineries produced more expensive, estatebottled wines at higher costs. Old winemaking families were joined by oil barons, engineers, and actors who revitalized old wineries and opened new ones.

By 1976, California wines were beating French vintages in European tastings. In the most famous tasting, the French wine industry's elite gathered in Paris to blind taste four white Burgundies against six California Chardonnays. The winner, to the surprise of

can match the growing conditions of the great north, especially the south central coast of Santa Barbara and San Luis Obispo counties.

Napa and Sonoma valleys

North of San Francisco, the valleys of Napa and Sonoma are the heart of California's Wine Country. The collection of small towns and villages are set amid miles of vineyards, whose premier grapes are the result of excellent growing conditions: temperate climate and rich, drainable soil. Napa Valley is especially famous for its Cabernet Sauvignon (Merlot and Sangiovese

> *California ranks first in wine consumption in the US, followed by Florida, then New York. There are more than 60,000 registered California wine labels.*

also do well here) and its high-end foodie scene.

Sonoma Valley has a more relaxed, less polished atmosphere than Napa. So far it remains less trafficked, especially compared to Napa Valley on weekends. Because of the valley's climate and soil variation (the county has more geologically distinct soil types than all of France), numerous varietals thrive in Sonoma County, including Chardonnay, Cabernet Sauvignon, Pinot Noir, Merlot, Zinfandel, Syrah, and Sauvignon Blanc.

Mendocino County

Some 35 miles (56km) long and 15 miles (24km) wide, the Mendocino Ridge Wine

Napa Valley Wine Train takes passengers from Napa to the village of St Helena and back.

the French judges, was Chateau Montelena's 1973 Chardonnay.

The Wine Country today

In the years since the 1976 grand tasting, California has become the world's fourth-leading wine producer. In the largest international wine competition, the Decanter World Wine Awards, two California wines received gold medals in 2012, and 35 received silver. Some 2,000 wineries cover the state, from Napa and Sonoma to the Gold Country and Santa Barbara. Indeed, grapes are grown in most of California's counties, and some vintners have discovered pockets of land in California that

A WINE PRIMER

Winemaking begins at the crusher, which frees juice from grapes. White wines are made from fermented juice; added yeast converts sugar to alcohol and carbon dioxide, with fermentation occurring in stainless steel tanks. Leaving yeast in creates dry wines; stopping yeast action makes sweeter wines. Sparkling wine begins the same way, then undergoes another fermentation. Carbon dioxide is trapped within the bottle, creating bubbles. For red wines, grape skin and pulp are included in the fermenting tank. After adding yeast, grape skins are pressed, then reds are aged in stainless steel or wooden tanks. The wine is clarified, then aged further before bottling.

Country, within Mendocino Country is a non-contiguous trio of burgundy-hued ridges that produce exceptional Zinfandel at high elevations. In 1988, the Kendall-Jackson Winery said the Mendocino Coastal Ridge was one of the world's greatest Zinfandel regions. The area is now being looked to as a new spot for Pinot Noir and Chardonnay grapes.

Monterey

An hour south of Silicon Valley, the Monterey Wine Country has 175 vineyards, largely in a 90-mile (145km) -long valley with just eight main viticulture soil types. The northern-most part of Monterey produces Pinot Noir and Chardonnay, while the valley's microclimates help support 42 different varietals. Pick up maps and winery information at Taste of Monterey (700 Cannery Row; tel: 1-888-646-5446), where you can also taste local wines.

San Joaquin Valley and the Sierra foothills

California's northern wineries produce just a fraction of the state's total output. Many of the grapes come from the hot, arid San Joaquin Valley, several hundred miles south, and are often used to make modestly priced "jug" wines.

The Sierra Nevada foothill's 10 counties are now home to more than 250 wineries, including Renwood in Plymouth (Amador Country). Many small and family-owned, these wineries excel at full-bodied Zinfandel, Syrah, and Petite Syrah. Rhone-style white varietals are also found here.

Santa Ynez Valley

Just 35 miles (56km) from Santa Barbara's beaches, the charmingly rustic Santa Inez Valley consists of six distinctive towns: Santa Ynez, Solvang, Los Alamos, Los Olivos, Ballard, and Buellton. Pinot Noir, Chardonnay, and Syrah can be tasted here, along with other varietals. Don't miss the Scandinavian-influenced Solvang either.

San Luis Obispo

In San Luis Obipso's Edna Valley, Arroyo Grande Valley, and Avila Valley, the rocky volcanic soil and marine influence produce grapes with complex flavors and intense varietal character. Small, family-owned wineries produce

primarily Pinot Noir, Chardonnay, Viognier, Syrah, Grenache, and Zinfandel. In Paso Robles, the three-day Paso Robles Wine Festival in May is the state's largest outdoor wine tasting.

Temecula Valley

The Temecula Valley (32miles/51km from San Diego) is emerging as California's southern-most wine country. A unique microclimate – with morning mist, cooling ocean air, warm midday sun, and clear nights – and granite-based soil are producing excellent Syrah, Cabernet, and Zinfandel grapes.

Chateau Montelena Winery sits at the base of Mt St Helena.

WINE-TASTING PRACTICALITIES

Most wineries are open 10am–4pm daily; some are by appointment only. A wine-tasting flight generally costs $10–20, and you may be given anywhere from four to six wines to try. Often, if you purchase bottles your tasting fee will be waived. Additionally, some tours include tastings. The best source for current information is the wineries themselves: call in advance to check on reservations, tasting fees, and discounts. Visitor centers are the best bet for contact details, or try www.winecountry.com. Try a tour (usually 1–2 hours) and a tasting at one of the larger wineries, then follow up with stops at a few of the smaller wineries.

Gloria Swanson in front of the street sign that immortalized them both.

THE MOVIEMAKERS OF SUNSET BOULEVARD

From such humble beginnings as filming in directors' living rooms, LA's movie industry became both star-maker and style-setter; while its heyday is in the past, the Hollywood neighborhood is still a magnet for people interested in the movie business.

Although its beginnings were elsewhere, Hollywood is what comes to most people's minds when they think of the film industry. In the first half of the 20th century, major changes were made, from silence to sound and from black-and-white to color. The early studios grew up on or around Sunset Boulevard, and the eponymous, quintessential movie about the industry's early days was released in 1950. Meanwhile, the story of California's movie industry has gotten more interesting ever since.

The start of the movie industry

The moving picture was actually invented as the result of a bet. In 1877, English eccentric Eadweard Muybridge helped California governor Leland Stanford win a $25,000 bet by using a series of 12 cameras to film a galloping horse and then printing the individual shots onto a revolving disk, thus proving that a trot-

Sound arrives with The Jazz Singer.

> William Laurie Dickson is on record at the Library of Congress as producer of the earliest movie: Fred Ott's Sneeze (1890), in which he captured an assistant sneezing.

ting horse has all four hooves off the ground simultaneously. Tripling his battery of cameras, Muybridge devised faster film, mounted his photographs on a wheel combined with light, and called his process Zoopraxiscope.

The Paris inventor Étienne-Jules Marey improved on this by developing a photographic gun with a long barrel for the lens and a circular photographic plate that rotated 12 times in the chamber during the single second the shot was being taken – the first movie camera. By 1888, George Eastman had produced celluloid film and the Kodak camera in New York, and in New Jersey Thomas Edison (who at first envisioned film as being merely a pictorial addition to his phonograph) added sprockets to synchronize the sound. Eadweard Muybridge died in 1904, unaware of the industry to which he had given birth, an industry that was about to move west.

The move to Hollywood

The first Hollywood census, in 1907, showed that among its population of 3,500 were 103 immigrants from England, 102 from Germany,

> *Charlie Chaplin was not impressed with LA when he first visited in 1910 while touring with one of Fred Karno's variety troupes. It was, he thought, "an ugly city, hot and oppressive, and the people looked sallow and anemic."*

86 from Canada, 20 from France, 28 from Ireland, 24 from Scotland, and 158 from New York. Also there was Francis Boggs, a film director visiting from Chicago's Selig Polyscope Studios, which had been battling over patents

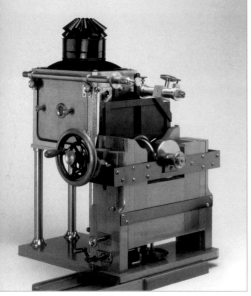

The first moving picture machine, Eadweard Muybridge's 1879 Zoopraxiscope.

with Thomas Edison's movie trust.

A year later, filming the *Count of Monte Cristo* during a severe Illinois winter, Boggs recalled the warmth of Hollywood and moved cast and crew to near Laguna Beach to complete the production, thereby earning his place in the reference books as the first director to shoot at least part of a film in California.

Four years later, Carl Laemmle's Universal Film Manufacturing Company began operations at Sunset and Gower, absorbing the Nestor Film Company, which had made Hollywood's first studio film, The Law of the Range. Eventually, his company moved through the Cahuenga Pass to found Universal

City. Meanwhile, Cecil B. de Mille, Jesse Lasky, Samuel Goldfish (who later changed his name to Goldwyn), and Arthur Friend formed a company under Lasky's name and planned to make *The Squaw Man*, starring Dustin Farnum, in Arizona, but found the scenery unsuitable. They continued westwards to Hollywood and completed the film at a rented barn one block north of Sunset at Vine and Selma.

The early years

Initially, films were shot quite casually around Hollywood, using private homes for domestic dramas, and banks during weekends for hold-up scenes, and passersby were conscripted on the spot for crowd scenes. But making movies soon became expensive because they were no longer simple. The easy days when sound pioneer Jack Foley was able to simulate galloping horses with coconut shells in a sandbox were giving way to times when the people required to make a film would include visual effects researchers, recording mixers, wranglers, gaffers, dialect coaches, and boom operators, not to mention caterers.

In 1924, both Metro and Goldwyn – studios which had moved onto the former lot on which the Pickford–Fairbanks studio had begun in 1922 – were merged. Mayer was quoted in *Motion Picture Weekly* as saying they aimed to produce 52 films per year, which he hoped would fill the 250,000 seats owned by the Loews theater chain.

This era saw the birth of the new system under which directors virtually ceased to be independent agents and became employees

D.W. GRIFFITH

The greatest name in early film, David Wark Griffith – "the teacher of us all," said Charlie Chaplin – started out as an actor and playwright, working in bit parts before becoming a director. Directing hundreds of stylish two-reelers for Biograph, he helped attract middle-class audiences, bringing respectability to an industry that had been largely for the working class who frequented nickelodeons. Boasting a still-impressive grandeur, *The Klansman* (later *Birth of a Nation*), was a sensation, introducing new techniques and sparking controversy with its apparent glorification of the Ku Klux Klan. Griffith is credited with many stylistic devices that define the modern film.

In the early days, Gower Gulch – at Sunset and Gower – was the rendezvous of would-be movie cowboys hoping to work for one of the small companies operating nearby. The formation of Central Casting eliminated this casual approach.

of "a massive, assembly-line organization." So began the great debate about studio versus artist, commercialism versus personal integrity, and "the desecration of great masterpieces and promising careers through the insensitivity of philistine management," wrote Gary Carey in the Mayer biography, *All the Stars in the Heaven*.

The talkies

By 1927, cinema attendances were slumping. The four Warner brothers – Harry, Albert, Sam, and Jack – had added a musical background to their film *Don Juan* (John Barrymore and Mary Astor), which was greeted enthusiastically. Then they had Al Jolson say a few words in *The Jazz Singer*. Although mostly background music with a few songs, the picture made millions and forced the other studios into sound.

The Birth of a Nation, a controversial movie directed by D.W. Griffith in 1915.

CENSORSHIP

From the beginning, there were reformers who wanted to censor the films and keep the industry under some restraints. In 1921 and 1922, such scandals as the Fatty Arbuckle rape case, actor Wallace Reid's drug death, and the (unsolved) murder of director William Desmond Taylor lent them ammunition at the same time as movies were appealing to wider and more middle-class audiences. Lewis Jacobs (author of *The Rise of the American Film*, 1968) wrote that "as the poor became less important as the mainstay of the movies, the ideals and tribulations of the masses lost some of their importance as subject matter."

Hoping to pre-empt the would-be censors, the movie industry invited Will H. Hays, an Indiana crony of President Warren G. Harding, to be its moral watchdog. Only months after taking office, Hays banned Arbuckle from the screen.

Hays's authority as head of the otherwise toothless National Association of the Motion Picture Industry was only moral – a smokescreen, charged some critics – although, for a while, most producers obeyed at least the letter of the law. But, late in the decade, such daring productions as Raoul Walsh's *Sadie Thompson*, in which actress Gloria Swanson portrayed the sad prostitute of W. Somerset Maugham's novel *Rain*, and the MGM filming of another banned title, Michael Arlen's *The Green Hat* as a vehicle for Greta Garbo, reduced the Hays office's credibility.

US Courts ruled in 1947 that the film studios' method of production and distribution violated anti-trust laws and that studios must divest themselves of their theater chains. It took Loews 10 years to finalize this move.

In July 1928, Warner released *The Lights of New York*, another instant hit. One month later, MGM's trademark, Leo the lion, roared from the screen showing a semi-documentary called *White Shadows in the South Seas*. The first

Pictures, 20th Century Fox, and RKO – while Universal, Columbia, and United Artists (which had been set up by Chaplin, Pickford, Fairbanks, and Griffith to distribute their work and that of other independents) played a minor role.

Accelerated by the Depression of the 1930s was the development of color on celluloid, which, by 1934, had progressed enough for Walt Disney to produce his first full-length animated feature, *Snow White and the Seven Dwarfs*, an assemblage of 250,000 individually painted frames. *Ben Hur*, which took

Charlie Chaplin and Jackie Coogan in The Kid, 1921.

MGM sound film was *Broadway Melody*. One scene was re-shot and MGM experimented with leaving the music as it was and having the players mime the number for the cameras – the beginning of pre-recording. It cost $280,000, grossed $4 million, and won an Oscar for the best picture in the Academy's third year of awards.

The Big Five

By the 1930s, the industry – one of America's top 10 – was dominated by the "Big Five" majors, all with production studios, large theater chains, and worldwide distribution – Warner Brothers, Loews Theatres (the theater chain that owned MGM), Paramount

around three years in the making, cost about $4 million.

Developed by David Selznick, *Gone With the Wind* was MGM's top-grossing release of 1939 and 1940. After Selznick borrowed money and Clark Gable from Mayer, Loews got to distribute the movie and MGM received 50 percent of the film's profits.

Movies and politics

By this date, there were almost 100,000 movie houses in the world – a third of them in Russia; only half that number were in the US. Every country's film industry needed foreign sales in order to be viable, which created a touchy situation for the US with the rise of Nazism because

Germany was a major market for US films. MGM was cautious and not until Germany had actually declared war on Poland did it start producing anti-Nazi films.

In 1947, the House Un-American Activities Committee (HUAC) targeted the industry for promoting communist propaganda, and influential columnists urged a boycott of "red" actors. The Hollywood Ten were cited for contempt and denied work. Most top stars escaped attention, although actress Katharine Hepburn, who had addressed a large gathering of people supporting Henry Wallace (a presidential candi-

been swept by social change so profound as that brought about in the old South by the Civil War. Overnight the coming of sound brushed gods and goddesses into obscurity. At first we saw [the heroine] as a kind of horror woman… an embodiment of vanity and selfishness. But as we went along, our sympathies became deeply involved with the woman who had been given the brush by 30 million fans."

Several former silent stars were approached: Mae West, then 55; Mary Pickford, 57; and Pola Negri, 51. All of them rejected the role as being too close to real life. The final choice, Gloria

Stephen Boyd and Charlton Heston in Ben Hur (1959), which won three Oscars.

In 1929, the very first American Academy of Motion Pictures awards (more commonly known as the Oscars) were presented in an award show that is now more popular than ever.

date who had been labeled a communist by far-rightists), came in for a good deal of criticism.

The ultimate Hollywood movie

When director Billy Wilder and producer Charles Brackett (together with co-writer D.M. Marshman) finished their script for *Sunset Boulevard* in 1949, they were "acutely conscious of the fact that we lived in a town which had

Swanson, 50, had left Hollywood a decade earlier after a 45-movie career that began in Mack Sennett comedies when she was still a teenager. Swanson embraced a lifestyle that typified its time – extravagant parties at which hundreds of the movie elite were presented with gold cigarette cases as party favors.

Sunset Boulevard, which portrayed the pathos of a former silent superstar in her declining years in a broken-down Hollywood mansion, struck a chord with critics as the ultimate inside-Hollywood movie. It garnered 11 Academy Award nominations and won three Oscars (best writing, score, and art direction). But not everybody in the city was pleased by the way the industry was depicted. "You

> *"The public wanted us to live like kings and queens,"* Swanson recalled. *"We were making more money than we ever dreamed existed and there was no reason to believe it would ever stop."*

bastard," shouted an outraged Louis B. Mayer to Wilder at a preview screening made on the Paramount lot. "You have disgraced the industry that made and fed you. You should be tarred and feathered and run out of Hollywood." Half

To be sure, Los Angeles still has a thriving industry – it often seems that every other person in Los Angeles is somehow connected to the movie business. Inevitably, many struggling actors and actresses find themselves waiting tables and bartending while waiting for their big break. The largest studios are still here, marketing and distributing films made by smaller production companies. Most TV shows are still produced in Los Angeles, and the San Fernando Valley is arguably the pornography capital of the world.

As for Hollywood itself? The neighbor-

Darth Vader and Wookie provide street entertainment on Hollywood Boulevard.

a century later, the success of Andrew Lloyd Webber's retelling of the tale in a stage musical demonstrated how timeless the story of Sunset Boulevard and the movies really is.

The modern movie industry

Today, the movie industry is much more decentralized. Once controlled by a small number of people, now it's an extremely complex network. Instead of a studio-based industry where the majority of films were shot on lots and film studios, today films are produced all over the world. California's tax code is partly to blame: high taxes for the film-making industry have pushed many producers to states that make it more affordable.

hood is mostly now a homage to days of yore, where tourists peruse the Hollywood Walk of Fame and would-be stars flock in hope of finding fame.

Movie stars themselves are a different breed than in the early days of cinema. They Tweet their fans, become entrepreneurs, and often live outside of Los Angeles: you likely won't see any celebrities in Hollywood unless its Oscars night. The movie stars tend to reside on the coast, in Malibu or Santa Monica, or else exclusive neighborhoods like Bel Air and Beverly Hills. The public has much more access to celebrities than in the past, but some things haven't changed: everyone wants to see one, meet one, or be one.

Sunset Boulevard, the quintessential movie about the film industry.

Rock climbing in Joshua Tree National Park.

THE GREAT OUTDOORS

Like a surfer waiting for a wave, the outdoors
enthusiast in California floats on a sea of
possibilities: from extreme mountain biking and
wilderness backpacking to gentle ocean-front bike
trails and fun on the ski slopes.

For many Californians – and visitors, too – the outdoors is synonymous with activity. And here there are endless ways to enjoy the breathtaking outdoor landscape of California, from hiking and climbing, to surfing and diving, to winters sports and whale watching. Whether you're a novice or an expert, California is filled with outdoor adventure schools, clubs, rental shops, outfitters, guides, and resorts to help you get going.

Camping

Looking to pitch a tent? Hiking and camping often go hand in hand in California, where many state parks have campgrounds as well. Whether you want to camp with your car nearby and have access to showers and bathrooms, or backpack into the wilderness for a few days, you'll find plenty of options to choose from all over the state. Just be sure to plan ahead; many campsites book up months in advance.

Zabriskie Point, Death Valley.

Cycling and mountain biking

Just north of the Golden Gate Bridge, opposite San Francisco, the Marin Headlands and Mount Tamalpais are considered the birthplace of mountain biking. Miles of scenic trails are the perfect routes for this bouncy recreation, though bikers share the trails with hikers and equestrians. Across the bay, road cyclists take long Wine Country tours on the rolling hills that wind through the scores of vineyards. California's central coast also has miles and miles of trails for bikers.

Up in Tahoe, summer adventurers can carry mountain bikes on the lifts of many ski areas to explore the alpine network of trails, some with bird's-eye views of Lake Tahoe. Meanwhile in the northeast corner of the state, bicyclists (of both the road and mountain variety) will find abundant trails and out-of-the-way roads to explore on two wheels, as long as the bikes are sturdy. (Be sure to have them checked out before you undertake a trip like this; garages are few and far between.)

Diving and snorkeling

Scuba diving is extremely popular in Monterey and along the coast south of the city. The kelp, long and spindly at the base and stretching up to form thick mats at the surface, ranges all along the coast, forming fantastic underwater

> On rainy spring days in the forest slopes above Sonoma, thousands of red-bellied salamanders come out of the woodwork (literally), crawling to the stream beds to spawn.

forests through which divers swim in search of the Garibaldi, ling cod, and many types of rockfish. Shark-diving (in cages) is also possible out by the Farallon Islands near San Francisco.

On the northwest coast, cold-water diving gear (a 7mm wetsuit, hood, booties, fins, mask,

be had pursuing surf smelt: the fisherman uses a big triangular net on a frame, plunging the net into oncoming breaking waves, and tends to get soaked completely. The nets are available for rent; the smelt, sometimes caught by the bucketful, are deep fried for dinner and then eaten whole.

Inland, up near Lassen Volcanic National Park and the surrounding national forest, many alpine lakes dot the area, and children will spend long days paddling driftwood logs like surfboards and watching the big, wary trout cruise slowly below.

Mountain biking in Mount Tamalpais State Park.

Pebble Beach Golf Links has hosted the US Open Championships five times and overlooks Carmel Bay.

snorkel, and 20lbs/9kg of lead to sink all that neoprene) equips you to hunt for abalone. This giant mollusk is a delicacy, but prying them off the rocks at depth is not for the casual swimmer (and needs a special permit; www.dfg.ca.gov/marine/faq.asp).

Diving is also increasingly popular among the kelp beds in the San Luis Obispo region, the Santa Catalina Islands, and Channel Islands National Park.

Fishing

At the coast, you can cast from rocks or piers, or embark on a "party boat" to probe the depths for salmon, ling cod, rockfish, and other denizens of the deep. Unusual, chilling sport can

> Sharks are under far more predatorial pressure from man than surfers and windsurfers are from them; many biologists fear that the prehistoric fish are being hunted to extinction out of misplaced fear and misunderstanding.

Fishermen, particularly fly fishermen who enjoy floating tiny nymphs in the surface film of chalk streams, will find abundant game and frequent caddis and mayfly hatches on the McCloud, Pit, and Fall rivers, as well as within the winding banks of Hat Creek, Hot Creek,

Battle Creek, and the many other notorious streams of the area.

Golf

From Napa Valley to Palm Springs to San Diego, you can play golf all over the Golden State, but a few destinations in particular should move to the top of the list for passionate golfers. First on the list is Pebble Beach, where you'll find the Pebble Beach Golf Links (home to the AT&T Pebble Beach National Pro-Am) and Poppy Hills. In February, the Buick Invitation Tournament takes place at Torrey Pines Golf

groves of giant sequoias and deep granite-walled canyons that were carved by glaciers. To walk among giant redwoods, visit Sequoia National Park, Muir Woods National Monument north of San Francisco, Redwood National Park, or Prairie Creek Redwoods State Park. Great hiking can also be had in Big Sur, Lake Tahoe, Anzo-Borrego, and parts of the deserts.

For a full list of state parks and information on the hundreds of hiking trails and campsites, visit www.parks.ca.gov. In general, most parks offer trails with various skill levels, and provide trail maps at visitor centers that help you plan your

Snorkeling at Laguna Beach, Orange County.

Course, where two championship courses offer players ocean views. See page 366.

Hiking

With numerous state parks, national parks, and wilderness areas, California provides superlative opportunities for hiking for all skill levels. Yosemite National Park offers everything from intense climbs with magnificent views of granite cliffs to easy trails along the valley floor. This is some of the Sierra's best backpacking country, where you can hike for many days without reaching a road (though careful planning and wilderness permits are required).

Kings Canyon, less accessible and more rugged than Yosemite National Park, has both

hikes. Some parks have a small day-use fee or parking fee.

Kayaking

A popular pastime in Monterey is to rent simple open-topped kayaks, called "scuppers," to paddle out to the local kelp beds. There you're likely to encounter one of California's most delightful wild animals, the winsome and intelligent sea otter, once hunted for its fur but now a favorite of animal lovers. The creatures are often seen floating on their backs with an infant sleeping on their belly, lolling about in the water, fastidiously cleaning their fur or crunching on a just-caught shellfish. Other great places for beginners are Morro

Bay, Sausalito, and Tomales Bay, while more experienced sea kayakers will love the Channel Islands, Santa Catalina Island, and La Jolla.

Rock climbing

California has some of the most diverse climbing in the country, with opportunities in both halves of the state. In Southern California, Joshua Tree National Park offers high desert climbing on 8,000 climbing trails, perfect for winter when other areas are too cold.

In April through October, climbers come to Yosemite for sheer granite cliffs, including the

The northwest coast is somberly beautiful: gray skies, long, empty beaches littered with driftwood, rugged sea cliffs, sawmills and fishing towns, and forests that end at cliff edges.

Monterey – and all along the Southern California coast. On a spring or summer afternoon, you're likely to catch sight of hundreds of windsurfers south of San Francisco, braving the cracking swells and blowing sands of Gazos

Whitewater rafting on the Truckee River.

famed El Capitan, with its 3,000ft (900-meter) face. In Northern California, Bishop and Lassen national parks are good options, as are Sequoia and Kings Canyon national parks.

Sailing and windsurfing

Sailing is possible in both Northern California – near San Francisco Bay, Santa Cruz, and

The Mojave – named after a Southwestern native tribe and pronounced mo-hahv-ee – covers much of the southeast portion of California, floating like a mirage out of Arizona and ending up against the precipice of the Sierras at their southern extreme.

Creek, Scott Creek, and Waddell Creek. The last is considered one of the best windsurfing spots in the country, where experts are often spotted jumping waves and pulling spectacular aerial maneuvers with names like "killer loop" and "cheese roll."

Windsurfing is also popular at Jalama Beach County Park on the end of Point Conception, the jutting corner of the state where the coast turns east. Wind that whips across the point propels windsurfers up and over the biggest and ugliest of the waves.

Surfing

Surfing is what California is most famous for, thanks to the Beach Boys. Both competitive and recreational surfers take the waves along California's coast. San Diego and Los Angeles coasts are particularly popular – the 130-mile (210km) area between the two cities stands out for the sharp blue line of the ocean. The water is warm here, pushed north by the Japan current, and the swells are manageable in most places, even for novice surfers.

But be aware that surfing has become a rather territorial pastime and has gained a somewhat unfriendly reputation. However, if you're willing to settle for something less challenging, try bodyboarding; you can paddle

Whale watching

During winter and spring, you can gaze from cliffs or boat cruises to spot migrating gray whales. There are numerous spots along the California coast to look for migrating whales. Dana Point, Point Reyes (including from the lighthouse), Redwood National and State parks, and Santa Cruz are all options in Northern California, while Santa Barbara and San Diego (especially Cabrillo National Monument at Point Loma) are good bets in Southern California. See page 96 for whale watching near San Francisco.

Hiking in Yosemite National Park.

For the most part, coastal swimming is best kept for Southern California. Because of undertows and riptides on the northwest coast, the waves can be powerful and dangerous, and are no place for the novice.

out at almost any non-surfing beach and be assured of a good time.

Other popular waves are found at San Luis Obispo's long beaches, which are interspersed with high cliffs. In the north, competitive surfing is found closer to Santa Cruz. Off the coast of Half Moon Bay, an annual surfing competition is held at Mavericks.

DEATH VALLEY NATIONAL PARK

At 282ft (86 meters) below sea level, Death Valley is the lowest point on the North American continent. At least five million years ago, this deep gap was formed by earthquakes and the folding of the earth's crust, creating what is known as a graben or rift valley. As you hike or camp, you may be lucky enough to spot California's horned lizard, a diamondback rattlesnake, a desert tortoise, or an endangered gila monster (North America's only poisonous lizard). Pack rats and kangaroo rats, bats, hawks, and low-swooping falcons make their home here, too. At night, you'll very probably fall asleep to the melancholy howling of coyotes.

"More free sunshine falls on this majestic range than on any other… It has the brightest weather, brightest rocks, …. and the brightest forests of silver firs and silver pines…" John Muir (1838–1914), founder of the Sierra Club.

Whitewater rafting

The Sacramento area is popular with whitewater rafters of all abilities, while adrenalin junkies seek out the thundering rapids of Burnt Ranch Falls on the Trinity, and the cataracts of Hell's

Spot whales off the central California coast.

Corner Gorge or the Ikes Falls on the Klamath. The breathtaking forest drops of the California salmon are at once beautiful and thrilling. On the other hand, you can float for many days in inflatable kayaks with nary a ripple on the lower Klamath River and parts of the Trinity. Within sight of fertile vineyards and cottage-style wineries, the Russian River and Cache Creek are popular rafting and canoeing streams.

Winter sports

Tahoe offers California's biggest and best concentration of snow sport opportunities. Attracting the most skiers are Squaw Valley on the North Shore, and Heavenly Mountain at the South Lake. Squaw has a giant hotel, an Olympic history, an ice-skating rink on top of the mountain, a climbing wall, a spa, and several shops. Heavenly is just as good; it's a question of choice. Many smaller areas – Kirkwood, Homewood, Sugar Bowl, Northstar, and Donner Ridge – are more friendly spots to ski, although the sheer vertical drops are not as great. In addition to downhill skiing and snowboarding, you can give cross-country skiing and snowshoeing a try.

On the Sierra's east slope, Mammoth Mountain is central California's premier ski area. Here, the mountains slope down to the desert plain of the Owens River Valley, not far north of the precipitous drop into Death Valley. Resorts generally offer equipment rentals, individual or group lessons for all skill levels, and day, weekend, or season passes. For more information on ski resorts in California, see page 367.

WHALE WATCHING NEAR SAN FRANCISCO

Just 27 miles (43km) from Fisherman's Wharf lie the Farallon Islands, once called the "Devil's Teeth." The islands themselves are off-limits to the public (only a limited part is inhabited, by researchers), but these jagged outcroppings provide a rich sanctuary for 23 species of marine mammals, including 18 types of whales and dolphins, plus seals, seabirds, and great white sharks that migrate here to breed in summer and fall.

A whale-watching excursion allows for the ultimate vantage point to observe these magnificent creatures as they frolic and cavort in their temporary environment. SF Bay Whale Watching runs full-day expeditions from Fort Mason to the Gulf of the Farallones on weekends from November through June. Get up close to gray, blue, and humpback whales, dolphins, seals, and sea lions as the boat sails from Fisherman's Wharf beneath the Golden Gate Bridge to the roiling waters of the Pacific Ocean.

A naturalist expert is on board the motor-catamaran to narrate throughout the trip, point out areas of special interest, and answer questions about local wildlife. Be sure to dress warmly, and be advised that water outside the Golden Gate can be quite choppy.

Surfing at Ocean Beach, San Diego.

EARTHQUAKES AND OTHER DISASTERS

California is not without its downsides: the state is prone to natural disasters including earthquakes and fires. Still, Californians usually view such risks as a small price to pay for all the advantages.

California is a major earthquake zone. In 1769, Gaspar de Portola's expedition felt the first recorded quake in the state, about 30 miles (48km) southeast of Los Angeles. Today, the southern part of the state alone has about 10,000 earthquakes each year, although only about 15–20 are greater than magnitude 4.0.

The reason is that the southern portion of the state straddles the boundary between the Pacific plate (extending as far west as Japan) and the North American plate (eastwards to Iceland). The former moves northwest at a rate of 1.25 inches (45mm) per year, about as fast as fingernails grow; if this rate continues for the next 15 million years, San Francisco and Los Angeles will become next-door neighbors.

The shift is not gradual and steady but a process where the earth stores up the energy, releasing it with the enormous burst that we know as an earthquake along one or another of the scores of fault lines. One of the state's major faults is the San Andreas fault, which is actually a more than 800-mile-long (1300km) fault zone with many segments, in some parts up to 10 miles (16km) deep. Although there have been recorded earthquakes since the 18th century, it was not until 1935 that Charles F. Richter devised the scale by which seismographs plot today's temblors.

Aftermath of a quake in the San Francisco Bay Area in October 1989 that measured 6.9 on the Richter scale, causing building and part of the two-level Interstate 880 highway to collapse.

Collapsed house in the hills north of Los Angeles, after the Northridge earthquake in 1994. It caused around US$7 billion in damage and left thousands of people homeless.

A sudden right slip movement of up to 16ft (4.9 meters) on the San Andreas fault caused the San Francisco quake in 1906 that measured 8.25 on the Richter scale, killing 315 people and causing a fire that took days to extinguish.

...e Williams brush fire in Angeles National Forest in 2012 covered ...000 acres and started near a campground. Brush fires destroy trees ...d hillsides, leaving the countryside vulnerable to flooding.

...ooding in the Sacramento delta.

Dead palm trees on the shore of Salton Sea, California's biggest lake, which has dried up and refilled numerous times, affected by human changes. Part of the San Andreas fault lies under the lake.

THE BIG ONES

The most disastrous earthquake in California history was the cataclysmic 8.25-magnitude quake that struck San Francisco on April 18, 1906, at 5:12 am. More than 300 deaths were reported, but today's estimate puts the toll at over 3,000, and 225,000 people lost their homes.

When will the next major earthquake hit? Scientists and California residents have long been anticipating the "Big One," a massive earthquake along the San Andreas fault. Research shows the southern portion of the San Andreas is long overdue for a large quake, leading some scientists to predict an 8.1 magnitude "wall-to-wall" quake running from the Salton Sea, a rift lake sitting directly on the fault line southeast of Palm Springs, to Monterey. Such a quake would release twice the energy of California's 1857 7.9-magnitude earthquake. Northern California's Hayward fault is also overdue for an earthquake. The fault averages a major quake every 140 years, and the last one occurred in 1868, meaning 2008 was the 140-year mark.

If you experience an earthquake, stay indoors and find shelter under something sturdy like a piece of furniture or door frame, and away from glass windows. If outside, avoid trees, power lines, buildings, and bridges.

Earthquake drill in a San Francisco school.

OCEAN

LOBBY

REGISTRATION

Getting away from it all with a ride through Deep Springs Valley.

Rush hour in Los Angeles.

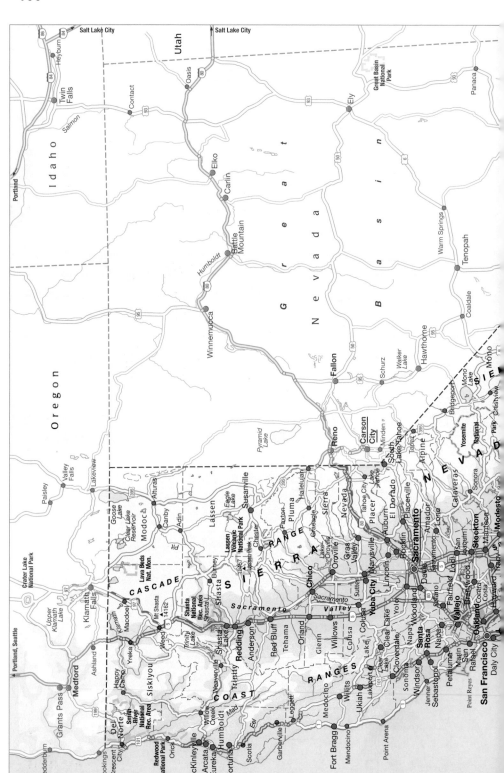

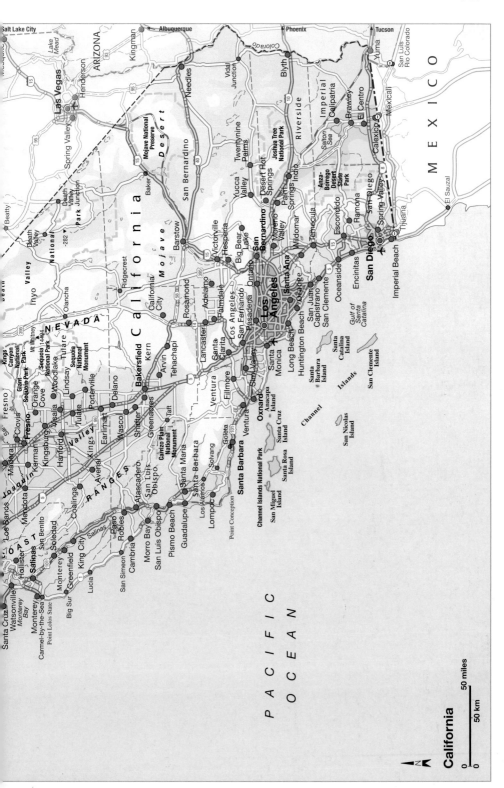

California

PACIFIC OCEAN

MEXICO

N

0 50 miles

0 50 km

Golden Gate Bridge viewed from the Marin County side.

NORTHERN CALIFORNIA

A detailed guide to Northern California, with principal
sites clearly cross-referenced by number to the maps.

*Grove of redwoods in
Northern California.*

Towering redwoods, granite cliffs, snowy peaks, picturesque vineyards, cosmopolitan cities... Northern
California is home to more natural and social variety
than found in any similar-sized territory in the world.

San Francisco is its most famous city, where vintage
cable cars crawl up incredibly steep hills, fog rolls eerily
around the Golden Gate Bridge, and boisterous sea lions
bark at Fisherman's Wharf. Millions of visitors explore this
open-minded metropolis every year, perusing farmers markets and fine art museums, and lounging in the sprawling
Golden Gate Park or on a ferry headed to the
world-famous Alcatraz island prison.

A journey of only a few hours in either
direction from San Francisco reveals entirely different
landscapes. To the south are Monterey's kelp forests and
peaceful tide pools, the spectacular rugged Big Sur coast,
and grand Hearst Castle; to the north, acres upon acres of
rolling vineyards in the serene Napa and Sonoma valleys
produce grapes that are used in the production of excep-
tionally fine wines.

Pacific coastline.

Further inland is the long, fertile Central Valley, the
heart of California's agricultural industry. It is also the
political heart of the state, home to the pretty state
capitol of Sacramento. Sacramento's historic Old Town
also is a starting point for exploring California's 1849 Gold Rush
history; not far from here in Gold Country's old frontier towns,
you can try your luck panning for gold in the rivers of the Sierra
Nevada foothills.

Climbing into the Sierra Nevada mountain range you find some
of the country's most stunning natural attractions. On the border of
California and Nevada, glittering Lake Tahoe draws hikers in summer
and hordes of skiers in winter. Sequoia and Kings Canyon national parks
protect the tallest redwood trees on earth, and awe-inspiring Yosemite
National Park shows off tremendous waterfalls, granite peaks, and
woodlands. Even more remote is the northeastern corner of the state,
which is dominated by Mount Shasta and Lassen Peak (both active volcanoes) and the town whose name is the state's official motto: Eureka,
meaning "I have found it!"

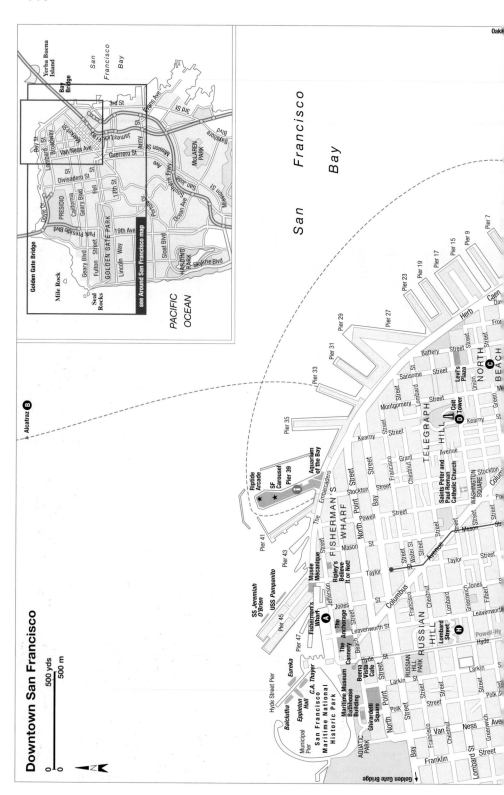

Downtown San Francisco

500 yds
500 m

N

San Francisco Bay

Oaki

PACIFIC OCEAN

Golden Gate Bridge

Mile Rock

Seal Rocks

Bay Bridge

Yerba Buena Island

San Francisco Bay

3rd St

Evans Ave

3rd St

Bayshore Blvd

McLAREN PARK

Guerrero St

Mission St

Army

Van Ness Ave

Lombard St

Broadway

Bay St

Divisadero St

California

Geary Blvd

Fell

17th St

Mission St

San Jose Ave

Ocean Ave

Southern Fwy

PRESIDIO

Doyle Dr

GOLDEN GATE PARK

Park Presidio Blvd

19th Ave

Lincoln Way

Geary Blvd

Fulton Street

Sloat Blvd

HARDING PARK

Skyline Blvd

see Around San Francisco map

San Francisco Bay

Alcatraz B

Pier 7

Pier 9

Pier 15

Pier 17

Pier 19

Pier 23

Pier 27

Pier 29

Pier 31

Pier 33

Pier 35

Pier 41

Pier 43

Pier 45

Pier 47

Caen

Herb

Fron

NORTH BEACH

TELEGRAPH HILL

Battery Street

Sansome Street

Montgomery Street

Lombard Street

Levi's Plaza

Union Street

Green

Kearny Street

Colt Tower D

C

Grant Avenue

Chestnut Street

Francisco Street

Saints Peter and Paul Roman Catholic Church

WASHINGTON SQUARE

Stockton

Colu

Po

Bay Street

Powell Street

Stockton Street

North Point Street

The Embarcadero

Aquarium of the Bay

Riptide Arcade

SF Carousel

Pier 39

Mason St

Taylor St

Jones St

Mason Street

Water St

Avenue

Columbus

Taylor Street

Francisco

Chestnut

Lombard

Greenwich

Jones

Filbert

Leavenworth

FISHERMAN'S WHARF

Musée Mécanique

Ripley's Believe It or Not!

Jefferson Street

Beach Street

Leavenworth St

SS Jeremiah O'Brien

USS Pampanito

Fisherman's Wharf A

The Anchorage

RUSSIAN HILL

Lombard Street H

Powell-Hy

Hyde

Larkin

Hyde Street Pier

Eureka

Balclutha

Eppleton Hall

C.A. Thayer

Municipal Pier

San Francisco Maritime National Historic Park

Maritime Museum Bathhouse Building

The Cannery

Ghirardelli Square

Buena Vista Cafe

RUSSIAN HILL PARK

Hyde St

Beach St

North Point

Larkin Street

Polk Street

Van Ness Ave

Francisco

Chestnut

Lombard Street

Greenwich

Bay

Franklin

AQUATIC PARK

Golden Gate Bridge

SAN FRANCISCO

Tony Bennett sang it like it is. The "City by the Bay,"
long celebrated in lyrics and postcards, wins visitors'
hearts straight away and effortlessly despite the
city's rather unpredictable weather.

San Francisco is without a doubt one of the most beautiful, vibrant, and diverse cities on the planet. Sitting like a thumb at the end of a 32-mile (50km) peninsular finger, this city of seven hills is surrounded by water on three sides and blessed by one of the world's great natural harbors. It is joined to the mainland by two acknowledged masterpieces of bridge design and construction, including the magnificent Golden Gate Bridge that glitters at night, often blurred by a blanket of fog.

Beyond the iconic San Francisco – the grand bridges, rattling cable cars, and barking sea lions – the city has far more depth than you might expect from a city only 49 sq miles (127 sq km) in area. It's easy to get caught up in the excitement of Downtown, but there are over a dozen distinct and wonderfully original neighborhoods to explore, each with its own appeal. And whether it's innovative cuisine, fine art, classical music, contemporary dance, sprawling parks, or boisterous street festivals you're after, you will be sure to find it.

San Francisco people

This truly endless variety of things to do is in many ways driven by the social and economic diversity of San Franciscans themselves. The 810,000 residents of this charmed city, the

nation's 14th largest, form an impressive demographic bouillabaisse. The descendants of early Italian, German, and Irish families are still found in snug neighborhood enclaves, but their numbers have fallen as many have moved to the rapidly developing suburbs, replaced by an influx of Asian and Latino people.

Regardless of their heritage, San Franciscans are all known for being left-leaning, environmentally conscious, gay-friendly, and very open-minded – eccentricity rarely raises an

Main Attractions
Fisherman's Wharf
Coit Tower
Chinatown
San Francisco Museum of
    Modern Art
Golden Gate Bridge
Mission Dolores
Golden Gate Park

View of the San Francisco skyline from Pier 40.

Mime artist at Fisherman's Wharf.

eyebrow. Embracing the beautiful and eclectic makes San Francisco the vibrant city it is today, and one that draws more than three million visitors a year to discover its magic.

Fisherman's Wharf

The city's touristy **Fisherman's Wharf** Ⓐ is one of the most visited places in San Francisco. A bright, family-oriented carnival of attractions, despite the crowds and occasional tackiness, the Wharf also has tons of seafood restaurants, good little stores tucked between the souvenir stands, and two garden parks with open space for picnicking.

In summer months, the narrow boardwalks are jammed with people and it's easy to forget that this is one of the city's most important historic spots. Along with hundreds of sailboats and yachts and the ferries packed with visitors and commuters, much of San Francisco's maritime past is moored here.

The waterfront retrospective start at the **Hyde Street Pier**, where a flee of vintage vessels is docked, including a sidewheel ferry and three schooner that carried heavy freight in the days of sailing ships. The tall masts and rigging at the water's edge belong to the graceful Scottish-built *Balclutha*, a 301ft (81-meter) clipper built in 1886 that made 17 trips around Cape Horn

These ships are all operated by the **Maritime Museum**, located in the Bathhouse Building (900 Beach Street; tel: 415-561-7000; free), which displays intricate models of boats and muralist Hilaire Hiler's surrealist vision of the Atlantis. It is located in **Aquatic Park**, a terraced greensward that leads out to a small beach and curving municipal pier sometimes dotted with fishermen.

South of the Maritime Museum and occupying the entire block bounded by North Point, Polk, Beach, and Larkin streets, Ghirardelli Square is a shopping center geared towards visitors. Ghirardelli Square was built as a wool mill during the Civil War era and later became a chocolate factory in 1893. Although the working factory

Fisherman's Wharf.

has moved, there is still a retail outlet and candy store.

If you're in the mood for something warmer, stop at the **Buena Vista Café** on the corner of Hyde and Beach streets for an Irish coffee (it was invented here) and watch the busy cable-car activity at the **Powell-Hyde Cable Car Turnaround.** A short walk east leads to **The Cannery** (2801 Leavenworth Street), once the largest fruit and vegetable cannery in the world, and now a three-story shopping complex.

Fish restaurants

An appetite for fruits of the sea can be satisfied by strolling down Jefferson Street, the wharf's main drag, where sidewalk vendors boil and steam shellfish all day long. Walk toward the waterfront to Pier 45, which remains as much of a working site as Fisherman's Wharf can offer. Fishermen depart before dawn and return with sand dabs, scallops, Dungeness crabs, and sea bass. Historically, Italians skippered and manned the boats and also ran the restaurants. A glance at the names of the restaurants indicates that not all that much has changed, with most restaurants in the area either serving Italian-inspired fare or some of the freshest fish in the city. Fisherman's Wharf is also a perfect place to try one of San Francisco's proudest legends, its crusty sourdough bread, which pairs perfectly with sweet butter, Dungeness crab, and a glass of crisp Chardonnay.

Moored at Pier 45 is the SS *Jeremiah O'Brien*, a World War II Liberty Ship. Also on Pier 45 at the end of Taylor Street is the **Musée Mecanique**, (tel: 415-346-2000; www.museemecaniquesf. com; Mon–Fri 10am–6pm, Sat–Sun 10am–7pm; free) an exercise in nostalgia with its coin-operated pianos, antique slot machines, and a 1910 steam-driven motorcycle.

Sea lions and an aquarium

To see the city's famous sea lions sunbathe and bark, head to **Pier 39.**

This 45-acre (18-hectare) collection of shops, arcades, fast-food restaurants, and other diversions lures tourists by the thousands to places like the **San Francisco Carousel**, the **Riptide Arcade,** and the **Aquarium of the Bay** (Embarcadero at Beach Street; tel: 1-888-732-3483; www.aquariumofthebay. org; charge). The oldest thing at Pier 39 is the **Eagle Café**, a fixture favored for decades by fishermen and longshoremen before it was moved intact from its original site a couple of blocks away.

Alcatraz Island

Set in one of the world's most beautiful harbors and accessible only by ferry, **Alcatraz ⑧** (daily tours depart from Pier 33; tel: 415-981-7625; www. alcatrazcruises.com and www.nps.gov/ altcatraz.com; charge) and its tales of legendary inmates have fascinated visitors since the days of Prohibition and American gangsters.

Just over a mile offshore from San Francisco, the hump of rock was sighted in 1775 by Spanish Lieutenant Juan Manuel de Ayala. Back then, the

Row of cells inside Alcatraz, the ones with the doors being for solitary confinement.

TIP

Less visited than
Alcatraz is the larger
Angel Island (www.
angelisland.com; tel: 415-
435-1915); accessible
by ferry from several Bay
locations. You can climb
to the top of Mt
Livermore to see all five
of the Bay's bridges, or
take a Segway tour or
hire a bike to explore the
perimeter road. There
are also picnic sites,
music events, and an
educational tram tour.

only occupants were pelicans, so Ayala named it Isla de los Alcatraces – the Island of Pelicans. Its strategic location in the bay suited it to military purposes and it was garrisoned with soldiers in the 1850s. Because escape from the island was a remote possibility (requiring a 1.5 mile/2km) swim through the frigid waters and swift currents of the San Francisco Bay), renegade servicemen were incarcerated on Alcatraz, to be followed by Apaches taken prisoner in Arizona during the 1870s Indian wars, and then prisoners from the Spanish-American War.

Alcatraz evolved into a federal prison that housed such hardened criminals as Mafia leader Al Capone and the notorious Machine Gun Kelly. Those few desperate inmates who managed to escape their cells in bids for freedom perished in the cold waters surrounding the island. The prison was finally closed in 1963 when the costs of repairing the constant ravages of wind and weather grew too great. It is now part of the Golden Gate National Recreational

The ruined Warden's
House on Alcatraz.

Area: park rangers give guided tours of safe parts of the island, including a peek at some of the cell blocks, while the evocative, award-winning taped audio tour features voices of some of the original prisoners.

North Beach

North Beach ◉ is many neighborhoods in one; the Little Italy of San Francisco (though nobody calls it that), the former haunt of Beat poets like Jack Keruoac, the city's strip club hub, and a destination for young nightowls looking to mingle at bars and dance clubs.

The once very tawdry **Broadway** strip has been gentrified a bit, but a number of strip clubs still beckon with promises of lap dances and naked girls. The historic **Condor remains, having** become famous when a waitress named Carol Doda peeled to the waist one night in 1964 and ushered in the topless boom. The venerable Carol Doda used to descend nightly from the ceiling atop a piano, wearing only a G-string.

North Beach is also where several of the city's comedy clubs are located. On Columbus, Woody Allen and Bill Cosby performed at the Hungry I, and the likes of Lenny Bruce, Jonathan Winters, and the Smothers Brothers plied their trades at the original Purple Onion.

The neighborhood has also long been congenial to writers, artists, and deep thinkers. A favorite haunt of wordsmiths is the **City Lights** bookstore at 261 Columbus Avenue (open late), which has been run since 1953 by poet Lawrence Ferlinghetti, one of the literary luminaries of the 1950s Beat era. Across Kerouac Alley – where quotes from Jack Kerouac, Lawrence Ferlinghetti, Maya Angelou, Confucius, and John Steinbeck are found in the sidewalk – is **Vesuvio**, an eclectic bar full of Beat nostalgia and intellectuals. Nearby, on Columbus, is the old **Tosca Café**, a bar where opera records play on the jukebox.

Columbus Street running north from Broadway is the real heart of North Beach. With the flavor of an old-fashioned Italian neighborhood, it is full of little cafés, Italian restaurants, and working-men's bars where elderly Italians sip red wine and muse about life. At the intersection of Columbus and Union is **Washington Square,** a grassy expanse for pick-up sports games, a morning Tai Chi location, and an ideal picnic spot. Overlooking the square is the Romanesque façade of 1924-built **Saints Peter and Paul Church**, where Joe DiMaggio and Marylin Monroe once posed for their wedding pictures.

Telegraph Hill

Above North Beach, at the end of Lombard Street, is **Telegraph Hill,** crowned by the 210ft (55-meter) **Coit Tower ①** (tel: 415-362-0808; summer 10am–5.30pm, winter 9am–4.30pm; charge to take elevator). Built in 1934 on the site of an early telegraph station and funded by heiress Lillie Hitchcock Coit, it lures visitors with momentous views and WPA frescoes in the style of Diego Rivera. Down the east side of Telegraph Hill are the lovely Filbert and Greenwich street staircases, flanked by attractive and lush private gardens. If you are lucky you will hear and spot the flock of wild red-headed parrots who live there, and who starred in the 2003 documentary *The Wild Parrots of Telegraph Hill*.

The steps end on Sansome Street, directly across from Levi's Plaza, the corporate headquarters of Levi Strauss & Co. A small but interesting museum in the main building's lobby chronicles the company's story and the development of the riveted blue denim jeans.

Chinatown

One of the largest outside Asia, this 24-block Chinatown is the quintessential city within in a city. The official entrance is the green pagoda-topped **Chinatown Gate ⑤** at the corner of Bush Street and Grant Avenue, which the Republic of China gifted in 1969. Through the gate, dragon-topped lampposts and crisscrossing lines of red lanterns run the length of **Grant Avenue**, Chinatown's main tourist street, and shop windows beckon with crowded displays of silk, porcelain, hand-painted vases, teak furniture, and the more usual and mainstream. Food ranges from tiny cafés and obscure eateries to popular dim sum lunches, for which waitresses push carts of dumplings and pastries from table to table like peddlers.

Two blocks north along Grant Avenue is **Old St Mary's Church**, the city's main Catholic cathedral from 1853 to 1891 and today a parish church. In the past this area was known for its seedy array of brothels, gambling houses, and opium dens; all attempts at clean-up failed until the 1906 fire destroyed most of the commercial establishments.

It's on the narrow streets intersecting Grant that Chinatown truly comes to life. Turn left on Clay Street to find **Waverly Place ⑤**, a colorful alley that

Coit Tower on Telegraph Hill.

TIP

Parking is very scarce near Coit Tower. To avoid the steep climb by foot, catch the No. 39 bus near St Peter and Paul's Church, and ride it all the way to the tower.

lent its name to one of Amy Tan's characters in *The Joy Luck Club*. After admiring the bright curved roofs and ornate balconies, you can climb three flights of stairs at No. 125 to visit the Tin Hou temple, dedicated in 1852 to the Goddess of the Seven Seas, where hundreds of red-and-gold paper lanterns flood the ceiling and incense fills the air. Waverly is just one of dozens of quiet alleys in Chinatown. Other alleys include Spofford Alley – notable for its cameo in *The Maltese Falcon* – and Ross Alley, home to an erhu-playing barber and a tiny one-room fortune cookie "factory" where you can see fresh fortune cookies folded.

On Washington Street, tiny, cluttered herb shops offer powders and poultices promising everything from rheumatism relief to the restoration of sexual powers. Outdoor produce and pastry shops also vie for your nose. A little farther west is **Stockton Street**, where all of Chinatown comes to grocery shop. Diminutive Chinese women clutch plastic bags in both hands as they go about their errands, while the old men smoke cigarettes and read Chinese-language newspapers.

When you're done exploring, head south of Grant on Washington or Clay Street to reach **Portsmouth Square**, Chinatown's small urban park, where Tai Chi devotees practice their balletic movements in the morning, children clamber on play structures, and men gather to bet over mahjong and Chinese cards. Here Robert Louis Stevenson used to watch the ships come in, biding his time until the married woman he loved would divorce her husband. Across Kearny Street and inside the Holiday Inn is the **Chinese Cultural Center** (www.c-c-c.org; Tue–Sat 10am–4pm; free), which offers art shows and guided tours.

Union Square

Considered the city's geographical center in pioneer days, **Union Square** Ⓖ and the surrounding blocks today comprise San Francisco's downtown hub for shopping, entertainment, and tourism. The land was set aside for public use in 1850 and received its name a decade later when pro-Union sympathizers rallied here before the Civil War. In the center of the square, a 90ft (27-meter) Corinthian column with a bronze winged *Victory* statue in the square commemorates another conflict – Commodore George Dewey's naval victory over the Spanish in 1898.

Just west of the square is the **Westin St Francis,** the city's second-oldest hotel and a majestic reminder of the past. For a spectacular view, take a ride in its glass elevators up to the 32nd floor. The St Francis' neighbors in Union Square are upscale department stores, including **Neiman Marcus** with its glorious rotunda, Barney's, and Macy's. Weave down Powell through the crowds of shoppers to the cable car turnaround. Two of the three cable car lines begin and end here, leading towards Fisherman's Wharf via slightly different routes.

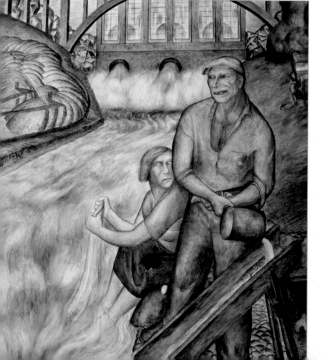

One of the frescoes in Coit Tower.

Visitor Center and theater district

Down the nearby stairs you'll find the **San Francisco Visitor Information Center** (900 Market Street; tel: 415-391-2000; www.sanfrancisco.travel; Mon–Fri 9am–5pm, Sat–Sun 9am–3pm, Nov–Apr closed Sun), offering maps, brochures, transportation passes, and advice in several languages. Cross Market Street to explore the elaborate Westfield Shopping Center, anchored on either end by Bloomingdales and Nordstroms department stores.

Just west of the Union Square area, San Francisco's theater (mostly spelled theatre here) district begins along Geary and Sutter streets. The Geary Theatre is the home of the **American Conservatory Theater**, one of the nation's best repertory companies and winner of several Tony awards. Next door, the Curran offers big hits and stars from New York. Theatres on Sutter Street include the **Lorraine Hansberry Theatre**; the nearby **Marines' Memorial Theatre**, which specializes in Broadway musicals; and the **Actors Theatre**, which

performs classics by luminaries like John Steinbeck.

In the other direction from Union Square, you can cross Stockton Street and wander down chic **Maiden Lane**, a quiet pedestrianized street of high-end boutiques that was named in the Gold Rush for the female company men found here during the tough Gold Rush era. At No. 140 is the only Frank Lloyd Wright-designed building in the city, which now houses a gallery.

Nob Hill and Russian Hill

The cable cars from Fisherman's Wharf and Union Square climb one of the city's best-known slopes, **Nob Hill**. Called the "Hill of Palaces" by writer Robert Louis Stevenson, the hill is celebrated mostly for the size and elegance of the mansions and hotels built there a century ago.

Here, the **Mark Hopkins Hotel** occupies the site of the former Mark Hopkins mansion, where the **Top of the Mark** bar (tel: 415-616-6916) on the 19th floor is a romantic and time-honored custom for visitors, offering a 100-martini menu and spectacular

Lombard Street.

views of the city and bay. The lovely **Stanford Court** and **Huntington** hotels were also built on the ashes of mansions, and the **Fairmont Hotel** retains an aura of (rebuilt) splendor, having been open only two days before being burned down in the fires that raged after the 1906 earthquake. It reopened for business just one year later. Across the street, the private Pacific Union Club is housed in the only Nob Hill mansion to survive the 1906 earthquake and fire, a sturdy brownstone built for silver magnate James Flood in 1855.

All these lavish structures encircle and provide the perfect setting for the grand neo-Gothic **Grace Cathedral**, inspired by Paris' Notre Dame. The doors are cast from Lorenzo Ghiberti's original *Doors of Paradise* in Florence, while the rose window was inspired by the blue glass of Chartres Cathedral. The acoustics are superb when the organ is played and the church's boys' choir sings. Northeast, at the corner of Washington and Mason streets, is the **Cable Car Museum** (tel: 415-474-1887; www.

cablecarmuseum.org; daily 10am–6pm, until 5pm in winter; free), which exhibits the city's transit history as well as the massive machinery and cables that still pull the glamorous transportation through the town.

Next to Nob Hill, Russian Hill is known for magnificent views, stately homes, hidden bistros, and a labyrinth of secret streets, stairways, and alleys like **Macondray Lane**, which connects Taylor and Jones streets. Russian Hill is home to **Lombard Street** , known as "the crookedest street in the world." Located between Hyde and Leavenworth streets, this one block takes cars on eight hairpin turns along a cobblestone roadway.

The Financial District

The original '49ers sailed into San Francisco Bay, dropped anchor, and set off north to pursue their dream of striking gold. It wasn't long before the city's original shoreline began to burgeon, contributing to the birth of today's soaring Financial District. Brokers, bankers, marketers, and software engineers now pursue wealth on

One of the city's iconic, rattling cable cars.

several acres of landfill on and around Montgomery Street.

The most obvious attraction in this neighborhood is the **Transamerica Pyramid ❶** on Montgomery Street, its 48 floors making it the tallest building in the city. When it was completed in 1972, a lot of people were appalled by its pointed, unorthodox appearance, but now almost everyone has come to appreciate its architectural eccentricity. Unfortunately visitors cannot enter the tower.

A little farther north on Montgomery is Jackson Square, one of the city's main destinations for antique shops and interior decorator showrooms.

South on Montgomery is the Wells Fargo History Museum (420 Montgomery Street; tel: 415-396-2619; Mon–Fri 9am–5pm; free), which displays Gold Rush relics alongside the history of the Wells Fargo company.

The sprawling $300 million Embarcadero Center takes up four-square-blocks; connected by bridges are numerous shops, restaurants and high-rise apartments, as well as the Hyatt Regency Hotel, which boasts a spectacular 20-story atrium lobby. Noticeable from any part of town is the Bank of America building, which is so tall its roof sometimes disappears in the fog.

Where Market Street ends, the bay begins with the **Ferry Building ❶**, whose design was influenced by the Cathedral tower in Seville, Spain. It's still the gateway for ferry riders from all over the bay, as well as a farmers market and upscale food esplanade. It's especially convenient for commuters who need only to cross the Embarcadero intersection to reach the **Financial District**.

South of Market (SoMa)

Stretching in wide blocks south of Market street to the bay, **SoMa** is one of the city's most forward-looking districts, fueled by artistic and entrepreneurial energy. As well as the locale

for some of the city's best nightclubs, restaurants, and museums, it emerged as the high-tech district, with many innovative Internet, design, and programming firms in residence. The bold **San Francisco Museum of Modern Art ❶** (151 Third Street; tel: 415-357-4000; www.sfmoma.org; Fri–Tue 10am–5.45pm, Thur 10am–8.45pm; charge) is the neighborhood's biggest attraction.

Across the street are the **Yerba Buena Gardens**, which started out as a lovely public park with a waterfall monument honoring Martin Luther King, Jr, and has now become a mecca for art and entertainment. Buildings around it house, for instance, the **Center for the Arts**, where plays, modern art exhibitions, and experimental multimedia performances are staged.

One of Yerba Buena's most innovative venues is the Children's Creative Museum, a visual arts facility geared toward young people. It includes an animation studio and a production studio where kids can make and star in their own music videos.

TIP

Buy cable car tickets ($6 for a single, regular ride; Muni & Cable Car Passports are also available and are much better value) at the booth at the corner of Market and Powell Streets, or in cash on the cable car when you board. If the line is long, try walking up a half dozen blocks to a stop further along the route.

THE FERRY BUILDING

Once a thriving terminal, the Ferry Building is now an upscale emporium designed to satisfy the local passion for food.

Before the rise of the automobile and the construction of bridges over San Francisco Bay, the Ferry Building was one of the world's most active transit terminals. Built in 1898 on the site of the original wooden ferry house at the foot of Market Street, the long and graceful building with its distinctive clock tower received thousands of daily ferry commuters from Marin County and the East Bay.

When speedier alternatives came on the scene in the 1930s, passengers abandoned the ferries. By the mid-1950s, the once-airy Grand Nave was clogged with offices, sealing out the natural light. Next, the building was walled off by the Embarcadero freeway. But after the freeway was damaged by the 1989 earthquake, it was demolished in 1991 and the Ferry Building, now in full view, inspired plans for the structure's regeneration. Meticulously restored, it now has a food hall that is open daily with artisan shops, restaurants, and cafes, and a farmers market twice a week. The ferries with their cross-bay commuters have returned, too.

Free walking tours are conducted at noon on Saturdays, Sundays, and Tuesdays.

Next to the Esplanade is the **Metreon** complex, with a 15-screen movie theater, an IMAX theater, a food court, and a Target store. Not far away is the largest structure in the heart of SoMa, the **Moscone Convention Center**, which hosts most of the major conventions held in the city.

Museums and Mint

Down on Mission Street are the **Cartoon Art Museum** (No. 655; tel: 415-227-8666; www.cartoonart.org; Tue–Sun 11am–5pm; charge), dedicated to pop cartoon art (and where children will particularly enjoy the comic playroom), the **museum of the California Historical Society** (No. 678; 415-357-1848; www.californiahistoricalsociety.org; Tue–Sun noon–5pm; free), and the Museum of the African Diaspora (No. 685; tel: 415-358-7200; www.moadsf.org; Sun noon–5pm, Wed–Sat 11am–6pm; charge), which explores the culture, history, and art of people of African descent.

Another signature building is the new home of the **Contemporary Jewish Museum** (736 Mission Street; tel: 415-655-7800; www.jmsf.

San Francisco Museum of Modern Art.

org; Sun–Thur noon–6pm; charge). It has three program spaces, designed by internationally renowned architect Daniel Liebeskind, and houses one of the world's leading collections of Jewish art and artifacts.

A couple of blocks away on 5th Street is another fine old building (c. 1875), San Francisco's **Old Mint**. Dating from the days when the city was still a Wild West town, it was in this massive building that silver from Nevada was first converted into dollars and then stored in huge safes in the cellar.

Palace Hotel

To the east bordering Market Street and New Montgomery Street is the venerable **Palace Hotel**. Opened in 1875, it is San Francisco's oldest and still one of its premier luxury hotels, notable for its 150ft (46-meter) Palm Garden, with a leaded-glass dome roof that bathes diners in light, and the Pied Piper bar with its beautiful Maxfield Parrish mural. Seven American presidents have stayed here, including Ulysses S. Grant, Franklin

Roosevelt, and Warren G. Harding, who died at the Palace in 1923 while still in office.

Civic Center

San Francisco's collection of historic buildings is centered in the Civic Center, bisected by Van Ness Avenue, the city's widest street. West of the large central square is **City Hall** ⓛ (tel: 415- 554-6139 for tours; Mon–Fri 10am, noon, and 2pm; charge), one of the most beautiful public buildings in the United States. It was designed by Arthur Brown, an architect so young and so unknown that he figured he might as well shoot for the moon in the early-20th-century competition to select the building design. To his surprise, Brown and his partner, John Bakewell, won with a design that called for the lavish use of costly marble, and a neoclassical dome that was influenced by Brown's time spent in Paris studying at the Ecole des Beaux-Arts. Built in 1914, City Hall is honeycombed with municipal offices, and

both civil and criminal courts. The full effect is best experienced from its Polk Street entrance, which faces the plaza. The magnificent stairway inside leads to the second-floor Board of Supervisors' chambers.

This is the building in which supervisor Dan White shot and killed Mayor George Moscone in 1978 for refusing to reappoint him to the seat White had resigned. White then shot and killed gay supervisor Harvey Milk. After White was convicted of manslaughter and given a remarkably lenient sentence, mobs descended on City Hall. The episode made headlines around the country and became a rallying cry for gay activists. Since then, the building has undergone sensitive retro-fitting and restoration in order to showcase its architecture and make the building earthquake-proof.

Opposite City Hall on Van Ness Avenue is a series of distinguished buildings. The **War Memorial Veterans Building** at the corner of Van Ness and McAllister streets was built in 1932 and houses the **Herbst**

City Hall.

THE NEXT EARTHQUAKE

No one can predict when the next earthquake will come and lay waste to the great beauty of San Francisco as it did in 1906 and, more recently, in October 1989.

This last quake cost many people their lives and caused billions of dollars of damage to the city (although most of the downtown remained intact). More people would have been killed during the quake had there not been a significant baseball game going on. The Bay Area's two home baseball teams were competing in the World Series, and most people were either at the stadium or at home glued to the television.

Although the 1989 quake was a major one, and there have been smaller "shivers" since, thankfully none has proven to be "the big one" Californians talk of someday facing.

TIP

The SF Museum and Historical Society sponsors a self-guided walk called the Barbary Coast Trail, indicated by bronze medallions set in the sidewalk linking 20 historic sites. For more information, go to www.sfhistory.org.

Theatre. Next to it is the **Opera House**, one of the country's greatest, and built in the same year as the Veterans Building. It has a summer opera festival and a regular season running from September to December. The opera company, which draws the foremost artists of the day to its stage, shares quarters with the highly regarded San Francisco Ballet. The **Opera Plaza** complex, where apartments go for astronomical sums of money, is a highly desirable address. Across the street from the Opera House is the lavish **Louise M. Davies Symphony Hall**.

Asian Art Museum

The **Asian Art Museum** moved from Golden Gate Park to occupy the 1917 Beaux-Arts style premises that once housed the old public library (the main branch of the **Public Library** is nearby). The museum (200 Larkin Street; tel: 415-581-3500; www.asianart. org; Tue–Sun 10am–5pm, Thur 10am–9pm; charge) houses the Avery Brundage Collection and is one of the largest museums of its kind outside

Asia, replete with Japanese paintings, ceramics, and lacquer; Chinese bronzes and jade; and sculpture from Korea and India. At the south end of the plaza is the **Bill Graham Civic Auditorium**, built in 1913 and renamed in honor of the city's late, great rock entrepreneur.

The north side of the plaza has the **State Office Building**, constructed in 1926. Together, they present an appearance of order and harmony. The brutal federal building standing behind the state building on Golden Gate Avenue is a reminder of how badly the Civic Center could have turned out had it been planned less carefully.

Pacific Heights

South of Union Street, the massive hills of one of the city's wealthiest neighborhoods, **Pacific Heights**, provide unparalleled views of the bay and are home to local luminaries like romance novelist Danielle Steele and the prestigious Getty oil family. Stunning mansions line every steep-and-wide street whose integrity is maintained by the upkeep

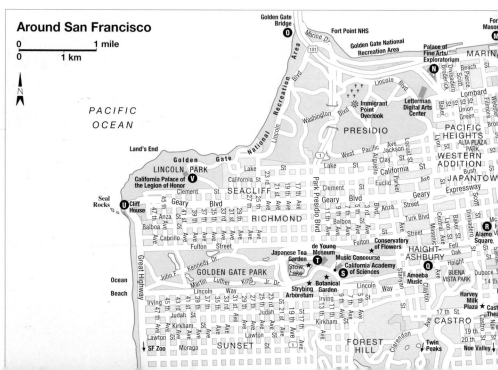

of underground telephone lines. A stellar example of Victorian Queen Anne architecture that is also open to the public is the beautiful **Haas-Lilienthal House** (2007 Franklin Street; tel: 415-441-3000; Wed and Sat noon–3pm, Sun 11am–4pm; one-hour guided tours; charge).

Japantown

Farther south, the hill crests at Jackson Street to mark the beginning of **Fillmore Street**. Further south of Fillmore itself at Post Street is the heart of **Japantown**. The **Japan Center**, the neighborhood's focal point, is an Asian-oriented shopping center that stretches three blocks and is filled with affordable Japanese restaurants and little stores featuring everything from kimonos to bonsai trees: a concentrated expression of Japanese culture in the middle of San Francisco. The handsome, distinctive five-tiered Peace Pagoda, designed by the Japanese architect Yoshiro Taniguchi, stands as a monument of goodwill between the Japanese people and those of the United States.

The Marina

The waterfront Marina District is popular with young urban dwellers, and encompasses the area all the way from Fort Mason to the Presidio, and inland to Chestnut and Union streets.

By day, Chestnut acts as one big outdoor café where the next generation of yuppies congregates in workout gear, when they're not shopping in the trendy boutiques. After dark, the same crowd meets in the plethora of tasty and inexpensive restaurants, then heads to the post-collegiate-type bars. Union Street is a more chic stretch of boutiques, antiques stores, gourmet shops, delicatessens, and classy restaurants.

On the waterfront, **Fort Mason** Ⓜ is a decommissioned military base whose long huts now house art galleries, ethnic museums, workshops, and a gourmet vegetarian restaurant called Greens that overlooks the harbor. The yachts in the harbor belong to the members of the **San Francisco Yacht Club**, whose clubhouse looks out on the bay, which is often alive with windsurfers. A little bit west is

TIP

East of Civic Center to Union Square and bordered by Market and Sutter streets is the gritty Tenderloin neighborhood, which can be dangerous and is notorious for drugs, crime, and homelessness. There are several different stories as to how the Tenderloin got its name; one stems from the eponymous cut of meat, the "soft underbelly" of the city, relating to the vice, corruption, and harsh realities of street life found there.

At the Museum of Asian Art.

Marina Green, beloved by kite flyers and joggers.

Palace of Fine Arts and Exploratorium

For a walk toward the bridge, follow the waterfront Golden Gate Promenade. One of the most beautiful man-made sights stands a few blocks inland from the promenade: the "Plaster Palace," across Marina Boulevard to the south, is the classic rococo rotunda of the **Palace of Fine Arts** . Designed by Bernard Maybeck, the palace was originally built of plaster of Paris for the Panama-Pacific Exposition of 1915. It wasn't meant to last, but somehow it did. Not until 1967 was it strengthened and made permanent. The palace houses the **Exploratorium** (3601 Lyon Street; tel: 415-561-0360; Tue–Sun 10am–5pm; charge), an interactive children's museum with more than 600 exhibits to awaken even the most dormant interest in science. This was founded by Frank Oppenheimer, brother of the inventor of the atom bomb.

Walk or cycle across the bridge, then take the ferry back across the bay from Sausalito.

Just west of the Exporatorium on the waterfront is **Crissy Field**, an airfield-turned-picnic area belonging to the 1,480-acre (599-hectare) **Presidio**. Established by the Spanish in 1776 and once owned by the US Army, the Presidio is a very unwarlike military installation. Decommissioned in 1992, its manicured grounds, which include stands of pine and eucalyptus and even a lake, are currently overseen by the National Park Service. After fierce debate concerning its fate, film director George Lucas was allowed to build a $300 million, 900,000-sq-ft (84,000-sq-meter) film studio in the park, the headquarters of Industrial Light & Magic and LucasArts at the Letterman Digital Arts Center.

Golden Gate Bridge

Whether sailing under the **Golden Gate Bridge** or taking in its enormity from the Marina's shore, it is interesting to consider that at one time many reputable engineers argued that it would be impossible to build a span at this point because of the depth of the water and the

powerful tidal rush in and out. The city authorized the first studies in 1918, but it was 1937 before the bridge was finished at a cost of $35 million and the lives of 11 construction workers. The full splendor of this vast, reddish-gold structure can be appreciated from a viewpoint near the access road on the south of the bridge. A bronze memorial of Joseph B. Strauss, the bridge's Chief Engineer, looks down on the throngs of visitors.

The Mission

The Mission is San Francisco's great melting pot of Latin American cultures. In the latter part of the 20th century, thanks to accessibility and lower rents, artists and musicians moved in too, earning the Mission its easygoing reputation for being the city's new bohemia. Now, with a wealth of trendy restaurants and hip nightspots, the neighborhood attracts an eclectic mix of people.

The district gets its name from **Mission Dolores** ❷ (3321 16th Street; tel: 415-621-8203; www.missiondolores. org; daily 9am–4pm; charge), the sixth

mission in the chain of Spanish settlements that stretched 650 miles (1,050km) from San Diego to northern California. Mission Dolores was founded less than a week before the American Declaration of Independence was signed in 1776, and its thick adobe walls still form what is the oldest building in San Francisco. The graves of many early pioneers, and thousands of native Costonoan Indians, can be found in the mission cemetery.

Valencia Street is full of popular boutiques, and hip restaurants and bars, while just a block east, Mission Street has an entirely different feel with discount shops, pawnbrokers, and produce stands. At the vast Dolores Park, families gather for birthday celebrations, gay sunbathers lie shirtless, and twentysomethings camp out on weekend afternoons.

In a town as condensed as this one, you need only go a few blocks to find yourself in an entirely different

The Golden Gate Bridge spans the bay separating San Francisco and Marin County to the north.

Mural on Mission Street.

THE GOLDEN GATE BRIDGE

On opening day in 1937, the *San Francisco Chronicle* described the bridge as "a thirty-five million dollar steel harp." In the 75 years since, the bridge has weathered political detractors, powerful wind, and an earthquake.

Romantic as the bridge is, the hard facts are undeniably impressive. Including its freeway approaches, the Golden Gate Bridge is 1.7 miles (2.7km) long, with the main suspended span stretching for 4,200ft (1,280 meters). When completed, the bridge was celebrated as being the longest suspension bridge in the world. The Art Deco towers stand 746ft (227 meters) above the water; when first built, they were the highest structures in the West. Its distinctive vermillion color, called International Orange, was chosen to stand out in the famous Bay fog.

community. To the west of Mission, near Dolores, the sunny districts of **Noe Valley** and the **Castro** are comprised of many well-kept Victorian homes and shopping streets.

The Castro

The **Castro** neighborhood is the world's most celebrated gay community. The streets are filled with same-sex couples, rainbow flags, hopping bars, and whimsical novelty shops, especially on Castro Street between 17th and 19th streets.

The **Castro Theatre** is a beautiful work of Spanish Baroque design. This Revival house features classic and cult films (including sing-along versions of *The Sound of Music, Mary Poppins, and Grease*) and film festivals, and sometimes a live organist plays on an ascending platform for a bit of nostalgia.

Another testament to the gay community is **Harvey Milk Plaza**, the plaza in front of a Muni bus stop that's been dedicated to celebrated gay resident Supervisor Harvey Milk who was shot and killed in 1978, along with

Mayor Moscone, by anti-homosexual Supervisor Dan White.

The Charles M. Holmes Campus at The Center, known locally as "The Center" (1800 Market Street; tel: 415-865-5555), is closer to the Mission than the Castro but has become the nexus for community events, classes, support groups, and information regarding the local LGBT community. Here, it's possible to attend a Mensa bisexual support group, view a show of Robert Rauschenberg, or obtain personalized legal services all in one place.

The westernmost section of the Castro leads into the Twin Peaks area, full of elegant homes. The neighborhood is named after the two 900ft (274-meter) hills that provide stunning views of the entire city, and are well worth the short ascent to the top.

The Haight

Heading north, back towards Downtown via Stanyan Street, is lively **Haight-Ashbury** and tranquil Golden Gate Park. Stanyan

Café in the Castro area.

AMERICA'S CUP

In September 2013, 72ft (22-meter) wing-sail catamarans will sail along the waterfront of the San Francisco Bay in an attempt to win the 34th America's Cup. This competition has been held since 1851, when the yacht *America* won the first race, off the Isle of Wight in England. The Golden Gate Yacht Club (GGYC) will be defending the America's Cup, their racing team, BMW Oracle Racing, having won the 2010 America's Cup.

With the competition taking place in San Francisco, this will be the first time the United States has hosted the America's Cup since 1995. Pier 27 will be the heart of the action for spectators. There, a spectator village will include a 10,000-seat amphitheater, live music and dance, and exhibitions of past America's Cup winners.

Street borders the eastern edge of the park and intersects **Haight Street**, a world-famous thoroughfare in the 1960s, when long hair, tie-dyed fabrics, hallucinogens, and a belief in the power of love and peace persuaded a generation that they could create an alternative lifestyle. They were called "hippies," openly smoked marijuana, took up forms of Eastern mysticism, declined to fight in foreign wars, and otherwise were a thorn in the sides of their elders, who sometimes sent police in riot gear to the middle of the **Haight-Ashbury** district to clean it up.

Haight Street was once so gaudy and bizarre that tour buses full of goggle-eyed tourists ran up and down it. Like most such radical departures from the social norm, the hippie experiment fell victim to time and fashion. The neighborhood still retains its anti-establishment roots, but today flower power has been replaced by piercing shops and tattoo parlors. It's still a vibrant, colorful stretch, however, with great shopping and a wide range of good, inexpensive restaurants and cafés.

Alamo Square

Nine blocks south, at the corner of Fulton and Steiner streets, a very different history is preserved. The "postcard rows" of perfectly maintained Victorian houses surrounding a grassy square with skyscrapers peeping over the top is called **Alamo Square ®** and the location of thousands of photographs of the streets of San Francisco. The harmonious beauties, called "Painted Ladies," are characterized by pointed gables and tiny oriel windows.

Golden Gate Park

Golden Gate Park (tel: 415-831-2700) is 3 miles (5km) long and half a mile (1km) wide, and consists of groves of redwoods, eucalyptus, pine, and countless varieties of other trees from all over the world. It is dotted with lakes, grassy meadows, and sunlit dells. There can be thousands of people within its borders, but Golden Gate Park is so large that one can easily find solitary tranquility in a misty forest grove or by a peaceful pond. More than a century ago, the park was painstakingly reclaimed from

WHERE

The Mission district is full of colorful murals and street art. One of the best examples is Balmy Alley, located five blocks east of Mission Street, between 24th and 25th streets, and at the Women's Building on 18th Street. Precita Eyes Mural Arts and Visitors Center runs tours on weekends (tel: 415-285-2287; www.precitaeyes.org).

Painting the Conservatory of Flowers, Golden Gate Park.

HIPPIES AND THE HAIGHT

For several hot months in the first Summer of Love, 1967, life became a costume party in a wonderland setting of brightly painted Victorian buildings. The neighborhood was a swirl of colors as flower children painted storefronts, sidewalks, posters, cars, vans, and, of course, themselves, with Day-Glo. The days and nights were filled with sex, drugs, and a pot-laced breeze, with a soundtrack provided by Janis Joplin, Jefferson Airplane, and the Grateful Dead, who all lived in Haight-Ashbury pads.

Things change, of course. Tourists still snatch up Summer of Love T-shirts, but today there are more homeless people than hippies on the streets, and the Victorians' color scheme has toned down. Nevertheless, vintage boutiques, music stores, and cocktail bars mean the neighborhood is happening again.

sand dunes through the Herculean efforts of a Scottish landscape architect named John McLaren. The park superintendent for 55 years, McLaren so disliked statuary that he shrouded all human likeness in dense vegetation. Most statues remain "lost" today.

Along John F. Kennedy Drive, about seven blocks into the park, is the hard-to-miss **Conservatory of Flowers**. The incredible glass structure was built in 1878, modeled after the Palm House at London's Kew Gardens. Housing wonderful collections of rare palms and other tropical flora, the atmosphere inside is one of color unleashed. A seasonal flowerbed in front is a natural announcement to its entrance, and the grounds around the conservatory have fine collections of fuchsias and azaleas.

The park has feasts for the mind as well as the eyes. Further along JFK Drive, a road branches off to the left for the **Music Concourse**, an esplanade built in 1894 offering Sunday concerts. On one side of the Music Concourse is the **California Academy of Sciences ⑤** (tel: 415-379-8000; www.calacademy.org; daily 9.30am–5pm,

Japanese Tea Garden in Golden Gate Park.

from 11am Sun; charge). With a ground-breaking design produced by Pritzker Prize-winning architect Renzo Piano, it is among the world's greenest museums, with a 2.5–acre (1-hectare) "living" roof of native grasses, porthole skylights, and solar panels that supply the museum's power. The complex also includes the **Steinhart Aquarium**, the **Morrison Planetarium**, coral reef exhibits, and a live rainforest with orchids, macaws, butterflies, bats, scorpions, turtles, and an enormous anaconda.

The fabulous **de Young Museum ❼** (50 Hagiwara Tea Garden Drive; tel: 415-750-3600; Apr–Nov Tue-Sun 9.30am–5.15pm, Fri 9.30am–8:45pm; charge) stands perilously close to the San Andreas fault, and the gallery was severely damaged in the 1989 earthquake. To withstand future seismic incidents, the new building – a bold, monolithic structure with a copper skin that will slowly turn green – is able to move up to 3ft (90cm). It has one of the best collections of American paintings in the US as well as art from Oceania, Latin America, Africa, and Meso-America. The tower at the northeast corner is 144ft (44 meters) high and has views all the way to Downtown and the Pacific Ocean.

Next door, the beautiful **Japanese Tea Garden** (www.japaneseteagardensf.com) is a harmonious blend of architecture, landscaping, and pools, and is one of the most visited and loved sites in the park. Built in 1894, it was created by George Turner Marsh, a successful dealer in Asian art. Marsh hired a renowned Japanese gardener, Makota Hagiwara, who planted traditional dwarf bonsai conifers, elms, and cherry trees. Hagiwara (whose family is said to have invented the fortune cookie) also designed the winding brooks with their moss-covered rocks, irises, and carp pond. A wooden gateway, a wishing bridge, and a five-story pagoda complete the landscape.

Across from the tea garden, the **San Francisco Botanical Garden**

(tel: 415-661-1316; www.sfbotanicalgarden.org; open daily 9am, for closing times check website; charge), is an urban oasis of extraordinary beauty that delights the senses with some 7,500 plant species on 70 acres (28 hectares). Specialty gardens include a Succulent Garden in which limestone walls warm giant aloe plants and cactus while woodpeckers nest, and the Moon Viewing Garden where magnolias, Japanese maples, and camellias surround a reflecting pond with a platform used to view the autumn moon.

Further north along Martin Luther King Jr. Drive is the lovely, sweet-smelling Garden of Shakespeare's Flowers, with "lady-smocks," rosemary, and 150 other species mentioned in Shakespeare's writings.

The beaches and northern coast

At the far western end of Golden Gate Park is Ocean Beach. Although the beach has dramatic ocean views, only the hardiest souls dip their toes into the ice-cold water.

Farther north along the coast is **Cliff House** Ⓤ, a restaurant that overlooks the Pacific Ocean, where you can peer down upon barking seals clinging wetly to the rocks below. The present Cliff House is the fifth to have been built here since 1863; each of its predecessors has burned down or suffered some other disaster.

North of the Cliff House is verdant **Lincoln Park**, whose 270 acres (109 hectares) include an 18-hole municipal golf course and the stunning neoclassical French-style **California Palace of the Legion of Honor** Ⓥ (100 34th Avenue; tel: 415-750-3600; www.legionofhonor.famsf.org; Tue–Sun 9.30am–5.15pm; charge). Smack-dab in some of the hottest real estate in town, the fine art museum, renovated at a cost of $35 million in 1995, is spectacular; at the entrance is one of five existing bronze casts of Rodin's *The Thinker*.

The cliffs wind east along a protected area known as the **Golden Gate National Recreation Area** (the largest urban park in the world), under the Golden Gate Bridge.

WHERE

The stretch of neighborhood north of the park is the **Richmond district**, fogbound much of the summer and renowned for its orderly streets which blend well into the **Sunset district**, equally conservative and flanking the south side of Golden Gate Park.

"Painted Ladies" at Alamo Square.

Spot pelicans at Pier 39 Marina.

SAN FRANCISCO'S CABLE CARS

Much more than just a means of transport, San Francisco's cable cars are an iconic feature of the city. They've been designated a National Landmark, starred in countless movies and TV shows, and featured on a postage stamp.

Even from their earliest days, San Francisco's famous cable cars impressed visitors. "They turn corners almost at right angles, cross over other lines and for aught I know run up the sides of houses," wrote Rudyard Kipling, who visited in 1889 on his way to India.

Operating on three routes – the Powell–Mason, Powell–Hyde and California lines – San Francisco's cable cars are among the last in the United States, at least 100 cities having abandoned them for buses. Underestimating the draw of this tourist attraction, San Francisco tried to get rid of the cars in 1947, but a vigorous local campaign saved them by a City Charter.

Today the cable cars transport over 9 million passengers a year, more than half of them local commuters. It is the visitors, of course, who buy the engraved knives, belt buckles, posters, and T-shirts emblazoned with pictures of the beloved cars, or dig into their wallets to pay for genuine cable car bells. The most enjoyable routes for visitors are the Powell–Mason and Powell–Hyde lines, which share a terminus at Powell and Market and then diverge in Nob Hill on different routes to Fisherman's Wharf (Powell–Hyde is more scenic, passing through Russian Hill and the top of Lombard Street).

Cable car winding machinery at the Cable Car Barn and Powerhouse Museum.

Cable car on Nob Hill. At the beginning of the 20th century, 600 cars rolled over 115 miles (185km) of track, but a fleet of electric trams powered by overhead wires hastened their demise.

Some of the tour buses are painted to resemble their more famous stablemates.

O'FARRELL.JONES &HYDE STREETS 74

The cable car turntable at Powell and Market streets is the starting point for two lines, the Powell–Mason and the Powell–Hyde. The third cable car line is the California Street line that runs east–west.

ANDREW SMITH HALLIDIE

The cable-car system was created in 1873 by Andrew Hallidie, a British-born engineer with a reputation for building suspension bridges and a background in mining engineering. Seven years before, it's said, he saw a horse slip, breaking a chain on the overloaded streetcar it was pulling uphill. Hallidie set about devising a system that would eliminate such accidents.

Although Hallidie and his friends put up $20,000 to get the cable cars operating, it was Benjamin Brooks, the son of a local lawyer, who was awarded a franchise in 1870 to operate a similar system, but failed to raise the necessary financing.

When the Hallidie plan came to fruition, skepticism was the order of the day. "I'd like to see it happen," said realtor L.C. Carlson, "but I don't know who is going to want to ride the dang thing."

Critics of the system still abide today. Although the cars run at only 9.5 mph (15 kmh), they can't duck potential collisions and their braking system has been called "unimprovable" or "blacksmith shop crudity at its worst" by columnist Dick Nolan.

Exhibit at the Cable Car Museum on Mason Street.

Cable cars on Market Street, c.1899.

Andrew Smith Hallidie.

Sailboats in Sausalito, Marin County.

GREATER SAN FRANCISCO BAY AREA

From the sequoias of Muir Woods to Jack London's Oakland, the people's Berkeley, and the high-tech communities of Silicon Valley, the Bay Area is as diverse as San Francisco itself.

O utside San Francisco are as many fascinating sights and delights as there are in the city. Mountains, redwood forests, and wonderful Pacific beaches beckon, as well as intriguing Silicon Valley, Oakland, and Berkeley. Travel is easy: several bridges span the bay; an underground train system (BART) links the East Bay and South Bay with the city; ferries crisscross the water; and trains run up and down the peninsula. Getting around by car, though, is the most attractive way to explore the coasts, hills, and valleys.

Marin County

Encircling San Francisco Bay from the north, and lying at the tip of a metropolitan area of some 5 million inhabitants, Marin County is home to tens of thousands of acres of pristine coastline, unspoiled redwood groves and mountain meadows, and pretty beaches. This luxurious green belt offers seemingly limitless options for hikers and nature-lovers, while old-fashioned towns and charming bed and breakfasts lend themselves to relaxed weekend getaways.

Sausalito

The first – or last – stop for most Marin visitors is **Sausalito ①**, tucked inside the bay to the east behind the Golden Gate. There is a ferry service to the Sausalito dock from San Francisco. The waterside shops, the warrens of pricey but perfect boutiques, and the houses perched behind them on a steep slope draw inevitable comparisons to towns on the Mediterranean Riviera. The Spanish word *saucelito* (meaning "little willow") is said to have been the name's origin. There is, in fact, very little to do in Sausalito except stroll around, have lunch or dinner in one of the restaurants – where California Cuisine is a specialty – and admire all the boats and pretty people.

Main Attractions

Sausalito
Mount Tamalpais
Muir Woods National
 Monument
Jack London Square, Oakland
Oakland Museum of California
University of California
Stanford University
Winchester Mystery House

View from Mount Tamalpais.

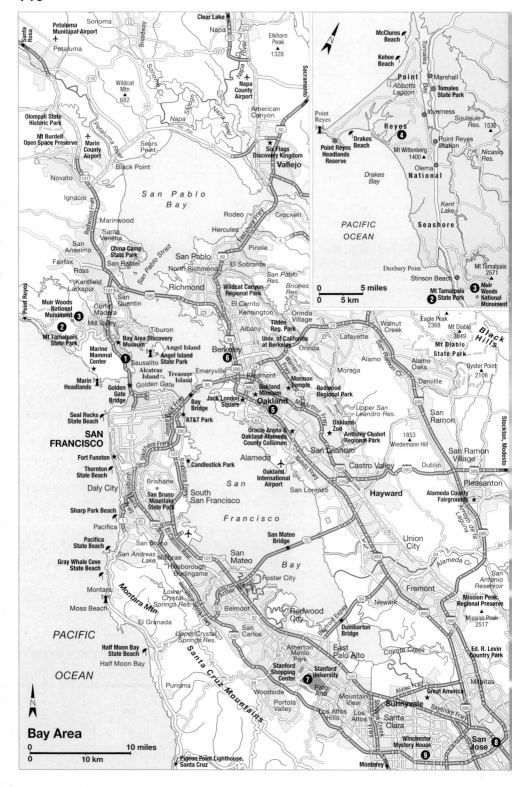

Bay Area

Mount Tamalpais

In recent years, **Mount Tamalpais ❷** has become a weekend traffic jam of hikers, mountain bikers, and runners. Still, there seems to be enough beauty to go around. Over 30 miles (50km) of trails wind their way through 6,000 acres (2,400 hectares), as well as many more miles of hiking in the contiguous watershed lands owned by the water municipalities. On Mount Tam's lower elevations, often shrouded in fog, are stands of virgin redwood. Above, the mountain's chaparral-covered high slopes jut proudly into the sunshine, overlooking San Francisco Bay and the Pacific. It's a fantastic sight.

Muir Woods

At the very base of Mount Tamalpais is wonderful, woodsy **Muir Woods National Monument ❸**. At the turn of the 20th century, the Marin Water District planned to condemn a property called Redwood Canyon, cut the timber on it, and with the profits build a dam and reservoir. The scheme so appalled one wealthy Marinite named William Kent that he bought the land outright, then cleverly deeded the redwood stand to the government, who turned it into a national monument. Kent modestly declined to have the monument named after him, out of deference to his old friend, naturalist John Muir.

About 1 million tourists a year visit the giant sequoia trees here, which grow to 200ft (60 meters) in height, 16ft (5 meters) in diameter, live up to 1,000 years, and are spread out through Muir Woods' 300-plus acres (120 hectares). Energetic walkers might be advised to leave parked cars behind and head up the steep slope of Mount Tam on the **Ben Johnson Trail** through deeply shaded glens rife with ferns and mushrooms, past ever-changing groves of bay, tan oaks, madrona, and nutmeg.

The Marin Headlands

Beyond Mount Tam, Marin County's green belt extends some 50 miles (80km) to the distant tip of Point Reyes National Seashore. The coastal country,

Muir Woods National Monument.

Sequoia trees in Muir Woods.

known as the Marin Headlands (easily accessible off Highway 1 just north of the Golden Gate Bridge), has miles of coastal and beach-bound trails. Stellar views can be had by driving up the Fort Baker Road.

Stinson Beach, at the foot of Mount Tamalpais, is San Francisco's favorite playground, popular among anglers hoping to hook surf perch and rockfish, and among bird-watchers who want to spy such out-of-the-way creatures as the sooty shearwater, brown pelican, Western grebe, killdeer, and millet. When the fog pulls back, the beach also attract hordes of sunbathers. Stinson gets especially crowded on fine weekends, or when sweltering inland weather drives home-dwellers as near to the sea as it's possible to get.

Point Reyes

A triangular peninsula, **Point Reyes** ❹ is separated from the rest of the world by the main fissure line of the San Andreas fault, which is nudging Point Reyes northeast at an average rate of 2ins (5cm) a year. This 65,000-sq-mile (105-sq-km) seashore

Point Reyes lighthouse.

park, which draws over 2 million visitors a year, is one of the most frequented of the country's national parks.

Add quaint inns and diners in the little towns of **Inverness** and **Point Reyes Station**, and it seems as close to untouched paradise as you can get. The epicenter of the 1906 San Francisco earthquake was a half-mile from where the main park headquarters now stands on Bear Valley Road. On **Earthquake Trail**, visitors can see where the quake moved one old stone fence a distance of at least 15ft (5 meters).

To get to the park headquarters and most of the trailheads in the National Seashore, drivers must travel up Highway 1 past the town of **Olema** to Bear Valley Road. The park is open only to those who are willing to walk or ride a horse. The terrain is varied, much of it very steep. Gloomy forests suddenly open on lush, sweeping meadows, while the coast is rockbound with occasional pocket beaches. Hikers may see owls, foxes, raccoons, bobcats, deer, and almost

every kind of bird imaginable, especially herons, egrets, and ducks.

A hike up wind-whipped, 1,400-ft (427-meter) **Mount Wittenberg** rewards out-of-breath hikers with a truly breathtaking view of the California coast: green-black forests and golden meadows that roll down to a coastline where the eye can track for miles without seeing a soul. Below is **Drakes Beach**, where the famous Elizabethan sea captain Sir Francis Drake is said to have set ashore in 1579 for ship repairs.

At the tip of the Point Reyes promontory perches a **lighthouse** that warns ships away from the treacherous coast. One of the foggiest places in Marin County, it usually has no view at all. When the fog lifts and at the right season, however, it is a good place from which to spot migrating whales.

On the northern edge of the seashore, Pierce Point Road meanders around to several beaches – **Abbotts**, **Kehoe**, and the most ruggedly dramatic, **McClures**. These beaches are not recommended for swimming because of the danger of sharks, undertow, and rip tides. It is better to head for Drakes Beach on the southern side, which is somewhat protected from winds.

The East Bay

From the Black Panthers to Chez Panisse, the East Bay is as revolutionary as San Francisco. Built around the ports and the University of California, Oakland and Berkeley offer a slightly slower pace than their sister city, as well as craftsman-style homes and leafy, winding neighborhoods. But don't mistake this for suburbia: the lively political culture, widely diverse demographics, museums, and intellectual centers make these cities thriving metropolitan centers with a distinctly urban edge.

Oakland

Despite author Gertrude Stein's infamous quip that "there is no there there," **Oakland ❺** long ago emerged from the shadow of its older sister to the west. In fact, things are looking pretty good in Oakland – especially for women: according to a recent US census, Oakland ranks third in

Inside the lighthouse on the Point Reyes promontory.

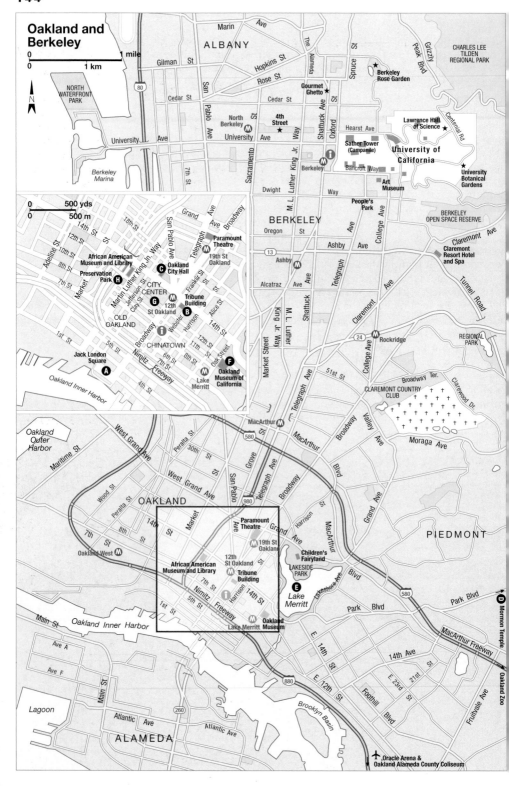

Oakland and Berkeley

0 ——————— 1 mile
0 ——————— 1 km

N

NORTH WATERFRONT PARK

Berkeley Marina

CHARLES LEE TILDEN REGIONAL PARK

ALBANY

Marin Ave
Gilman St
Hopkins St
Rose St
Cedar St
Cedar St
The Alameda
Spruce St
Peak Blvd
Grizzly
CHARLES LEE TILDEN REGIONAL PARK

Berkeley Rose Garden ★
Gourmet Ghetto ★

North Berkeley M
4th Street ★
University Ave
Hearst Ave
Oxford St
Shattuck Ave

Lawrence Hall of Science ★
Centennial Rd

Sather Tower (Campanile) ★
University of California
Berkeley M i
Bancroft Way
Art Museum ★
University Botanical Gardens ★

University Ave

San Pablo Ave
Sacramento St
7th St

Dwight Way

BERKELEY
BERKELEY OPEN SPACE RESERVE

Oregon St
Ashby Ave
Telegraph Ave
College Ave

Claremont Ave

Claremont Resort Hotel and Spa

People's Park ★

Ashby M
13
Alcatraz Ave

Tunnel Road

Detail Inset

0 ——— 500 yds
0 ——— 500 m

18th St
14th St
12th St
10th St
8th St
7th St
Adeline St
Market St
Grand Ave
Broadway
Telegraph Ave
San Pablo Ave
Martin Luther King Jr. Way

Paramount Theatre
19th St Oakland M

African American Museum and Library
Preservation Park H
Oakland City Hall C
CITY CENTER
G 12th St Oakland M
Tribune Building B
OLD OAKLAND
Jefferson St
Clay St
Webster St
Harrison St
Franklin St
Alice St
Broadway
CHINATOWN
11th St
7th St
8th St
12th St
13th St
14th St
Oak Street

Jack London Square A
5th St
Nimitz Freeway
4th St
Oakland Inner Harbor
i

Oakland Museum of California F
Lake Merritt

Market Street
M.L. Luther King Jr Way
Telegraph Ave

24
Rockridge M

REGIONAL PARK

51st St
College Ave
Broadway
Valley Ave
Grand Ave

CLAREMONT COUNTRY CLUB
Broadway Ter.
Claremont Ave
Claremwood Dr.

Moraga Ave

Oakland Outer Harbor

Maritime St
West Grand Ave

OAKLAND
Peralta St
30th St
West Grand Ave
San Pablo Ave
Grove St
Telegraph Ave
Broadway
Harrison St
MacArthur Blvd

MacArthur 580

Oakland West M

7th St
8th St
14th St
Market St
Peralta St
Wood St

Paramount Theatre
Ave
980
19th St Oakland M
12th St Oakland M
African American Museum and Library
Tribune Building
i
Harrison
Children's Fairyland
LAKESIDE PARK
Lake Merritt E

PIEDMONT

Nimitz Freeway
1st St
5th St
7th St
14th St
Oakland West M
Lake Merritt M
Oakland Museum

Oakland Inner Harbor

Grand Ave
MacArthur Blvd
580
Park Blvd

Lakeshore Ave

Park Blvd
MacArthur Freeway

D Mormon Temple
Oakland Zoo

Main St
Oakland Inner Harbor
880

Ave A
Ave F
ALAMEDA
Lagoon
260
Atlantic Ave
Atlantic Ave
Main St

Brooklyn Basin
E 14th St
E 12th St
E 14th St
E 23rd St
21st Ave
Foothill Blvd
Fruitvale Ave

✈ Oracle Arena & Oakland Alameda County Coliseum

the number of businesses owned by women.

Oakland's version of Fisherman's Wharf is the restaurant and shopping pedestrian walk called **Jack London Square A**. The author of *The Sea Wolf* and *The Call of the Wild*, who died in 1916, might not be impressed to see the overpriced restaurants and souvenir stores, but he'd be able to munch crab, listen to live music, and watch the sailboats pass by.

The **First and Last Chance Saloon**, which London frequented, is popular with tourists, and nearby is his sodroofed Yukon cabin, moved from Alaska to the waterfront in tribute to the city's most famous son.

Moored in the harbor is the USS Potomac, President Franklin D. Roosevelt's "floating White House," and now a National Historic Monument (www.usspotomac.org; dockside tours Wed, Fri, and Sun 11am–3pm; charge).

On Sundays a farmers market is held in the part of the city called Old Oakland (around Washington Street at 8th Street; www.oldoakland.org), a neighborhood with stores, restaurants, and shops in its renovated buildings. Nearby, Oakland's Chinatown is more negotiable than its cousin across the bay.

Oakland's many landmarks include the handsome **Tribune Building B**, with its distinctive tower, and the post-1989-earthquake renovated **Oakland City Hall C**, with its wedding-cake cupola. The Art Deco palace, the Paramount Theatre, is the home of the Oakland Ballet and the Paramount Organ Pops, and shows old movies and newsreels. Other cultural attractions in Oakland are the Fox Theatre and monthly Art Murmurs (www.oaklandart-murmur.org), events promoting local art and culture. In the hills above, the fivetowered, white granite **Mormon Temple D** is the only Mormon temple in the state. From its lofty heights are wonderful views of the bay.

On the eastern edge of town is a natural landmark, **Lake Merritt E**.

This large saltwater lake and wildlife refuge, rimmed by Victorian houses and a necklace of lights, is the location of a 10-acre (4-hectare) theme park, **Children's Fairyland** (see margin).

Not far from the lake is the **Oakland Museum of California F** (1000 Oak Street; tel: 510-318-8400; www.muse-umca.org; Wed–Sun 11am–5pm; charge; free on first Sun of every month).

Landscaped with terraces and gardens and occupying three levels, it is considered the finest museum in the state for information on California's art, history, and natural science. The Cowell Hall of California History has a huge collection of artifacts, while the Gallery of California Art is known for its oil paintings.

Among Oakland's newer attractions are the **City Center G**, a pedestrian mall with quaint restaurants, jazz concerts, and art exhibits; **Preservation Park H**, a restored Victorian village complete with 19th-century street lamps and lush gardens; and the **African American Museum and Library** at 659 14th Street. For many black Americans,

First and Last Chance Saloon.

Oakland has a special significance; it was here in the 1960s that the Black Panther Movement was founded. The politics espoused by the Panthers spread from here to the East Coast and then to college campuses around the country.

Berkeley

Just north of Oakland is **Berkeley** ❻, another East Bay rival of San Francisco. A city famous for social experimentation and the birth of the Free Speech movement, Berkeley has, in recent times, become slightly less flamboyant and slightly more commercial.

On the approach to Berkeley from Oakland, two buildings catch the eye. On a hillside toward the south is a fairy-tale white palace, otherwise known as the **Claremont Resort and Spa** (tel: 510-843-3000), which, like San Francisco's Palace of Fine Arts, was finished just before the Panama-Pacific Exposition of 1915. The other landmark is a tall, pointed structure, the university's bell tower. Its official name is **Sather Tower**, but it is known to everyone simply as "the campanile"

because it's modeled after St Mark's campanile in Venice, Italy. Sather Tower belongs to the **University of California** (tel: 510-642-6000), known simply as "Cal" and considered one of the country's finest public universities. Berkeley grew from a humble prep school operating out of a former fandango house in Oakland, to become part of the ninecampus University of California system.

To get the feel of Berkeley at its liveliest, visitors should take a walk down Telegraph Avenue from Dwight Way to the university. Students, townspeople, and "street people" pick their way between street vendors offering jewelry and pottery, and stores catering to modern students.

Berkeley's climate (it can be foggy in San Francisco but sunny across the bay) produces sweet scents in the **University Botanical Gardens** in Strawberry Canyon. Over 12,000 species thrive in the research facility here. Elsewhere in the Berkeley hills are other nature-based attractions: **Tilden Regional Park**, the **Berkeley Rose Garden**, and the **Lawrence Hall of Science**.

The Peninsula

The San Francisco **Peninsula**, a roughly 55-mile (89km) swath of high hills, tall trees, and beautiful estates, is wedged between the Pacific Ocean and San Francisco Bay. To its north is San Francisco. At its southern end lies the sprawl of **Silicon Valley** – or what used to be known as the Santa Clara Valley when apples and pears, not computers and silicon chips, were harvested here. In the valley, the peninsula's highlands segue into the affluent, high-tech communities of Palo Alto, Los Altos, Sunnyvale, Santa Clara, and San Jose. As the drive south on **El Camino Real** – the main thoroughfare that runs through all these cities down to San Jose – will prove, the only true borders between peninsula cities seem to be stoplights.

University of California, Berkeley.

Where the commercial and spartan-finish industrial strips end, the wealthy suburban homes begin, spread like a heat rash across the ample flatlands.

The style of the peninsula is sophisticated, shamelessly commercial, and contemporary. Stanford University is the hub of academic and cultural activity. Mixed with the high-mindedness, however, is lots of new money (millionaires from scratch as common as tennis courts) and old money (San Mateo is one of the four wealthiest counties in California). Both types shop at the impressive **Stanford Shopping Center**.

Stanford University

A farm – a blue-blooded horse ranch – is exactly what the campus of renowned **Stanford University** ❼ (tel: 650-723-2300) was a little over a century ago when Leland Stanford and photographer Eadweard Muybridge began their experiments with moving images (which were to lead to the creation of motion pictures). Today, it is the academic lifeblood of the peninsula, located in the northwestern corner of **Palo Alto**, a city known for its strict environmental policies and praised as one of the best "model little cities of the world." Architecturally, Stanford's handsome, rough-hewn sandstone buildings are Romanesque in style, though the red-tiled roofs, the burnt adobe color of the stone, and the wide arches give the university a Spanish mission look. The exception to the overall prosaic qualities is beautiful **Memorial Church**, which dominates the **Inner Quad** (also known as the central courtyard). The church is resplendent in stained glass and with a domed ceiling.

San Jose

San Jose ❽ was the first pueblo to be founded in Northern California by the Spanish, in 1777. Until 1956, the San Jose area was providing America with half its supply of prunes. But the orchards of five decades ago have now sprouted condominiums and industrial parks. Today, San Jose is the third-largest city in California, with a

Colorful Californian.

FREE SPEECH FOR ALL

The Free Speech movement of 1964 put Berkeley on the map. At issue was a UC Berkeley administration order limiting political activities on campus. This touched off massive student protests and, in turn, similar protests on campuses nationwide. Since then, the campus has been a center of political action.

In 1969, students took to the streets to stop the university's expansion in an area they wanted to preserve as **People's Park**. They prevailed, despite the intervention of 2,000 National Guard troops and violence that led to the death of an onlooker. Years on, People's Park drew more drug dealers and drifters from the city's homeless than it did students. But today, student unrest has turned more to rest and recreation, so the city has added basketball and volleyball courts to the park.

WHERE

While you're in San Jose, take a look at the Tech Museum of Innovation in the city center (201 South Market Street; tel: 408-294-8324; www. thetech.org). It's a hands-on museum with galleries documenting innovations in areas such as health and biotechnology, energy, exploration, and the development of local industry. Don't miss the Tech Test zone, where you can experience the technology of the future.

City Hall, San Jose.

population that is booming due to the influx from around the world of high-tech personnel and like-minded groupies.

It is a busy, fast-paced community (population over 960,000), with several major hotels, nightclubs, and no fewer than 100 shopping centers that cater to all the techies with money to burn. Of these the most renowned is Santana Row. The **San Jose Museum of Art** (110 South Market Street; tel: 408-271-6840; www.sjmusart.org; Tue–Sun 11am–5pm; charge) boasts nearly 1,500 works of art, new media, and installations, including glass sculptures by Dale Chihuly and photographs by Ruth Bernard. For entertainment of a more eccentric bent there is the red-roofed, sprawling, touristy but nonetheless fascinating **Winchester Mystery House ❾** (near Interstate 280 and State Highway 17; tel: 408-247-2000; www.winchestermyseteryhouse.com; daily, but hours vary; charge) in downtown San Jose. It was built in convoluted stages by local eccentric Sarah L. Winchester, who inherited the fortune of her

father-in-law, the famed gun manufacturer. Sarah was a spiritualist who believed that she would live as long as she kept adding to her house. Sixteen carpenters worked on the mansion for 36 years, adding stairways that lead to nowhere and doors without any rooms.

The spiritual realm is also the basis and reason for the **Rosicrucian Egyptian Museum and Planetarium** (tel: 408-947-3635) in San Jose, on the way to **Santa Clara**. A recreated walk-in tomb of 2000 BC and the West Coast's largest collection of Egyptian, Babylonian, and Assyrian artifacts are contained within the building. The Ancient Mystical Order Rosae Crucis is an international philosophical order said to have been established nearly 3,500 years ago.

Anyone longing for fresh air and the sound of the sea should nip over to Highway 1 west of San Jose near the little town of **Pescadero,** where there is a particularly atmospheric site – **Pigeon Point Lighthouse**, the second-tallest lighthouse in the United States.

Silicon Valley

Endowed with the enterprising spirit of pioneers, Silicon Valley nurtured many of the technological advances that catapulted the world into the electronic age.

Silicon Valley stretches about 20 miles (32km) from the lower San Francisco peninsula to San Jose. Google, Adobe, Cisco, Yahoo, Apple, Facebook, and Intel are just a selection of the famous IT names based here. A large part of any history of modern computing will be a list of Silicon Valley milestones.

Formerly known as Santa Clara Valley and settled by farmers in the mid-1800s, it is bounded to the east by the San Francisco Bay and to the west by the Santa Cruz mountains. It embraces 16 cities, including Palo Alto, home of Stanford University. In 1938, two Stanford students, David Packard and William Hewlett, living at 367 Addison Street in Palo Alto (now a State Historical Monument), founded what would one day become one of the world's corporate giants, Hewlett-Packard.

Local heroes

After receiving the Nobel Prize for the electronic transistor in 1956, Valley native William Shockley intended to build an empire, but the eight young engineers he hired all left to form Fairchild Semiconductor. It was here, in 1959, that Bob Noyce developed the miniature semiconductor set into silicon. Noyce, known to many as the father of Silicon Valley, co-founded Intel with Gordon Moore in 1968.

At 2066 Crist Drive in a Cupertino garage, Steve Jobs and Steve Wozniak turned out their first computer and later formed Apple Computer. Apple's headquarters are still located in Cupertino.

During the 1980s, personal computers replaced arcade games as the entertainment of choice. Then came email and the World Wide Web. At first these were mainly electronic noticeboards for tech geeks; now they are indispensable tools. When the internet started to catch on, with an estimated 18 million users in 1995, a frenzy began. Entrepreneurs were eager to dig from the emerging market, and people flocked to Silicon Valley, much as they had to the Sierras looking for gold in 1848. This time, instead of picks and pans, they brought business plans and laptops. Through the tumult and excitement of the dot-com boom, many got burned and the industry suffered a huge crash in 2002.

Life rose from the rubble. The world discovered Google as a search engine; on its stock flotation Google overtook Time-Warner as the world's most valuable media corporation; eBay gobbled up many of the old "bricks and mortar" auction houses; and Apple Computer took a market out from under Sony, replacing the Walkman with the iPod.

Social media mania quickly became the next Silicon Valley phenomenon with the rise of Facebook and Twitter. The communication, marketing, business, and political landscapes were forever altered by these powerful media tools. A movie on the origins of Facebook, *The Social Network*, was nominated for a Best Picture Oscar at the 2011 Academy Awards.

Google Android foam robot and phone at the Google headquarters, Mountain View.

Cycling in Mount Tamalpais State Park.

Stained glass in Rhine House,
Beringer Vineyards, Napa Valley.

WINE COUNTRY

Wine is grown all over the state, but the Napa and Sonoma valleys represent California Wine Country for most visitors. Apart from wineries, the region has plenty to entice the visitor, from trails to spa towns, and gorgeous scenery.

From the summit of Mount St Helena, a vast, rolling expanse of emerald vineyards stretches for miles below. Supported by a temperate climate and rich, drainable soil, the grape vines blanket the beautifully bucolic Napa, Sonoma, Mendocino, and Lake counties, together forming one of the most famous wine-growing regions in the world. Although wine is the main allure – for both San Francisco day-trippers and international visitors – the region also boasts a renowned farm-to-table restaurant scene, spas fed by hot springs, ballooning excursions, plenty of opportunities for biking, hiking, and camping, and even a wild animal park.

Napa Valley

Rural Napa Valley, with its wealthy and genteel aura, was catapulted into wine industry fame after beating French wines in a 1976 tasting. Today it is the most famous of California's wine-producing regions. The 30-mile (50km) thrust of flat land nestles between the pine-forested Mayacamas Mountains and the buff-colored Howell Mountains, pinched off in the north by Mount St Helena. State Highway 29 and the Silverado Trail run parallel through the valley, passing long expanses of vineyards broken up by farmhouses, stone wineries, and a series of small towns. If you are staying overnight, any of these

World-class vineyards.

towns makes a good launching point for exploring the valley. Otherwise, simply choose the wineries you want to visit and hit the road (with a designated driver, of course).

Napa

The first Napa Valley town you enter when heading north from San Francisco is **Napa** ❶ (www.visitnapa valley.com). The charming small town (whose name means "plenty" in the local Indian dialect) is a compact collection of shops, country inns,

Main Attractions

Napa Wine Train
Oxbow Public Market, Napa
Yountville
Silverado Trail
Old Faithful Geyser
Downtown Sonoma

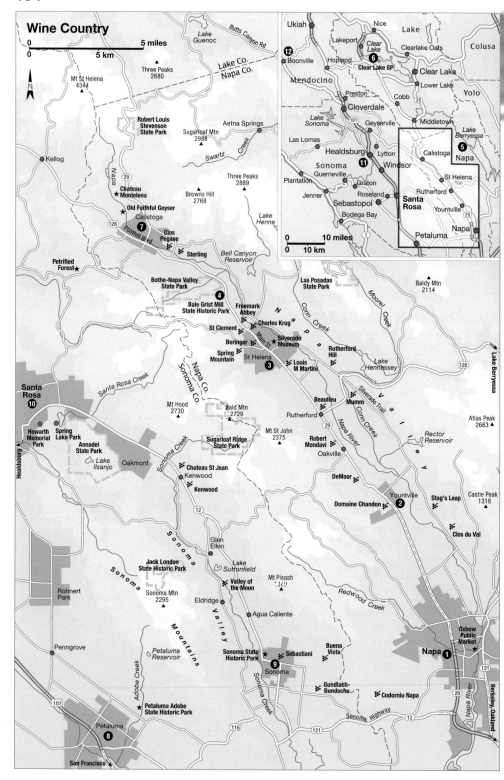

Wine Country

0 — 5 miles
0 — 5 km

N

Three Peaks 2680

Mt St Helena 4344

Lake Guenoc

Butts Canyon Rd

Lake Co.
Napa Co.

Robert Louis Stevenson State Park

Sugarloaf Mtn 2988

Aetna Springs

Swartz Creek

Kellog

Chateau Montelena

Old Faithful Geyser

Calistoga

Three Peaks 2889

Browns Hill 2768

Lake Henne

Petrified Forest★

7

Clos Pegase

Sterling

Bell Canyon Reservoir

Foothill Blvd

Napa

128

29

Bothe-Napa Valley State Park

4

Bale Grist Mill State Historic Park

Freemark Abbey

Charles Krug

St Clement

Beringer

Spring Mountain

Silverado Museum

St Helena

3

Louis M Martini

Rutherford Hill

Las Posadas State Park

Baldy Mtn 2114

Moorel Creek

Corn Creek

N a p a

Lake Hennessey

128

Lake Berryessa

Santa Rosa

10

Santa Rosa Creek

Napa Co.
Sonoma Co.

Mt Hood 2730

Bald Mtn 2729

Mt St John 2375

Beaulieu

Mumm

Rutherford

Robert Mondavi

Oakville

29

Napa River

Corn Creek

Silverado Trail

V a l l e y

Atlas Peak 2663 ▲

Rector Reservoir

Howarth Memorial Park

Spring Lake Park

Annadel State Park

Lake Ilsanjo

Oakmont

Sonoma Creek

Sugarloaf Ridge State Park

Chateau St Jean

Kenwood

Kenwood

DeMoor

Domaine Chandon

Yountville

2

Stag's Leap

Castle Peak 1318 ▲

Clos du Val

Healdsburg

12

Rohnert Park

S o n o m a

Jack London State Historic Park

Sonoma Mtn 2295

Eldridge

Glen Ellen

Lake Suttonfield

Valley of the Moon

Mt Pisgah 1349

Agua Caliente

Redwood Creek

Oxbow Public Market

Penngrove

Petaluma Reservoir

M o u n t a i n s

S o n o m a

V a l l e y

Sonoma State Historic Park

9

Sonoma

Sebastiani

Buena Vista

Napa

1

101

Adobe Creek

Petaluma Adobe State Historic Park

Sonoma Creek

Gundlach-Bundschu

Codorniu Napa

Sonoma Highway

121

29

Napa River

Berkeley, Oakland

Petaluma

8

116

121

12

San Francisco

Inset map (top right)

Ukiah

Nice

Lake

Lakeport

Clear Lake

Clearlake Oaks

Colusa

12

Boonville

Hopland

Clear Lake SP

6

Clear Lake

Lower Lake

Yolo

Mendocino

Preston

Cobb

29

Cloverdale

Lake Sonoma

101

Geyserville

Middletown

Lake Berryessa

Las Lomas

Healdsburg

Lytton

Calistoga

5

Napa

Sonoma

Guerneville

Windsor

St Helena

Plantation

Graton

Rutherford

Jenner

Roseland

Sebastopol

Santa Rosa

Yountville

11

Bodega Bay

29

0 — 10 miles
0 — 10 km

Napa

Petaluma

1

vineries, and eateries. Peruse boutiques on the main street through the quaint Downtown, grab a bite at an upscale restaurant, then get on the road to taste your way through wineries like Darioush, Paraduxx, Ceja, Frogs Leap, Vintners Collective, and Schramberg. If you don't feel like driving, consider a ride on the Napa Valley Wine Train (see box).

On Tuesdays and Saturdays, the Napa Farmers Market is held at the Oxbow Public Market (610 and 644 First Street; www.oxbowpublicmarket. com; open most days 9am–7pm). All week long, you can choose from dozens of restaurants and specialty food purveyors, including Three Twins, serving scoops of organic ice cream; Hog Island, dishing out fresh oysters; and Ritual Coffee Roasters, pouring some the Bay Area's best coffee.

Yountville

In what must surely be one of history's most lucrative contracting deals. George Yount received his huge land grant for roofing General Vallejo's Petaluma adobe. Today, Yount's grave at the pioneer center is found across from Yountville's city-park picnic stop. The renovated brick and stone buildings in **Yountville ②** are home to exceptional restaurants, from Thomas Keller's world-renowned French Laundry to the more relaxed Girl and the Fig.

Of course, the focus here is also on wine. **Domaine Chandon Winery** (tel: 707-944-2280; www.chandon. com) just west of town is owned by Chandon of Moët and Chandon fame, and produces sparkling wine in the *méthode champenoise*; that is, it is fermented in the same bottle from which it is poured. Just north of Oakville is the **Robert Mondavi Winery** (tel: 707-968-2000; www.robertmondavi.com/ rmw), a sleek operation, as befits such a famous local name.

St Helena

The undisputed capital of the Napa Valley is **St Helena ③**, noted for its dozens of wineries, historic stone buildings, picnic parks, chic shops, pricey hotels, and the CIA (see page 159). The **Silverado Museum** (1490 Library Lane; tel: 707-963-3757; www.silverado

On the Napa Valley Wine Train.

NAPA VALLEY WINE TRAIN

A one-of-a-kind fine-dining experience, with exceptional locally sourced Napa wines, awaits the passenger on this popular Wine Country attraction. The lavishly restored 1915 Pullman dining and lounge cars lend an air of opulence to this tasteful journey. The train whizzes past wineries along 36 miles (58km) of track in the heart of the Napa Valley during the three-hour tour. The Wine Train operates year-round and offers a variety of packages – from champagne brunch to a moonlight escape. Special trains operate on all holidays, and they offer winemakers' dinners and murder mystery rides. Optional excursions include tours of Domaine Chandon Winery and Grgich Hills Estate. For more information: tel: 707-253-2111; www.winetrain.com.

Chefs at work in the kitchens of Sonoma's The Girl and the Fig restaurant, producing seasonal, French-inspired food.

The Girl and the Fig restaurant in Sonoma.

museum.org; Tue-Sat noon-4pm; free) is stuffed with Robert Louis Stevenson memorabilia and collectables like first editions of his work and souvenirs of his global jaunts.

South of town, the **Louis M. Martini Winery** (tel: 707-963-2736; www.louismartini.com), run by one of the valley's oldest winemaking clans, offers reasonably priced wines in an unpretentious setting. Two historic wineries lie just north of St Helena. Jacob and Frederick started the **Beringer Vineyards** (tel: 707-963-7115; www.beringer.com) in 1876, modeling the Rhine House (1883) after their ancestral estate in Mainz, Germany. They dug limestone caves for aging wine. Today's winery, owned by Foster's (yes, the Australian beer people), features Fumé Blanc and Cabernet Sauvignon in the mansion tasting room. Outside, spacious lawns and a regal row of elms fronts the winery.

The building of the other founding father, **Charles Krug Winery** (tel: 707-963-5057; www.charleskrug.com), dates from 1874. The lavish Greystone building nearby was the world's largest stone winery when it was erected in 1889 by mining magnate William Bourn; today, the mansion is run by the California headquarters of the **Culinary Institute of America**, a brilliant cooking school with a restaurant that is open to visitors.

To take a break from wine tasting, visit the **Bale Grist Mill State Historic Park** ❹ (tel: 707-942-4575; open Sat–Sun 10am–5pm), 3 miles (5km) north of St Helena. The center of Napa social activity in the mid-19th century, the historic 1846 mill is where settlers once ground their corn and wheat into flour or meal. Milling demonstrations and historic tours are held on weekends.

Between Bale Grist and the town of Calistoga are two excellent places to stop. **Sterling Vineyards** (tel: 707-942-3344; www.sterlingvineyards.com) – part Spanish mission, part fantasy – reigns over the upper valley atop a knoll. A sky tram whisks visitors 300ft (91 meters) up for a self-guided tour. The tram fee is offset against the purchase of Sauvignon Blanc and other wines. Close by is **Clos Pegase** (tel: 707-942-4981; www.clospegase.com), designed in 1986 by architect Michael Graves in sleek, modern style. Clos Pegase is known almost as much for its art collection as for its wines.

Lake County

St Helena is also the turn-off to a warm-water paradise. The tragedy-ridden Berryessa family lost sons and soil in the Mexican War; today, their Napa land grant is better known as **Lake Berryessa** ❺, reached via State Highway 128 from St Helena or State Highway 121 from Napa. Fishermen pull in trout, bass, and catfish, while sailors, waterskiers, campers, and swimmers have their choice of several resorts around this lake, which has more miles of shoreline than Lake Tahoe. Bring along some of your favorite vintage and enjoy your wine in a picnic setting.

Back on State Highway 29 and past **Robert Louis Stevenson State Park,** the road heads towards **Lake County** and its bold, friendly, visitor-seeking wineries scattered around **Clear Lake** ❻, California's largest natural lake (Lake Tahoe lies partly in Nevada). Besides producing Cabernet Sauvignon, Zinfandel, and Sauvignon Blanc grapes, Lake County is famous for Bartlett pears and walnuts. Resorts and campgrounds ring the lake, and there's good walking in **Clear Lake State Park** at the foot of conical **Mount Konocti**, an extinct volcano.

Calistoga

The one-street spa town of **Calistoga** ❼ is a little gem. Wooden hangings shading the shopfronts give it a Wild West feel, while treatment centers including Indian Springs, Calistoga Spa Hot Springs, and Spa Solage make use of mineral springs and hot,

*Beringer Vineyards'
historic Rhine House.*

Bottle of white from the Beringer Vineyards, where Cabernet Sauvignon, Merlot, Pinot Noir, Chardonnay, and Sauvignon Blanc are produced.

Chateau Montelena produces Zinfandel, Riesling, Cabernet Sauvignon, and Chardonnay.

therapeutic mud. After treatments, head to on-site pools heated by hot springs to completely relax.

Calistoga is surrounded by numerous wineries. Of note for its historic (1882) lakeside setting with a Chinese feel is **Chateau Montelena** (tel: 707-942-5105; www.montelena.com), which produces classic Chardonnay and Cabernet Sauvignon. A limited number of reservations are accepted for the picnic sites on Jade Lake in view of the pagoda.

Two miles (3km) north of town, Old Faithful Geyser (tel: 707-942-6463; www.oldfaithfulgeyser.com; daily, winter 9am–5pm, summer 9am–6pm; charge) spouts jets of boiling water 60–100ft (18–30 meters) into the sky every half-hour. Although the tickets are somewhat expensive for what takes place, there are tables inside the little waiting area, so you can have a pleasant picnic while waiting for the water to take off. Just to the west is the Petrified Forest (4100 Petrified Forest Road; charge), where redwoods were turned to stone millions of years ago. Docent-led tours (included in

the admission price) guide visitors through an ash fall, meadow, and view of Mount St Helena, and discuss the area's geology, flora, and fauna.

Seven miles (11km) north of Calistoga is Robert Louis Stevenson State Park, named for the famous author of Treasure Island, who honeymooned there in 1880. On a 5-mile (8km) hike to the top of Mount St Helena, a marker notes where his cabin once stood. On clear days, Mount Shasta can be seen 192 miles (309km) away from the peak.

Sonoma Valley

More slow-paced and rustic than Napa, Sonoma County is a patchwork of country roads, towns, orchards, ridges, and hills. West of Napa, Sonoma is only about one hour's (jam-free) drive from San Francisco. US 101, the Wine Country's only freeway, runs the length of **Sonoma County** north to south, entering it near **Petaluma** ❽. The freeway continues on through Santa Rosa, Healdsburg (gateway to the Alexander, Dry Creek, and Russian River valleys), and Cloverdale, which is located on the Mendocino County

border. State Highway 12 runs through Sonoma Valley to Santa Rosa, passing the towns of Sonoma and Kenwood.

The **Sonoma Valley** is steeped in wine and wineries, and literary and political history. *Sonoma* is a native Patwin word meaning "Land of Chief Nose," after an Indian leader with a prominent proboscis. Founding father Mariano Vallejo romanticized Sonoma Valley as the "Valley of the Moon" (author Jack London later borrowed the name for a book about frazzled urbanites rejuvenated by clean country living).

Sonoma

Father Altimira founded California's last mission, **San Francisco de Solano**, in 1823. General Vallejo set up the town in 1835, making **Sonoma ⑨** the northernmost outpost of a Catholic, Spanish-speaking realm that, at its peak, extended all the way to the tip of South America. It briefly became a republic after the Bear Flag Revolt in 1846, when Americans stormed Vallejo's home. Although Vallejo and the missionaries at Mission San Francisco de Solano dabbled in winemaking, the local residents really only recognized the region's vinicultural potential after Hungarian political refugee Count Agoston Haraszthy founded Buena Vista Winery in 1957 and began winemaking in earnest.

Today, downtown Sonoma is picturesque, relaxed, and well-heeled. Upscale restaurants and art galleries ring its tree-shaded **Sonoma Plaza**. Several restored adobes are also found around the plaza and on nearby streets, including the Mission (tel: 707-938-9560); Vallejo's old house, **Lachryma Montis** (tel: 707-938-9559); and the **Sonoma** Barracks (707-939-9420), all part of the **Sonoma State Historic Park** (363 3rd Street West; www.parks.ca.gov; Tue–Sun 10am–5pm; charge).

Two blocks from the plaza stand **Sebastiani Vineyards** (tel: 707-933-3230; www.sebastiani.com), on lands once cultivated by the people of the San Francisco de Solano Mission. This winery is still owned by the Sebastiani family.

East of Sonoma, the **Buena Vista Winery** Tasting Room (tel: 1-800-926-1266; www.buenavistawinery.com) retains connections with Count Haraszthy; his original cellars are still standing and his image adorns the label of the winery's Founder's red wine. South of town, the Gundlach and Bundschu families were involved in winemaking for more than 125 years, and Gundlach-Bundschu (tel: 707-938-5277; www.gunbun.com) wines are exported around the globe.

Nearby, the pricey, beautifully decorated **Fairmont Sonoma Mission Inn and Spa** (tel: 707-938-9000; www.fairmont.com/sonoma) offers health and fitness facilities (with its own source of thermal mineral water).

North on State Highway 121, the **Valley of the Moon Winery** (tel: 707-996-6941; www.valleyofthemoonwinery.com) occupies part of George Hearst's 19th-century vineyards (George was the father of tycoon William Hearst). North on State

EAT

Before the Culinary Institute of America (CIA) was founded, many cooks were so secretive about their recipes that it was hard for a novice to break into the profession. Today, the California branch works hard to ensure that knowledge is preserved and shared with the public. Expect tasty tidbits, paired wines, and up-and-coming chefs at the teaching school (Wine Spectator Greystone Restaurant; 2555 Main Street, St Helena; tel: 707-967-1010; www.ciarestaurants.com; daily 11.30am –9pm, Fri–Sat until 10pm).

Old Faithful Geyser, Calistoga.

TIP

.Not into wine? Enjoy a
few rounds on the links,
instead. Golfing options in
Napa Valley include the
Silverado Resort and Spa,
which has hosted tour
events since the 1960s
(www.silveradoresort.com),
Chardonnay Golf Club
(www.chardonnaygolfclub.
com), Eagle Vines Golf
Club (www.eaglevinesgolf
club.com), or Napa Golf
course (www.playnapa.com).

Highway 1 is the town of Kenwood. The **Kenwood Winery** (tel: 707-833-5891; www.kenwood1vineyards.com) features Zinfandel, Cabernet Sauvignon, and Chenin Blanc, while Chardonnay lovers head for **Château St Jean** (tel: 707-833-4134; www.chateaustjean.com), with its medieval-style tower and excellent whites.

Santa Rosa

Famed botanist Luther Burbank picked the area around **Santa Rosa** ⑩ , on State Highway 12, as "the chosen spot of all the earth" to conduct his plant experiments in hybridization. He developed more than 800 new plants, including many fruits, vegetables, and flowers, yet relished few of them except asparagus. Visitors can tour the **Luther Burbank Home and Gardens** (tel: 707-524-5445; www.lutherburbank.org; check for tour and visiting information; charge). Children will want to head for Santa Rosa's **Snoopy's Gallery**, selling the widest range of Snoopy products in the world, thanks to the fame of Santa Rosaite and dog creator Charles Schultz.

Sonoma Valley vines.

The town's trinity of adjoining parks form a 5,000-acre (12,000-hectare) urban oasis with a children's amusement park and lake in **Howarth Park**; camping, picnicking, and boating in **Spring Lake Park**; and hiking and equestrian trails in **Annadel State Park**.

Alexander, Dry Creek, and Russian River valleys

North of Santa Rosa, **Healdsburg** ⑪ is where the Alexander, Dry Creek, and Russian River valleys meet. A beach on the river encourages swimming, fishing, and canoeing. There's also a tree-shaded, Spanish-style plaza dating from the 1960s. The Healdsburg Museum on Mattheson Street, housed in the old Carnegie Library building, displays Pomo tribal artifacts and 19th-century exhibits from the region.

There are more than 60 wineries within a half-hour's drive of Healdsburg, and the industry's growth and the concomitant rise in tourism have been bringing almost a million visitors a year to this pretty town. Opposite the 130-year-old Belle

du Jour Inn on Healdsburg Avenue is the tasting room of the Simi Winery (daily 10am–5pm; tours at 11am and 2pm). One entry in the 1942 guest-book is by Alfred Hitchcock, who drew a sketch of himself and noted, "The port here is far too good for most people." There are numerous other wineries in the area, especially in the picturesque Alexander Valley, east of US 101. State Highway 253 snakes westward from US 101 just south of Ukiah to join northbound State Highway 128 at Boonville. This narrow, often-wooded country road meanders through the valley past grazing sheep, vineyards, and orchards all the way to Navarro and beyond to the coast.

Winemaking first began here more than a century ago, when many frustrated gold-seekers settled and planted vineyards. **Boonville** ⓬ is a delightful little place. You can eat well and stay comfortably at the Boonville Hotel (tel: 707-895-2210), which calls itself a "roadhouse," defined in Funk and Wagnall's 19th-century dictionary as "an inn or restaurant in a rural locality

which caters especially to transient pleasure-seekers."

Other worthwhile stops include the Anderson Valley Historical Society Museum (12340 Hwy 128; www.andersonvalleymuseum.org; Feb–Nov Fri–Sun 1–4pm; free), in a red, one-room schoolhouse north of Mountain View Road; the Buckhorn Saloon; and the Anderson Valley Brewing Company (www.avbc.com; tours summer daily 1.30pm and 3pm, winter Thur–Mon).

Getting hitched at a vineyard.

Lavish parties are held when vintners congregate from around the world for the Napa Valley Barrel Auction.

MONTEREY PENINSULA AND THE BIG SUR COAST

The stretch of State Highway 1 from Santa Cruz to Big Sur is arguably California's most scenic route, passing beautiful state parks, rustic country inns, and great spots to surf.

Highway 1 south from San Francisco may be the most spectacular route in America. A series of razor-sharp switchbacks hug hills, plunge into valleys, and skirt the coast the entire way. Steep, rugged mountains loom on the left of the road, while on the right is nothing but a sheer drop to the wild, crashing waves below. The climate changes every few miles, from fog to rain to blinding sunshine. This is the *real* California.

Santa Cruz

At the northern end of Monterey Bay is **Santa Cruz ❶**, a cool, green, redwood-shingled beach 77 miles (120km) southeast of San Francisco. The **University of California** opened its Santa Cruz campus in 1965 and within a few years this influx of academic activity transformed what had previously been a quiet backwater town into an activist community. Santa Cruz was rejuvenated with excellent restaurants, cafés, pastry shops, and bookstores. Old buildings were refurbished, with cement block and aluminum replaced by natural redwood and hanging ferns.

Sunny Santa Cruz has sparkling clean air and is usually unaffected by the fog and chilly winds that hover off the coast, north and south.

Popular beaches include Natural Bridges State Beach, Bonny Doon, Pleasure Point Beach, and Twin Lakes State Beach. Surfing is very popular in Santa Cruz; to learn more, visit the Santa Cruz Surfing Museum (701 West Cliff Drive; tel: 831-420-6289; www.santacruzsurfingmuseum. org). Santa Cruz Pier is the place for all things fishy – fish restaurants, fish markets, and fishing facilities. One of the most popular attractions in Santa Cruz is the **Santa Cruz Beach Boardwalk** (www.beachboardwalk.

Main Attractions
Santa Cruz Beach Boardwalk
Monterey Bay Aquarium
Carmel
Big Sur
Bixby Bridge
Hearst Castle
Pinnacles National Monument
Año Nuevo State Reserve

Decorative tiles at Carmel Mission.

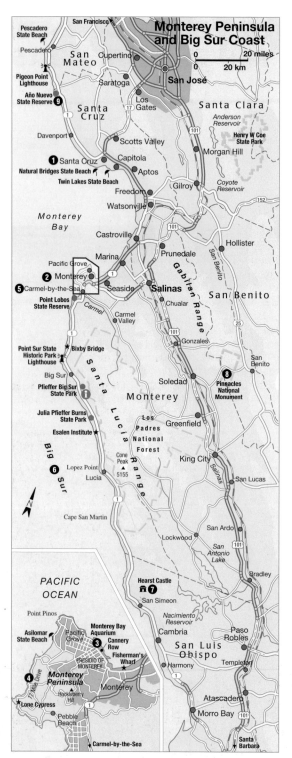

Monterey Peninsula and Big Sur Coast

com), with its 1911 carousel with hand-carved horses, the thrillingly rickety Giant Dipper rollercoaster built in 1924, an old-fashioned arcade containing shooting galleries, and a giant Ferris wheel. On Fridays in the summer, the Beach Bandstand hosts free live oldies concerts at 6.30 and 8.30pm.

Leaving Santa Cruz, Highway 1 follows the coast in a beautiful arc around Monterey Bay. During the springtime, marigolds carpet the high sand dunes. The road passes near the beach town of **Capitola**, then stretches dramatically toward Big Sur. Break at produce and peanut stands for snacks, or at wineries in the mountains behind Santa Cruz for tastings (www.scmwa.com).

Monterey

The city of **Monterey** ② is located at the northern end of Monterey Peninsula. During World War II, Monterey was the sardine capital of the western hemisphere, processing some 200,000 tons a year. After the war, for reasons variously blamed

on overfishing, changing tidal currents, and divine retribution, the sardines suddenly disappeared from Monterey Bay and all the canneries went broke.

Cannery Row, located along the waterfront on the northwest side of town just beyond the Presidio, has become a tourist attraction, its old buildings filled with lusty bars, gaudy restaurants, a wax museum, dozens of shops, a carousel, and food vendors. Cannery Row is also home to one of the world's premier aquariums: the **Monterey Bay Aquarium** ❸ (886 Cannery Row; tel: 831-648-4888; www.monterey bayaquarium.org; daily 10am–6pm; charge). The enormous building, with its outdoor pools overlooking the sea, stands on the site of what was Cannery Row's largest cannery, the Hovden Cannery. Showcasing the incredible diversity of marine life from near and far, more than 100 galleries and exhibits include over 350,000 specimens, from sea otters, leopard sharks, bat rays, and giant octopuses, to towering

underwater kelp forests. Although always crowded – it's the biggest aquarium in the US and attracts nearly 2 million visitors each year – this spectacular sanctuary is worth any amount of waiting time.

In downtown Monterey, the main visitor attraction is **Fisherman's Wharf**, lined with restaurants and shops, with fish markets, an organ grinder with a monkey, and noisy sea lions which swim among the pilings, among the attractions. The real working wharf is found two blocks east.

To see the rest of Monterey, a 3-mile (5km) walking tour, called **The Path of History**, leads past key historical buildings and sites. These include the Customs House, the oldest public building in California, now a museum; Pacific House, a two-story adobe with a Monterey balcony around the second floor; and impressive historical exhibits from the Spanish, Mexican, and early American periods.

Other attractions include **Colton Hall**, a two-story building with a classical portico which was the site of the

One of the entrances to Santa Cruz's beach boardwalk.

The Looff Carousel on the beach boardwalk at Santa Cruz is hand-carved and is a National Historic Landmark, having been in operation since 1911.

Feeding time in the kelp forest tank at Monterey Bay Aquarium.

as the **Defense Language Institute Foreign Language Center** for the US government. Other points of interest in Monterey are the **Monterey Museum** of Art (www.montereyart.org), which focuses on Californian art and photography from the 19th century onwards, and the **Museum of Monterey** (5 Custom House Plaza; 8331-372-2608; www.museumofmonterey.org; Tue–Sat 10am–5pm, Sun noon–5pm; charge), which includes models of sailing ships and boats, photography, and historic and decorative objects. In mid-September each year, the hugely popular **Monterey Jazz Festival** (tel: 831-373-3366; www.montereyjazzfestival.org) attracts many of the biggest names in music to the Monterey Fairgrounds; this is where Jimi Hendrix was brought to the attention of the world.

Diving is popular in Monterey, as is kayaking, which offers a delightful opportunity to get out among the otters and sea lions. The Monterey Visitors Bureau (401 Camino El Estero; tel: 1-888-221-1010; www.

state's first (1849) constitutional convention; Stevenson House, a smaller former hotel where the romantic (and sickly) Robert Louis Stevenson lived for a few months while courting his wife; and the **Royal Presidio Chapel**, in constant use since 1794 and where US President Herbert Hoover was married.

The **Presidio**, founded in 1770 by Gaspar de Portolá, was one of a series of "royal forts" built on the west coast by Spain and now serves

MONTEREY'S FISHY PAST

In the heady early years of Monterey's canning industry, the beaches were so deeply covered with fish guts, scales, and flies that a sickening stench covered the whole town. When the fishing boats came in heavy with their catch, canneries blew whistles and residents streamed down the hill to work amid the rumbling, rattling, squealing machinery of the canning plants. When the last sardine was cleaned, cut, cooked, and canned, the whistle blew again and the wet, smelly workers trudged back up the hill.

John Steinbeck famously described former Ocean View Avenue, now Cannery Row, as "a poem, a stink, a grating noise, a quality of light, a tone, a habit, a nostalgia, a dream." Today, thankfully, the beaches are bright and clean, and the air is sparkling fresh.

seemonterey.com; daily, check website for opening times) provides information on local companies that operate tours out to see the gray whales on their migration between Alaska and Baja California.

17-Mile Drive and Pebble Beach

Just north of the foot of Ocean Avenue is the Carmel Gate entrance to the lovely **17-Mile Drive ❹**, which meanders around the Monterey Peninsula, via the **Del Monte Forest**, to Pacific Grove. There is a charge to take the road, and you should watch out for golfers. The drive takes around three hours.

Close to the **Ghost Tree** cypress is a big, atmospheric stone mansion that looks like something seen in a lightning flash in a horror film. The **Lone Cypress**, a single gnarled and windswept tree near the top of a huge wave-battered rock, is a much-photographed sight.

The drive's other famous attraction is the **Pebble Beach Golf Links**, site of some of the most prestigious

tournaments in the US. The 17-Mile Drive is undeniably beautiful but the attitude of the Pebble Beach Company toward tourists is somewhat condescending, and the landscape is littered with "no trespassing" signs threatening fines and imprisonment.

Carmel-by-the-Sea

The southern gateway to the Monterey Peninsula is the town of **Carmel-by-the-Sea ❺**. A few chance factors made Carmel what it is today: starving

Carmel Beach.

Cadillac on Cannery Row.

One of the striking jellies in Monterey Bay Aquarium, which has hypnotic, beautifully lit tanks of different jelly fish.

celebrities such as Sinclair Lewis, Ansel Adams, Robert Louis Stevenson, and Clint Eastwood. When the evening fog rolls in from the bay, the lights inside the cozy houses, combined with the faint whiff of wood smoke from roaring fires, give Carmel the peaceful feeling of a 19th-century European village.

Carmel's best-known attraction is **Carmel Mission**. Dating from 1771, it is the burial place of Father Junípero Serra and one of California's largest missions. Masses are conducted daily, and self-guided or docent-led tours of the church and grounds are available.

Although some 3 or 4 million people visit each year – its popularity was boosted when actor Clint Eastwood became mayor for a couple of terms – Carmel has resisted the glare of neon signs, fast-food franchises, and even street numbers. The plazas and little shopping malls attract pedestrians to wine shops and antiques stores, art galleries, and over 500 boutiques, especially on Ocean Avenue between San Antonio and Junipero avenues.

writers and unemployed painters in flight from the devastation of the 1906 San Francisco earthquake; and canny property developers who, in order to reduce their taxes, covered the treeless acres with a thick, lush carpet of Monterey pines.

The result is one of the most charming seaside towns on the West Coast, one that has attracted artists and

In the residential parts of town, the streets meander through the forest, sometimes even splitting in two to accommodate an especially praiseworthy specimen of pine. Sandy Carmel beach, at the bottom of the hill and within easy distance of the town, is undeniably stunning. For tours, contact Carmel Walks (tel: 831-642-2700; www.carmelwalks.com).

South of Carmel is **Point Lobos State Reserve**, a rocky park overlooking the sea. Nature trails crisscross the reserve, and big natural rock pools are home to lolling sea lions. Be sure to take water and a picnic: there are no food facilities.

Highway 1 south of Point Lobos begins to swoop and curve in dramatic fashion. The Santa Lucia Mountains rise steeply to the left; the foamy sea to the right changes shape and color constantly. Only the two-lane road separates the two, which means the curling ribbon of road has its own distinct weather pattern. Although the sun may be shining brightly on the other side of the mountains, and can often be seen through the trees, Highway 1 can be distinctly chilly, and the fog comes on very quickly.

Big Sur

Arguably California's most beautiful stretch of coastline, **Big Sur** ❻ is a 90-mile (140km) stretch from Carmel to San Simeon, between the Santa Lucia range and the Pacific Ocean.

The stunning **Bixby Bridge**, north of Big Sur village, spans the steep walls of Rainbow Canyon and is one of the highest single-span concrete bridges in the world.

Until 1945, Big Sur was mainly populated by ranchers, loggers, and miners. But soon literary people began arriving, attracted by the idea of living cheaply, growing marijuana in remote canyons, and communing with what long-time resident Henry Miller called "the face of the earth as the creator intended it to look." The **Henry Miller Memorial Library** (tel: 831-667-2574), near **Nepenthe** restaurant (where everyone goes to enjoy a sunset over dinner), has works by and about this local hero.

Carmel Mission.

Pinnacles National Monument is a release site for endangered California condors, the largest land birds in North America. Their population of thousands began to decline during the Gold Rush; in the 1980s their population in the wild numbered just 27 but today, thanks to the success of a captive breeding program and their subsequent release into the wild, the population in the wild now numbers around 200, with half that number living in California.

Trail through Pinnacles National Monument.

Big Sur village is really little more than a huddle of shops and a post office. Places to stay in Big Sur are scarce, and, if you're planning a weekend visit, book early for any of them. In addition to a couple of campsites, a couple of motels and inns, there are a few very luxurious rustic resorts, notably the **Ventana Inn** (tel: 1-800-628-6500; www.ventanainn.com) and the **Post Ranch Inn** (tel: 831-667-2200; www.postranchinn.com), designed by local architect Mickey Muennig.

There are numerous local parks and wilderness areas to explore along this stretch of coast. Of special note is the stunning **Julia Pfeiffer Burns State Park**, with its twisting nature trails and silvery waterfall.

After winding past several state parks south of Big Sur village, Highway 1 passes the entrance to 1960s alternative haven the **Esalen Institute**, which has hot spring baths on a ledge over the ocean, before ending 16 miles (25km) north of **Hearst Castle ❼** (see page 176).

Beyond Hearst Castle, Highway 1 branches off to hug the coast, passing close to **Morro Bay**, dominated by a 576ft (176-meter) rock just offshore. To take the fast track back to San Francisco, turn at Morro Bay onto State Highway 41, which eventually joins US 101.

Heading north, US 101 passes through the town of **King City** to **Pinnacles National Monument ❽**, a 24,000-acre (9,700-hectare) destination ideal for hikers, climbers, campers, and bird-watchers. It is named for the unusual rock formations – massive monoliths and spires – formed by water and wind eroding volcanic rock.

If Big Sur has made you long for the coast, head for **Año Nuevo State Reserve ❾**, off Highway 1, 20 miles (32km) north of Santa Cruz near the San Mateo–Santa Cruz county line. Here, whiskered and roly-poly elephant seal pups are born in January, when entire seal families are visible from lookout points along the beachfront. It's a popular attraction, however, so book a place in October for this unique natural spectacle.

AÑO NUEVO RESERVE

On the wild and undeveloped shores of the Año Nuevo State Reserve, northern elephant seals come ashore every winter to give birth to pups and breed. Starting in mid-December, the 2.5-ton bulls fight for breeding access to females. Already pregnant females come on shore to have pups in late December and January, and then nurse for about a month before weaning, mating, and departing to sea. In March, pups learn to swim in the tide pools before heading out to sea.

For a chance to watch the action, reserve tickets for the 2.5-hour naturalist-led tours (tel: 1-800-444-4445; charge). To see them up close in a more subdued state, visit between April and August when they spend time on land molting. Weather can be extreme here, so come prepared for rain and muddy trails.

Paragliding over Monterey Bay.

HEARST CASTLE AT SAN SIMEON

Tycoon William Randolph Hearst, the newspaper magnate, was larger than life and so is his mansion. Indeed, it is so lavish that it is often referred to as Hearst Castle, but he just used to call it "the ranch".

The massive, Baroque Hearst Castle was built by media tycoon William Randolph Hearst, who was the model for Orson Welles' 1941 movie *Citizen Kane*.

It was Hearst's father George, a multimillionaire from his gold, silver, and copper mines, who first acquired the 275,000-acre (111,300-hectare) ranch. On his parents' death, the younger Hearst hired his favorite architect, Julia Morgan, to design the highly ornate twin-towered main house, which ended up with 38 bedrooms, a Gothic dining room, two swimming pools, and three sumptuous guest houses.

Next, he stocked the grounds with exotic animals and filled the buildings with carvings, furnishings, and works of art from European castles and cathedrals. To hide from view a water tank on the adjoining hill, Hearst planted 6,000 pine trees. All in all, craftsmen had labored for 28 years to create La Cuesta Encantada, "the Enchanted Hill," with its acres of gardens, terraces, pools, and walkways, and four grand buildings with a total of 46 rooms and almost as many fireplaces.

Hearst, who at his death in 1951 was at the helm of a media empire including the country's largest newspaper chain, 14 US magazines, and 11 radio stations, lived in his 130-room hilltop mansion at San Simeon for 20 years until ill health caused him to move to Beverly Hills in 1947. The property is now a State Historical Monument.

Hearst Castle is at 750 Hearst Castle Road, San Simeon (tel: 1-800-444-4445; www.hearstcastle.org). Walking tours run most days, reservations are required, and there is a charge for entry.

The indoor Roman swimming pool took over three years to build. Replete with decorative tiles in Venetian glass and hammered gold, the pool room is big enough to hold twin tennis courts on its roof.

William Randolph Hearst.

Neptune Pool, an enormous outdoor swimming pool, was the favorite among the castle's guests. Marble colonnades and white marble statues front an impressive Greco-Roman temple facade.

ost nights the publisher would preside over dinner at the
th-century monastery table in the dining room. Liquor was
ictly banned (so guests drank in their rooms). After dinner,
earst often showed an as-yet-unreleased movie. Gone With
e Wind, for example, was screened six months before its
emiere in December 1939.

ne of the lavish bedrooms.

HOLLYWOOD HIGHLIFE

Hearst Castle frequently welcomed moviedom's elite. A special train with a jazz band and open bar brought party guests 210 miles (340km) from Hollywood to San Luis Obispo; limousines then transported them through the estate's grounds filled with lions, bears, ostriches, elephants, and leopards. Guest were free to wander, except during the mandatory late-night dinner. There were also special occasions: among the hundred guests at a covered-wagon party were the Warner Brothers, the Gary Coopers, and William Powell.

Marion Davies.

"The society people always wanted to meet the movie stars so I mixed them together," wrote actress Marion Davies, Hearst's longtime mistress. "Jean Harlow came up quite frequently. She was very nice and I liked her. She didn't have an awful lot to say… all the men used to flock around her. She was very attractive in an evening dress because she never wore anything under it." Clark Gable was another regular guest. "Women were always running after him but he'd just give them a look as if to say 'how crazy these people are' and he stayed pretty much to himself."

One of the three guest houses.

ALONG THE NORTH COAST

California's huge stands of protected redwood trees
and a tight legislative reign on development mean
that urban civilization has been kept at bay on
this wild coastline.

Few places in America are as beautifully wild as California's North Coast. North of Sonoma Valley, stunning coastline links together state parks and sleepy seaside towns such as Bodega Bay and Mendocino, which offer scenic bluff views and plenty of opportunities for beachcombing, hiking, and wildlife spotting. In the upper reaches of the rugged north, it is easy to contemplate miles of majestic coastline, inland hills, and towering redwood groves without spotting a living soul.

The absence of development is partly due to the California Coastal Commission, formed in the 1970s when the state seemed fated to become a 400-mile (600km) ribbon of private marinas and ocean-view condominiums. Visitors hardly complain – the quiet north coast is all the more lovely for the relative solitude you can find here.

Bodega Bay to Fort Ross

North of Point Reyes National Seashore is Bodega Bay ❶, named for the Spanish explorer Juan Francisco de la Bodega y Quadra. Bodega Bay's bluffs offer sweeping views from Point Reyes to Fort Ross, and are a popular whale-watching spot from January through April. For more wildlife-spotting, the bird sanctuary at Doran Beach is arguably the

best bird-watching site in Sonoma County. Visit the Sonoma Coast Visitors Center (850 State Highway 1; tel: 707-875-3866; www.bodegabay.com) for more information.

North of Bodega Bay, most of the Sonoma County coast is a state beach, with no camping but comfortable access, plenty of parking, thrilling views, and appropriate beach names like **Mussel Point**, **Salmon Creek**, **Hog Back**, **Shell Beach,** and **Goat Rock**. As you travel north on Highway 1 from Bodega Bay, the prevailing

Main Attractions
Bodega Bay
Fort Ross
Mendocino
Whale watching
Avenue of the Giants
Redwood National Park

Bodega Bay.

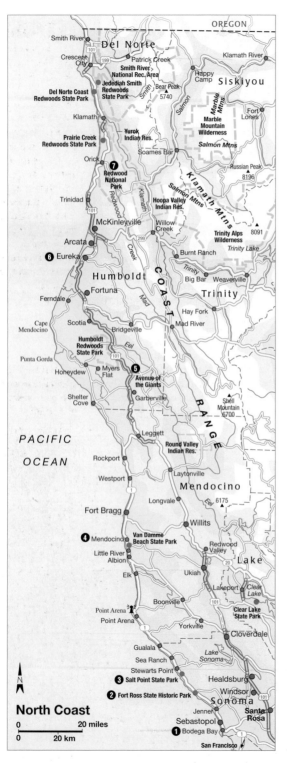

North Coast

0   20 miles

0   20 km

scenery is cypress trees, pines, old barns, and grazing sheep and cows, often shrouded in fog. As real estate, this grazing land is so valuable that local ranchers are termed "boutique farmers," because they don't really have to farm: they could sell the land for easily more money than they'd make in a lifetime of farming.

North of **Jenner**, Highway 1 weaves through daily fog, rolling pastures, and sudden canyons that drop 1,000ft (over 300 meters) into the blue and foamy Pacific. The road passes historic **Fort Ross** ❷ (www.fortross.org; Fri–Sun; charge), a careful reconstruction of the original fort built by Russian traders in the early 19th century. There are tours, but the best way to see the fort is to stroll through and around on your own. The small Russian Orthodox chapel is worth a special stop.

One compelling way to pass an afternoon in north Sonoma County is to visit the coastal tide pools. At **Salt Point State Park** ❸, a popular place for abalone divers, visitors can explore the rocky tide pools at low tides to see marine life up close. Additional park

activities include hiking, horseback riding, fishing, and diving.

Mendocino County

Travelers enter Mendocino County just north of Sea Ranch, at **Gualala**, **which is** notable for its fine old hotel in the center of town. Fifteen miles (24km) north, a coastal access path leads to **Point Arena**, a tiny bayside beach that comprises several dozen weathered mobile homes, two disintegrating and dangerous piers, and a few shops selling bait and fishing tackle. However, bed and breakfast inns are springing up all along the coast as city dwellers buy up Victorian homes, preserve them, fill them with antiques, and surrender with relief to a lifestyle change in the countryside.

The Coast Guard's **Point Arena Lighthouse** occupies the point of the US mainland closest to Hawaii. Many ships have crashed near Point Arena; lots of free literature is available to tell visitors which ships, and where, and what was lost as a result.

Set 156 miles (251km) north of San Francisco on a long bluff above a small bay, **Mendocino** ❹ is a cultured town with an arts center (with year-round events) and many galleries. A century-old former logging village, Mendocino was all but deserted in the early 20th century, but saw a cultural renaissance in the 1950s as artists and musicians moved in.

Today it's a lovely, low-key place, much of the pleasure coming from just strolling around. Gingerbread houses cling to windswept headlands, and there are white picket fences and ancient wooden water towers. Still, with more than 20 bed-and-breakfast inns, the small town becomes hectic on weekends. Two nearby state parks, **Van Damme** and **Russian Gulch**, offer camping, hiking, birdwatching, fishing, beachcombing, and other quiet pleasures. To the north, the city of **Fort Bragg** is a down-to-earth, working-class town established in 1857 as a US military post. A mill built in 1885 served the town's lumber industry until 2002; its closure then was a huge blow to the local economy. Some of the best of its unpretentiousness can be found in **Noyo Harbor**, a

Mendocino has attracted creative types since re-inventing itself in the 1950s.

sunny inlet lined by docks, characterful boats, and seafood restaurants.

Humboldt County

Much of the North Coast's mystique is due to the majestically tall redwood trees, which have survived attempts to transform them into everything from lumber and ashtrays to mulch for suburban rose gardens. Most of California's remaining old-growth redwoods are now protected in parks.

North of Garberville, a breathtaking 33-mile (53km) scenic drive called the **Avenue of the Giants ❺** follows the South Fork of the Eel River through 55,000-acre (22,000-hectare) **Humboldt Redwoods State Park**. The giants – redwood trees, otherwise known as *Sequoia sempervirens* – are breathtakingly tall and sometimes surprisingly wide. Their size can, and has been, marketed: "Drive through a living tree" is the come-on from the **Drive-Thru Tree** in the town of **Myers Flat**.

Those seeking to avoid this kind of commercialism can take the difficult road west from Garberville

over the **King Mountains** to **Shelter Cove**. North of this isolated outpost is **Petrolia**, site of California's first oil well.

An honest glimpse into the spirit of the early settler life along the North Coast is aptly afforded by **Scotia**, a crisp little company town built entirely of redwood – the wooden visitor center is in the style of a classic Greek temple – and dominated by the **Pacific Lumber Company mill**, the world's largest redwood mill. The company owns the town and keeps it tidy.

Eureka

From the moment you arrive, it is obvious that **Eureka ❻** is a good place to buy such commodities as sewer pipe, lumber, a slab of redwood burl, a life-sized statue of a lumberjack carved from a redwood log, or a fresh fish dinner. Often shrouded in fog, it is the largest Pacific Coast enclave in North America north of San Francisco. A sprawling, busy, industrial place, still with a large fishing industry, Eureka is also the location of the

Victorian architecture in Eureka's Old Town.

North Coast's only institution of higher learning, called, appropriately enough, **Humboldt State University**.

Eureka's ubiquitous and impressive Victorian architecture in the **Old Town** is highlighted by the **Carson House** at the end of 2nd Street. Visitors can't go inside this much-photographed house because it is now a private men's club, which makes it seem all the more Victorian. Anyone interested in this type of architecture will want to head to the little town of **Ferndale**, 10 miles (16km) southwest of Eureka, which has a very good sampling of well-maintained Victorian buildings.

Redwood National Park

Orick is the gateway to **Redwood National Park ❼**, established in 1968 to consolidate 40 miles (60km) of majestic forested coastline under federal jurisdiction.

The 106,000-acre (42,900-hectare) national park encompasses three state parks: Prairie Creek Redwoods, **Del Norte Coast Redwoods State Park**,

and **Jedediah Smith Redwoods State Park**.

There are five visitor centers throughout the park (most open daily 9am–5pm), and many campsites (tel: 1-800-444-7275; www.nps. gov for reservations). The Kuchel Visitor Center (tel: 707-465-7765) is located 1 mile (1.6km) south of Orick on US 101 and gives out trail maps, directions, and shuttle-bus information for excursions up

The coast around Mendocino.

Gray whale breaching.

WHALE WATCHING

One of the highlights of a trip to California is the chance to see whales. Every year, 20,000 California gray whales migrate south from Alaska to breeding grounds in Baja California, and then after a short stay head north again, with the moms bringing their new calves. From the end of December through April, the Mendocino coast is a prime spot to sight them on their journey.

To see whales without leaving the shore, try the Mendocino Headlands, Point Cabrillo, the MacKerritcher State Park (tel: 707-964-8898), or Chapman Point just south of Mendocino. All these have good vantage points.

You can also book a charter boat that will get you quite close (although by law the boats have to keep a certain distance). For more information on booking a ride on a boat, visit www.mendocino.com.

Amongst the redwoods.

Marijuana is legal for medicinal use in California.

Redwood Creek, to the southeast. There, three of the tallest trees ever identified are clustered in the **Tall Trees Grove**. The tallest, at 368ft (112 meters) in height, was the world's tallest known tree when it was discovered in 1963.

Other notable sites include the Lady Bird Johnson Grove, an old-growth forest named for the former First Lady. It is difficult to recommend much of the scenery north of the **Klamath River** bridge, however, because you probably won't see much of it; fog can come in thick and fast and without warning. Be sure to take a sweater, just in case.

Crescent City

Crescent City – a grim, gray gathering of plain houses and vacant lots around a semi-circular harbor – has never fully recovered from a 1962 typhoon which devastated the town, and the traveler's best bet is to head inland to higher and hotter ground. Fifteen minutes east of Crescent City, on US 199 heading toward Grants Pass, Oregon, the last undammed river in California flows gin-clear through the 90°F (32°C) summer twilight.

Although the **Smith River** is wild, its accommodations are civilized. There's a lodge on **Patrick Creek** with a restaurant and bar. There are clean campgrounds, public and private, under the peeling red madronas. The attractions here are simple: boulder-lined banks, clear pools, good fishing – and no redwood souvenirs.

HASH CROP

In Humboldt County, notices tacked to buildings and utility poles offer "Sinsemilla Tips." Says another bulletin: "Don't get caught with your plants down." The plant in question is marijuana, which until 1981 was listed in Mendocino County's agricultural report as the largest local cash crop. Since then, officials have chosen not to include the estimated marijuana gross value.

California was the first state in America to establish a medical marijuana program, enacted in 1996. In 2009, a bill to legalize cultivation, possession, and use of marijuana lost by 46 percent to 54 percent, but in 2010, a new law effectively reduced the charge of possession; for anyone who is caught with up to one ounce, the fine is $100, with no mandatory court appearance or criminal record.

Although there are no drive-through trees in Redwood National Park, there are three located along the Pacific Highway: the Klamath Tour Thru Tree, the Shrine Drive-Thru Tree, and the Chandelier Tree.

On the road to Mendocino.

CENTRAL VALLEY

Gold-seekers flocked here in the late 1800s, followed by thousands of Dust Bowl families during the Great Depression. Today, this important agricultural region is home to the state's capital, and many recreation areas and historic Gold Rush-era communities.

A large, flat basin in the heart of California, the 450-mile (720km) -long Central Valley encompasses California's capital city of Sacramento, a vast agricultural region, and the historic Gold Country.

The region first really became known to the world in 1848, when James Marshall discovered gold in the Sierra foothills, sparking a mass migration to the Mother Lode, California's richest mineral vein. Tucked just below the fork of the Sacramento and American rivers, Sacramento flourished as an arrival point for miners heading to the Sierra Nevada foothills to pan for gold. The Gold Rush is still a major part of the region's identity, especially in Sacramento's Old Town and towns along the Mother Lode that have been expensively restored to their former pioneer glory.

Today, the Central Valley's main source of wealth is agriculture. The San Joaquin valley is the lifeline of California's farming industry, producing more than half of the state's annual $25 billion in farm goods. Fresno County alone accounts for a significant portion of that, making it the number-one farming county in America.

Sacramento

Located about two hours northeast of San Francisco and nestled in the middle of the Central Valley, the area surrounding **Sacramento ❶** is home to spacious tree-lined roads, expansive shopping malls, countless industrial parks, suburban tracts, and a tangle of multi-lane highways that joins it all together. The city itself boasts the state capitol and fascinating historic museums, and continues to develop rapidly as more residents from San Francisco and Los Angeles come to Sacramento in search of affordable housing.

In contrast to its glamorous coastal neighbor, San Francisco, Sacramento is a blazing furnace in midsummer,

Main Attractions
Old Sacramento
California State Capitol
Sutter's Fort
Mark Twain's Cabin
Mercer Caverns
Auburn State Recreation Area
Gold panning

Governor's Mansion, downtown Sacramento.

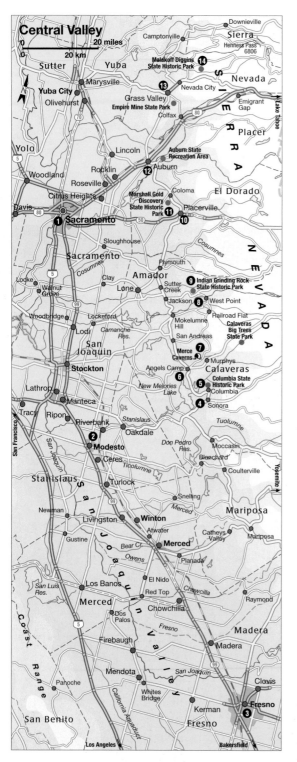

Central Valley

with temperatures often passing 100°F (38°C) for days at a time. But the weather can still be pleasant, as humidity is low, it seldom rains for long, and the prevailing wind is a marine breeze from San Francisco Bay that cools the nights. In the winter, the city, which lays low in the 150-mile (240km) -long Sacramento Valley, is a resting bed for thick tule fog (a type of ground fog peculiar to the Central Valley), which, like the summer sun, can last for many weeks.

Old Sacramento

Beneath the imposing facade of Sacramento's mirrored-glass office buildings and slightly away from all the traffic lies the nostalgic neighborhood of **Old Sacramento** Ⓐ, a 28-acre (11-hectare) historic district along the Sacramento waterfront. Established in 1849, it was here that steamers from San Francisco once let off passengers headed for the gold fields. Today, wooden buildings, horse-drawn carriages, and cobblestone streets convey a distinct image of the Old West. The *Delta King* is a 1920s paddle steamboat that once regularly shuttled passengers between Sacramento and San Francisco on the Sacramento River. Today, it's permanently moored in Sacramento and operated as a hotel and restaurant.

Once the western terminus of the Pony Express overland mail service, Sacramento was also the western terminus of the Transcontinental Railroad. The station is now part of the **California State Railroad Museum** (125 I Street; tel: 916-445-6645; www.csrmf.com; daily 10am–5pm; charge), which delights kids and adults alike with its 50-plus restored engines.

The **Sacramento History Museum** is housed in a reproduction of the 1854 City Hall and Water Works building. Exhibits focused on the Sacramento region reflect on everyday life in the Native American period, celebrate the

Pony Express, and commemorate the role Chinese immigrants played in the Gold Rush.

Another important collection is at the **Crocker Art Museum** ❸ (216 O Street; tel: 916-808-7000; www.crocker artmuseum.org; Tue–Sun 10am–5pm, until 9pm Thur; charge). The oldest art museum west of the Mississippi River, it boasts one of the state's premier collections of Californian art, including works from the Gold Rush era to the present. Stop off at the **Visitor's Center** (1608 I Street; tel: 1-800-292-2334) for a complete list of historic sites in Old Sacramento.

Downtown

Downtown Sacramento is dominated by the nicely restored **California State Capitol** ❸ (between 10th and 16th and L and N streets). Daily tours of the capitol building are offered on the hour (tel: 916-324-0333; daily 9am–4pm; free).

The capitol is surrounded by the 40-acre (16-hectare) **Capitol Park**, a manicured arboretum that has a vast collection of California flora

and examples of plants from different climates and continents. Not far from Capitol Park, **the California Museum** ❻ (1020 O Street; tel: 916-653-7524; www.californiamuseum. org; Mon–Sat 10am–5pm, Sun noon–5pm; charge) is a fascinating mix of treasures from the California State Archives and cutting-edge multimedia exhibits, all designed to educate adults and children about California's history and influence on the world.

A 400-seat IMAX **theater**, next to the **Convention Center**, is another popular attraction. Also, while downtown, don't miss the handsome **Governor's Mansion** (corner of 6th and H streets; tel: 916-323-3047; Wed–Sun 10am–5pm; charge), an 1877 Victorian building, complete with Italian marble fireplaces and gold-framed French mirrors, where 13 California governors lived between 1903 and 1967.

Sacramento's Old Town, which migrants from San Francisco passed through en route to the gold fields in the 19th century.

Actors in period dress in Old Sacramento.

Sutter's Fort

Now almost overtaken by suburbs, **Sutter's Fort ⓔ** (2701 L Street; tel: 916-445-4422; charge) was once one of the most important in the West. It was an employee of John Sutter's who discovered gold in 1848, but 11 years earlier Sutter had already established the fort as a rest stop and refueling station for immigrants crossing the frontier from the east. The present site, which includes a prison and a bakery, has been reconstructed to give one of the most authentic pictures of pioneer life in the state.

Sacramento River Delta

When the temperature gets too hot to handle, take the cue of thousands of recreational houseboaters, waterskiers, anglers, and sailors, and head south on State Highway 5 or 99 toward the **Sacramento River Delta**, where hundreds of miles of interconnected river channels percolate slowly toward San Francisco Bay and the Pacific Ocean.

This river country contains hundreds of islands; much of the area is accessible only by water. Still, even landlocked car passengers can choose from a variety of charming olde-worlde towns such as **Walnut Grove** and Locke.

Locke, created by Chinese laborers brought in to build the railroads, has a porticoed street with wooden sidewalks that is right out of the Old West. The deepwater port of **Stockton**, the "Gateway to the Delta," has 1860s homes, the **Haggin Museum** (www.hagginmuseum.org), which is full of local history, and several wineries.

San Joaquin Valley

Though its name is often mistakenly applied to California's entire Central Valley, the San Joaquin comprises just the southern two-thirds of this region. It follows the course of the **San Joaquin River**, flowing south to north, to the Sacramento–San Joaquin Delta, where both rivers empty into San Francisco Bay.

It doesn't take long to see that the valley is the lifeline of California. Interstate 5, running the length of it, is the main link between Los Angeles and the Bay Area, and the east–west

Tour guide at the reconstructed Sutter's Fort State Historic Park.

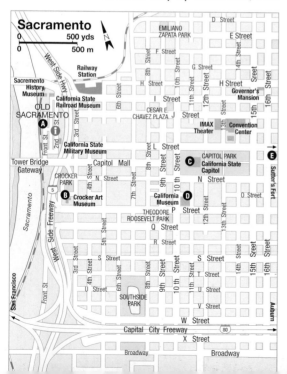

Sacramento

routes to Lake Tahoe and the Sierras all cross the valley. The freeways are full of trucks hauling bottled tomato catsup, ripe golden melons, or crates of canned peaches.

Recently, with substantial growth in population, the area's cities have experienced a boom as commercial and manufacturing centers, but employment in the valley is most closely tied to farming and rainfall. The San Joaquin Valley's soil, covering more than a million irrigated acres (405,000 hectares), supports some of the most productive farming in the world.

It is the abundance of that most precious of the state's resources – water – that makes the San Joaquin Valley a recreational as well as an agricultural heartland. Aside from the Sacramento River Delta and the mammoth irrigation projects it supports, several great rivers flow through the area – the San Joaquin, the **Stanislaus**, the **Tuolumne**, the **Merced**, the **Kings,** and, farther south, the **Kern**. Most are renowned for outstanding – and occasionally terrifying – stretches of whitewater rafting. This sport is for serious

enthusiasts only, but there are gentler stretches of water where the faint-hearted will also feel at home.

Lodi to Merced

In the northern part of the Central Valley and just 37 miles (60km) south of Sacramento, Lodi is recognized as a major center of wine production, especially Zinfandel. Robert Mondavi grew up here, and his well-known Woodbridge winery is located nearby in Woodbridge.

Another 45 minutes south is **Modesto ❷**. Like much of California, Modesto is a creation of Leland Stanford's Central Pacific Railroad. The Tuolumne River runs almost unnoticed through the southern fringes of town, but an early-20th-century steel arch along the main thoroughfare promotes the town's virtues: "Water, Wealth, Contentment, Health." As in most of the valley, food production is king – here you can find an almond

Statue of a Pony Express rider in Sacramento, once the western terminus of the Pony Express overland mail service.

Sutter's Fort, Sacramento.

The highlight of the summer in Sacramento is the family-friendly California State Fair, a colorful occasion (running for around 18 days before Labor Day) with all kinds of concerts, exhibits, and other events, which attracts thousands of people from all over the county.

San Joaquin Valley has some of the world's most productive farmland.

exchange, a mushroom farm, a cheese processor, a Hershey chocolate plant, and more local wineries.

Halfway between Modesto and Fresno, **Merced** is a major access point to Yosemite. The biggest attraction Merced County can call its own may be **Castle Air Force Base**, where lumbering B-52s provide a somewhat chilling background to the **Castle Air Museum's** collection of vintage fighters.

Fresno

The sleeping giant of central California, **Fresno** ❸ is the only community in the United States within little more than an hour's drive of three national parks. From a simple train station by the edge of a wheat field, Fresno has become a city with 11 freeway exits and rows of high-rises. The financial and cultural as well as service and commercial center of the San Joaquin Valley, it is also as ethnically diverse, with large Mexican, Asian, Armenian, and Basque communities. Cultural institutions include

the **Community Theater** and the **Fresno Philharmonic Orchestra**.

For people with children, **Roeding Park**, right off State Highway 99 in west Fresno, features a number of family amusements – a zoo, a Playland with rides, and Storyland, a quaint walk-through village where plaster fairytale figures tell their stories. **Woodward Park** in central Fresno has a Japanese Garden and a bird sanctuary.

Perhaps the most bizarre attraction is **Forestiere Underground Gardens** (tel: 559-271-0734; reservations required; charge). The gardens were once the beloved domicile of sculptor-horticulturist Baldasare Forestiere, a Sicilian immigrant, who single-handedly carved out the maze of 100 rooms, passageways, and courtyards over a period of 40 years.

Gold Country

The Gold Rush may have ended, but it wasn't because they ran out of gold. They just ran out of the gold lying near the top of the ground. As the holes got deeper and more dangerous, the work got harder, slower, and

CALIFORNIA'S MIDWEST

Stuck between the magnificent California coast and the awe-inspiring Sierras, the San Joaquin Valley suffers the kind of image problem more associated with the Midwest than the Golden State. That's because, in many ways, it is the Midwest. Perhaps as many as 500,000 so-called "Okies" – the Dust Bowl victims of the Great Depression that gave life to John Steinbeck's The Grapes of Wrath – migrated here from Oklahoma and other places in the Midwest. Like ants on a honey trail, they piled into overloaded flivvers and streamed west on old US Route 66, through the chalk-dry Mojave Desert, past "bum barricades" and the abuse heaped on them by native Californians.

What became of them? One-eighth of the current California population – or nearly 3.75 million residents – claim Okie ancestry, and the core of that gritty, family-based community is still here in the heart of the San Joaquin. Stop by any town in San Joaquin Valley and, as one Dust Bowl survivor said himself, "You might as well be in Tulsa or Little Rock or Amarillo… Same music, same values, same churches, same politics." The music influence is felt in Sacramento too: The Dixieland Jazz Jubilee, held each May in Old Sacramento, is the world's largest celebration of Dixieland jazz, featuring more than 120 bands from around the world.

more expensive, until finally it was no longer cost-efficient to dig.

Geologists say there is at least as much gold in the Mother Lode today as was taken out in the past 100-odd years. Latter-day gold miners say the 7 million lbs (3.2 million kg) extracted by the old-timers was only 10 percent of the wealth that nature had deposited there. Either way, there is a good deal left – and quite a few people are looking for it. Modern mining operations dig deeper and deeper into the Sierra with automated machinery, but there are still the rough-hewn old-timers who crouch by mountain streams, squinting for the glimmer of gold flakes in shallow tin pans.

There's another rush going on in the Gold Country foothills from Mariposa to Nevada City, but it's real estate, not valuable minerals, that is at stake. Travelers on State Highway 49, the Gold Country's main highway, are likely to see more real-estate signs than ghost towns. The modern miner now competes with housing developers – not claim jumpers – for land. Still, for the most part, it is tourism, not treasure, that plays a key role in the area's resources.

Sonora

Sonora ❹, named for the Mexican state from which many of its first '49ers came, is a city and one that may be losing a struggle with the real-estate hustlers. But the houses and shopping centers have sprung up because Sonora is as beautiful as it was during the Gold Rush – and its quaint Downtown has remained true to the miners' spirit.

In the 1870s, there was a pocket mine at the north end of Sonora where the operators found a vein of nearly pure gold and recovered, they say, $160,000 worth of gold in one day. It was part of *La Veta Madre*, otherwise known as "**The Mother Lode**," from which the legends sprang. It is the kind of story that still keeps miners at work today, toiling in the dark tunnels.

Columbia

A real gem of Tuolumne County these days is the town of **Columbia**.

FACT

In spring, the roadsides from the Central Valley towns of Sacramento, Stockton, and Fresno are crowded with wild mustard, an edible plant that adds piquancy to a salad and covers the beef-cattle grazing land with yellow blossoms. A succession of wildflowers moves up the hills and turns entire mountainsides blue and purple with lupine and brodiaea, along with other plants such as larkspur, purple vetch, and baby blue eyes.

Farmland in the San Joaquin Valley is used to grow grapes, citrus fruits, vegetables, and nuts.

Mercer Caverns.

*Vintage airplane at
Castle Air Museum.*

Just a few minutes north of Sonora and just off State Highway 49, this old town has been restored as the **Columbia State Historic Park ❺** (tel: 209-588-9128; www.parks.ca.gov). Columbia once had a population of 15,000, 50 saloons, competing daily newspapers, and at least one church. Nearly $90 million in gold was mined there over a 20-year period. Much of restored Columbia is closed to cars, but the easy layout of the town makes it well worthwhile parking and walking around. The best sites are the Wells Fargo Express Office; the old schoolhouse, used until 1937; and the old city hotel.

Around Columbia, as in many of the Gold Country towns, there are several rock or gold shops whose proprietors may be willing to show visitors where to look for gold and perhaps even teach them how to mine. There are even tour companies that will set up trips to local mines.

Calaveras County

Back on State Highway 49, still headed north, a sign indicates the way to the summit of **Jackass Hill**. It is named for the animals so central to gold prospecting, and it is the place where Mark Twain lived in 1864. Twain's **cabin** has been reconstructed around the original hearth. During the time Twain lived in the cabin, he wrote one of his most famous yarns, *The Celebrated Jumping Frog of Calaveras County*. The actual jumping frogs were supposed to have been a bit to the north in **Angels Camp ❻**, where they can still be found.

From the Angels Camp area, a detour leads up into the mountains to the town of **Murphys**, a Gold Rush period settlement far enough

off the track to be a natural museum. The impressive **Mercer Caverns** ❼ (www.mercercaverns.com), which are well worth a visit, are in this area. You descend 208 steps to see giant stalactites, stalagmites, and other cave formations formed by the dripping of limestone over centuries. Discovered in 1885, the cave is especially known for its rare frost-like aragonite flosferri, which won a Grand prize at the 1900 Paris World Exposition. Farther up State Highway 4 is **Calaveras Big Trees State Park**, with magnificent sequoia trees.

San Andreas is another town whose present is a triumph of development interests, but whose past is alive with romantic echoes. Black Bart, a real stagecoach bandit, was tried here in 1883 for some of the 28 robberies he allegedly committed. Bart, a San Franciscan with expensive tastes and little income, embarked on a series of polite, bloodless robberies of the gold-laden stages. His shotgun was always unloaded and no one was ever hurt, but he served six years in San Quentin's rough prison. Then he disappeared.

In good weather, the drive from San Andreas to **West Point** ❽ on the Mountain Ranch and Railroad Flat roads is beautiful. A few of the 500 local mine shafts are now used as a site for ore-crushing, and even welcome visitors. If you stand in the mouth of a mine shaft, even in midsummer, you can see your breath condensing in the cold air seeping up from thousands of feet beneath the ground. Modern techniques of deep-rock mining differ little from those used by the '49ers. The gold pan and sluice boxes used by weekend miners are essentially the same tools that were used 100 years ago.

From West Point, it is possible to loop back west to **Mokelumne Hill**, a town once so rich in gold that its claims were limited to 16 sq ft (1.5 sq meters) in size. According to legend,

Storyland in Roeding Park, near Fresno, is an old-fashioned village with fairytale characters.

Playland in Roeding Park.

Columbia State Historic Park.

Statue of a gold miner in Auburn, where gold was discovered.

the lust for wealth ran so high that there was a murder a week here for more than four months. On a more benign note, Mokelumne Hill is the site of the founding of the **E. Clampus Vitus Society**, a group devoted to good deeds and good times. The society is still around and active, and generally has an entry in any local parade or fair.

From **Sutter Creek** to Grass Valley, about 75 miles (120km), the countryside surrounding State Highway 49 is mostly a commuter suburb of Sacramento. For a more authentic look at the Old West, drive east to **Chaw'se Indian Grinding Rock State Historic Park** near the town of Jackson, one of the largest Native American sites in the United States. The park and its museum are a celebration of the contributions made by the Miwok tribe.

Placerville, Coloma, and Grass Valley

At the junction of State Highways 49 and 50 is **Placerville** once called Hangtown because of its chosen method of execution. Placerville was the nexus of wagon, mail, Pony Express, and telegraph routes, and consequently a busy and exciting place. Now it may be the only town in America with its own gold mine. The **Gold Bug Mine** (www.goldbug park.org), north of town, is located in a public park where there are several other mines, and is open to visitors for inspection.

North of Placerville on State Highway 49 is **Coloma**, the birthplace of the Gold Rush. The **Marshall Gold Discovery State Historic Park** is now at the spot where, in 1848, James Marshall was building a waterway for John Sutter's lumber mill and

was distracted by something glittering in the water. The state has reconstructed the mill, though not exactly at the same place, since the **American River** has changed its course in the past century. Daily interpretive programs are held at the replica sawmill, and visitors can try their own hand at panning for gold.

At the junction of State Highway 49 and busy Interstate 80 is **Auburn** ⓬, home to the Auburn State Recreation Area. Located south of Interstate 80 on two forks of the American River, it stretches from Auburn to Colfax. Here you can hike, fish, camp, pan for gold, and ride whitewater rapids – some 30 private outfitters are licensed to offer whitewater trips in the area. When you tire of river recreation, visit the **Placer County Museum** (daily 10am–4pm; free) in Auburn; with its collections of Native American artifacts as well as gold-mining paraphernalia, it is counted as one of the best cultural attractions in the mountains. Nearby is the quirky Old Town Auburn **Firehouse**.

Auburn is a good place to jump off for a visit to Lake Tahoe (up Interstate 80) with a return via State Highway 20 near **Emigrant Gap**. Highway 20, the old Tahoe–Pacific Highway, is one of California's great drives. It rejoins State Highway 49 in the Nevada City–Grass Valley area.

Grass Valley ⓭ was once the center of the deep mines, and there are several splendid places to get a sense of what they were like. Some of them, including the **North Star**, have shafts that go hundreds of feet below sea level, though these shafts are now closed and flooded. The **Grass Valley Museum** (tel: 530-273-5509) in the town of Grass Valley is good for local history. **Empire Mine State Park**, east of town, is the site of the oldest and richest mine in California, which once produced no less than $100 million worth of gold before it was closed down in the mid-20th century.

Grass Valley is now very much in the 21st century and a center of high-technology industry, most notably the manufacture of equipment for television broadcasting.

TIP

For those who don't want to spend all their time meditating on history, Coloma is a pleasant place for a raft trip. A number of companies offer one-day and longer trips rafting down the American River, or check www.coloma.com.

Panning for gold at Columbia State Historic Park.

Nevada City's old factories and miners' stores were converted into restaurants and antiques stores, amongst much else, and have since been restored.

Pleasantly old-fashioned Nevada City.

Nevada City

Nevada City is as old-fashioned as Grass Valley is up-to-date. It is the kind of place that attracted city people early. They busily converted the old factories and miners' stores into restaurants, museums, antiques stores, and theaters, many of which have now been restored. There are a couple of pleasant bars, and the **National Hotel** (tel: 530-265-4551) puts up overnight visitors in rooms furnished with antiques.

Ten miles (16km) north of Nevada City is a large state historic park at the old **Malakoff Diggins** ⑭, a place that generated one of the very earliest pieces of environmental legislation. Visitors to the Malakoff mine can see the effects of hydraulic mining, a method of gold extraction in which high-powered streams of water were directed from cannons at the side of the mountain. This method was highly effective, but it devastated the mountain, and waterways were clogged with mud as far away as San Francisco Bay. The technique was banned as early as 1884 but the scars, which have been only slightly healed by time, are still grimly awesome.

It's an hour's drive from Nevada City to **Downieville**, which marks the end of this tour of the Gold Country. The country here is higher, cooler, and much less crowded than further south. From **Camptonville**, midway along the route from Nevada City, the pretty **Henness Pass Road** veers off into the mountains. In good weather, it is a lovely side trip and there are a number of campgrounds a few miles toward the pass. Downieville itself is picture-perfect. It is a remote place hemmed in by steep hillsides, with a population of under a thousand people. Despite its size and seclusion, however, there are a few places for visitors to have a meal or relax for the night, taking in the sweet mountain air.

*Paddle steamer on
Sacramento's river.*

Whitewater rafting on the Truckee River.

LAKE TAHOE AND THE SIERRA NEVADA

There's a reason why both Californians and out-of-state visitors gush about Tahoe ski slopes and jaw-dropping views in Yosemite – they're just about as good as it gets.

Lake Tahoe straddles both California and Nevada, and is a major tourist attraction for both states. Surrounded by the Sierra Nevada mountain range, the lake is a haven for nature lovers and sports enthusiasts in winter and summer.

LAKE TAHOE

"The lake burst upon us," wrote Mark Twain in *Roughing It*, "a noble sheet of blue water lifted 6,300 feet above the level of the sea, and walled in by a rim of snowclad mountain peaks… I thought it must surely be the fairest picture the whole earth affords."

Many would agree with this picture of **Lake Tahoe ❶**, located high in the Sierra Nevada about 50 miles (80km) southwest of Reno, Nevada. The crystal-blue lake, its 71-mile (114km) shoreline, and the surrounding region attract outdoor enthusiasts year-round, who come for skiing, snowboarding, hiking, biking, watersports, and lakeshore fun. The outdoor attractions do have competition for visitors' attention, however: roulette wheels and craps tables sing their sirens' call out from South Lake Tahoe casinos.

Getting there

Getting to Lake Tahoe is easy and relatively inexpensive from San Francisco. The drive takes four to five hours in good weather and light traffic. On

Friday nights the weekend exodus from the San Francisco Bay area begins streaming up Interstate 80 or US 50 toward the lake, and traffic can be slow. In the winter, carry chains in case of ice and snow. Package tours are easy to find in the large cities, and can include transportation, ski lift tickets, accommodation, and food vouchers. See page 367 for details.

Tahoe in winter

Outdoor recreation is the lake area's lifeblood. In winter, that means

See page 367 for details.

Main Attractions

Lake Tahoe
Yosemite National Park
Sequoia and Kings Canyon
    national parks
Bodie State Historic Park
Devils Postpile National
    Monument

Lake Tahoe.

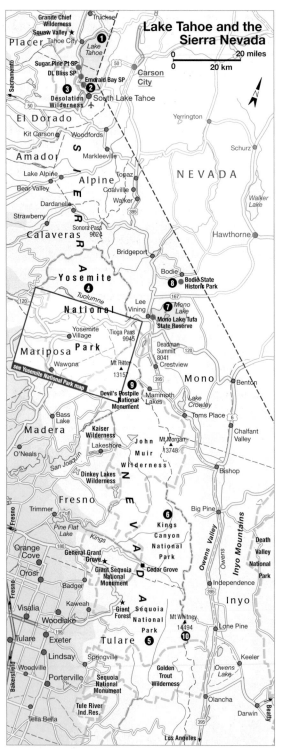

downhill and cross-country skiing, and lots of snowboarding. If you don't care for skiing, the outdoors can still be the central focus. To get off the beaten track, **Lake Tahoe Adventures** (tel: 503-577-2940) leads snowmobile tours through meadows, lakes, and mountain forest. Wilderness dinners, weddings, and overnights in igloos can be arranged. To take the wintry chill off, try a hot soak at **Walley's Hot Springs Resort**, located 12 miles (19km) east of South Lake Tahoe on Foothill Road in Genoa.

Tahoe in summer

When the snow has gone, rent in-line skates or a bicycle to explore the local roads, or a mountain bike to blaze down the bare ski runs at Squaw Valley. Several parks and reserves have well-marked hiking trails. The lake offers great fishing, as well as jet-skiing, waterskiing, and kayaking. There is usually good river rafting on the **Truckee River**. Check the local tourist office for information on operators and rental shops.

A great way to see Lake Tahoe is to take a ride on one of the large vessels that cruise around the lake all year round, which offer lunch, dinner, and dancing cruises, as well as sightseeing trips along the shoreline and through spectacular **Emerald Bay ❷** an isolated, tree-lined wilderness tucked into the southwest corner of the lake.

Hikers and backpackers usually head for **Desolation Wilderness ❸**, a lake-studded area located west of Tahoe's Emerald Bay. A wilderness permit must be obtained for backpacking in Desolation Wilderness – it's a popular place that often fills to capacity in summer. The 165-mile (265km) **Tahoe Rim Trail** offers magnificent views and can be accessed from several points around the lake. The **Granite Peak** area is also good for backpacking, and the extremely pretty **Emerald Bay State Park**, as well as **DL Bliss** and **Sugar Pine Point** state parks, are excellent for short walks and picnics.

On any summer weekend, joggers and bicyclists take to the roads ringing the lake. The 75-mile (120km) circle makes a strenuous one-day bike ride or a leisurely two-day trip.

South Lake Tahoe

The busiest part of the lake and just a stone's throw from Nevada, the town of South Lake Tahoe has both ski resorts and casinos. The latter can come in handy for skiers in the evening – most offer inexpensive all-you-can-eat buffet dinners to lure customers. Gambling is, of course, the area's biggest and most lucrative business.

YOSEMITE

Absolutely magnificent, **Yosemite National Park ❹** is one of America's most visited national parks, drawing some 4 million visitors each year to see its striking granite rock formations, pouring waterfalls, and lovely groves and meadows.

To its original inhabitants, the indigenous Ahwahneechee, Yosemite ("*yoseh-mih-tee*") Valley was a holy place. Because of its isolation, the tribe managed to keep its mountain paradise a secret from outsiders until 1851, a full year after California attained statehood, when the US Cavalry arrived and herded the tribe members across the Sierras to a barren reservation near Mono Lake. As with much of the American West, subjugation of the Indians paved the way for settlement. During the decade following its "discovery," Yosemite Valley was fenced, farmed, and logged by homesteaders. Today, 94 percent of the park's 747,956 acres (302,687 hectares) is designated wilderness.

Yosemite Valley

Although the valley comprises only 8 sq miles (21 sq km) of the park's 1,169-sq-mile (3,027-sq-km) area, it plays host to more than 90 percent of all Yosemite's overnight visitors.

But there's a reason why the crowds come in such numbers. From the Yosemite Valley, many well-known sites can be seen, including Half Dome and Rainbow Falls. If you visit during a busy period, book your lodgings six months to one year in advance and be prepared for the Yosemite Valley to be very full.

Nowhere else in the world are there so many big waterfalls in such a small area, including 2,425ft (739-meter) **Yosemite Falls ❹**, the highest in North America. When Ice Age glaciers scoured out an 8-mile (13km)-long, 1-mile (1.5km)-wide Yosemite Valley, they left behind several smaller hanging valleys on either side high but not dry conduits for free-leaping torrents whose very names suggest their infinite variety: **Ribbon**, **Bridalveil**, **Silver Strand**, **Staircase**, **Sentinel**, **Lehamite**, **Vernal**, **Nevada**, **Illilouette**. Visitors should note, however, that falls are often dry out of season, from late July through fall.

As the prehistoric ice melted and retreated, it exposed the colossal building blocks of the Sierra Nevada, shaped and polished into scenery on a grand scale – **El Capitan ❹**, **Cathedral Rock**, **Three Brothers**, **Royal Arches**, **Clouds Rest**.

TIP

Another way to see the area is from above. HeliTahoe tours (tel: 530-544-2211) take off from the Lake Tahoe airport in South Lake Tahoe. The Heavenly Gondola goes 2.5 miles (4km) up the mountain for views and trails departing from an observation deck. The Squaw Valley Cable Car also offers great panoramas year-round.

Snowboarding at one of Lake Tahoe's seven ski resorts.

Hiking the Mist Trail, which takes in two waterfalls and the combined view of Nevada Falls, Liberty Cap, and the back of Half Dome.

Hiking in the Lake Tahoe area.

In the daredevil world of technical rock climbing, El Capitan is a major challenge.

Roads in the east end of the valley near **Mirror Lake** have been restricted to shuttle buses, bicycles, and pedestrians. You can arrange to take a guided horseback trip at the valley stables near **Yosemite Village** ⦿ (the first large developed area on the Yosemite loop road). Bicycles may be rented at the village and at **Yosemite Lodge** (tel: 801-559-4884),

and several bikeway trails make two-wheeled travel the most efficient choice of locomotion. Lodgings runs the gamut from inexpensive cabins at the village to the palatial suite atop the **Ahwahnee Hotel**, with Yosemite Lodge somewhere in the middle.

Glacier Point

To the south, State Highway 41 climbs 9 miles (15km) to **Chinquapin** junction, where a 15-mile (25km) paved road departs for **Glacier Point** ⦿. From this famed viewpoint, 3,200ft (980 meters) above the floor of Yosemite Valley, the entire park comes into unforgettable, stomach-clutching focus. No less compelling is the 80-mile (130km) vista to the east and south, a panorama of lakes, canyons, waterfalls, and the rugged peaks of Yosemite's High Sierra. Close at hand are the granite steps of the **Giant's Staircase** ⦿, where the Vernal and Nevada falls drop the raging waters of the **Merced River** 320 and 594ft (98 and 181 meters), respectively.

From Glacier Point, **Half Dome** ⦿ is the most prominent landmark, a great solitary stone thumb thrusting skyward. What became of Half Dome's other half? In fact, the dome never had another half of solid rock, only slabs of granite on the sheer north face that were peeled away like onion skin by advancing Ice Age glaciers.

At the height of glaciation, 250,000 years ago, Glacier Point itself lay under 700ft (200 meters) of ice, and interpretive markers explain how the 2,000ft (600-meter) -thick Merced and Tenaya glaciers ground down from the high country to merge near Half Dome and hollow out vast Yosemite Valley. The mighty glacier filled the valley to its brim, and extended all the way down the Merced canyon to **El Portal**, 15 miles (24km) to the west.

Mariposa Grove

Five miles (8km) south of **Wawona**, just inside the park's southern boundary, a short side road leads to the

Mariposa Grove ⓖ of giant sequoias, a preserve containing more than 500 mammoth redwood trees. It was here that naturalist John Muir and President Theodore Roosevelt slept under the stars. Roosevelt was persuaded by Muir that the forest should be added to the infant Yosemite National Park. The grove's largest tree, the **Grizzly Giant**, 200ft (60 meters) high and with a girth of 94ft (29 meters), is at least 3,800 years old. The best way to experience the trees is on foot, wandering among living things that were already giants when Christ walked the Holy Land.

Tuolumne Meadows

If Wawona and the Mariposa Grove are Yosemite's Black Forest, **Tuolumne Meadows ⓗ** is its Switzerland. Reached by an hour's drive north from Yosemite Valley on the scenic road to the **Tioga Pass ⓘ**, and situated at 8,600ft (2,600 meters) above sea level, Tuolumne is the gateway to an alpine wilderness. The only way to see the more remote areas of the backcountry is to pick up your feet and hike, with the minimum

of creature comforts carried in a backpack that may tip the scales at 50 lbs (23kg) or more. A less arduous alternative on some of the smoother trails is to arrange a horse-packing trip, details of which can be discovered locally or by calling Yosemite Park information services (tel: 209-372-0200).

Tuolumne is also the site of **Tuolumne Meadows Lodge**, central star in the summer constellation of high Sierra camps. Arranged roughly

The Ahwahnee Hotel in Yosemite National Park. The wood on its facade is actually concrete stained to look like redwood, in order to protect the building from fire.

Tunnel View in Yosemite.

Upper and Lower Yosemite Falls.

in a circle, about 9 miles (14km) apart, these six permanent tented camps provide lodging, meals, and hot showers to hikers and horse-packers on the popular High Sierra Loop trail. Elevations of the camps vary from 7,150ft (2,180 meters) to 10,300ft (3,140 meters), and a night of acclimatiza-tion in Tuolumne is recommended before departure. In a typical year, camps are open from June 14 through September 1, with advance booking essen-tial (www.recreation.gov).

SEQUOIA AND KINGS CANYON NATIONAL PARKS

Sequoia National Park ❺ and **Kings Canyon National Park ❻** are less visited than Yosemite, but still attract 1.5 million each year. In some ways, these parks can out-boast Yosemite:

the 7,000ft (2,000-meter) -deep Kings Canyon exceeds Yosemite Valley in sheer vertical relief, and the sequoia forests of the southern park are larger and more numerous than Yosemite's groves.

Sequoia/Kings Canyon is a wilder-ness park, with only two developed areas near its western boundaries. The back-country extends across the west slopes of the Sierras as far as the crest of the range, encompassing the head-waters of the Kern and San Joaquin rivers and the highest Sierra summits, including Mount Whitney.

A majority of the park's mountain trails are most easily reached from trailheads out of Lone Pine, Big Pine, and Bishop on the Sierra's east side, a 250-mile (400km) drive from park headquarters near **Three Rivers**. Permits are required for overnight back-country camping. The most sce-nic approach to the Kings Canyon sec-tion of the park, State Highway 180, begins in the sprawling agricultural city of Fresno (see page 196). A 52-mile (84km) drive from there through the Sierra foothills leads to the **General**

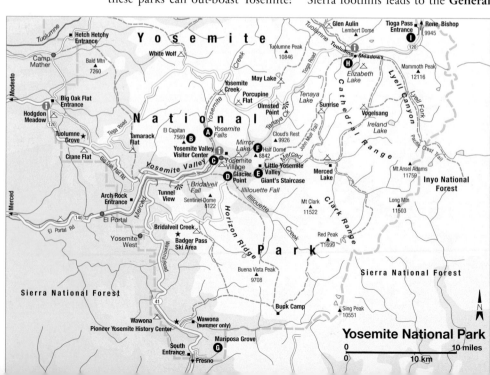

Yosemite National Park

0   10 miles

0   10 km

Grant Grove, a stand of massive 3,000-year-old sequoia trees notable for the wide-open parkland that surrounds their bases.

Thirty-eight miles (61km) past the Grant Grove (where campground sites are available by advance reservation), State Highway 180 drops into Kings Canyon at **Cedar Grove**. In contrast to Yosemite Valley, this gaping chasm is V- rather than U-shaped; the smaller flow of the **Kings River** has yet to deposit enough alluvium to level out the canyon's floor. Two trailheads lead north and east toward the High Sierra, but the 6,500ft (1,980-meter) climbs on south-facing (and sun-broiled) slopes are only for the fit and experienced.

After backtracking to Grant Grove, visitors can proceed into the Sequoia section by following State Highway 198 south for 28 miles (45km) to **Giant Forest**. A short nature trail leads to the **General Sherman Tree**, a redwood much loved by photographers, who like to pose very small persons next to the very tall tree for contrast. The tree is believed to be the earth's largest living thing. In recent years the park has removed many facilities in an attempt to restore the forest floor to its original ecosystem. With its **Giant Forest Museum**, built to showcase the huge sequoias and the diverse flora and fauna, Giant Forest is the closest thing to an urban center in the area. State Highway 198 continues southward past good camping and boating at **Lake Kaweah**, and drops back into the San Joaquin Valley at **Visalia**, 50 miles (80km) from the park boundary.

THE EASTERN SIERRA

Approached from the west, through the foothills of the Gold Country and on into Yosemite or Sequoia and Kings Canyon, the Sierra Nevada begins gently. Low, rolling hills studded with oak trees give way to pine-blanketed higher hills, which in turn give way to an accelerating crescendo of granite domes, spires and ridges. These culminate in the 13,000 to 14,000ft (4,000 to 4,300-meter) peaks of the crest. But there is nothing gradual about the Sierra

TIP

In early June, one of the rarest of Yosemite sights – the "moonbow" at the foot of lower Yosemite Falls – sometimes appears. It shows up only in the spring, when the falls are running full, and only in the days around the full moon, when the moonlight shines on the spray from the falls, producing a ghostly rainbow.

Climbing El Capitan.

BEAR COUNTRY

Grizzly bears no longer live in Yosemite, but the park is home to up to 500 wild black bears, which, despite their name, have mostly brown, cinnamon, and blonde fur. With a sense of smell seven times that of a bloodhound, bears are extremely good at finding your food; they'll even tear up your car for a piece of fruit or toothpaste hidden in the trunk. In fact, bears break into an average of 100 cars a year while looking for food. As a result, it is very important to use food storage lockers in the park.

Attacks on humans are extremely rare, but they can be aggressive about food or their cubs. If you do see a bear and you are in a developed area (parking lot or campsite), make as much noise as possible by yelling very loudly. For more information, see www.nps. gov/yose/planyourvisit/scarebears.

Buddhist visitor walking to Mariposa Grove, a stand of more than 500 giant redwood trees.

View of Half Dome from Cook's Meadow, Yosemite.

longest contiguous roadless area in the United States outside Alaska.

Mono Lake to Mammoth Lake

At **Deadman Summit**, north of June Mountain, US 395 begins a long descent into Mono Basin, once the site of an inland sea. **Mono Lake** , the last remnant of that sea, is the oldest continuously existing body of water in North America, and islands near the lake's northern shore are breeding grounds for 90 percent of the world's California seagulls. Eerie calcified rock formations on the shoreline are called tufa, and some of the best examples are strikingly preserved at **Mono Lake State Tufa Reserve**.

when approached from the east, up US 395 from Southern California. On the east side, the mountains of the crest drop precipitously nearly 10,000 vertical feet (3,000 meters) in the space of a few miles, a single great front nearly 200 miles (300km) long. From **Walker Pass** at the southern end of the range to Tioga Pass on the eastern Yosemite boundary, not a single highway cleaves the scarp, the

From May through November, or until the first winter snow falls, the town of **Lee Vining** on Mono Lake's western shore is the east entry to Yosemite National Park, via 9,990ft (3,045-meter) Tioga Pass. From Lee Vining, Tuolumne Meadows is a 45-minute drive away; it takes at least two hours to reach Yosemite Valley. Campgrounds are spaced every 15

WHEN TO VISIT YOSEMITE

In spring, wildflowers carpet the meadows, and the roar of wild water resounds throughout the valley. In summer, Yosemite Valley's singular concentration of natural beauty has its far less felicitous human analogue, complete with crowded campgrounds and traffic jams.

Autumn brings a rich gold to the leaves of the oak trees, and the sun's lowering angle etches the granite domes and spires into sharper relief. Autumn also brings herds of wild deer, migrating to winter forage in the Sierra foothills.

Yosemite Valley is emptiest in winter, when the action shifts to the ski resort of Badger Pass, 21 miles (34km) away and 3,000ft (900 meters) higher. Badger's gentle slopes are ideal for family groups and novice-to-intermediate skiers who don't mind the 45-minute commute by car or bus from the valley.

miles (24km) or so, and, unlike the rest of the park's sites, can*not* be reserved in advance; just show up and see if space is available.

North of Mono Lake, the Sierra crest begins to lower, although "lower" in this case still means snowy summits 11,000ft (3,400 meters) high. Just under 12 miles (18km) north of Lee Vining, a graded side road leads 13 miles (21km) to **Bodie State Historic Park ❽**, which offers both an excellent panorama of the northern Sierras and a reasonably authentic glimpse into the life of a '49ers boomtown. Once the wildest camp in the West, Bodie was home to a ragtag collection of miners and confidence men who made silver fortunes by day and squandered them by night in opium dens, saloons, and bawdy-houses. Both professional and amateur photographers love Bodie Park, whose eerie, abandoned buildings perfectly evoke an era long past.

South past Tioga Pass is **Devils Postpile National Monument ❾**, just west of Mammoth Lakes. Its abrupt geometric pickets (80ft/24 meters high, 350yds/meters long) testify to the power of the twin forces that shaped the Sierras – fire and ice. There's some camping in summer at **Agnew Meadows** (just before the monument boundary on State Highway 203) and **Red's Meadows** (just after the boundary).

Winter sun fanatics head for **Mammoth Lakes**, one of the largest downhill ski resorts in America. In the snowy season, Mammoth is where Los Angeles goes skiing, and it is not uncommon to share lift lines with 20,000 other powder hounds. On the plus side, Mammoth offers gourmet dining at several eating establishments, plus good wine and cheese shops and, in summer, lots of outdoor activities, including hiking, canoeing and kayaking, fishing, golf, hot-air ballooning, and bird-watching.

Posing by the General Sherman Tree in Giant Forest.

Zumwalt Meadow in Kings Canyon National Park.

*National Park Service
ranger at Roaring
River Falls, Kings
Canyon.*

*Sunset over Mount
Whitney from
Alabama Hills.*

Owens Valley

Heading south further still, there is more dramatic scenery to be found at the shores of **Owens Lake**, near the hamlet of **Olancha**. To the west, the tawny, unforested peaks of the southern Sierras rise abruptly, cresting in granite pinnacles 12,000ft (3,600 meters) high. To the east, across the wide, shimmering lakebed, the softer, more rounded contours of the somewhat lower **Inyo Range** dissolve into black and purple foothills. These are the portals of **Owens Valley, the** deepest in America, and "The Land of Little Rain". The vegetation here is hardy desert flora, consisting as it does of scrub oak, mesquite, and sagebrush, but Owens Valley and the Inyos receive less than 10ins (25cm) of rain every year.

Just past the northern end of the lakebed, 21 miles (34km) north of Olancha, State Highway 136 departs east for Death Valley. Located at this junction is the **Visitor Center,** which dispenses maps, information, and wilderness permits for the extensive public lands under federal jurisdiction. In wintertime, the visitor center is a mandatory stop for the latest word on campground closures and road and weather conditions. In the busy summer season, rangers will direct travelers to campgrounds with vacant spaces.

On a patio outside the Visitor Center, telescopes are trained on the summit of **Mount Whitney ❿**, at 14,494ft (4,418 meters) the highest mountain in the United States outside Alaska. A trail leads to the very top of Whitney, where portable latrines have been set up to cope with the tide of visitors. It's a strenuous three-day hike (two up, one down), but no technical skills are required, and thousands make the trip every summer. The hardest part can prove to be acquiring a reservation: many Mount Whitney trail permits are reserved up to a year in advance. For details or more information, call tel: 760-873-2485.

Gondola on Heavenly Mountain, Lake Tahoe. A mid-station observation platform, The Deck, provides sweeping views of Desolation Wilderness and the shores of Lake Tahoe.

Ski resorts

Ski resorts in the Lake Tahoe area all offer equipment rentals and private and group lessons for both skiing and snowboarding, for kids and adults.

The ski season is usually November through May, and season, weekend, or day passes are available. Serious skiers tend to prefer the northern half of the lakeshore on the California side, particularly the area around **Tahoe City**. It's quieter and cleaner, and there's a bigger selection of ski areas. In addition to Squaw Valley, skiers can choose **Alpine Meadows**, **Sugar Bowl**, and **Northstar**. For cross-country skiing, the 90-trail Royal Gorge Cross-Country Ski Resort and the smaller Tahoe Cross Country Ski Area are both options in addition to the resorts below.

Where to go

Alpine Meadows (2600 Alpine Meadow Road, Tahoe City; tel: 1-800-403-0206; www.skialpine. com) The 14-lift Alpine Meadows is preferred by experienced skiers, as of its more than 100 runs, those rated "expert" make up 40 percent of the terrain, but kids' programs and ski and snowboard lessons are also available.

Heavenly (South Lake Tahoe; tel: 775-586-7000; www.skiheavenly.com)

On the south side, the very popular Heavenly straddles California and Nevada. It has a total of 29 lifts including five high-speed detachable quads plus a snowboard park, and a half-pipe. There are also tubing lanes for racing, and childcare for infants and kids up to 6 years old. The Heavenly Gondola takes passengers up to an observation deck at 9,200ft (2,800 meters). Located in South Lake Tahoe, Heavenly is the favorite ski area for those who like to duck into the casinos at night.

Kirkwood (State Highway 88, Kirkwood; tel: 209-258-6000; www.kirkwood.com) Although it's a bit further away from the action, Kirkwood is one of the best ski resorts in the area, with 12 lifts and 65 trails. You can also get outfitted for cross-country skiing and snowshoeing here.

Northstar (100 North Star Drive, Truckee, NV; tel: 530-562-1010; www.northstarattahoe.com) One of the top options on the West Coast, this 2,420-acre (980-hectare) resort has 70 runs spread over two mountains. Here you can also cross-country ski, snowshoe, and ice-skate.

Sierra-at-Tahoe (1111 Sierra, Twin Bridges; tel: 530-659-7452; www.sierraattahoe.com) Another local favorite, the family-run resort west of South Lake Tahoe has bunny slopes and wide runs for beginners, and 200 acres (80 hectares) of backcountry for experts to explore.

Squaw Valley (Olympic Valley, CA; tel: 530-583-6955; www.squaw.com) The majority of Squaw Valley's 4,000 acres (1,600 hectares) are better for beginning and intermediate skiers. But experts ski here too – Squaw Valley hosted the Olympic Winter Games in 1960.

Sugar Bowl (Norden, CA; tel: 530-426-9000; www.sugarbowl.com) Opened in 1939, Sugar Bowl is a medium-sized resort that is particularly popular with skiers from the San Francisco Bay Area who want a shorter drive.

Lake Tahoe caters to downhill and cross-country skiers and snowboarders.

Upper Yosemite Falls, Yosemite National Park.

The Sundial Bridge in Redding was designed by architect Santiago Calatrava, who designed a similar one in Buenos Aires, Argentina.

THE HIGH NORTH

The key to unlocking the secrets of the north is State Highway 299. This two-lane blacktop cuts across some of the state's least-populated wilderness areas.

Mountainous State Highway 299 should be savored like a fine wine and at least five days should be allowed to travel its route. On its winding trek, it cuts across a remote domain of mountains, valleys, volcanoes, rivers, canyons, basins, and, at its end, barren desert. The best time to visit is mid-April to mid-November, but even under the best of weather conditions, rockslides and heart-stopping curves make driving this road no experience for the timid or the impatient.

The Klamath Mountains

Coming from the Pacific Coast, State Highway 299 branches off US 101 at Arcata, north of Eureka, and crosses the low **Coast Range** to reach the wilderness realm of the **Klamath** and **Trinity** rivers. These two principal rivers drain the Coast Range and **Klamath Mountains**. The Klamaths comprise a series of smaller ranges: the **Siskiyou**, the **Trinity**, the **Trinity Alps**, the **Marble**, the **Scott Bar**, the **South Fork,** and the **Salmon** mountains. They cover about 12,000 sq miles (31,000 sq km) of Northern California and southern Oregon. **Mount Hilton** is the highest peak in the region.

There is something very wild about the Klamaths: with more than 70ins (1,800mm) of annual rainfall in some parts, they sustain a lush forest of

ferns, hemlocks, pines, and spruce. Except for the highest of the Trinity Alps, glaciers are rare, so most peaks retain a raw, jagged quality and river canyons lack the graceful horseshoe shape of their glaciated Sierra Nevada counterparts.

Some native tribes still inhabit the area. The Hoopa and Klamath tribes own ancestral fishing rights and still set their traps and dip their nets at the foot of Ishi Pishi Falls. Guides with graceful rowboats, called "MacKenzies," will lead you to

Main Attractions
Trinity Alps Wilderness Area
Lassen Volcanic National Park
Mount Shasta
Lava Beds National Monument

Lake Siskiyou, near Mount Shasta.

The Taoist temple in Joss House State Historic Park looks at the role Chinese immigrants played in the state's early history.

the finest holding pools. Stealthy visitors are sometimes rewarded with sightings of eagle, river otter, great blue heron, duck, fox, bobcat, and the occasional great bear.

The rivers and streams bear names that join in a confluence of Native American mythology and the whims of 19th-century prospectors: Klamath, Ukunom, Trinity, Salmon, Smith. Fishing and floating on these rivers is by no means limited to natives; the streams are big and cool in hot summers, and rafting and fishing guides take visitors down many of the most inviting canyons. Salmon and steelhead trout still spawn in these rivers and the fall run is unparalleled in the state.

Three national forests contain most of California's Klamaths – Klamath, Shasta, and Trinity. Within these forests are more strictly protected wilderness areas. The best-known and most popular is the vast **Trinity**

Alps Wilderness Area ❶, a region of high, craggy peaks and sparkling lakes, laced with hundreds of miles of trails for hiking and camping. Ranger stations along State Highway 299 at **Burnt Ranch**, **Big Bar** and Weaverville, and on State Highway 3 at **Trinity Center**, will issue free permits, answer flora and fauna questions, and provide up-to-date information on weather and trail conditions.

Redwood trees can be found here, especially in the old-growth state parks of these northern coastal mountains. Some of these majestic giants, 1,000 years old and reaching 300ft (90 meters) into the sky, are the largest living things on earth. Sun filtering through the redwood canopy as if through leaded glass, the cool enveloping shade, and the imposing sense of age often draw comparisons to the cathedrals of Europe.

About 10 miles (16km) east of the Trinity River bridge marking the Humboldt–Trinity county line, near the community of Burnt Ranch, State Highway 299 passes just south of

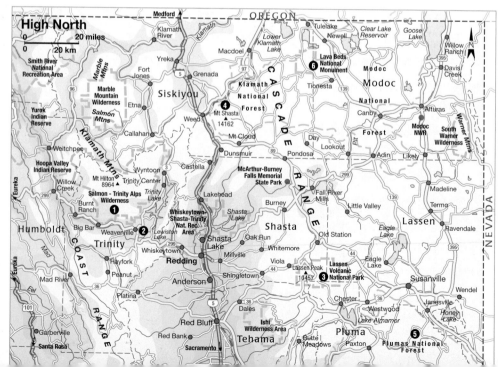

Ironside Mountain (5,255ft/1,602 meters). Ironside's sheer, scenic face is the eroded, exposed tip of a much larger piece of granite – the Ironside Mountain Batholith. About 165 million years old, this batholith is typical of other such intrusions in the Sierra Nevada and Klamaths, which distinguish the Klamaths from the neighboring Coast Range.

Weaverville

For residents of Trinity County a "night on the town" usually means a trip to **Weaverville ❷**, the county seat, with a population of around 3,100. It saw its glory days during the mid-19th century, when it was a supply post for Klamath region gold prospectors. Gold hunters still haunt the creeks of Trinity County, but lumbering sustains the economy.

Weaverville is the site of the **Joss House State Historic Park**, a tribute to Chinese history in California, particularly of the Gold Rush days. Here, the oldest Chinese temple still in use in the state is open daily; guided tours are available. Nearby is the eclectic **JJ "Jake" Jackson Museum,** focusing on local history.

Weaverville is also the gateway to **Trinity and Lewiston lakes**, part of the expansive **Whiskeytown National Recreation Area.** A short drive north of town, these lakes were created in the 1960s with the damming of the upper Trinity River. They offer outdoor recreation opportunities in the form of fishing, hiking, boating, and camping.

Although lumber ranks first, marijuana ranks second in Trinity County's cash crops. This juxtaposition of enterprises – one traditional, one contraband – is typical of Trinity. Trinity County's population breaks into two groups – true locals, and those who have come here since the end of the 1960s. Generally, old-timers tend to be conservative, the newcomers less so

Chinese temple in Joss House State Historic Park.

Whitewater rafting on the Trinity River.

Mount Lassen.

– but both groups share an individualism and a jealous regard for the natural environment. While Trinity often votes Republican, it also displays an abiding sensitivity to ecological issues. This is less ideology than simple self-interest.

Many residents hunt for their own food and draw water directly from springs, rivers, and creeks. (The bedrock of granite and serpentine is too impermeable for aquifers.) So when the county's residents recently tried to stop the federal government from spraying Trinity's woodlands with an herbicide many feared would end up in water supplies, no politicians – Democrat or Republican – openly opposed the grassroots effort. This closeness to one another and to the land breeds a native suspicion of outsiders.

The Cascades

The **Cascades** run almost due north from California to Canada's British Columbia. In California, the range stretches 40 to 50 miles (70 to 80km) across. Farther north, glaciers dominate the range. Here in California, only the highest peaks bear these relics from the Ice Age. The dominant snow-capped Cascade peaks are young volcanoes; some, like Washington's Mount St Helens, are still active. Unlike the Klamaths, the higher Cascade peaks present a sharply vertical profile of high conical peaks surrounded by lower mountains of the 4,500 to 5,000ft (1,400 to 1,500-meter) range.

There are few better places to study volcanology than **Lassen Volcanic National Park ❸**. The park is reached via State Highway 36 stretching east from **Red Bluff**, State Highway 44 east from Redding, or State Highway 89 south from State Highway 299 beyond Burney. Backpackers will find hot springs and geysers throughout the huge park. Lassen Peak (elevation 10,457ft/3,187 meters) marks the southern terminus of the Cascade Range, and is one of only two Cascade volcanoes to have erupted in the 20th century: Mount Lassen blew its lid in 1914.

Much of 108,000-acre (43,700-hectare) Lassen Park lies within a caldera,

the giant crater left by the collapse of an ancient volcano. Out of this caldera, Lassen Peak later rose to dominate this expanse of wilderness, but there are small volcanoes in the park as well; check out the bubbling mudpots of **Bumpass Hell**, a steaming valley of active geothermal pools and vents. There are lakes, rivers, meadows, pine forests, and fine trails for hiking and camping.

Just east of Lassen Park lies **Eagle Lake**, an anomalous, highly alkaline body of water straddling the Eastern Sierras on one side, sage desert on the other, and home to a splendid species of oversize Eagle Lake rainbow trout found nowhere else in the state. As the name of the lake implies, osprey, golden eagle, and bald eagle – the national bird – are often seen skimming this lake for unsuspecting fish.

Nearby Lake Almanor, a massive man-made reservoir, is a resort area with plentiful opportunities for waterskiing, sailing, lake trolling (slowly dragging a fishing line through deep water), and sunbathing.

All the mountains of this region are notorious for their massive deer herds, stealthy cougar (aptly called "mountain lions," but smaller and much more solitary than their handsome African cousins), black bear, and North America's only antelope, the pronghorn.

Northwest of Lassen, near the town of Weed, an ancient volcano named **Mount Shasta ④** (14,162 ft/4,317 meters) and the southern point of the volcanic Cascade Range that extends all the way to Alaska, stands solitary sentinel at the head of the Sacramento Valley. The glacier-capped peak is a moderately difficult all-day climb in the summer, with climbers offered a sweeping view of the Central Valley to the south, the Trinities to the southwest, and the Sierras to the southeast. In the winter, the mountain is buried in snow, but still open to enthusiastic skiers.

It is thanks to the collapse of an ancient volcano, leaving a giant crater in which Lassen Park lies, that visitors can enjoy geothermal features such as bubbling mudpots and steaming pools and vents.

Bumpass Hell.

TIP

Come summer, the man-made Shasta Lake is popular for houseboating vacations. It is possible to rent boats for a few days or an entire week (tel: 1-888-454-8825; www.houseboating.org/shasta/overview.cfm).

Most of the California Cascades fall within two national forests, **Lassen** and **Shasta**. At Shasta's southern boundary lies another prime wilderness, **Plumas National Forest ❺**. These upland woods cover the northern end of the Sierra Nevada and cradle the **Feather River**, one of the state's best-known wild streams.

Between Redding and Burney, a distance of 53 miles (85km), State Highway 299 climbs into a gently undulating country of ranches and volcanic debris. The red rocks that litter the landscape and pastures to the south of the road were deposited by hot mud flows from the eruption of Mount Maidu 7 million years ago. This posthumously named volcano collapsed to form the caldera within Lassen Park. Just beyond the lumber and livestock marketing center of **Burney** is the State Highway 89 intersection.

Lava tunnel at Lava Beds National Monument.

Falls and forests

About 6 miles (10km) north of Burney is pretty, moss-covered 129ft

(39-meter) **Burney Falls**. East of Burney is **Fall River Mills**, and from here to the Nevada border, State Highway 299 runs across the basins and fault-block mountains of the **Modoc Plateau**, a lava plain similar to the Columbia Plateau to the north. For a large section of its route, the highway follows the deep canyon of the Pit River, the plateau's main drainage. The plateau extends over some 13,000 sq miles (34,000 sq km), taking in the whole of Modoc County and parts of Lassen, Shasta, and Siskiyou counties. Vestiges of volcanism make up much of the **Modoc National Forest**, a wonderful green expanse covering 1.97 million acres (800,000 hectares). A pristine example of this volcanic past is **Glass Mountain**, a huge flow of obsidian lava on the forest's western edge.

But the main focus of any geological tour of this region has to be **Lava Beds National Monument ❻**. A more impressive example of basalt flows cannot be found than this moonlike landscape of lava flows, columns, and deep, dark caves.

OPEN RANGE

There are a few things to bear in mind when driving through this area.

Trinity County, like most of California's north, has open range, which means that cattle wander beyond their owner's unfenced rangelands. Cattle have never been a major part of the economy here, and open range is mostly a symbolic vestige of the region's frontier heritage. It also means you need to be extra vigilant, as any driver whose vehicle strikes a cow has just purchased damaged livestock.

Hikers must be careful to stay away from creek bottoms on which gold prospectors have staked claims.

Likewise, those who come across a patch of marijuana should leave quickly before they are either shot at by its owner or arrested on suspicion of being its growers.

Mount Shasta, southern point of the Cascade Range.

Enticing empty road in Lassen
Volcanic National Park.

Brewery in Weaverville.

View over Los Angeles from the Griffith Observatory.

Riding dune buggies
at Pismo Beach.

SOUTHERN CALIFORNIA

A detailed guide to Southern California, with principal
sites clearly cross-referenced by number to the maps.

*Classic VW bus parked in the Ocean Beach
neighborhood of San Diego.*

Southern California is one of the
few places on the planet where a
few hours' drive can transport you
from gorgeous sun-drenched beaches to
majestic snow-capped mountains and
from fertile green farmland to parched
desert landscapes.

The diversity of the geography is
mirrored by the varied cities and attrac-
tions packed into the region. Modern Los Angeles, a sprawling, thriving, and often smoggy metropolis, is home to the cinema
mecca of Hollywood and the thousands of
stars and fame-seekers it attracts, as well as
the blockbuster attractions of Disneyland and
Universal Studios, and constantly evolving
restaurant, nightlife, and cultural scenes. The
state's second-largest city, sunny San Diego,
boasts surfer-packed coastlines, easy access to
Mexico, and one of the best zoos in the world.
And the smaller cities have their own claims to
fame, too: Palm Springs is globally renowned
for its hot-spring-fed spas, Anza-Borrego for its
spring flood of wildflowers, Pismo Beach for
its massive sand dunes, and Ojai Valley for its
exceptional wine.

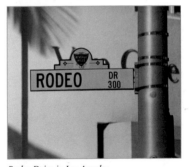

Rodeo Drive in Los Angeles.

After all this, the desolate and scorch-
ing hot Mojave Desert and Death Valley
seem like another planet. But elsewhere
in the Southern California region,
balmy weather is the norm; it seldom
rains between April and November.
The sunny climate not only feeds a
thriving agricultural sector that has
made California the country's agricultural powerhouse, but it has also helped
create the healthy, upbeat attitude that
Southern California is known for.

Services warning sign on Kelbaker road.

THE CENTRAL COAST

From beautiful beaches to an increasingly popular
Wine Country, California's central coast and its small,
relaxed towns make lovely escapes for city folk.

California's central coast south from San Luis Obispo to Los Angeles is a lovely collection of small towns and scenic attractions. There's the sleepy college town of San Luis Obispo and nearby Pismo Beach, famous for its sand dunes and monarch butterflies. Nearby, the Santa Ynez and Santa Maria valleys are home to over 100 wineries, along with quaint towns like Scandinavian-influenced Solvang and flower-filled Lompoc.

Then comes Santa Barbara, a beautiful coastal city with Spanish-style architecture and a relaxed, wealthy vibe – it's fittingly nicknamed the "American Riviera." For a detour, head inland to artsy Ojai or set off from seaside Ventura to explore the uninhabited Channel Islands. All of these towns can be explored easily by car – a drive directly from San Luis Obispo to Los Angeles takes about 3.5 hours. There are also small regional airports in Santa Barbara and San Luis Obispo.

San Luis Obispo

Roughly halfway between San Francisco and Los Angeles is the town of **San Luis Obispo** ❶. It owes its beginnings to the 1772 Catholic mission, and its continued development to the 1894 arrival of the Southern Pacific Railroad. Today, the pleasant town is a frequent stopover for visitors to the nearby Wine Country, as well as home to the students at Cal Poly (California Polytechnic State University).

The pedestrian-friendly downtown hosts a popular Thursday night farmers market on Higuera Street that turns into a proper street festival, with entertainment and barbecues plus stalls selling produce such as flowers, herbs, nuts, honey, and marmalades.

Main Attractions

Guadalupe-Nipomo Dunes Preserve
Solvang
Stearns Wharf, Santa Barbara
Mission Santa Barbara
Channel Islands National Park

Gold Rush Steak House at the Madonna Inn Resort and Spa.

Riding a dirt bike on the sand dunes at Pismo Beach. Beach buggies and quad bikes can also be hired.

Windmill in Solvang, the town founded by a group of Danes and built to resemble a Danish settlement.

the grounds. The San Luis Obispo Children's Museum (1010 Nipoma Street; tel: 805-545-5874; www.slocm. org, charge) caters to visitors with shorter attention spans.

If time permits, leave US 101 at the **Los Alamos ❷** turnoff to view the virtually one-block town with its antiques stores and frontier-style buildings. The **1880 Union Hotel** has a wonderful saloon and pool room as well as bedrooms and a restaurant furnished completely in 19th-century style. Even more unusual rooms are offered by the famously pink and kitschy **Madonna Inn** (tel: 805-543-3000; www.madonnainn.com), which can be admired from US 101 just after San Luis Obispo.

The Victorian homes in the **Old Town** neighborhood around Buchon and Broad streets are worth exploring; download self-guided historic walking tours to smartphones in advance at www.historycenterslo.org.

Mission San Luis Obispo

At the 1772 Mission San Luis Obispo de Toloso (751 Palm Street; tel: 805-543-6850; www.missionsanluisobispo. org), visitors can view Chumas Indian artifacts in the museum and explore

Pismo Beach

If you're craving beach time, **Pismo Beach** delivers. It's the only real shore community on US 101 between San Francisco and Santa Barbara, and is ideal for sunning and surfing. Here also is the stunning **Guadalupe-Nipomo Dunes Preserve ❸** (tel: 805-342-2455; www.dunescenter.org),

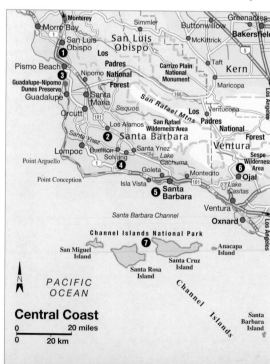

Central Coast map

including the Mussel Rock Dunes, the world's highest coastal dunes.

Pismo Beach is famous for its clams, which can grow to almost 8ins (20cm), but they've almost disappeared because of overharvesting. Nevertheless, a Clam Festival is still held every October. If you want to try clamming, you must have a salt-water fishing license and a caliper to ensure they are of legal size (minimum 4.5ins (11.5cm). The limit is 10 per day and they can only be taken between a half-hour before sunrise and a half-hour after sunset.

From late November through February, hordes of colorful Monarch butterflies come to winter in groves of eucalyptus and Monterey pines. The groves are accessible from State Highway 1 at the southern city limits of Pismo Beach (daily guided walks 11am and 2pm).

Santa Ynez and Santa Maria valleys

Napa and Sonoma may be the best-known wine-producing regions in California, but the emerging and increasingly well-regarded **Santa Ynez and** Santa Maria **valley** wineries are well worth a visit. Spotlighted in the movie Sideways, the rural region is home to 100-plus wineries, including the high-profile **Firestone Vineyard** (tel: 805-688-3940) and the **Fess Parker Winery** (tel: 805-688-1545). For a current list of local wineries and information on their tours and tastings, contact the Santa Barbara County Vintners' Association (tel: 805-688-0881; www.sbcountywines.com).

One of this Wine Country's most notable towns is **Solvang** ❹, an amusing and slightly camp replica of a Scandinavian town with horse-drawn streetcars, windmills, and Danish bakeries. The Hans Christian Andersen Museum (The Book Loft Building, 1680 Mission Drive; tel: 805-688-2052; daily 10am–5pm; free) has first, early, and illustrated editions of Andersen's works and original photographs and letters. To learn more about the history of Solvang and heritage of Denmark, visit the Elverhoj Museum (1624 Elverhoy Way; tel: 805-686-1211; www.elverhoj.

TIP

On man-made Cachuma Lake in the Santa Ynez Valley, there are guided cruises led by park naturalists (Fri–Sun); in winter you can view a rare flock of migrating bald eagles; in spring and summer, resident birds can be seen building their nests.

1880 Union Hotel, Los Alamos.

Danish-style Solvang.

Stearns Wharf, Santa Barbara.

Charles Nordhoff glowingly touted its mineral springs. The sunny "American Riveria" is still an alluring getaway destination, boasting a Mediterranean climate, picturesque white stucco buildings topped with red-tiled roofs, and 5 miles (8km) of palm-tree-lined beaches, perfect for leisurely jogging, biking, rollerblading, and sunbathing.

One of the shore's main landmarks is the century-old **Stearns Wharf** Ⓐ, the oldest pier on the West Coast. Here visitors choose among seafood stands, restaurants, wine tasting, fishing, and the Ty Warner Sea Center (211 Stearns Wharf:; tel: 805-962-2526; www.sbnature.org; daily 10am–5pm; charge), where local jellyfish mesmerize visitors with their graceful undulations, and small sharks patrol a touch pool.

org; Wed–Thur 1-4pm, Fri–Sun noon-4pm; free).

Continuing south on US 101, the highway skirts past gorgeous beaches before passing through **Goleta**, home of a University of California branch, and then arriving in Santa Barbara.

Santa Barbara

Beautiful **Santa Barbara** ❺ first found admiration as a health resort in the 1870s after New York journalist

If you are looking for larger marine life, whale-watching boat trips depart from Stearns Wharf most days from February through September. They are out to spot the heavyweight mammals heading north from the Baja coast with their offspring.

Take a short diversion to Chapala and Montecito streets to admire the massive **Moreton Bay fig tree** **B**, native to Australia and said to be the largest of its kind in America. Planted here in 1914, its branches have since grown to cover, at their widest spread, a length of 160ft (49 meters) and often shade the city's down-and-out homeless community. A bit further along the harbor is the Santa Barbara Maritime Museum, with its ship models and floating exhibits.

For some beach life, Stearns Wharf is lined on either side with volleyball-court-filled beaches; East Beach is the long stretch of sand alongside Chase Palm Park, with showers, picnic facilities, and a playground.

Further down the eastern end of the shore, expensive hotels and the multicolored 21ft (6-meter) high **Chromatic Gate** stand on the waterfront. The latter was the work of Herbert Bayer, last survivor of the seminal Bauhaus school, who spent the years before his death in the town. Nearby, the petite Santa Barbara Zoo (500 Ninos Drive; tel:

805-963-5693; www.sbzoo.org; daily 10am–5pm; charge) houses 160 species – including gorillas, snow leopards, tropical birds, and giant anteaters – along with a small train and a petting zoo.

To explore downtown Santa Barbara, head up State Street, the main thoroughfare running northwest from the coast through Downtown. Turn right at E. De La Guerra Street to admire the **Casa de la Guerra** **C** (1827), the original home of the Presidio's commander and his family. Here the city council first met in 1850, an event still celebrated every August with a fiesta. The enticing cobbled area, **El Paseo** ("the street" in Spanish), is an attractive place to shop and sip coffee at outdoor cafés around the fountain.

The next block of E. De La Guerra, bordered by the **Canedo Adobe** (1782), is where the city began, centered around the **Presidio** **D** with its chapel, restored adobes, and the **Historical Society Museum**. Continue up Anacapa Street and turn right on Carrillo to visit the

Museum exhibit at Mission Santa Barbara. The Mission is still home to a group of Franciscan friars, and has a retreat center as well as the church and museum.

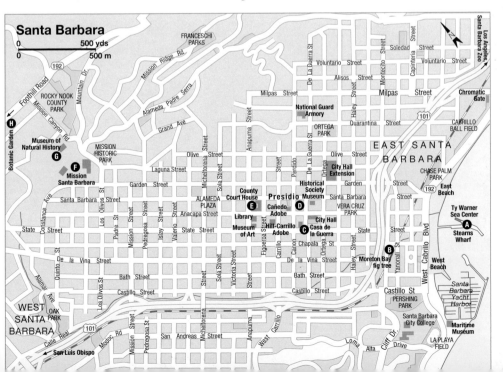

Spanish-Moorish style of Santa Barbara's Court House.

Mission Santa Barbara.

Hill-Carrillo Adobe. The city's first home with a wooden floor, it was built by Daniel Hill in 1826 for his Spanish bride.

Further up Anacapa is the handsome 1929 Spanish-Moorish **Court House ❸** (1100 Anacapa Street; tel: 805-962-6464; Mon–Fri 8am–5pm, Sat–Sun 10am–4.30pm; free). Admire the lobby's mosaics and murals, then take the elevator up to the tower for a lovely view of gently sloping roofs and the multilevel lawn below. The Santa Barbara Public Library is around the corner on Anapamu Street and the **Museum of Art** is close by on State Street.

A short drive up State Street and right on E. Los Olivos Street brings you to **Mission Santa Barbara ❺** (Laguna and Los Olivos streets; tel: 805-682-4149; www.santabarbaramission.

org; daily 9am–5pm; charge), one of the most beautiful of the remaining missions. Founded in 1786, it was damaged in both of the area's major earthquakes (1812 and 1925) but lovingly restored, and is still in use as a parish church. The museum displays relics from the days when Chumash Indians lived and worked at the mission.

Just two blocks north, the **Museum of Natural History ❻** (2559 Puesta del Sol; tel: 805-682-4711; www.sbnature.org; daily 10am–5pm; charge), shares more about Native American and in particular Chumash life, and also has collections focusing on animals, birds, reptiles, and fish. A mile to the north up Mission Canyon Road, trails at the **Botanic Garden ❼** (tel: 805-682-4726) meander through 78 acres (32 hectares) of native flowers, shrubs, and cacti.

Ojai

Hidden away on the edge of the Los Padres National Forest, **Ojai ❻** (pronounced *Oh*-hi) is a sleepy but happy town full of artists and writers. From the Pacific Coast Highway, take Highway

MONTECITO

Just on the southern outskirts of Santa Barbara, Montecito has long been a good place to spot celebs. The charming Montecito Inn (tel: 805-969-7854; www.montecitoinn.com) was popular with refugees from Hollywood in the 1920s when one of its original owners was Charlie Chaplin.

Montecito's other legendary hotel is San Ysidro Ranch (tel: 805-565-1700; www.sanisidroranch.com), where John F. Kennedy honeymooned with his wife, Jackie, and where Lauren Bacall says she fell in love with Humphrey Bogart. It is also the site of a midnight wedding in 1940 between Laurence Olivier and Vivien Leigh.

Today Butterfly Beach (at Olive Mill Road) is often frequented by celebrities; it lies across the street from the posh Biltmore Hotel.

30 for 15 miles (24km), or head inland 35 miles (56km) from Santa Barbara on highways 101 and 150.

On the main street, a graceful tower offsets a row of shops behind a covered arcade. The predominantly Spanish-style architecture owes its origins to glass tycoon Edward Drummond Libby, who in 1917 built the elegant **Oaks Hotel** opposite the library.

To see exhibits on the environmental, cultural, and historical factors that shaped the Ojai valley, visit the **Ojai Valley Museum** (130 W. Ojai Avenue; tel: 805-640-1390; www.ojaivalleymuseum.org; Tue–Sat 10am–4pm, Sun noon–4pm; charge). It is located in the St Thomas Aquinas Chapel (c.1918) and doubles as the **Ojai Visitor Center.**

Large annual events in Ojai include a spring tennis tournament, an arts festival in May, a classical music festival in June, and a film festival in October.

West of Ojai, you can take State Highway 150 to wind along some 60 miles (100km) of the shoreline of **Lake Casitas**, but the scenery is even better along the coast.

Ventura and the Channel Islands

Just north of Los Angeles, **Ventura** is dominated by an ostentatious city hall perched on the hillside. The grand civic giant is outshone in style and grace, however, by the 230-year-old **Mission San Buenaventura** (211 E. Main Street; tel: 805-643-4318; www.sanbuenaventuramission.org) with its pretty garden. Founded in 1782 by Father Junípero Serra, it sits on the edge of a restored "**Olde Towne**" area filled with antiques shops.

Ventura also serves as a main departure point for the **Channel Islands National Park ❼**. The only national park in Southern California, it encompasses the Anacapa, Santa Cruz, San Miguel, Santa Rosa, and Santa Barbara islands. The beautiful and desolate Santa Barbara Island is especially popular, with its 640 acres (260 hectares) offering a haven for birds, sea lions, and seals. For trip-planning help, visit the National Park Service Visitors Center (1901 Spinaker Drive; tel: 805-658-5730; www.nps.gov/chis/index.htm).

TIP

The Downtown–Waterfront Shuttle provides frequent service along State Street and the Waterfront area. Shuttle buses and bus stops are marked with blue and black sailboat symbols and the shuttles travel on State Street from Sola Street to Stearns Wharf and along Cabrillo Boulevard. The shuttle fare is 25 cents one-way. State Street service stops every block and runs daily every 10 minutes (10.15am–6pm).

Webster Point area of Santa Barbara Island.

CHANNEL ISLANDS

One of the least visited of America's national parks, the isolated Channel Islands are often called the "North American Galapagos."

Over 150 endemic or unique species are found here, including the island fox, island spotted skunk, and island night lizard. The pygmy mammoth once lived here too, standing just 4–8ft (1–2 meters) high at the shoulders, compared to the 12–14ft (3.5–4-meter)-tall mainland mammoths. Separated from their mainland counterparts, these mammoths evolved as food scarcity put smaller animals at an advantage.

Today, 99 percent of Southern California sea birds nest and feed here, including bald eagles and peregrine falcons, while sea lions, whales, dolphins, and giant black sea bass swim in the surrounding waters.

Wildflowers bloom on a central Californian hillside in the spring.

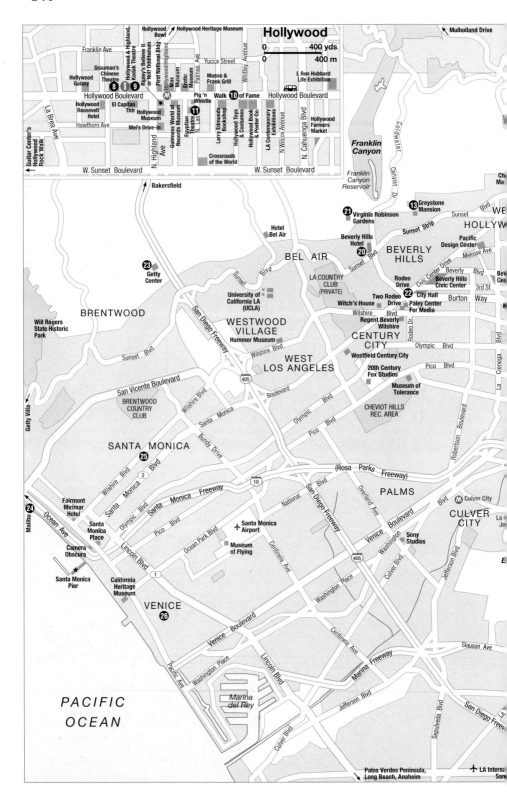

Hollywood

0   400 yds
0   400 m

Mulholland Drive

Franklin Ave

Hollywood Bowl
Hollywood Heritage Museum

Hollywood & Highland, Kodak Theatre
Ripley's Believe It or Not! Odditorium
First National Bldg

Grauman's Chinese Theatre
Hollywood Galaxy
Hollywood/Highland
Hollywood Wax Museum
Erotic Museum
N Palmas Ave
Yucca Street
Whitley Avenue
Musso & Frank Grill
L Ron Hubbard Life Exhibition

Hollywood Boulevard
Pig 'n Whistle
Walk of Fame
Hollywood Boulevard

Hollywood Roosevelt Hotel
El Capitan Thtr
Hollywood Museum
Mel's Drive-in
Guinness World of Records Museum
Egyptian Theatre
N. Las
Larry Edmunds Bookshop
Hollywood Toys & Costumes
Hollywood Book & Poster Co.
LA Contemporary Exhibitions
N Wilcox Avenue
N. Cahuenga Blvd
Hollywood Farmers Market

Hawthorn Ave

Crossroads of the World

W. Sunset Boulevard
W. Sunset Boulevard

Guitar Center's Hollywood Rock Walk
La Brea Ave
N. Highland Ave

8 **i** **9**
10
11

M

Bakersfield

Greystone Mansion
Virginia Robinson Gardens
Sunset
WE
HOLLYW

Hotel Bel Air
Beverly Hills Hotel
Sunset Strip
Pacific Design Center
Melrose Ave

BEVERLY HILLS

Getty Center
BEL AIR
LA COUNTRY CLUB (PRIVATE)
Rodeo Drive
Beverly Hills Civic Center
Bev
Cer
Beverly Blvd
Civic Center Drive
3rd St

University of California LA (UCLA)
Two Rodeo Drive
Witch's House
City Hall
Paley Center For Media
Burton Way

Wilshire Blvd
Regent Beverly Wilshire
Rodeo Dr.

BRENTWOOD

Will Rogers State Historic Park

Sunset Blvd

San Diego Freeway

WESTWOOD VILLAGE
Hammer Museum

CENTURY CITY
Olympic Blvd

Wilshire Blvd

WEST LOS ANGELES
Westfield Century City
20th Century Fox Studios

Pico Blvd

La Cienega
La

Santa Monica
Boulevard

Museum of Tolerance

San Vicente Boulevard

Olympic Blvd

CHEVIOT HILLS REC. AREA

BRENTWOOD COUNTRY CLUB

Wilshire Blvd

Robertson Boulevard

Getty Villa

Santa Monica

Bundy Drive

Pico Blvd

SANTA MONICA
25

Wilshire Blvd
Santa Monica Blvd

(Rosa Parks Freeway)

Fairmont Mirimar Hotel
Santa Monica Place
Camera Obscura
Ocean Ave
Malibu
24
Olympic Blvd
Santa Monica Freeway
National Blvd
Overland Ave
San Diego Freeway
Venice Boulevard
Washington

PALMS

Culver City
M

Santa Monica Airport
Ocean Park Blvd
Pico Blvd
Museum of Flying
Centinela Ave
Sony Studios
Culver Blvd
Jefferson Blvd

CULVER CITY
La
Je
E

Santa Monica Pier
California Heritage Museum
Lincoln Blvd

VENICE
26

Venice Boulevard
Washington Place
Lincoln Blvd
Centinela Ave
Slauson Ave

Pacific Ave

Washington Place

Marina Freeway

PACIFIC OCEAN

Marina del Rey

Culver Blvd

Jefferson Blvd
Sepulveda Blvd
San Diego Freew

Palos Verdes Peninsula, Long Beach, Anaheim
LA Interna
San

Coldwater

Franklin Canyon

Franklin Canyon Reservoir

Ch
Ma

13
21
20
22
23

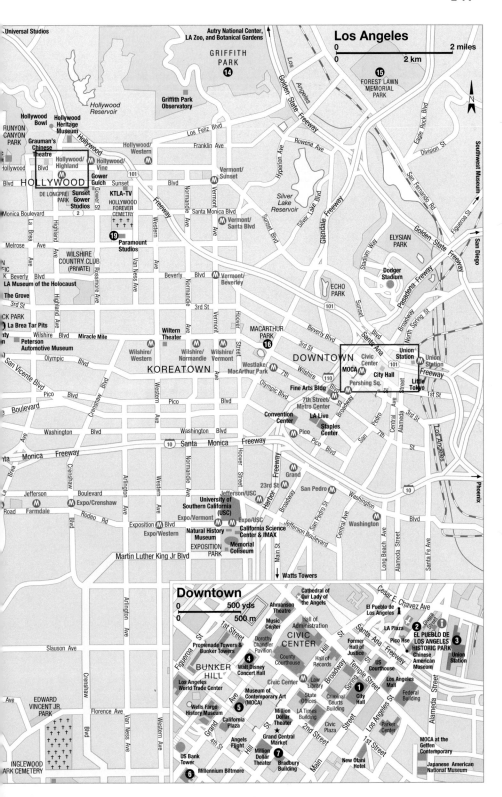

Los Angeles

0 _____ 2 miles
0 _____ 2 km

Universal Studios

Autry National Center, LA Zoo, and Botanical Gardens

GRIFFITH PARK
14

15
FOREST LAWN MEMORIAL PARK

Hollywood Reservoir

Griffith Park Observatory

Los Feliz Blvd

N

RUNYON CANYON PARK

Hollywood Bowl
Hollywood Heritage Museum

Grauman's Chinese Theatre

Hollywood Blvd

HOLLYWOOD

Hollywood/Western

Hollywood/Vine
Hollywood/Highland

Gower Gulch

DE LONGPRE PARK

Sunset Gower Studios

KTLA-TV

HOLLYWOOD FOREVER CEMETERY

Franklin Ave

Vermont/Sunset

Vermont/Santa Blvd

Santa Monica Blvd

Sunset

Silver Lake Reservoir

Rowena Ave

Hyperion Ave

Eagle Rock Blvd

Division St

Southwest Museum

San Fernando Rd

Golden State Freeway

ELYSIAN PARK

Dodger Stadium

San Diego

19
Paramount Studios

Melrose Ave

La Brea

Highland

WILSHIRE COUNTRY CLUB (PRIVATE)

Rossmore Ave

Van Ness Ave

LA Museum of the Holocaust

Beverly Blvd

Vermont/Beverly

ECHO PARK

Pasadena Freeway

Figueroa St

The Grove

3rd St

La Brea Tar Pits

Wilshire Blvd

Miracle Mile

Peterson Automotive Museum

Olympic

San Vicente Blvd

Pico Blvd

Washington Blvd

Crenshaw

Arlington Ave

Normandie Ave

Western Ave

Vermont Ave

Hoover St

MACARTHUR PARK
16

3rd St

Beverly Blvd

Westlake/MacArthur Park

Wilshire

Olympic Blvd

Fine Arts Bldg

7th Street/Metro Center

DOWNTOWN

Civic Center

Union Station

MOCA

City Hall

Pershing Sq.

Little Tokyo

Union Station

1st St

3rd St

Central Ave

San Pedro St

Alameda St

Santa Fe Ave

Wiltern Theater

KOREATOWN

Wilshire/Western

Wilshire/Normandie

Wilshire/Vermont

Convention Center

LA Live

Staples Center

Pico

Grand

23rd St

San Pedro St

Washington Blvd

Santa Monica Freeway

Jefferson Blvd

University of Southern California (USC)

Expo/Vermont

Expo/USC

Expo/Western

Natural History Museum

California Science Center & IMAX

EXPOSITION PARK

Memorial Coliseum

Martin Luther King Jr Blvd

Watts Towers

Phoenix

Expo/Crenshaw

Jefferson Boulevard

Farmdale

Rodeo Rd

Exposition Blvd

Downtown

0 _____ 500 yds
0 _____ 500 m

Cesar E. Chavez Ave

Cathedral of Our Lady of the Angels

Ahmanson Theatre

El Pueblo de Los Angeles

EL PUEBLO DE LOS ANGELES HISTORIC PARK

Olvera St

2

3

Music Center

Hall of Administration

CIVIC CENTER

Dorothy Chandler Pavilion

LA Plaza

Pico Hse

Union Station

1st Street

Promenade Towers & Bunker Towers

BUNKER HILL

4
Walt Disney Concert Hall

County Courthouse

Hall of Records

Former Hall of Justice

US Courthouse

Chinese American Museum

Los Angeles World Trade Center

Civic Center

Law Library

Los Angeles Mall

Federal Building

Wells Fargo History Museum

Museum of Contemporary Art (MOCA)

5

State Offices

Criminal Courts Building

1
City Hall

California Plaza

Million Dollar Theater

LA Times Building

Civic Plaza

Parker Center

US Bank Tower

Angels Flight

Grand Central Market

Bradbury Building

New Otani Hotel

MOCA at the Geffen Contemporary

6
Millennium Biltmore

Million Dollar Theater

7

Japanese American National Museum

EDWARD VINCENT JR. PARK

INGLEWOOD PARK CEMETERY

Slauson Ave

Florence Ave

Crenshaw Blvd

Van Ness Ave

Western Ave

Bugatti Veyron parked on Rodeo Drive, Beverly Hills.

LOS ANGELES

Sun-drenched beaches, Hollywood celebrities,
fabulous food, blockbuster theme parks... La La land
is a vast metropolis with many identities and
many cities within one.

A huge, sprawling city of 18 million people, Greater Los Angeles is California's biggest city and a metropolis with multiple (and often opposing) personalities. There's the MOCA's modern art and the cliff-side Getty Center, innovative fine dining from celebrity chefs and street-side food carts, slick clubs and hipster dives, and designer Rodeo Drive and tiny vintage shops. Movie buffs can soak up Hollywood and television show tapings, while beach lovers have plenty to keep them busy: from the exclusive Malibu colony to the roller-blading boardwalk of Venice, Los Angeles wouldn't be Los Angeles without its photogenic beaches. A forward-looking city from the start, Los Angeles has been a mecca for the young and hopeful since the 1950s, and it is still a magnet for the adventurous, for those seeking to begin a new life, and especially those looking to become a star or at least see one.

Downtown

It isn't the bustling central hub of the city you might expect given its name, but the Downtown district of Los Angeles still represents both new and old faces of the city. Millions of dollars have been spent to spruce up the neighborhood with modern architecture, cultural institutions,

and high-end lofts, now interspersed among the ornate movie palaces and other unforgettable fixtures of the city's past.

One such historic landmark is the restored **City Hall ❶**. In keeping with its public-spirit function, the mortar with which City Hall was built contained sand from every California county and water from every mission. You can take a fascinating walking tour of this landmark and its magnificent rotunda through the Los Angeles Conservancy (tel:

Main Attractions
El Pueblo de Los Angeles
Museum of Contemporary Art
Hollywood Walk of Fame
West Hollywood
Griffith Park and Observatory
LA County Museum of Art
La Brea Tar Pits
Getty Center
Getty Villa
Venice Beach Boardwalk

*Hand- and footprints outside Grauman's
Chinese Theatre.*

Dancers celebrate at a Hispanic festival in El Pueblo de Los Angeles.

213-623-2489). A quirky claim to fame of City Hall is that it featured as part of the Daily Planet building in TV's Superman series.ßFrom City Hall, you can drive or take a bus to **El Pueblo de Los Angeles ❷**, the oldest section of the city. It was here in 1780 that the city's El Pueblo de Nuestra Señora a la Reina de Los Angeles came into being on what was then Wine Street. Busy **Olvera Street,** a lively pedestrian market-place, teems with working craft-speople, Mexican stalls, and strolling mariachi who serenade diners sipping frozen margaritas under the sidewalk awning of La Golondrina, the city's first brick building (*c.*1855). This was home to the Pelanconi family whose piano, a neighborly gift, sits across the street in the older Avila Adobe. The Avila Adobe, the home of a prosperous rancher who died in 1832, was deserted for years and condemned by the city as unsafe. It was saved from demolition by a civic-minded group and acquired by the state in 1953. Since then, it has been restored pretty much as it was left by

his widow when she died, using some of the original furnishings.

Other preserved buildings include Pico House, the city's first three-story building and once its finest hotel with 82 bedrooms, 21 parlors, two interior courtyards, and a French restaurant; the Garnier Building (1890); and the Hellman Quon building, which was originally a Chinese store but is now managed by the Parks Department who offer morning tours of the neighborhood. In the firehouse is a picture of Blackie, the city's last fire horse.

Adjacent to the marketplace is **LA Plaza de Cultura y Artes (LA Plaza)**, the nation's premier center of Mexican-American culture and arts, which opened in 2011 (www.lapca.org). Here you'll find interactive exhibits, a re-creation of 1920s-era Main Street, a short film series, and a large public garden.

Nearby is majestic **Union Station ❸**. Opened in 1939, it is one of the country's last grand railway stations. Its leather seats, marble floors, and stratospheric ceiling have been seen

in scores of old newsreels. Just behind the station is the glass-roofed Gateway Transit Center, the mural- and fountain-filled transportation hub of the region today.

Not far from Union Station, the austere **Cathedral of Our Lady of the Angels** (555 West Temple Street; tel: 213-680-5200; www.olacathedral. com; Mon–Fri 6.30am–6pm, Sat 9am–6pm, Sun 7am–6pm) is the home of LA's Catholic archdiocese. Designed by architect José Rafael Moneo, the exterior is all jutting angles, while inside, daylight seeps through thin alabaster panes into a cavernous, polished space. Visitors can park in the underground garage (entrance on Hill Street), and grab a simple lunch in the plaza's café.

The grand **Walt Disney Concert Hall** ❹ (111 South Grand Avenue; tel: 323-850-2000; www.laphil.com; free tours most days), where the LA Philharmonic performs, is just a block and a half away from the cathedral. Opened in 2003, it was designed by renowned architect Frank Gehry to be one of the world's most acoustically sophisticated concert halls. The exterior's striking stainless steel curves make the main auditorium a bit of a surprise: it's warm and inviting with golden-hued Douglas fir panels and an enormous organ centrepiece. The Hall is part of the Music Center's campus, which includes the Dorothy Chandler Pavilion, the Ahmanson Theatre, and the Mark Taper Forum.

A block further along Grand Avenue is the **Museum of Contemporary Art (MOCA)** ❺ (tel: 213-626-6222; Mon and Fri 11am–5pm, Thur 11am–8pm, Sat–Sun 11am–6pm; charge), which harbors American and European art from the 1940s to the present, including work from Mark Rothko, Diane Arbus, and Franz Kline. In addition to this postmodern architectural gem designed by Arata Isozaki, the permanent collection is also housed in the **Geffen Contemporary** (152 North Central Avenue; tel: 213-626-6222; www.moca-la.org; charge) in Little Tokyo, and at West Hollywood's Pacific Design Center. California Plaza is a good

Walt Disney Concert Hall.

spot for a quick lunch, with take-away food counters, numerous tables, and a spectacular waterfall.

A few blocks away up Bunker Hill are the LA Central Library at 5th and Grand streets, and Pershing Square, flanked by the awe-inspiring **Millennium Biltmore** ❻, with its ornate lobby and photographs of attendees at the 1937 Academy Awards. It was here that MGM's art director is said to have used a napkin to sketch a design for a still-unnamed Oscar statue. Not far away, admire the gilded façade of the **Figueroa Tower**, built in 1989. A subtle fountain by Eric Orr stands outside the Figueroa at Wilshire building while inside one of the 80ft (24-meter) high Art Deco lobbies, among acres of brown marble, sit two of the largest plants ever seen in captivity. A remarkable late-1980s addition to LA's soaring skyline is the **US Bank Tower**, one of the tallest buildings in the west of the country.

At 7th and Fig, a stylish mall with a sunken plaza and open-air food court sits among three-story palm trees shading stores. Scattered around are several artworks, including a stooping bronze businessman on the north side of Ernst & Young Plaza.

At 811 West 7th, the Fine Arts Building has a medieval-style lobby with 15 chandeliers and a tiled fountain, and hosts exhibitions. The stepped, white form of the 777 Tower ("subtle profiles and strong silhouettes," says one critic) was created by Argentine-born Cesar Pelli, also responsible for the distinctive Pacific Design Center (known locally as "the Blue Whale") in West Hollywood. A few blocks away, adjacent to the **Staples Center,** is the **LA Live entertainment complex,** where you can catch a show at the Nokia Theatre, or peruse the four-floor Grammy Museum, dedicated to the history of the Grammy Awards.

Back on Broadway is the ornate, 1893-built **Bradbury Building** ❼, whose winding iron staircases, open elevators, and rich woodwork have long endeared it to moviemakers. It

The Watts Towers sculpture in the Downtown suburb of Watts.

WATTS TOWERS

In the Downtown suburb of Watts, in Los Angeles' South Central area, is one of the city's most astonishing sculptures: the Watts Towers (1727 E. 107th Street; tel: 213-847 4646). Created between 1921 and 1954 by Simon Rodia, a penniless Italian tilesetter, the trio of lacy columns was intended as an affectionate tribute to his adopted land.

Composed of broken bottles, pottery shards, tiles, pebbles, and steel rods all stuccoed together and covered with 70,000 seashells, the towers are a set of sculptures so far ahead of their time that they were unappreciated for years: vandals tried to destroy them and the city planned to pull them down.

The towers, the highest of which reaches 100ft (30 meters), were reprieved after attempts to dismantle them using steel cables pulled by a tractor – in full view of TV cameras – were thankfully unsuccessful. In time, the towers started to accumulate the adulation they had long deserved, but Rodia died in poverty in 1965 at the age of 86, having left town and deeded the site to a friend.

The towers can be seen behind the fence even when the adjoining Watts Towers Arts Center, which displays works by African-Americans, is closed.

featured in Ridley Scott's cult movie *Blade Runner* and also passed for private eye Philip Marlowe's down-at-the-heels office in the 1969 adaptation of Raymond Chandler's *The Little Sister*.

Opposite the Bradbury is the lively **Grand Central Market**, which adjoins one of the city's earliest movie palaces, the Million Dollar Theater at 307 South Broadway. Founded by showman Sid Grauman, it had a gala opening in 1918 with Charlie Chaplin, Mary Pickford, and Lillian Gish in attendance. The last of the grand movie palaces, S. Charles Lee's Los Angeles Theatre, which opened with the premiere of Charlie Chaplin's City Lights (in 1931), is still operating down the street. Three other notable buildings are the Mayan Theater (Hill and 11th streets), now a nightspot, where Norma Jean Baker is said to have appeared as a stripper long before she became Marilyn Monroe, and the 1928 Oviatt Building (South Olive and 6th streets), whose lobby has more than 1 ton of Lalique glass.

Head east to explore **Little Tokyo**, where you'll encounter interesting shops in Little Tokyo Square, lush Japanese gardens, Buddhist temples, and the **Japanese American National Museum** (100 N. Central Avenue; tel: 213-625-0414; www.janm.org).

Hollywood

Home to Grauman's Chinese Theatre, the Hollywood Walk of Stars, the Hollywood sign, and the Hollywood Bowl, Hollywood is one of Los Angeles' iconic neighborhoods.

Start off at **Grauman's Chinese Theatre ❽**, the famous landmark most notable for its forecourt of famous footprints. Nearby are the Hollywood First National Bank Building (a neo-Gothic structure created by the same architects, Meyer and Holler) at the corner of

Head to Little Tokyo to find an enclave of Japanese culture.

Grauman's Chinese Theatre.

Star on the Hollywood Walk of Fame.

Concert at the Hollywood Bowl.

The Kodak Theatre, where the Oscars ceremony is staged, is part of the shop- and restaurant-filled **Hollywood and Highland Center** ❾. In 30-minute guided tours (tel: 323-308-6363; www.kodaktheatre.com; charge for guided tours), visitors get access to VIP areas and the low-down on the gossip and glitz of the event.

The old Max Factor building (a former speakeasy) on Highland just south of Hollywood is now the **Hollywood Museum** (tel: 323-464-7776; Wed–Sun 10am–5pm; charge), which displays hundreds of costumes, film posters, and artifacts, including Cary Grant's Rolls-Royce.

Highland Avenue, and, east of La Brea, the glamorous Hollywood Roosevelt Hotel, site of the first public Oscars ceremony in 1929. The hotel once contained a treasure trove of memorabilia, including the first Technicolor camera, used in Disney's Silly Symphonies cartoons. Now, such artifacts reside in the Hollywood Entertainment Museum, currently seeking a new home after a decade on the boulevard.

Across the street is the approach to the **Hollywood Bowl,** an 18,000-seat amphitheater staging "Symphonies Under the Stars" concerts all summer, not to mention jazz, world music, and major rock performances.

The **Hollywood Walk of Fame** ❿ is the area today that most visitors think of as the heart of Hollywood: the celebrated brass and terrazzo stars along it run along Hollywood Boulevard westwards from Vine

Street, with Marilyn Monroe's star positioned outside the McDonald's restaurant. The walk was part of a major restoration of the street back in 1958 when the first batch of stars to be cemented into the sidewalk included Burt Lancaster, Ronald Colman, and Joanne Woodward. Only one star, Barbra Streisand, in 1976, failed to make the obligatory appearance at a dedication ceremony, although it's presumed that she or her agent paid the usual fee of around $15,000 to be commemorated in this quintessential Hollywood way.

After years of neglect, Hollywood Boulevard is making a comeback: witness the **Egyptian Theatre** ⑪ in the 6700 block. The theater is a 1,700-seat replica of a palace in Thebes; in its heyday, the theater had a man on the roof in white robes announcing the times of the movie screenings. Now the property of the American Cinematheque, this restored theater presents a movie about Hollywood history on weekends; classics and previews of independent films are also screened (tel: 323-461-2020: www.

egyptiantheatre.com; monthly tours; charge.) There is also the spectacular **Pantages**, which wows visitors with its grand lobby and Art Deco chandeliers.

Other nearby landmarks include the **Musso & Frank grill**, a rendezvous built in 1919 and frequented by writers Nathanael West, William Faulkner, and Raymond Chandler; and Larry Edmunds Bookshop, a peerless source of Hollywoodiana, the best place for movie souvenirs in town.

Not far from **Frederick's of Hollywood** (6751 Hollywood Boulevard; tel: 323-957-5953), with its infamous bras and lingerie, steep Whitley Terrace heads up to **Whitley Heights**, a community of elegant mansions much favored by movie stars of the Gloria Swanson era, preceding the rise of Beverly Hills.

Access is easier, however, off Highland Avenue, just before the big yellow barn (moved here long ago) that served as the original de Mille and Lasky studio, now the **Hollywood Heritage Museum** (tel: 323-874-2276; www.hollywoodheritage.org).

The iconic Hollywood sign on Mt Lee in the Hollywood Hills.

West Hollywood

Tourists often assume that the "Sunset Strip" refers to the entire length of Sunset Boulevard. In reality, it begins and ends at West Hollywood's city limits, one of LA's most hip and happening neighborhoods. Just a few decades old, "WeHo" has a large gay community and a stylish outlook. By day, a chic crowd meanders from elegant art gallery to bohemian clothing shop to intimate café; by night the same people glide between classy bistro, slick hotel lounge, and pulsating music club.

The castle-like **Chateau Marmont** ⑫, on Sunset near Laurel Canyon (tel: 323-656 1010) is almost an historic monument, in part because of guests such as Greta Garbo and Howard Hughes, and its notoriety as the place where John Belushi died; in part because of its current laid-back but starry ambience.

The hotel is, loosely, the eastern edge of the Strip. From here, temples of cool march down the boulevard on ever-higher heels, its role-call including the Standard and Mondrian hotels, the House of Blues, the Comedy Store, the Whiskey a Go-Go, and the Roxy.

Some delightful Spanish-style architecture can be found in the West Hollywood blocks lying between Sunset Boulevard and Fountain Avenue, west of Crescent Heights. The Villa Primavera (1300 North Harper), as well as the Patio del Moro (8229 Fountain) and the Villa Andalusia (1473 North Havenhurst), were the work of the husband-and-wife architectural team of Arthur and Nina Zwebell; others, including Villa D'Este (1355 North Laurel), were done by the Davis brothers, Pierpont and Walter. All date to the 1920s, as does the apartment house located at 1305 North Harper where Marlene Dietrich is said to have stayed when she first arrived in 1930.

Mi Casa (1406 North Havenhurst) is the genuine foreign article: an irresistible row of balconied apartments around twin patios brought over from Ronda, Spain, in 1926, and since designated as a national historic place. The city's denizens have always had

LA COUNTY MUSEUM OF ART

Established in 1961, the LA County Museum of Art (LACMA) is the largest art museum in the western United States, and attracts about 1 million visitors each year. Housed in a seven-building complex spanning 20 acres (80 hectares), the collection includes more than 100,000 objects from ancient times to the present. When planning a visit, decide what are your priorities and head straight there or you risk being overwhelmed and exhausted before you've even begun.

Particular strengths include its significant Asian art – the LACMA boasts the most comprehensive Korean art holdings outside of Korea and Japan – and its Southeast Asian art galleries, which are particularly notable for their early Tibetan and Nepalese paintings, sculpture, furniture, and decorative arts.

It also has a significant 1,700-piece Islamic art collection, including glazed ceramics, enameled glass, carved wood and stone, inlaid metalwork, and calligraphy.

Strong Latin American holdings range from pre-Columbian masterpieces found in Mexico and Peru to modern and contemporary works by the likes of Diego Rivera, Frieda Kahlo, Rufino Tamayo, and Jose Clemente Orozco.

Among its European masterpieces are Georges de la Tour's *Magdalen with the Smoking Flame* (c.1638–40), Rembrandt van Rijn's *Raising of Lazarus* (c.1630), Edgar Degas's *The Bellelli Sisters* (1862–64), and Paul Cézanne's *Sous-Bois* (1894).

In December 2007, the museum expanded its modern art holdings with the gift of the Janice and Henry Lazaroff collection, including works by Edgar Degas, Pablo Picasso, Camille Pissaro, and Alberto Giacometti.

A further addition in 2008 was the Broad Contemporary Art Museum, designed by Italian architect Renzo Piano. This fabulously bold and modern building is a stunning display space for changing exhibitions of contemporary art.

In 2012, the museum inaugurated artist Michael Heizer's monumental sculpture titled *Levitated Mass*. Originally conceived in 1969, the sculpture consists of a 456ft (139-meter) -long concrete slot, over which sits a 340-ton granite boulder.

an ambivalent attitude about the local architecture and what survives seems to be largely a matter of chance.

Dominating the hill above Sunset is **Greystone Mansion** ⑬. The 18-acre (7-hectare) garden is a popular spot for visitors, although the house (905 Loma Vista Drive) itself usually remains closed. It is, however, often rented out to movie companies for location filming. Built at a cost of $6 million in 1926 by the city's first oil millionaire, Charles Doheny, the 50-room mansion is now owned by the city of Beverly Hills.

Down La Cienega at Beverly Boulevard is the Beverly Center. For 30 years, until 1974, an amusement park and oil wells stood on the site of what is now an eight-level mall with 140 shops and restaurants and 13 movie theaters.

Griffith Park

Griffith Park ⑭ (tel: 323-913-4688) is an immense preserve that begins at Los Feliz Boulevard and extends all the way to the Ventura freeway. At 4,000 acres (1,620 hectares), the park is the nation's largest, and is home to a **zoo**, a wonderful **observatory**, an **open-air theater**, a **train museum**, numerous recreation areas, and the excellent **Autry National Center** (tel: 323-667-2000; www.theautry.org; charge), **which focuses on the diverse people of the American West**, but is otherwise more for motorists than for exploring by foot. Not too far away is one of the country's best collections of Native American art, on display at the **Southwest Museum** (234 Museum Drive; tel: 323-221 2164).

Perched on the south-facing slope of Mount Hollywood in the park is the Griffith Park Observatory (2800 East Observatory Road; tel: 213-473-0800; www.griffithobservatory.org; Tue–Sun noon–10pm, Sat–Sun from 10am; free). In addition to is grounds, massive telescopes, and exhibits, the observatory offers public star parties and

Griffith Observatory.

planetarium shows (charge), the latter in the impressive 285-seat Samuel Oschin Planetarium, arguably the best in the world.

Forest Lawn Memorial Park ⑮ (the park literature studiously avoids the word "cemetery") has two peaceful locations flanking Griffith Park: **Glendale** and the **Hollywood Hills** (tel: 1-800-204-3131). The Glendale location was the inspiration for Evelyn Waugh's *The Loved One*, and is a must-see. Ultimately a final resting place

La Brea Tar Pits.

Farmers' Market.

(for many Hollywood stars, including Clark Gable, Carole Lombard, Nat King Cole, and Jean Harlow), Forest Lawn also has reproductions of famous churches from around the world, a stained-glass interpretation of da Vinci's *The Last Supper*, and the world's largest religious painting, *The Crucifixion*, by Jan Stykam, measuring 195 by 45ft (59 by 14 meters).

The Hollywood Hills site is dedicated to early American history, and features bronze and marble statuary, including a replica of the Liberty Bell in Philadelphia. Later residents include Buster Keaton, Stan Laurel, and Liberace.

Westlake, Miracle Mile, and La Brea

West of Downtown, Wilshire is showing its age nowadays, although the Metro Line subway has brought life to otherwise seedy **MacArthur Park** ⑯ and the Art Deco landmark of the former Bullock's department store has been refurbished and now houses a law library. The Ambassador Hotel once stood at 3400 Wilshire

Boulevard, drawing showbiz types to its Coconut Grove and in the 1960s becoming infamous as the site of Robert Kennedy's assassination.

Miracle Mile's Museum Row, on Wilshire near Fairfax, has Old Masters and other fine paintings, which hang in the **LA County Museum of Art** (**LACMA**) ⑰ (tel: 323-857-6000; Thur–Tue noon–8pm; charge).

Focusing on a much older collection, the **La Brea Tar Pits** ⑱ at the Page Museum (tel: 323-934-7243; daily 10am–5pm; charge) is a major tourist attraction. In the 1860s, Rancho La Brea had been bought for $2.50 an acre by Major Henry Hancock, who quarried asphalt and shipped tar to San Francisco to pave streets. The oil company geologists who, in 1989, started uncovering fossils here identified some of the bones as belonging to extinct sabre-toothed tigers, dire wolves, and giant sloths.

After a decade of oil drilling, Henry's son, George, allowed LA County to examine the site, deeding the 23-acre (9-hectare) ranch to the county in 1913. The skeleton of

a woman from 9,000 years ago was found, but no other humans among what were literally millions of bones. The museum opened in 1972; excavations for the building uncovered skeletons of complete animals, which had been trapped in the tar as they came to drink.

There's alfresco eating just a few blocks north at the **Farmers Market**, where, from 1934, farmers parked their trucks and sold produce from the back. Next door is a huge open-air shopping mall, **The Grove**, complete with several dozen stores (ranging from Coach and Kiehl's to Topshop and Anthropologie), a movie theater, and restaurants. The mall and market are connected by a free shuttle service.

In 2010, the **Los Angeles Museum of the Holocaust** (www.lamoth.org), opened its new permanent home next to the Holocaust Memorial in Pan Pacific Park. Here you'll find the West Coast's largest archive of documents, relics, and other primary source materials from the Holocaust period, a moving testament to the horror.

The studios

Most of the movie studios that earned Hollywood its reputation have gone, but the famous gate seen in the film Sunset Boulevard still guards the entrance to **Paramount Studios** ⑲, (5555 Melrose at Van Ness Avenue; tel: 323-956-5000), where *The Ten Commandments* and all the Godfather movies were also made. Fans who were not even born when silent star Rudolph Valentino died in 1926 seek out his grave (and those of Douglas Fairbanks, Cecil B. de Mille, Eleanor Powell, and Marion Davies) in the adjoining Hollywood Forever Cemetery, formerly the Hollywood Memorial Park Cemetery.

Memories of all the low-budget Westerns churned out in moviedom's early days are evoked by the aptly named **Gower Gulch** now the site of a shopping center resembling a Western movie set, opposite Sunset Gower Studios on the corner at Sunset and Gower. Across the street, at Columbia Square, is where Hollywood's first film studio, the Nestor Film Company,

TIP

Hollywood Walk of Fame CityPASS ($59 adults, $39 children, valid 9 days) includes tickets to Starline Tours' "Homes" Tour, Red Line Tours' "Behind-the-Scenes" Hollywood tour, either the Hollywood Wax Museum and Guinness World Records Museum or Madame Tussauds Hollywood, and either the Hollywood Museum or Kodak Theatre Guided Tour.

Shopping in Beverly Hills.

paid just $40 to rent a defunct tavern in 1911.

Four blocks east, the KTLA TV station replaced the old **Warner Brothers studios**, where, in 1927, Al Jolson emoted in The Jazz Singer. Just north of Sunset on nearby Vine Street, Cecil B. de Mille and Jesse Lasky in 1913 filmed The Squaw Man, Hollywood's first full-length feature.

A bust of Rudolph Valentino stands in the minuscule **De Longpre Park** (below Sunset at Cherokee), named after the turn-of-the-20th-century flower painter whose gorgeous house and gardens near Wilcox Street and Hollywood Boulevard was Hollywood's first tourist attraction. Kansas-born Harvey Wilcox and his wife, Daeida, were the founders late in the 19th century of a temperance community they called "Hollywood" that encircled their orchards.

Beverly Hills

Drilling for oil on what was once the Rancho Rodeo de las Aguas is what led to the birth of Beverly Hills; the unsuccessful oil prospectors

BEVERLY HILLS HOTEL

The Beverly Hills, the famous pink palace, is a legend in Los Angeles. Here Elizabeth Taylor honeymooned in a bungalow and reclusive resident Howard Hughes ordered pineapple upside-down cake from room service almost every night. For a long time, Katharine Hepburn took lessons from the hotel's tennis pro and one day, after six sets, dove in the pool fully clothed. She was also known to curl up outside Spencer Tracy's locked door, waiting for him to let her in after a drinking bout. Greta Garbo chose the hotel as a hideaway in 1932 and Clark Gable checked in to dodge the press after separating from his wife, Rita. At the Fountain Café, Marilyn Monroe and Yves Montand romanced over afternoon tea in 1959.

When the world's then richest man, Hassanal Bolkiah, Sultan of Brunei, bought the hotel for $185 million in 1987, he ordered extensive renovations. The number of rooms was cut from 253 to 194 and gilded ceilings were added to the lobby. New additions included a kosher kitchen. Finally, 1,600 gallons (6,100 liters) of "Beverly Hills Pink" were computer-matched to old paint samples, so the new extensions' decor matched the old.

Some things, of course, stayed the same. The menu of the Polo Lounge, where Will Rogers and Darryl Zanuck dropped in after their matches, still features the Neil McCarthy salad, named for the polo-playing millionaire who died in 1972.

subsequently decided to develop the land. One-acre lots were offered for under $1,000 along the length of Sunset Boulevard. In 1912, Burton Green built the **Beverly Hills Hotel** ⓴ to be the focal point of the new community.

One of Beverly Hills' earliest homes is the **Virginia Robinson House and Gardens** ㉑ (tel: 310-276 5367; tours by appointment), built in 1911 for the son and daughter-in-law of the owner of the Robinson department store chain. Lushly landscaped gardens include a mini-forest of palm trees and flower-filled terraces.

Filmdom's elite built ever-bigger homes in this elegant area, fanning out into the hills and canyons, and around **Mulholland Drive**, the spectacular highway that runs for 50 miles (80km) along the crest of the Santa Monica Mountains all the way down to the coast just north of Malibu.

Greta Garbo and John Gilbert shared idyllic poolside afternoons together in a mansion at Seabright and Tower Grove Drive; Rudolph Valentino luxuriated in Falcon's Lair at 1436 Bella Drive; not too far away, the home of Roman Polanski and Sharon Tate at 10050 Cicelo Drive was the scene of the 1969 murders by members of the infamous Charles Manson "family."

At the canyon's lower end, along immaculate **North Roxbury Drive**, lived Marlene Dietrich (No. 822), Jimmy Stewart (No. 918), Lucille Ball (No. 1000), and Jack Benny (No. 1002). Greta Garbo's home was nearby at 1027 Chevy Chase Drive and William Randolph Hearst's mistress, Marion Davies, had a home at 1700 Lexington Road. At the time of his death in 1951, Hearst was living with Ms. Davies in a house on Beverly Drive, noted for the huge palms that line the street. With some 30,000 trees, Beverly Hills has almost one per resident.

Land was cheaper down around Santa Monica Boulevard when the community first began, but these days you'd hardly know it considering the prices along famous **Rodeo Drive** , especially between Santa Monica and Wilshire where designer stores with foreign names like Gucci, Hermès, Chanel, Fendi, and Cartier have branches – "the most staggering display of luxury in the western world," says novelist Judith Krantz. Two Rodeo Drive, with its cobbled street and bow windows, is a replica of what only Hollywood could believe to be an olde-worlde European backwater; across the street, the late entrepreneur Fred Hayman's red-and-yellow boutique-cum-bar has a working fireplace surrounded by photos of celebrity customers.

Even **City Hall**, with its handsome tiled dome, is a splendid sight, part of the Spanish Renaissance-style Beverly Hills Civic Center. More interesting architecturally, however, is the intriguingly bizarre **Witch's House**, at 516 Walden Drive, which began life as a 1921 movie set designed to look like the home of the fairy tale witch in Hansel and Gretel. It was later moved to this site. Conscious of its worldwide fame, Beverly Hills maintains an informed, active Visitors Bureau at 239 S. Beverly Drive (tel: 310-248-1015; Mon–Fri 8.30am–5pm).

If you happen to be in LA on a rare rainy day, head for the **Paley Center for Media** (465 North Beverly Drive; tel: 310-786-1000; Wed–Sun noon–5pm; free), where visitors can listen to news and watch old TV shows. About a mile (1.5km) south is the **Museum of Tolerance** (9786 West Pico Boulevard; tel: 310-553-8403; www.museumoftolerance.com; Sun–Fri, check website for hours; charge), a sobering look at the history of racism in the US and the Holocaust experience in Germany.

Santa Monica and Wilshire boulevards intersect at the far side of Beverly Hills, beside the **Electric Fountain** that caused sightseeing traffic jams when it was first built in the 1930s. Santa Monica Boulevard heads west past the skyscrapers (filled mostly with corporate law offices and the like) of Century City, centered around the luxurious Century Plaza Hotel and another

> **FACT**
>
> Wilshire Boulevard, running more or less parallel with Sunset Boulevard, 3 miles (5km) to the south, became the major road out to the coast when Sunset was little more than a dusty track leading out of the original Mexican plaza. It started out as a clearing in the barley field of Henry Gaylord Wilshire (1861–1927).

Malibu Beach.

FACT

A movieplex and mall stands on the site of the former Schwabs Drugstore at 8024 Sunset, where F. Scott Fitzgerald once suffered a heart attack while buying cigarettes, and composer Harold Arlen said the light coming from the windows as he walked past one day inspired him to write "Over the Rainbow."

The Getty Villa is a museum of ancient art in Malibu.

upscale shopping center, before terminating at Santa Monica. Century City's 180-acre (73-hectare) site was once part of the studio back lot of 20th Century Fox.

Westwood, Bel-Air, and Brentwood

Wilshire Boulevard swerves slightly to the northwest heading out of Beverly Hills along the southern flank of the shopping complex **Westwood Village**, once the headquarters of William Fox's newsreel operations and now home to the interesting Hammer Museum (10899 Wilshire Boulevard; tel: 310-443 7000; www. hammer.ucla.edu; Tue–Sun, check website for hours; charge), which exhibits a mix of European paintings, da Vinci drawings, and traveling art shows. The movie theaters at Westwood are often the places for sneak previews and low-key movie premieres; it's also one of the places where off-duty movie stars take their kids on Saturday afternoons.

Westwood also adjoins the tree-shaded **University of California** (UCLA) campus. UCLA's 130 buildings include Schoenberg Hall (named after the composer who taught here), Bunche Hall Library, and the New Wight Gallery, all open to the public. The college's main entrance is on Hilgard Avenue, south of Sunset. A first stop should include one of 11 information and parking booths around the campus.

The gated community of ultra-chic Bel Air is north of Sunset, the road up through Stone Canyon passing what some think of as LA's most beautiful hideaway hotel, the **Hotel Bel Air**. Grace Kelly lived here for much of her movie career.

Back on Sunset, the boulevard begins a series of dizzying loops and curves passing through Brentwood, site of the impressive **Getty Center** ㉓ (see page 268). One of Raymond Chandler's many homes was at 12216 Shetland Place and Marilyn Monroe died in a bungalow at 12305 Fifth Helena Drive; both located just off Sunset. Sunset continues through Pacific Palisades before sweeping down to the Pacific Coast Highway.

On the way to the coast, it's worth turning off to the right for the challenging, uphill drive to the Will Rogers State Historic Park. The cowboy philosopher, who had been America's top box-office star, died in a plane crash in 1935. Ten years later, the ranch was turned over to the state, which has maintained it as a museum pretty much as it was when Rogers lived.

Malibu

Head west on Pacific Coast Highway (PCH) to reach the wealthy seaside community of **Malibu** ㉔, with its free state beach and pier. Southwest of the pier is the historic **Adamson House** (tel: 310-456-8432; Wed–Sat 11am–3pm; charge for tours). The Adamson House was built in 1929 by Rhoda Adamson, daughter of Frederick Rindge, Malibu's founder and major landholder. (Frederick Rindge bought hundreds of acres of surrounding land for as little as $10 an acre back in 1892.) The house is as attractive outside as it is inside, and even when it is closed you can drive or walk up the lane (or even come in from off the beach) and admire the tiled terrace, the lovely fountains, bottle-glass windows, and well-kept gardens.

A display in the museum, which features old photographs, explains that the real Malibu Gold is real estate: Bing Crosby's house cost him $8,700 in 1931 and was bought for almost $2 million by Robert Redford half a century later. Harold Lloyd's 1928 house cost him $6,400, but singer Linda Ronstadt paid $1.3 million in 1985. Now they sell for tens of millions.

Just northeast of the lagoon (a preserved wetland in which you can sometimes spot ducks, herons, and pelicans) is **Malibu Pier**, built by Rindge just before he died in 1905. The pier is open to the public and is a fun place to while away an amusing hour or two.

Dozens of stars live hidden away here, some of them along the well-guarded beachfront Malibu Colony at the junction of PCH and Webb Way, but the only place they're likely to be seen in public is the Colony shopping center about a mile to the west of the pier.

Broad Beach, like so much of the Malibu coastline, is private but only

Decorative tiles in Adamson House, Malibu.

GETTY VILLA

Where Sunset hits the Pacific Coast Highway (PCH) is 1 mile southeast of the Getty Villa (www.getty.edu; Thur–Mon 10am–5pm; free, but fee for parking; timed ticket required).

The villa, one of America's most beautiful museums, has reopened as an evocative and highly suitable permanent home to the Greek and Roman exhibits. These treasures were formerly displayed in highly cramped quarters or more often, packed away in storage.

But when the Getty Center (see page 268) opened and many items moved to the clifftop museum, the Getty Villa came into its own.

For a break from culture, up the highway from the villa is Topanga County beach, with a full range of public facilities, but somewhat territorially minded surfers.

down to the mean high-tide line – meaning that as long as you stay on wet sand, you have every right to be there. Easily missed access to the beach is in the 3100 and 3200 block of Broad Beach Road. Zuma Beach and Point Dume State Beach are public and often crowded. Up in Malibu's Santa Monica Mountains, the environmentally friendly **Ramirez Canyon Park** (tel: 310-589-2850; by appointment) occupies the 22.5-acre (9-hectare) site of what was formerly one of Barbra Streisand's estates, donated by the singer in 1993. Walking paths shaded by sycamore, walnut, and pine trees wind along Ramirez Creek.

Santa Monica

Once, it took a full day's stagecoach ride to get to **Santa Monica** ㉕ from Downtown, but, when the freeway opened in 1966, the trip was cut to half an hour: Los Angelenos had discovered the beach. Whereas previously the city's seashores had been the preserve of fishermen and those wealthy enough to build bungalows by the sea, suddenly everyone was sporting

Ferris wheel on Santa Monica Pier.

a tan and hanging ten. Today Santa Monica is the largest coastal town in the 100-mile (160-km) stretch between Oxnard and Long Beach.

This deceptively casual town embraces both a metropolitan sophistication and a beach-town atmosphere. Many people in the media, arts, and design choose to live here, and almost every visitor to Los Angeles under the age of 35 chooses to at least visit, or more often, stay here. It's a great place to walk around and, so unusual for LA, no car is necessary. The Visitor Information kiosk at 1400 Ocean Avenue, open daily 10–5pm (until 4pm in winter), is a great place to start. To the south is a Camera Obscura, for which the (free) admission is via the Senior Recreation Center.

At the northern end of Santa Monica, the enormous mansions along the beach were mostly built by moviedom's elite. The grandest, at 415 Pacific Coast Highway, was the 118-room compound designed by William Randolph Hearst's favorite architect, Julia Morgan, for the newspaper tycoon and his paramour, Marion Davies. In

LA DETECTIVES

Raymond Chandler, writer of hard-boiled detective fiction, documented the seamy side of Los Angeles life in the 1940s. Chandler felt LA was a city "rich and vigorous and full of pride… a city lost and beaten and full of emptiness."

The "Bay City" setting of many of Chandler's detective novels is where Wilshire and Sunset boulevards meet the ocean. Chandler's biographer Frank MacShane said he felt the detective story was an entirely appropriate form for LA because such stories "could involve an extraordinary range of humanity from the very rich to the very poor and can encompass a great many different places."

Chandler used the detective story to create the whole of Los Angeles in much the same way that Dickens and Balzac created London and Paris for future generations.

1945, the house was sold for $600,000 to Joseph Drown, owner of the Hotel Bel Air, who turned it into a beach hotel and club (today it is the public Annenberg Community Beach House).

In those days, before the breakwater extended the beach, the sea came to within 50ft (15 meters) of most of these homes. It was another famous architect, Richard Neutra, who created Mae West's home at No. 514, while Wallace Neff, who designed Pickfair (Douglas Fairbanks' and Mary Pickford's estate), was responsible for the home of Louis B. Mayer's son-in-law, producer William Goetz, at No. 522.

The century-old **Santa Monica Pier** has numerous amusement arcades, a carousel you might recognize from *The Sting* and *Forest Gump*), and eating places and fishing stands from which visitors have gorgeous views of Pacific sunsets and beaches curving gently around the bay. Unfortunately, the ocean here is often too polluted for safe swimming.

Affluent "industry" people stop by Santa Monica from Malibu or their offices nearby to shop or use the

excellent library, and people from all over the area frequent the spacious pedestrian mall, the **Third Street Promenade**. The promenade leads to attractive Santa Monica Place, an upscale mall designed by acclaimed local architect Frank Gehry, replete with major department stores, scores of eating places, and several cinemas nearby.

Eucalyptus-fringed **Palisades Park**, overlooking the pier, was given to the city in 1892 for use "forever" by Santa

Venice Beach.

Santa Monica Pier is a great place to watch a Pacific sunset.

Monica's founders, Col. Robert Baker and his partner, silver tycoon John P. Jones. Jones's house at the corner of Wilshire was where the **Fairmont Miramar Hotel** now sits; the enormous fig tree outside the lobby was planted by a member of his family more than a century ago. Greta Garbo spent her first three years living at the Miramar when she first came to the US in 1924. The pool was seen in the "Bermuda" sequence of *That Touch of Mink* with Cary Grant and Doris Day.

South of the pier, a walkway and bicycle path extends all the way down to Venice. Buses run up and down Ocean Avenue, close to Main Street with its terrific shops, cafés, and California Heritage Museum (tel: 310-392 8537; Wed–Sun 11am–4pm; charge). On Main Street is Santa Monica's primary Visitor Information Center (tel: 310-393-7593; daily 9am–6pm).

Venice

The closer you get to **Venice** ㉖, the odder the ambiance. An early favorite of such silent moviemakers as Charlie Chaplin and Carole Lombard, **Venice**

Junk-food shops mix with vendors of marijuana for medicinal purposes on Venice Beach's boardwalk.

Boardwalk is today jammed almost around the clock with characters who appear to be auditioning for some unannounced contemporary epic. Sights and sounds are likely to include guitar-bearing rollerbladers in robes and turbans, bikini-clad beach bunnies, rainbow-haired punks, lunatic dreamers, outrageous con men, barely dressed cyclists, psychics, chain-saw jugglers, and the bicep-bound boasters of Muscle Beach.

But there is another, less-explored Venice a few blocks to the east. After noting the building on Windward Avenue whose colonnaded arches are meant to evoke visions of San Marco Square in Venice's Italian namesake, walk east to the post office, which was where once most of the canals met. Many are now paved over, but a walk of a few blocks to the southeast will bring you to what remains of the watery network, a charmingly tranquil area of shallowly filled canals lined with houses in myriad styles, mostly with gardens full of flowers that thrive in the hot sunshine, and where ducks and geese roam the walkways. If you are

driving, the route is down Dell Avenue across the humpback bridges. The creator of this area was Abbott Kinney, whose name has been memorialized in Abbott Kinney Boulevard – connecting Main Street with Marina del Rey – along which can be found interesting little cafés, restaurants, and lots of shops.

Some of the city's most interesting murals can be seen around Venice – Christina Schlesinger's Marc Chagall Comes to Venice Beach at 201 Ocean Front Walk and Emily Winters' Endangered Species six blocks down are notable – not far from the headquarters of SPARC (www.sparcmurals. org), an organization which sponsors such public art such as the half-mile Great Wall of Los Angeles beside the Los Angeles River in Van Nuys.

Marina del Rey

This seaside place is close to the Los Angeles international airport (LAX), and is a good place for a stopover. The marina's tourist attraction is the charming but phony Fisherman's Village (the "lighthouse" is a fast-food stand) with a multitude of restaurants

for lunch. These range from reasonably priced Mexican fare to more upscale Shanghai Red's, which has the appealing ambiance of a century-old inn but has actually been there for only 40 years or so, since the marina began.

At the end of Basin D is a shallow-water family beach known as **Mother's Beach.** All the restaurants overlook the harbor – the world's largest artificial harbor for small craft – with its berths for 6,000 boats. From Beverly Hills, the bus runs down Robertson Boulevard all the way to Marina del Rey, which is also accessible by Santa Monica's Big Blue Bus.

Back on Ocean Avenue, take the Big Blue Bus up a few blocks to Ocean View Park and transfer to the bus that runs along the north side of Santa Monica Airport. At Clover Park, walk a couple of blocks down to the Museum of Flying (3100 Airport Avenue; www.museumofflying.com), which focuses on the Douglas Aircraft Company (which built the DC-3 here in 1977) and houses about two dozen aircraft plus aviation art, artifacts, and the California Aviation Hall of Fame.

EAT

Straddling the border with Venice on Rose Avenue at Main Street is the Rose Café, where locally created artworks are sold in a small shop that's part of this lively set-up. Sip espresso and nibble sinfully rich pastries while sitting on stools at high tables or on the outside patio.

Venice's canals were created from marshland.

VENICE

When tobacco magnate Abbott Kinney invested millions in creating his Venice worthless marshland in the early 1900s, he lined the canals with Japanese lanterns, imported gondolas, encircled the project with a miniature railroad, and sold scores of housing lots. Visitors who paid 25¢ to take the new railroad from Downtown ended a busy day on the (now-abandoned) pier watching an armored trumpeter serenade the sunset from a replica of Juan Cabrillo's medieval flagship before retiring for the night in the St Mark's Hotel, modeled after the Doge's Palace in the town's original namesake.

Despite Kinney's ambitious plans, which included hiring Sarah Bernhardt and the Chicago Symphony Orchestra for his 3,500-seat auditorium before scaling down the attractions for more plebeian audiences, the project gradually deteriorated. Its collapse was speeded by the discovery of oil (there were 163 wells in the area by 1931) and by the shortage of fresh water. Like so many neighboring communities, Venice was obliged to come under the aegis of Los Angeles if it wanted a regular water supply. With incorporation came less tolerance for canals when paved roads could occupy the space. Moreover the envisaged water circulation system proved unworkable and the canals became stagnant. Since then extensive renovations have helped dredge the canals, refill them with water, repair the paths, and rebuild some of the bridges.

J. PAUL GETTY MUSEUM AND THE GETTY CENTER

The Getty Center, comprising art collections, gardens, a research center, and more, has been likened to a Tuscan hilltown by its award-winning architect, Richard Meier.

The white city on the hill high above the intersection of the Santa Monica and San Diego freeways has – like most examples of modern architecture – provoked both praise and criticism. Detractors have claimed it resembles an oversize refrigerator or a strip mall while one admirer claims it is "too good for Los Angeles." Richard Meier, winner of architecture's highest honor, the Pritzker Prize, was chosen for the commission after a worldwide search. He described the site as the most beautiful he had ever been invited to build upon, one whose light, landscape, and topography provided the cues for his design. The center, he says, "is both in the city and removed from it… evok[ing] a sense of both urbanity and contemplation."

The Museum at the Getty Center houses European artwork, ranging from sculpture to paintings, and European and American photographs.

Irises (1889), by the Dutch artist Vincent Van Gogh, is on sho at the Getty Center's Museum.

The J. Paul Getty Museum's collections include European drawings, paintings, illuminated manuscripts, sculpture, French 17th- and 18th-century decorative arts, and photography, which are displayed in a series of five interconnecting buildings. But the site also includes six other buildings, including a research institute, a library, an auditorium, and a restaurant, most offering breathtaking views of the city, the sea, and the mountains. Between the museum and the research institute is a playful and imaginative central garden, designed by artist Robert Irwin.

The Getty Center, 1200 Getty Center Drive; tel: 310-440 7300; www.getty.edu; Tue–Sun 10am–5.30, Jun–Sep Fri–Sat to 9pm; free, but fee for parking.

J. Paul Getty, c.1935.

THE RECLUSIVE BILLIONAIRE

Minneapolis-born oil billionaire J. Paul Getty, who refused to fly and lived his last years as a virtual recluse in England, never saw the museum that bears his name. When his Malibu ranch house opened to the public to exhibit his art and antiquities, he was no longer in the country. From the oilfields of Kuwait in May 1954, he telegraphed regrets that he could not attend the opening: "I hope this museum, modest and unpretentious as it is, will give pleasure…"

Later, he remotely directed the construction of a new site, an elaborate reproduction of a Pompeian villa (now called the Getty Villa), which opened in 1974. When Getty died two years later, aged 83, Getty oil stock was left to the museum; this $700-million endowment has ballooned into billions. Planning for the ambitious Getty Center began almost immediately, but family lawsuits (eventually running up $26.4 million in legal fees) held up events until 1982.

With five marriages and innumerable mistresses, Getty had 26 children, but only one – his third son, Gordon – is connected with the museum today.

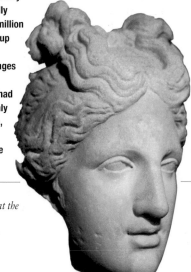

Ancient sculpture at the Getty Villa.

...*wing British artist J.M.W. Turner's Modern Rome – Campo ...ino (1839).*

...Museum at the Getty Villa in ...ibu is dedicated to Greek, Roman, ...Etruscan pieces.

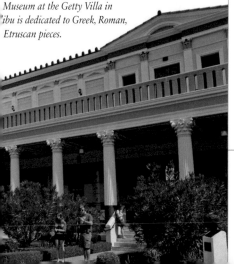

Amusement park ride at Knott's
Berry Farm.

DISNEYLAND AND AROUND LA

Pasadena, the San Fernando Valley, Anaheim... the fringes of the Los Angeles region offer historic houses, gardens galore, not to mention the magic of Disneyland and other family-friendly attractions.

Heading north of the Los Angeles Basin, in which the whole of downtown Los Angeles sits, you reach the San Fernando Valley. Better known locally as "the Valley," this valley encircled by the Traverse Ranges is home to beautiful gardens, historic missions, plenty of malls, and some 1.7 million people.

East of Los Angeles, Pasadena boasts noteworthy gardens of its own at the Huntington Library, Art Collections and Botanical Gardens, not to mention an annual New Year's Day parade featuring elaborate floats made entirely of flowers. For year-round entertainment, head just south of Los Angeles. Despite the great popularity of newer theme parks, there's nothing quite like the original Disneyland, or the other family attractions around Anaheim.

PASADENA AND ENVIRONS

To the east of the San Fernando Valley and bordering almost on the San Gabriel Mountains, **Pasadena ❶** comes fully alive once a year during the Rose Bowl football game and the famous Tournament of Roses Parade, held on New Year's Day. Any other day of the year, the city's houses, museums, and gardens take center stage.

Near the freeway is the 18-room **Fenyes Mansion** (1905), home of the **Pasadena Museum of History** (tel:

626-577-1660; Wed–Sun noon–5pm; charge) where D.W. Griffith shot one of his first films. Half a block away is the impressive **Gamble House** (tel: 626-793-3334; Thur–Sun noon–3pm; charge), built for David Gamble (of Procter & Gamble, America's biggest soap company) in 1908. Technically a California-style "bungalow," the terraced, wood-tiled house is a product of the turn of the 20th-century Arts and Crafts Movement of which the Greene brothers, Charles Sumner and Henry Mather, were noted members. Its

Main Attractions
Norton Simon Museum
Huntington Library, Art Collections and Botanical Gardens
Universal Studios
Disneyland
Knott's Berry Farm

Loop-the-loop at Knott's Berry Farm.

FACT

Brothers Charles and Henry Greene established the architectural firm Greene and Greene in Pasadena in January 1894. The brothers became famous for their "ultimate bungalows," Craftsman-style bungalow homes built on a large and very detailed scale. Signature features include the use of tropical woods and inlays in wood, mother-of-pearl, and metal. The 1908 Gamble House is one of the best examples.

interior is a knockout, but its impressive exterior makes it worth seeing even when the house is closed.

Just south of the freeway is the **Norton Simon Museum** ❷ (411 W. Colorado at Orange Grove; tel: 626-449-6840; Wed–Mon noon–6pm; charge), where one the world's most impressive private art collections is held. Norton Simon (1907–93) was an industrialist who acquired a remarkable collection of both European and South and Southeast Asian art. Some of the most famous pieces in his collection are Madonna and Child with Book (c.1502–03) by Raphael, Portrait of a Boy (c.1655–60) by Rembrandt van Rijn, Mulberry Tree (1889) by Vincent van Gogh, Little Dancer Aged Fourteen (1878–81) by Edgar Degas, and Woman with a Book (1932) by Pablo Picasso. In addition to Simon's collection, the museum's 12,000-artwork collection includes pieces from the former Pasadena Art Museum. Each year, about 1,000 of the museum's 12,000 artworks are displayed.

The main local attraction, however, is the **Huntington Library**, **Art Collections, and Botanical Gardens** ❸ (1151 Oxford Road, San Marino; tel: 626-405-2100; www.huntington. org; check website for opening hours; charge), the former gardens and library of multi-millionaire railroad magnate Henry Edwards Huntington. With his wife Arabella, Huntington assembled one of the most important collections of art and rare books in the country.

The main art gallery has several world-famous paintings: Thomas Gainsborough's *Blue Boy* (c.1770), Thomas Lawrence's *Pinkie* (1794), Sir Joshua Reynolds' *Sarah Siddons* (1784), and John Constable's *View on the Stour* (1822). The library has an astonishing five million items. Among those on display are a 1410 edition of Chaucer's *Canterbury Tales*, a Gutenberg Bible, Audubon prints, and an early Shakespeare folio.

The tranquil gardens occupy more than 100 acres (40 hectares). Beyond the lily pond are the colorful Subtropical Garden, the Australian Garden, and the Japanese and Zen

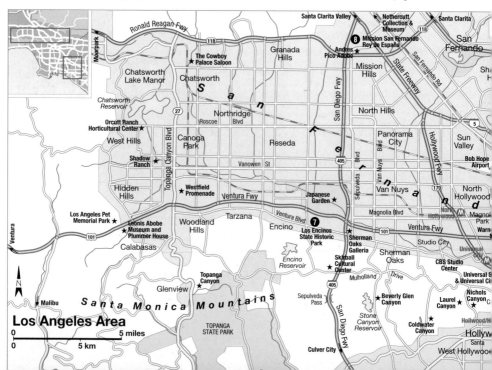

gardens flanking a delightful 19th-century Japanese house. After crossing a little red bridge over the carp-filled lake and climbing some steps, you can take tea at the charming **Rose Garden Tea Room** (reservations required).

North of Pasadena, off the Angeles Crest Highway exit on Interstate 210 is fragrant **Descanso Gardens** ❹ (1418 Descanso Drive, La Cañada Flintridge; tel: 818-949-4200; daily 9am–4.30pm; charge), which cover what remains of a 30,000-acre (12,000-hectare) ranch. The 165-acre (67-hectare) gardens can take several hours to explore. The oak and camellia woodlands constitute one of the largest camellia collections in the world, with more than 600 varieties. The woodlands began as carefully planned landscaping along the private drive leading to a magnificent 22-room house built in 1938 by the energetic *Daily News* publisher E. Manchester Boddy.

The woodlands collection is augmented by winding trails, a lilac garden, the International Rosarium (a timeline of roses from Cleopatra's day to the present), and

the Japanese Garden and Teahouse, which serves refreshments in summer. Something is always in bloom whenever you arrive: daffodils, tulips, and lilacs in the spring, chrysanthemums in the fall.

Donning costumes for the Cinco de Mayo (Fifth of May) festival in Pasadena.

SAN FERNANDO VALLEY

Were it a city unto itself, the San Fernando Valley would be the

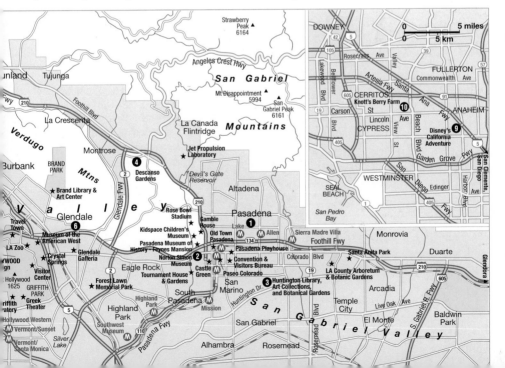

TIP

Admission is free at Universal Studios but there is a parking fee; budget-conscious visitors can take the Metro Red Line from Downtown or Hollywood to the Universal City station.

Arts and Crafts-designed Gamble House, Pasadena.

fifth-largest in the country, topped only by New York, Chicago, Houston, and Los Angeles. Despite sporadic efforts to secede, the valley is not its own city, however – with the exception of holdouts Burbank and Glendale, which are separate cities. All the differently designated areas are merely neighborhoods in the City of Los Angeles, and compose nearly one-third of LA's population.

In contrast to neighboring areas, the valley – about 24 miles (39km) wide and 12 miles (19km) north to south – is a staggeringly flat expanse of land bounded by the Ventura county line on the west, the San Gabriel mountains to the north, the Verdugo range on the east, and the Santa Monica Mountains and Hollywood Hills on the south. The west and south sides are the more affluent: cities like **Encino**, **Tarzana**, **Woodland Hills** and **West Hills** display few signs of opulence, but a quiet wealth predominates. Heavy industry is almost all concentrated in the northern area, around Pacoima, Sylmar, and San Fernando.

Movie and TV studios

West of Griffith Park, in the Cahuenga Pass that joins Hollywood to the valley, is **Universal Studios** ❺ (Hollywood 101; tel: 800-864 -377; www.universal-studioshollywood.com; see website for hours; charge), whose daily tours offer glimpses of the studio in what is in effect an amusement park. A 45-minute tram ride visits King Kong and the giant shark from *Jaws*, and negotiates the perils of a collapsing bridge, an avalanche, an earthquake, and the parting of the Red Sea. Other additions include *Jurassic Park* – The Ride, the fiery *Backdraft*, the comical *Shrek 4-D*, the unpredictable *Fear Factor Live*, and *Terminator 2: 3D*. You can see numerous outdoor sets, including the Bates mansion from *Psycho* and the facades from *Back to the Future*. Directly next door to the studios, **Universal CityWalk** (tel: 818-622-4445) is a glittery mall with one-of-a-kind shops, a contemporary art gallery, and a 19-screen cinema.

To the west, in **Studio City**, is CBS **Studio Center** (tel: 818-655-5000) where sit-coms like Seinfeld have

LA'S VALLEYS

Of the three main valleys of Los Angeles, the smallest is the Santa Clarita, known for its abundance of produce stands; next in size is the San Gabriel, which stretches through Pasadena and Monterey Park toward Riverside and San Bernardino. But the sprawling San Fernando Valley is the one to which local people are usually referring when they simply say "the valley."

Various passes and canyons are byways to and from the valley: Sepulveda Pass connects it to West LA via the San Diego Freeway; the Cahuenga Pass takes it to Hollywood. Laurel Canyon connects Studio City and West Hollywood, and Coldwater Canyon connects Sherman Oaks to Beverly Hills. The last of the large canyons, Topanga and Malibu, offer dramatic routes from the landlocked valley to the ocean.

been made; there are no tours, but the public can apply for tickets to be members of the audience. Other tours can be enjoyed in Burbank at the NBC **Television Studios** (tel: 818-244-6397; charge) and **Warner Brothers Studios** (tel: 818-972-8687; charge). Also in Burbank, but not open to the public, is the unbelievably successful **Walt Disney Studios**.

Glendale

A few miles northeast, in the town of **Glendale ⑥**, the **Brand Library and Art Center** (1601 W. Mountain Street at Grandview Avenue) usually houses the art and music section of the city's public library in a Moorish-style mansion. Inspired by the East Indian Pavilion at the 1893 Chicago World's Fair, it was built in 1904 by Leslie C. Brand, and the peaceful, landscaped grounds are perfect for picnicking. It's under renovations until 2014; until then the collections will be held at the Central Library.

The *Great Wall of Los Angeles* **mural** (west wall of the concrete flood control channel on Coldwater

Canyon Boulevard between Burbank Boulevard and Oxnard Street, North Hollywood) claims to be the world's longest mural. It recounts the history of California from dinosaurs to the present, and doesn't leave out the nasty bits.

One of the murals on The Great Wall of Los Angeles, Glendale.

From Van Nuys to Encino

Heading west along the Ventura Freeway, several great homes and gardens dot the valley neighborhoods.

San Fernando Valley.

Universal Studios.

The **Japanese Garden** (6100 Woodley Avenue, Van Nuys; tel: 818-756-8166; www.thejapanesegarden.com; charge), a 6-acre (2-hectare) botanical delight, is little-known despite having been created over two decades ago on the Donald C. Tillman Water Reclamation Plant. Morning tours (Mon–Thur) visit three areas of the property designed in distinctly different styles: a dry karen-sansui, a wet garden, and an authentic tea ceremony garden with a tatami mat tea room. In summer, popular "sunset" tours are offered on weekdays.

Orcutt Ranch Horticultural Center (23600 Roscoe Boulevard, Canoga Park; tel: 818-346-7449) perfectly recalls a vanished moment in California history, with citrus groves bounded by ancient, majestic, and stately oaks. When the Orcutts purchased the 200-acre (80-hectare) estate in 1917, they named it Rancho Sombra del Roble, "ranch in the shadow of the oak," which is quite literally the case. There is one magnificent valley oak, 33ft (10 meters) in circumference, that is estimated to be at least 700 years old. The orange

groves are only open to the public on one weekend announced in July.

Shadow Ranch (22633 Vanowen Street, Canoga Park; tel: 818-883-6397; Mon–Fri 9am–9pm, Sat–Sun 9am–5pm) is a restored 1870 ranch house built by LA pioneer Albert Workman and located on the remaining 9 acres (4 hectares) of a 60,000-acre (24,000-hectare) wheat ranch. It reopened in 2001, seven years after being damaged in the Northridge earthquake. The stands of eucalyptus are purported to be parents of the towering trees that now blanket the state, and the ranch is currently used as a community center.

At the valley's western end, near Mulholland Drive, is the **Leonis Adobe** (23537 Calabasas Road at Mulholland Drive; tel: 818-222-6511; Wed–Fri and Sun 1–4pm, Sat 10am–4pm; donation suggested), a two-story 1844 Monterey-style ranch house transformed by "King of Calabasas" Miguel Leonis into this charming home, fully restored and furnished with livestock and artifacts. Located on the same property is the

Plummer House (serving as the **park visitor center**), a pretty Victorian cottage which was transported from Hollywood to avoid demolition.

Los Encinos State Historic Park ❼ (16756 Moorpark Street, Encino; tel: 818-784-4849), originally the site of a Native American village, later became a ranch belonging to the de la Ossa family, who planted vineyards and orchards, and raised cattle. Amid the 5 acres (2 hectares) of manicured lawns, duck ponds, and eucalyptus and citrus groves is the de la Ossa Adobe, built in 1849 and restored with period furnishings. A stone blacksmith shop and a two-story French provincial home, built by the ranch's second owners, are also located here.

Near the junction of Iinterstates 5 and 405 in Mission Hills is the historic and interesting **Mission San Fernando Rey de España** ❽ (tel: 818-361-0186; daily 9am–4.30pm; charge), California's 17th mission, founded in 1797. Its history has been shaped by destruction in two earthquakes (1806 and 1971) and reconstruction. The tour of the working, sleeping, and recreation areas, and an extensive collection of artifacts, vividly recreate a sense of day-to-day early mission life.

Nearby, the **Andres Pico Adobe**, the oldest home in San Fernando and second-oldest in the Greater LA area, was built by Mission San Fernando Indians in 1834. After years of disuse, it was purchased and restored in 1930 by the curator of the Southwest Museum, housing the **San Fernando Valley Historical Society**. Just to the northeast are the very different **Nethercutt Museum** and **Nethercutt Collection** (15151 and 15200 Bledsoe Street, Sylmar; tel: 818-367-2251; www.nethercuttcollection. org), two private facilities owned and operated by the Merle Norman Cosmetic Co. They offer the visitor a world-class and sizeable collection of antiques, vintage automobiles, rare musical instruments, and music boxes. Tours of the collection require reservations.

Remains of a eucalyptus tree at Shadow Ranch. The eucalyptus trees here are thought to be the first planted in the state.

Inside Mission San Fernando Rey de España.

Mexican banner inside Andres Pico Adobe, which houses the Mark Harrington Library and is also the headquarters of the San Fernando Valley Historical Society.

Andres Pico Adobe.

DISNEYLAND: THE MAGIC KINGDOM

Despite the great popularity of newer theme parks, there's nothing quite like the original **Disneyland** ❾ (1313 Harbor Boulevard, Anaheim; tel: 714-781-4000; www.disneyland.disney.go.com; hours vary; charge), first opened with the tagline "Magic Kingdom" in 1955. Walt Disney once said that Disneyland grew out of his search for a clean, safe, friendly park where he could take his own daughters.

One of Disney's early designers, John Hench, referred to Walt's knack for putting "little touches of humanity" in everything he did. Hench said that Mickey Mouse's appeal has something to do with his body shape – all circles, all round, harmless and non-threatening. In fact, because of a height restriction – you can't have Mickey towering too much over his

fans – most of the besuited Mouse persons in Disneyland are actually girls.

There's still no successful way to avoid the crowds and the lengthy line-ups, especially in summertime. Obviously, it helps to get there as soon as the gates open and head straight for the most popular rides. To avoid backtracking, cover the park one "land" at a time, including the ever-pleasing and hugely ambitious worlds of Fantasyland, Adventureland, Frontierland, Critter Country, and jazzy New Orleans Square.

The Disney lands

Main Street is the place to get information and maps (City Hall), exchange foreign currency and get money from an ATM, hire a stroller or wheelchair (just inside the main entrance), stash your surplus items in a locker (adjoining Disney Clothiers), and attend to your infant (Baby Center, near the Magic Castle).

Fantasyland is often a favorite for younger children, home to Sleeping Beauty's Castle and rides like the It's a Small World cruise, the 68-horse

King Arthur Carrousel, Mad Tea Party teacups, and miniature circus train that tours Storybook Land. Some of the other rides in Fantasyland, such as Peter Pan's Flight, **Matterhorn**, Mr Toad's Wild Ride, **Snow White's Scary Adventures**, and Alice in Wonderland, seem to be aimed as much at adults. The first two are especially interesting, demonstrating how much illusion owes to darkness and luminous paint.

Fantasyland is also a key place to meet characters. Disney Princess Fantasy Faire offers little ones a chance to meet princesses like Snow White, Aurora, Cinderella, and Mulan. Over in Pixie Hollow, you can snap photos with Tinkerbell and her fairy friends. Then head over near the Pinocchio's Daring Journey ride to meet Rapunzel and Flynn Rider from Disney's Tangled.

Another spot youngsters enjoy is Mickey's Toontown, where you can explore Mickey's House, Minnie's House, Goofy's Playhouse, Donald's Boat, and the Chip 'n' Dale Treehouse.

Adventureland is home to the popular Indiana Jones Adventure, a ride into an ancient temple full of giant snakes and screaming mummies. For a tamer experience, the Jungle Cruise, Tarzan's Treehouse, and the Enchanted Tiki Room are fun options. The tiki room was first visualized as a restaurant, but grew into a major attraction. The audio-animatronics pioneered with the moving, speaking figure of Abraham Lincoln on Main Street culminated in the 225 talking, moving birds, flowers and figures of the **Enchanted Tiki Room**.

In Critter Country, paddle along the Rivers of America in a canoe, then cool off on Splash mountain, a water flume ride that finishes with a five-story plunge.

Frontierland is home to the amusingly hokey Big Thunder Mountain Railroad, the Mark Twain Riverboat, an infrared shooting gallery, Pirate's Lair on Tom Sawyer Island, and a recreated 1880 ranch with a petting zoo. This is also where the pyrotechnic nighttime spectacular **Fantasmic!** takes place, for which crowds start jostling two hours' before it starts to get a good view.

WHERE

South of Encino, west of Interstate 405, lies the Skirball Cultural Center (2701 North Sepulveda Boulevard; tel: 310-440-4500; www.skirball.org; Tue–Fri noon–5pm, Sat–Sun 10am–5pm; charge for museum). Visitors are treated to Jewish historical exhibits, comedic performances, classic films, and world music concerts.

Sleeping Beauty's Castle at Disneyland.

Theme park rides at Disneyland.

Head to Fantasyland and Mickey's Toontown to meet Disney princesses, Mickey and Minnie, Goofy, and Donald Duck.

Try not to miss **New Orleans Square**, with its spooky **Haunted Mansion** and the nearby **Pirates of the Caribbean**. Talking about his cast of 64 humans and 55 animals in Pirates, sculptor Blaine Gibson explained: "In a ride system you have only a few seconds to say something about a figure through your art. So we exaggerate their features, especially their facial features, so they can be quickly and easily understood from a distance... we have to instantly communicate 'good guy' or 'bad guy.' We try to provide the illusion of life."

In addition to the Disneyland Park, you can visit **Disney's California Adventure**, a 55-acre (22-hectare) theme park with a 750-room luxury hotel and a huge shopping, dining, and entertainment center, aptly named the **Downtown Disney District**. Rides like Soarin' Over California, Radiator Springs Racers, and the Twilight Zone Tower of Terror are fun for older kids, along with the thrilling California Screamin' and Grizzly River Run. Littler ones can play games with Woody and Buzz on Toy Story

Pointing the way to Tomorrowland is Astro Orbitor, which has colorful rockets circling a series of moving planets. People pilot their own spaceships as they soar through an animated "astronomical model" of constellations. Tommorowland is also home to one of the park's most famous attractions: the Space Mountain roller coaster. After a thrilling turn on Space Mountain, hop on the Disneyland Railroad or Disneyland Monorail for a relaxing ride.

DISNEYLAND TIPS

Anaheim is best known for its amusement parks and similar attractions, of which Disneyland is by far the most famous and well-attended. If you want to visit Disneyland when there are fewer visitors, come Tuesday to Thursday during mid-September through mid-November, mid-January through mid-March, or mid-April through mid-May.

To save time waiting in line, use Disneyland's free FASTPASS service (subject to availability). These passes save your place in line for Space Mountain, Big Thunder Mountain Railroad, and other popular attractions while you explore the rest of the park.

If you're traveling with children and have two or more adults in your party, you can use the rider swap program that lets you go on the ride while one adult waits with the child. You then "swap" to enable the other adult to enjoy the attraction as well.

If you don't want to drive, MTA bus 460 travels all the way to Disneyland from Los Angeles, as does a train from Union Station. To make the trip more relaxed, you could stay in the Anaheim area overnight. Pushing itself heavily as a convention destination, there's not a lot to see, but it will save traveling. Disneyland itself has pricey but amusing hotels located on its grounds, but there are cheaper motels on surrounding roads; most branches of major hotel chains operate free shuttle buses to the park.

Mania! or dive beneath the waves on The Little Mermaid: Ariel's Undersea Adventure. Tickets can be bought for both parks, although you really need more than one day to visit them.

KNOTT'S BERRY FARM

A few miles north of Disneyland is the 160-acre **Knott's Berry Farm** ❿ (8039 Beach Boulevard, Buena Park; tel: 714-220-5200; hours vary; charge). A recreated 19th-century gold town, Knott's Berry Farm grew out of a roadside snack bar operated by farmer Walter Knott and his wife Cordelia, whose reputation spread far and wide for tasty chicken dinners and slabs of boysenberry pie (served on the couple's wedding china). The oldest theme park in the county, predating its bigger and much more famous rival by a few years, is just as interesting but a little funkier. The characters are more primitive than high-tech and the staff charm tourists with individual attention. The **Ghost Town** offers panning for gold, a stagecoach ride, a watery log ride, and stunt and vaudeville shows.

In the contemporary side of the park, the various other theme areas include stomach-dropping rides such as the 20-story-freefall Supreme Scream. Thrill-seekers will also enjoy GhostRider, Silver Bullet, Xcelerator, and the Sierra Sidewinder, a new spinning coaster. Tributes to Southern California's beach culture include the 13-acre (5-hectare) water park with 17 slides, **Soak City**, and the surf-inspired dual roller coaster, Rip Tide. Meanwhile kids love the cartoon-themed **Camp Snoopy** with its miniature train and other rides. As a tribute to Spanish California, Knott's **Fiesta Village** entices visitors with mariachi bands, ferocious rides like Jaguar! and **Montezooma's Revenge**, as well as scrumptious and reasonably priced tacos, fajitas, and burritos.

You can continue the theme-park theme over dinner at **Medieval Times** in Buena Park (tel: 1-888-935-6878), where hundreds of enthusiastic customers dine every night, egging on pretend knights in jousting battles in a castle-like area while eating with their bare hands.

SHOP

Shopping is a popular pastime in the valley. There are mega-malls like the Sherman Oaks Galleria, which is halfway between Westfield Topanga to the west and Glendale Galleria nearer to LA; also at the western end are Westfield Promenade in Woodland Hills, and Town and Country Shopping Center and Plaza de Oro in the town of Encino. There's also 21-mile (34km) -long Ventura Boulevard, the valley's upscale artery of restaurants and pricey shops.

Scream-inducing ride at Knott's Berry Farm.

HALLOWEEN HAUNT

For over 35 years, Knott's Berry Farm has presented the world's largest (and most famous) theme park Halloween event: the annual Halloween Haunt. From late September to Halloween night, Knott's Berry Farm becomes Knott's Scary Farm, treating fear-lovers to several spooky mazes, where you'll encounter murderous mutants, deadly arachnids, lurking vampires, cursed pirates, and the infamous Grendel.

In addition, you'll see irreverent comedy routines, magic shows, and "psychobilly" concerts. Some might find the experience corny, but it's definitely worth a look. Be aware that Halloween Haunt is a special ticket event (not covered by regular theme park admission and not recommended for young children).

Newport Beach.

Avalon, Santa Catalina Island.

SOUTH BAY AND THE ORANGE COAST

Pristine beaches, ecological preserves, and a Surfing
Walk of Fame are just a few of the coastal
attractions south of Los Angeles.

Driving down the coast from Los Angeles towards San Diego takes a little longer than whizzing down the freeway, but the seaside route along the Pacific Coast Highway ("the PCH") is much more beautiful and interesting. Starting in the South Bay neighborhood of Palos Verdes (still part of Los Angeles County) you explore a string of beach towns – Long Beach, Seal Beach, Huntington Beach, Newport Beach, Laguna Beach – before hitting Del Mar. Along the way, Catalina Island and San Juan Capistrano are delightful detours.

Palos Verdes peninsula

The **Palos Verdes** peninsula is home to magnificent seaside houses as well as more humble natural attractions. Next to a lighthouse, the **Point Vicente Interpretive Center** ❶ (31501 Palos Verdes Drive West; tel: 310-377-5370; daily 10am–5pm; donation requested) includes exhibits focusing on the peninsula's natural and cultural history, such as a relief map showing how mountainous the peninsula's terrain is, an informative whale-watching video, and earphones to hear the whales' mournful voices. Look through telescopes to spot passing whales (December to spring), then pick up a leaflet that identifies plants along the Botanic Trail, or picnic on

the grassy grounds. More nature fun is found at **Abalone Cove** beach, west of Narcissa Drive, which is an ecological preserve perfect for diving and exploring tidepools.

About 2 miles (3km) further on is the wood-and-glass **Wayfarers Chapel** (5755 Palos Verdes Drive; tel: 310-377-1650; daily 10am–5pm), designed by Frank Lloyd Wright's son, Lloyd, whose inspiration is said to have been Northern California's majestic redwood trees. It was built in 1951 as a memorial to the

Posing on the Surfing Walk of Fame, Huntington Beach.

Avocados are grown along the coast from central to south California thanks to the soil type, amount of sunshine, and ocean breeze combining for ideal growing conditions.

18th-century Swedish theologian Emanuel Swedenborg. In the peaceful gardens, songbirds warble and a fountain and stream gurgle. Services are held in the chapel every Sunday.

San Pedro

Eastwards along the coast is **San Pedro**, headquarters of Southern California's fishing fleet, which once distinguished this town as a genuine fishing port. All the authentic old parts of what eons ago was a little fishing town are gone now, replaced by a pseudo construction called **Ports O'Call Village**. It is surprisingly imaginative: several blocks of saltbox-type, apparently weathered New England shops – all in appealing, matching styles. Harbor tours and fishing trips can be taken from here, as well as a classic sailing ship and the *Catalina Express* (tel: 1-800-833-6685; www.

catalinaexpress.com), which sails to Santa Catalina Island.

A few miles south is San Pedro's **Cabrillo Beach ❷**, which has earned a reputation as one of the best places in the area to windsurf. Beginners especially favor the sheltered waters inside the harbor breakwater. Some visitors also relish the nearby Cabrillo Marine Aquarium (3720 Stephen M. White Drive; tel: 310-548-7562; www.cabrillomarine aquarium.org; charge) and elevated coastal trail. Palos Verdes Drive segues into 25th Street, from which a left turn on Gaffey (State Highway 110) and up to Highway 47 over the **Vincent Thomas Bridge** takes you straight ahead through Long Beach on Ocean Boulevard.

Out in the bay take a close look at the palm-fringed island with the tall towers that are illuminated at night: it's actually one of four man-made islands created by a consortium of oil companies to hold (and conceal) all the working oil derricks that tap one of the richest offshore fields in the United States.

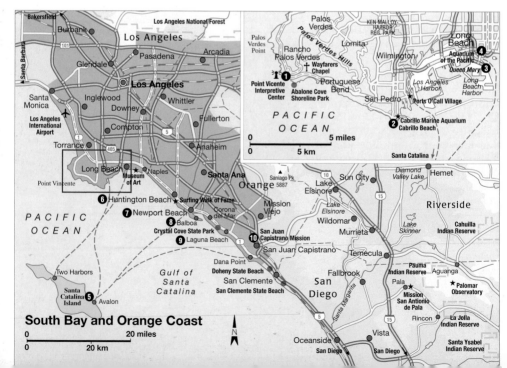

South Bay and Orange Coast

Long Beach

The most famous attraction in the town of **Long Beach** is the wonderful, historic *Queen Mary* ❸ (1126 Queens Highway; tel: 562-435-3511; www.queenmary.com; charge), a retired ocean liner that made 1,001 trips across the Atlantic Ocean since it was launched in 1936. Today the Art Deco halls, restaurants, and lounges have been beautifully restored. Tours are available, as is dinner or a hotel room on the ship itself.

On the Rainbow Harbor across the water from the *Queen Mary* is the **Aquarium of the Pacific** ❹ (100 Aquarium Way; tel: 562-590-3100; daily 9am–6pm; charge). One of the country's best, it houses 11,000 ocean animals representing more than 500 species, from mesmerizing jellyfish to leopard sharks and barracuda.

Art offerings include the local Museum of Art (2300 East Ocean Boulevard; tel: 562-439-2119; www.lbma.org; Thur–Sun 11am–5pm, until 8pm Thur; charge). Long Beach is also well known in particular for its video art and street murals.

One of the most attractive suburbs of Long Beach is **Naples**, with its winding streets, waterside houses, and one-hour **gondola tours** on boats that cruise elegantly along a series of canals.

Santa Catalina Island

A temperate outcrop 26 miles (42km) off the coast, lovely **Santa Catalina Island** ❺ is home to rugged canyons and 54 miles (87km) of coastline. Two-thirds of the scenic island is protected, making it a quiet (and relatively car-free) weekend excursion, though if time is short, it can all be squeezed into one day.

Begin early in the day by taking the *Catalina Express* (tel: 1-800-481-3470) from Long Beach, zipping across to the charming capital of **Avalon** in one hour; with extreme luck you may even spot a whale en route. Ferries also run from San Pedro, Newport Beach, and

The Art Deco casino in Avalon, Santa Catalina Island, is a ballroom and movie theater; despite its name, no gambling takes place.

Retired ocean liner Queen Mary.

Navigating Avalon by golf cart, the main personal transportation on Santa Catalina Island.

Gondola cruise in Naples, a suburb of Long Beach.

Dana Point. The five-minute walk into town passes a couple of places that rent bicycles or the ubiquitous golf carts, which are the main personal transportation on the island.

Head to the far end of the harbor to take the 45-minute inspection of the **Casino, the island's most recognizable landmark**. It achieved national fame more than half a century ago with broadcasts of such famous bands as Count Basie and Kay Kyser playing in the Art Deco ballroom for as many as 6,000 dancers at a time. Built in 1929 at a cost of $2 million, the casino's ground-floor theater with a full-size organ was the first in America to be built especially for the new talking pictures.

Water and island tours can be booked with companies on the pier. A 45-minute trip in a glass-bottomed boat from the **Pleasure Pier** traverses shallow waters filled with multicolored fish (mostly olive or blue with the occasional orange garibaldi) darting in and out of a seaweed "garden." Fronds of kelp sway to the motion of the glass-bottomed boat, and at night little fish are replaced by nocturnal creatures, including "wimpy" lobsters that lack the formidable claws of their Maine cousins.

Inland motor tours often head up through the mountains to the island's airport, where historical pictures and a diorama featuring local animals are displayed. Apart from some flights to San Diego – which offer probably the most spectacular views of the island – the airport is used mostly by a freight company and a few private plane owners. A bus running from Avalon five times daily provides an alternative way to get into the mountains from town.

Motor tours also stop at **El Rancho Escondido**, the Wrigley-owned ranch where Arabian horses are reared, before traversing the old stagecoach route across the island to various ancient Indian sites and secluded bays. The best parts of Catalina are these wilderness areas, popular with campers and hikers. You may even spot a

CATALINA ISLAND

Although "discovered" by Portuguese navigator Don Juan Rodríguez Cabrillo in 1542 and claimed for Spain 60 years later, Catalina was inhabited by Native Americans for thousands of years prior. But within two centuries of the Spaniards' arrival, the Native Americans had been virtually eliminated by Russian hunters searching for sea-otter pelts.

Descendants of General Phineas Banning, who operated the earliest legendary stagecoach routes across the West, once owned most of Catalina Island and began the process of turning it into a tourist resort, building the luxury Hotel St Catherine at Descanso Beach.

Chewing-gum tycoon William Wrigley continued this development when he acquired the island after the great fire of 1915. He built the Hotel Atwater, an aviary, the Casino, and a mansion on Mount Ada (now the Inn on Mount Ada bed and breakfast). The Wrigley family still owns about 11 percent of the island, having donated the remainder to the non-profit Island Conservancy.

Since the Conservancy took over, much of the damage has been repaired. Fauna such as bald eagle, fox, and wild boar have been protected and their numbers expanded. The Catalina gray fox is endemic to the island.

couple of bison – descendants of a herd brought here (and then never taken away) when the movie of Zane Gray's book, *The Vanishing American,* was shot on the island in 1925. The house Grey once owned is now the **Zane Grey Pueblo Hotel**.

Huntington Beach

In busy **Huntington Beach** ❻, slow down to avoid the surfers carrying their boards across the road to white-sand beaches fronting great waves. North and south of the 1,800-ft (540-meter) Huntington Pier is the 3-mile (5km) Huntington City Beach. It and the Huntington State Beach to the south have lifeguards, changing rooms, concessions, and parking. To the north, the Bolsa Chica State Beach is less crowded. Opposite the beach is a hotspot for bird-lovers: the Bolsa Chica Ecological Reserve, where hundreds of species including great blue herons have been spotted in the 1,180-acre (480-hectare) salt marsh.

Many of the communities around here dispute which most deserves the title "Surf City," but Huntington Beach may have the best case: the professional US Open surf competition is held here each July, a **Surfing Walk of Fame** commemorates legendary surfers on Main Street at the Pacific Coast Highway, and the International Surfing Museum (411 Olive Avenue; tel: 714-960-3483; www.surfingmuseum.org; Mon, Wed–Fri noon–5pm, Tue noon–9pm, Sat–Sun 11am–6pm; free) displays classic surfboards and memorabilia.

Newport Beach

In chic **Newport Beach** ❼, the Balboa peninsula's 6 miles (10km) of sandy shore enclose Newport Harbor, home to 10,000 boats, many of them expensive yachts. On Main Street, it's hard to miss the **Balboa Pavilion**, built in 1906 as a railroad terminal, with its distinctive but totally unnecessary steeple. Behind it, you'll find fishing boats unloading their catch early in the morning.

Next to the pavilion is the ferry that makes the three-minute trip from Palm Street to **Balboa Island** ❽. There you can gawk at million-dollar cottages and then shop and relax

Sailboats in Avalon's harbor.

International Surfing Museum, Huntington Beach.

Balboa Pavilion and Newport Harbor.

Harbor Nautical Museum (tel: 949-675-8915; www.nhnm.org; charge), which is great for kids. Almost a dozen luxury beachfront hotels have been built or are under construction along the coast between here and San Diego.

South of Newport, **Corona del Mar** has gorgeous beaches, especially **Corona del Mar State Beach**. There are two reefs for snorkeling, plus volleyball courts, firepits, and restrooms on shore. En route to Laguna Beach, Crystal Cove State Park is a spot for beachgoers, tide-pooling, hiking, and mountain biking.

Laguna Beach and Dana Point

Ten miles south of Newport Beach, **Laguna Beach ❾** is another beautiful coastal community. This oceanside paradise has a decided creative streak. In the early 1900s, the California Plein Air (paintings created outside and not in a studio) art movement began here; today the Laguna Art Museum (307 Cliff Drive; www.lagunaartmuseum.org; charge) displays American art, fine art galleries and jewelry shops fill the streets, and the annual **Pageant of the**

in cafés on Marine Avenue. Former homes of John Wayne and cowboy star Roy Rogers are on nearby islands. From **Balboa Pier**, you see kiteflyers, frisbee-throwers, body-surfers, and sunbathers. Check out the diner at the end of the pier – the original branch of Ruby's – before finishing up at the **Balboa Fun Zone**, with its rides and video arcades, and the **Newport**

Masters – first held in 1932 – presents tableaux of famous paintings with costumed participants each summer.

Before turning inland, the harbor at **Dana Point** is worth a stop to browse in the shops and have a drink in the upstairs bar of the Jolly Roger. Then it's off on Del Obispo Street to Camino Capistrano to visit a historic mission.

San Juan Capistrano

Nicknamed "The Jewel of the Mission" **San Juan Capistrano Mission** ⑩ (26801 Ortega Highway; tel: 949-234-1300; www.missionsjc.com; daily 8.30am–5pm; charge) is seventh in the chain of 21 missions established by Franciscan padres in the 18th and 19th centuries (see page 36).

Father Junípero Serra founded several of the missions, this one included, and his statue stands beside the ruins of the Great Stone Church to the right as you enter. Behind the **Serra Chapel**, which is currently being restored, is the oldest still-in-use church in California. Pick up the free, annotated map, which points out what there is to see here, from the bells to the left of the church

to the location of the famous San Juan Capistrano swallows' nests, during their nesting season.

At the mission's far-left corner, where the tanning vats, metal furnaces, and tallow ovens can still be inspected, is the archeological field office, whose archaeologists still uncover old relics from time to time. The lovely gardens were added during the last century, but the main courtyard itself was always the central focus of the mission. It was also the site of rodeos in the old days, with eager spectators watching from the surrounding roofs, including that of the west wing, which now houses the **Mission Museum**.

San Clemente to Rincon Springs

Just north of the controversial San Onofre Nuclear Generating Station is the town of **San Clemente**. Located 40 miles (65km) north in Yorba Linda, the **Nixon Presidential Library and Museum** (18001 Yorba Linda Boulevard; tel: 714-993-5075; Mon–Sat 10am–5pm,

Taking the Catalina Express ferry from Long Beach. The journey takes one hour and there are departures all year round.

Laguna Beach.

Visitors can snorkel, surf, dive, and spot marine life in tidepools at Laguna Beach, whose coast has been designated a Marine Protected Area (MPA).

Sun 11am–5pm; charge) chronicles the life and times of the former US president, who operated his western White House from San Clemente. San Clemente and Doheny state beaches allow camping for a small fee.

An interesting drive inland is along State Highway 76 (near Oceanside) to the village of **Pala**. The village is notable for the Mission San Antonio de Pala, an *asistancia* (extension mission) built in 1816. Located on the Pala Indian Reservation, it is the only California mission still serving Indians and has celebrated its Corpus Christi Festival, with an open-air mass, dances, and games, on the first Sunday of every June since 1816.

The road continues southeast to **Rincon Springs**, a community to the north of Escondido on Road S6, and the gateway to **Palomar Mountain**. Rising 5,500ft (1,700 meters) above sea level and stretching for some 20 miles (32km), this is the home of the Hale Telescope and the Oschin Telescope, contained inside **Palomar Observatory** (Palomar Mountain, at the end of the S6 Road; tel: 760-742-2119; www.astro.caltech.edu/palomar; daily 9am–3pm, until 4pm in summer; charge), which is owned and operated by the **California Institute of Technology**. Public tours (May–Oct Sat–Sun 11am and 1pm; charge) cover the history and scientific research of the observatory. Check the latest information before you set out as the observatory is closed in poor weather and hazardous travel conditions.

Off State Highway 76, you can catch Interstate 15 south towards San Diego.

SAN JUAN CAPISTRANO SWALLOWS

The famous cliff swallows of San Juan Capistrano historically arrived at the mission on or around March 19th, St Joseph's day, when they were greeted with a festival. "Scout swallows" tip off their return, arriving a few days before the rest of the flock. Come autumn, they would leave the mission on or near the Day of San Juan, October 23rd, flying 6,000 miles (10,000km) south to winter in Argentina.

Legend has it that the swallows first came to the mission seeking safety after a shopkeeper destroyed their gourd-shaped mud nests. Now their protection is guaranteed: The city prohibits destroying their nests, both in the church ruins and elsewhere in the Capistrano Valley.

While an innkeeper may have driven the swallows to the mission, they likely stayed because of the mission's location near two rivers, which provided plenty of insects for the swallows to feast on.

The swallows became truly famous after Leon Rene recorded "When the Swallows Come Back to Capistrano" in 1940. The hit song was also later recorded by Glenn Miller and Pat Boone.

Today, many of the swallows have relocated farther from town, a result of the area's development, which has reduced the number of insects in the area. Still, the town and Mission celebrate their return each year with a festival and Swallows Day Parade (www.swallows parade.com).

Mesquite Dunes, in the Stovepipe
Wells area of Death Valley.

Mormon Point in Death Valley.

THE DESERTS

California's deserts attract those seeking extremes: the striking rock formations of Joshua Tree National Park, a bouyant sea, and the desolate landscapes of the Mojave and Death Valley are some of the deserts' highlights.

California's deserts feature some of the state's most unusual and uniquely stunning landscapes. The 800,000-acre (300,000-hectare) Joshua Tree National Park is a Dr Seuss-like landscape of twisted trees, granite monoliths, and rugged canyons. The Anza-Borrego Desert State Park is renowned for its deluge of bright wildflowers every spring, and the buoyant Salton Sea for its ability to make everything float more easily. Colored sandstone towers and limestone spires punctuate the Mojave Desert, while Death Valley is home to the jagged Devil's Golf Course and an extinct volcano. Compared to all this desolation, the luxury spa resorts of Palm Springs are a veritable oasis, and make an easy entry into California's desert regions.

From LA to Palm Springs

The San Bernardino freeway, then the I-10, will bring you to Palm Springs (population 50,400) from Los Angles in just under three hours, but the Pomona Freeway (the continuation of the Santa Monica Freeway) is an alternative route, which takes you closer to the city of **Riverside ❶**.

Architect Charles Moore once observed that if you could see only one building in Southern California, downtown **Riverside's Mission Inn**

Riding at Cottonwood Canyon Ranch, near Palm Springs.

(3649 Mission Inn Avenue; tel: 951-784-0300; www.missioninn.com; free 75-minute tours) should be it.

Opened in 1903, the grand hotel catered to Riverside's influx of wealthy residents and visitors: by the 1890s, Riverside had become the richest city per capita in the country. Albert Einstein, Henry Ford, Susan B. Anthony, Sarah Bernhardt, and Joseph Pulitzer are just a few of the dozens of celebrities who have visited the inn, along with political visitors have included Richard and Pat Nixon, who

Main Attractions
Palm Springs Aerial Tramway
Joshua Tree National Park
Anza-Borrego Desert State Par
Salton Sea
Lake Havasu
Mount Whitney
Devil's Golf Course
Scotty's Castle

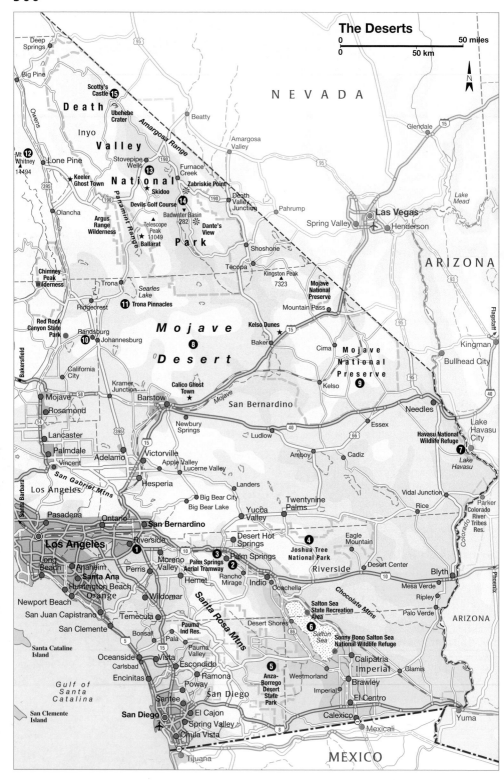

The Deserts

0   50 miles
0   50 km

NEVADA

ARIZONA

MÉXICO

held their wedding party in the hotel, and Ronald and Nancy Reagan, who chose it for their honeymoon.

The beautiful hotel, complete with gargoyles, flying buttresses, and spiral staircases, was reopened in 1992 after a seven-year renovation that preserved its Tiffany stained-glass windows, the gold-leaf altar from a 17th-century Mexican church, a 120-year-old Steinway piano, and the special chair built to accommodate one overweight visitor, President William Howard Taft.

A few miles east of Riverside, State Highway 60 joins Interstate 10. Just beyond that, giant model dinosaurs tower 30ft (9 meters) above the highway at Cabazon truck stop; you can stop at the Wheel Inn on the left of the freeway to get a closer look. From this point, the hillsides become covered with row after row of state-of-the-art steel wind turbines for the generation of electric power.

Palm Springs

From Interstate 10, turn onto State Highway 111 to enter the affluent town of **Palm Springs** ❷, where stressed-out Angelenos come on weekends to indulge in golf, spas, and pampering. **Indian Canyon Drive** and the aptly named **Palm Canyon Drive** are the parallel main streets around which the town is structured. Follow the latter to see the charming **Village Green Heritage Center** (tel: 760-323-8297), with **its** restored adobe, a handful of 1800s buildings, and a recreated general store from the 1930s.

Other cultural attractions include the **Palm Springs Art Museum** (101 Museum Drive; tel: 760-322-4800; www.psmuseum.org; Tue–Wed and Fri–Sun 10am–5pm, Thur noon–8pm; charge), with its contemporary paintings and sculpture, Meso-American art, miniatures, and celebrity photographs.

Nature lovers will love the city's **Moorten Botanical Garden** (1701 South Palm Canyon Drive; tel: 760-327-6555; www.moortengarden. com; charge). The attractive "living museum" established in 1938 is home to giant cacti, desert plants, flowers, and shaded nature trails.

WHERE

A half-hour southeast of Riverside, between Interstates 15 and 215, the Perris Valley airport is a lift-off point for hot-air balloonists, and, at Perris Valley Skydiving, would-be parachutists can take a training course that concludes with an actual jump. For people who can't decide, there's even an option to parachute out of a hot-air balloon.

Wedding party at Mission Inn.

Variety of cacti at Moorten Botanical Garden.

If you're tired of cooling off in your hotel's pool, join the younger crowd at the seasonal **Knott's Soak City** water park (1500 Gene Autry Trail; tel: 760-327-0499; www.soakcityps.com; 10am–5pm; charge) to enjoy water slides, a lazy river, and a wave pool.

Coachella Valley

Just north of the city is the **Palm Springs Aerial Tramway ❸** (One Tramway Road; tel: 1-888-515-8726; www.pstramway.com; Mon–Fri 10am–8pm, Sat–Sun 8am–9pm; charge), where an awesome 10-minute ride pulls you up the sheer cliffs of Chino Canyon to a 8,516ft (2,596meter) peak of the **San Jacinto Mountains. The views are** magnificent!

The 200-sq-mile (518-sq-km) Coachella Valley below is huge enough to accommodate 10 cities and a wildlife preserve, whose star is a rare lizard whose "fringe toes" allow it to swim through the sand as readily as a fish in water.

As might be imagined, the area abounds in luxury resorts, many of whose guest registers are a litany of famous names. The **La Quinta Resort**

and Club (tel: 1-800-598-3828), for example, is where Frank Capra checked in to polish the movie script of *Lost Horizon* and Irving Berlin composed *White Christmas*, a song all the more poignant perhaps due to the hot sunshine outside. Renovations uncovered sketches on the lobby's high ceilings by artist Diego Rivera.

If you don't have time to explore the real thing, **The Living Desert** (47900 Portola Avenue, Palm Desert; tel: 760-346-5694; www.livingdesert.org; charge) can give you a quick taste of the region's desert wilderness. Located 15 miles (24km) southeast of Palm Springs, the nature park is filled with eagles, irresistible exotic animals such as zebras, gazelles, and lovable meerkats, along with desert shrubs, flowers, and cacti.

Joshua Tree National Park

Head north from Palm Springs on **Indian Canyon Drive** (which becomes Indian Avenue) to pass the city of **Desert Hot Springs** and eventually reach the **Joshua Tree National Park ❹** (tel: 760-367-5500; www.nps.gov/jotr; charge). Established in 1936,

the vast parkland is filled with strange rock formations, fascinating flora and fauna, and the tall, fibrous plants after which it is named (Mormon explorers named the plant in 1851). However, it's unlikely you'll see any of the mostly nocturnal animals – kangaroo rats, rattlesnakes – other than the occasional coyote and lizard, unless you stay overnight in one of the camping grounds.

The easiest way to visit this area, the similarly unspoiled Santa Rosa Mountains, and the Indian Canyons with their cool palm oases, is with one of the local adventure tour companies. Among the places they visit, **Indian Canyons** (tel: 760-325-3400; charge) are rich in flora and fauna. Hawks and bald eagles circle overhead; tiny kangaroo rats and fleet-footed bighorn sheep can occasionally be seen on the slopes. **Palm** and **Andreas canyons** have the largest stands of palm trees in the world.

Anza-Borrego Desert State Park

The 600,000-acre (200,000-hectare) **Anza-Borrego Desert State Park ❺**

(tel: 760-767-5311) is the state's largest park. Its numerous canyons and gullies are easily accessible by car. Camping is permitted in the park, which is populated by jackrabbits, coyotes, kangaroo rats, and lizards, as well as more than 150 species of birds. The vegetation is equally varied, ranging from junipers and pines growing at the 5,000ft (1,500-meter) level to palm trees at sea level. A 3-mile (5km) hike from Campfire Center to Palm Grove reveals plants used by the Cahuilla Indians for medicines, dyes, and food.

Wildflowers in Joshua Tree National Park. Depending on autumn and winter rainfall levels and spring temperatures, wildflowers may begin blooming in February, but March and April are usually the best months to see them.

Palm Springs Aerial Tramway.

The Joshua Tree is a member of the Agave family, and produces white-green flowers in spring if conditions are suitable. It is thought that Mormon migrants named the tree after the Biblical figure Joshua, seeing the tree's branches as similar to limbs stretching out, guiding the travelers.

Hiking the Boy Scout trail in Joshua Tree National Park.

Indio and the Salton Sea

The town of **Indio**, on Interstate 10 about 10 miles (16km) east, has been popular with tourists since 1921 when it began staging its annual National Date Festival (tel: 760-863 8247). The week-long celebration in February includes an Arabian Nights pageant, and ostrich and camel racing. South of Indio and north of the Salton Sea is **Lake Cahuilla** (tel: 760-564-4712; charge). The lake is stocked with rainbow trout, striped bass and catfish. For non-anglers, there are hiking and equestrian trails, shady picnic spots, campsites, and a children's play area on the sandy beach – away from the fishermen.

The **Salton Sea** ❻, 35 miles (56km) long and 9 to 15 miles (14 to 24km) wide was, in fact, all a big mistake. In 1905 engineers attempted to divert some of the Colorado River to the Imperial Valley, but the river changed course and reflooded the ancient Salton Basin, 235ft (72 meters) below sea level. This formed a sea of 360 sq miles (932 sq km) with royal blue water filling the area where the Coachella and Imperial valleys merge. The sea's saltiness creates unusually high buoyancy that water skiers and swimmers particularly enjoy. The salt waters also provide a habitat for salt-water game fish. Adjoining marsh-lands are a refuge for bird-watchers.

The Salton Sea State Recreation Area is an 18,000-acre (7,300-hectare) park with both developed and primitive campsites. There is a Bird Watch and Nature Trail (tel: 760-393-3059) and, 26 miles (42km) away on State Highway 86, a boat basin at Varner Harbor (currently closed), where geology buffs often have a field day with ancient shorelines and layers of marine fossils visible along the base of the Santa Rosa Mountains.

Yuma, Arizona, and Lake Havasu

About 58 miles (93km) due east of the city of El Centro is **Yuma**, Arizona, a desert town built on the banks of the Colorado River where it enters Mexican territory. The Colorado forms the entire eastern border of Southern California from Mexico to Nevada. Several dams built across it have created reservoirs while also providing hydroelectric power for the metropolises of Los Angeles and San Diego.

Lake Havasu ❼ (tel: 928-855-4115), 46 miles (74km) long, and no more than 3 miles (5km) wide, is the reservoir trapped behind Parker Dam. Those who don't want to drink the water enjoy playing in it. Along Arizona State Highway 95 between Parker and Lake Havasu City are recreational-vehicle parks, marinas, and campgrounds with room for tens of thousands of visitors. Everyone, from water sportsmen and outboard boaters to yachtsmen, water skiers, and sailboarders, love the lake. There's fishing for bass, bluegills, and crappies. Small game populates the rugged southeastern (Arizona) shore of the lake that constitutes Lake Havasu

State Park. Birds are everywhere, and the entire body of water is contained within the **Havasu National Wildlife Refuge** (tel: 760-326-3853).

Lake Havasu City, nonexistent as recently as the late 1960s, has exploded into a resort center of over 56,000 residents, and has become a popular vacation spot for collegiate types at spring break. Developed by the late millionaire Robert P. McCulloch Sr., its most famous landmark is the original **London Bridge**. (A popular story is that McCulloch thought he was buying the more decorative Tower Bridge.) The bridge was shipped in pieces to the US, then trucked to the "British town" the tycoon created at its feet.

The Mojave Desert

The **Mojave Desert** ❽ (named after a Southwestern native tribe, and pronounced "mo-hahv-ee") lies between US 395 and Interstate 40, adjoining the Nevada state border. Great, brightly colored columns of sandstone rise off the desert floor on either side of the highway: sculpted towers in the foothills of the eastern Sierras. Today

the desert is relatively little-explored, despite its geological importance. On weekends, state rangers give guided nature walks and facilities include picnic tables and about 50 primitive campsites for tents and recreational vehicles. Visitors must bring their own food and water.

The gateway to the **Mojave Desert** is the small town of Mojave, at the junction of State Highways 14 and 58. From borax to the B-1 bomber, it has seen more history than places many times its size. Near Edwards Air Force Base, Mojave was part of the Antelope Valley aerospace boom, serving as a temporary community for the aerospace workers, as well as those employed in agriculture and railroads. The winter season is its busiest time, when weekend skiers, heading to and from Sierra slopes, pack the motels and roadside cafés.

East of Mojave, near the town of **Barstow**, paleontologists are still carrying on the work of the late Dr. Louis Leakey, the leader of a team of eminent scientists who believed they had found a prehistoric "tool factory" estimated

Aerial view of Yuma.

England's original London Bridge, at Lake Havasu City.

to be some 200,000 years old. The so-called **Calico Early Man Site** (www.blm.gov/ca/st/en/fo/barstow/calico.html) is open for public viewing, with guided tours some days of the week. Arrangements can be made with the Federal Bureau of Land Management office (tel: 760-252-6000) in Barstow, a bustling desert town, which is largely the suburb of a military community. Situated at the junction of Interstates 15 and 40, it has a 5-mile (8km) stretch of motels, gas stations, and grocery stores that makes it a very good base for stocking up.

Near **Barstow**, you can also explore the **Calico Ghost Town. The town of Calico** was established by silver miners in the 1880s. Today, it is half history and half Hollywood; the town was restored by LA's Walter Knott of Knott's Berry Farm fame. Part authentic mining town, part theme park, it's fun to discover which is real and which is whimsy, and visitors can explore mining tunnels, ride the ore train, and browse in old-fashioned dry-goods shops.

Continuing east on Interstate 15 or 40 brings you to the 1.6 million-acre (650,000-hectare) **Mojave National Preserve** ❾ (www.nps.gov/moja). The scenic Kelbaker Road, a 56-mile (90km) paved road, connects the town of Baker on the I-15 and Ludlow on the I-40. Kelso Depot, 34 miles (55km) south of Baker, is the park's main information center. A further 7 miles (11km) from Baker are the impressive Kelso Dunes, standing about 600ft (200 meters) high and covering 45 sq miles (120 sq km). Other top attractions include the 1,500ft (460-meter)-high Cima Dome (reach it via the paved Cima Road from the I-15), which passes through the world's largest, densest Joshua tree forests.

Red Rock Canyon State Park and Randsburg

An alternative to heading east to explore the **Mojave National Preserve** is to head north. About 25

THE CAHUILLA TRIBE

The Cahuilla Indians survived in the hostile desert region not only because of their knowledge of desert plants and animals, but also because of the curing techniques of their shamans, or medicine men.

Among the Cahuilla, as with other Native Americans, shamans – "technicians of the sacred" – were believed to possess supernatural powers and mediated between the world of mortals and the world of spirits. Because they employed both plant remedies (which have enriched medicine ever since) and sacred power, they occupied a more prominent place in the community than doctors do in modern society. They gave advice on political decisions, cured diseases, and searched nature for signs from the spirit world.

The origin and meaning of the word Cahuilla is unknown: "master" (in both mental and physical strength) has been suggested. Their territory ranges from valleys as high as 5,000ft (1,500 meters) altitude, in the Santa Rosa Mountains, to the desert around the Salton Sea, 200ft (60 meters) below sea level. South of Palm Springs, the tribe still owns the five Indian Canyons in which their villages used to sit. There are still some traces of house foundations, ditches, and dams.

miles (40km) north of Mojave along Highway 14 is **Red Rock Canyon State Park** (tel: 661-942-0662). Here, in the middle of the 19th century, prospectors discovered gold nuggets on the surface of dry stream beds, prompting a mini-boom that removed about $16 million worth of ore, including one 5lb (2.27kg) nugget.

   Nearby is **Randsburg ⑩**, a 19th-century ghost town that is still home to a tiny community, about 20 miles (32km) east of Red Rock Canyon on US 395. Named after one of the gold towns of South Africa, Randsburg struck it rich three times between 1895 and 1947, first with gold, then with silver, and finally with tungsten. After its discovery late in the 19th century, the Yellow Aster mine yielded $20 million in gold before it was exhausted. Turn-of-the-20th century Randsburg was as wild and wooly as any Western boomtown, with saloons and dance halls, scoundrels and rogues.

   Among the ramshackle remains of the original wood-and-corrugated-iron buildings on Randsburg's main street today is the **Desert Museum** (open weekends only), with its collection of mining and geological artifacts. Also open are the town saloon, dance hall, and barber shop, which have been quaintly converted into shops offering rocks, bottles, and mining curios. At the **Randsburg General Store**, wayfarers can sip a chocolate soda at the same swivel-chaired soda fountain that was hauled into town by mules over a century ago.

China Lake and the Trona Pinnacles

China Lake is a dry basin near Ridgecrest off US 395. It is best known as the focus of the important China Lake Naval Air Warfare Center. Near the main gate of the naval station is the small **Maturango Museum** (tel: 760-375 6900; daily 10am–5pm; charge). The museum occasionally conducts field trips to study Native American rock inscriptions found nearby, possibly the best such collection in the state. As a result of the discoveries made at China Lake, some scientists are tempted to say that humans migrated from Asia at least

Beachfront hotel at Lake Havasu City, Arizona.

*View from Amboy
Road, which runs
through the landscape
between Mojave
National Preserve and
Joshua Tree National
Park.*

40,000 years ago, perhaps even 100,000 years ago.

Not far from China Lake, near the banks of the equally dry Searles Lake, are the **Trona Pinnacles** ⑪. This great pincushion of ancient limestone columns in the middle of the Mojave Desert is both rare and bizarre. The spooky stone spires are "national natural landmarks," probably the most outstanding examples of tufa formations in North America, and a challenging moonscape to explore for hikers and rock climbers. The Trona Pinnacles are situated on the west side of bleakly awesome **Searles Lake**, access to which is via State Highway 178 north from **Johannesburg**. Camping is permitted at the Pinnacles. Ninety-four miles (151km) north of Johannesburg on US 395 is **Lone Pine**, a picturesque village that has been a popular location for Hollywood Westerns.

Mount Whitney

From here, **Mount Whitney** ⑫, at 14,494ft (4,418 meters) the highest peak in the continental United States, is accessible, although it's an 11-mile (18km) challenge from the end of

Whitney Portal Road to reach the summit. After the climb, a good place for a break is **Keeler**, a ghost town about 10 miles (16km) from Lone Pine. About 50 miles (80km) to the east, beyond Towne Pass, State Highway 190 runs into the Panamint Mountains, some of whose rugged canyons bustled with people and activity in 1873.

The town of **Panamint**, now abandoned, came into being when the robbers of a Wells Fargo express discovered silver while hiding out in **Surprise Canyon**. Persuading two state senators to make a deal with the express company in return for part ownership of the lode, they presided over an instant boomtown with stores, saloons, boarding houses, and banks, all along a main street that occupied the entire width of the narrow canyon. Within a year, the boom was over, but the canny miners cast their silver in the form of 700lb (318kg) cannon balls, a burden too heavy for robbers to carry away.

Indian Ranch Road, an unpaved track off the Trona–Wildrose road and which forks off up Surprise Canyon, continues down to **Ballarat**. Only

crumbling adobe walls and ruined shacks remain here of what was once an important supply town for the miners, to which the stagecoach used to run all the way from Johannesburg.

Another deserted mining town, off Emigrant Canyon Road, is **Skidoo**. Its name was derived from the phrase "23 Skidoo," it having been 23 miles (37km) from Telescope Peak. Skidoo is famous for its "million-dollar slope," from which $1 million in gold ore was taken early in the 20th century: "it could be scraped out in wheelbarrows," boasted its former owner.

But Skidoo has gone down in legend more than this as "the town that hanged its killer twice," after an incident in which a drunken saloon keeper killed a popular town banker. Skidoo's citizens were wary of what kind of justice might be administered from the nearest lawmen at Lone Pine, so they took it upon themselves to promptly hang the killer. The next day, when a reporter from the big-city *Los Angeles Herald* arrived, they dug up the body and hanged it again so the newsman could get a picture.

Death Valley

Death Valley National Park 🔞 (www.nps.gov/deva/index.html) was first established as a national monument in 1933. Its namesake 120-mile long (193-km) valley is the result of a geological phenomenon. At least 5 million years ago, the deep gap between the Panamint and Funeral mountains was formed by earthquakes and the folding of the earth's crust. This created, technically, not a valley but what geologists tend to call a graben.

Coyote in Death Valley. Despite seeming like an unlikely environment for life to flourish, the National Park supports 51 species of native mammals, 36 reptile species, three amphibian species, and 307 species of birds.

SURVIVAL IN THE DESERT

The first settlers who wandered into Death Valley in 1849 found the name to be unfortunately true, but travel these days is infinitely easier and safer, with well-supervised roads and accommodations (including two inns and a luxury resort). Autumn through spring, the climate is ideal for exploring, with daytime temperatures in the 60s and 70s Fahrenheit (about 16–26°C), although it is chillier at night. Summer temperatures (May–Oct) are exceeded only in the Sahara: the July average daily high is 116°F (47°C). It commonly soars past 120°F (49°C), and once hit a national high of 134°F (57°C). It is quite literally life-threatening to remain under the desert sun for too long.

The vast Mojave covers roughly the combined area of the states of Massachusetts, Rhode Island, and Connecticut. It's easy to get lost and, with conventional vehicles, even to get stranded off the main roads. Take adequate provisions, and adequate precautions. Have your car checked out thoroughly before setting off, paying particular attention to the tires and any problems concerning overheating. Pack food, water, and sunscreen, for use even while in the car (do not make the journey in a convertible), and try to let someone know your route and expected arrival time. If you have car trouble, rangers suggest you wait where you are: do not wander off to look for help.

Alternate Energy

California is at the forefront in researching and implementing alternative forms of energy.

In the 1970s, tax credits helped establish a new wind and solar industry. Wind turbines began snaking along California hills, particularly on the Altamont Pass near San Francisco, Tehachapi Pass near Bakersfield, and San Gorgonio Pass near Palm Springs.

The early experiments with solar energy in the Mojave Desert known as Solar Two (which closed in the late 1990s) used hundreds of giant mirrors to concentrate the sun's rays on a 300ft (90-meter) tower and heat, to a temperature of 1,050°F (566°C), a molten nitrate salt stored in an insulated tank. When needed, the molten salt – a yellowish syrup that retains heat better than water or oil – will convert water into the steam required to power a turbine generator.

California's alternate energy industry really gained momentum after the deregulation of the electric utilities in 1998, after which the California

Wind turbines near Palm Springs.

Energy Commission launched a new Renewable Energy Program. Following a decade of legislation pushing for renewable energy laws, real change can now be seen. In 2009, 11.6 percent of California's electricity was coming from renewable resources such as wind, solar, geothermal, biomass, and small hydroelectric facilities; an additional 9.2 percent came from large hydro plants. Other energy sources are also being explored. California has the largest geothermal generating capacity in the country, biomass plants produced 2.1 percent of the state's electricity in 2007, and ocean energy projects are being explored.

Making it law

In 2011, California Governor Jerry Brown signed into law the country's most ambitious renewable energy mandate: by the end of 2020, state utilities need to obtain one-third of their power from renewable energy sources such as solar panels and wind turbines. All three of the state's major investor-owned utilities – Southern California Edison, Pacific Gas and Electric, and Sempra's San Diego and Electric – currently will need to meet these goals or else pay hefty fines. The main hurdles may be in getting renewable projects built: development can be delayed, permits are hard to obtain, and legal opposition from local residents is expensive.

Some of the mature renewable energy sources, however, are getting cheaper. The Electric Power Research Institute reports that the cost of producing wind energy has decreased four-fold since 1980. On the solar front, over 30 large solar thermal power plants have been proposed in California's deserts.

The state is encouraging residents to participate in this renewable energy initiative as well: the California Energy Commission and the California Public Utilities Commission have teamed up to run the Go Solar California! program, which encourages Californians to install solar energy systems on homes and businesses, through rebates and tax credits.

The environment is extremely marsh, yet about 900 different species of plant grow in the national park. In many ways, Death Valley's human population of 200 or so seems just as indomitable, enduring terrific heat and isolation. However, the growth of Las Vegas, Nevada, 140 miles (225km) away, inspired the development of the town of Pahrump. It's now only a 60-mile (97km) drive from Death Valley to the nearest big grocery store.

Today the valley's fearsome reputation seems to attract as many as it intimidates. Winter or summer, sightseers, hikers, and amateur naturalists come to scramble up the sand dunes near **Stovepipe Wells**. They also want to marvel at the views, study old mines and abandoned charcoal kilns, explore old ghost towns, and snap scores of pictures at sites such as humble **Badwater**, 282ft (86 meters) below sea level, the lowest spot in North America, and throughout the park.

Years ago, it was traditional for all concessions to close down in the summer, but the tourists kept on coming. Nowadays, in the town of **Furnace Creek,** the **Furnace Creek Ranch** and the nearby **Stovepipe Wells Village** complex stay open throughout the year, and neither is ever empty. Tour groups also arrive in the white-hot summer months from Las Vegas, albeit sheltered from the worst elements by desert-tough, air-conditioned vehicles.

Furnace Creek is a good focal point for a visit to Death Valley. Located not far from Badwater, its **Visitor Center** (tel: 760-786 2331; admission charge for park) is open daily all year round. Although Furnace Creek Ranch's 18-hole golf course is said to be the lowest course on earth, nobody would hire a caddy for the valley's other "links," the so-called **Devil's Golf Course** ⓮, an otherworldly expanse of rugged salt crystals that point to the sky in jagged little edges. It lies between the former sites of the Eagle Borax mill, southwest of Badwater, and the Harmony Borax Works, just north of Furnace Creek, where the former workers' quarters were developed into a resort. At the **Harmony Borax Works**, an old

TIP

Native Americans have moved into the gaming business with enthusiasm. Tribes formed partnerships with MGM Mirage and Donald Trump that created lavish casinos in downtown Palm Springs and elsewhere, to rival those in Las Vegas. Las Vegas, of course, isn't too far: only a two-hour drive from the Mojave National Preserve, or less than five hours by car from Palm Springs.

Devil's Golf Course, Death Valley.

Rhyolite Ghost town, Death Valley, deserted in 1916.

Scotty's Castle.

located southeast of Furnace Creek in the Black Mountains near interesting **Twenty Mule Team Canyon**; **Artists Drive** and the **Golden Canyon**, with its vivid displays of color among old outcroppings; and empty **Ubehebe Crater**, an extinct volcano nearly 2,000 years old at the north end of the national park.

Near Ubehebe Crater is the 25-room Death Valley Ranch, also known as **Scotty's Castle ⓯** (tel: 760-786 2392; daily; charge), a $2 million palace that is a facsimile of a Spanish-Mediterranean villa. Death Valley's biggest visitor attraction, Scotty's Castle is operated by the National Park Service, which runs hourly tours. Work on the castle began in 1926, at the foot of a natural spring-fed canyon at an elevation of 3,000ft (900 meters). About 2,000 hard-working men assembled the castle, completing it in 1931, all at the expense of a young, enthusiastic Chicago millionaire by the name of Albert Johnson. Today Scotty's Castle contains beautiful continental furnishings and objets d'art.

cleanser-processing plant has been stabilized to show interested visitors the now very primitive 19th-century manufacturing methods.

Overlooking Badwater to the east is **Dante's View** (5,475ft/1,669 meters) and, in the west, **Telescope Peak**, the highest point in the Panamint Range (11,049ft/3,368 meters).

Among Death Valley's other natural beauty spots are **Zabriskie Point**, made famous by a 1960s movie and

SCOTTY'S CASTLE

Touring the grounds of Scotty's Castle, Death Valley's biggest visitor attraction, visitors might well wonder how such a villa came to be in the desert, and who was Scotty?

Its builder was Chicago millionaire Albert Johnson, who had been charmed into investing thousands of dollars in a fruitless search for gold by an affable roustabout named Walter Scott, popularly known as "Death Valley Scotty."

After years of waiting, Johnson's patience ran out, but not before he had grown so fond of Death Valley that he decided to build a summer retreat there.

The Chicago financier and his wife lived on and off at the castle for many years until his death in 1948. "Death Valley Scotty," the good-natured rogue, also lived nearby; his grave lies along a trail just behind the castle.

Surfers heading for Ocean Beach, San Diego.

Balboa Park, San Diego.

SAN DIEGO

Beautiful beaches, a world-class zoo, museum-filled Balboa Park, and the trendy Gaslamp Quarter help attract families, surfers, and culture-hounds to sunny and relaxed San Diego, the state's second-largest city.

Home to 77 miles (124km) of beautiful Pacific coastline, the busy, elegant harbor town of San Diego is the state's birthplace. It was here, in what is now the historic Old Town, that a group of Europeans first settled in 1769; today the city has a population of 1.3 million, second only to Los Angeles.

Twenty-first-century **San Diego** ❶ is a vibrantly modern and evolving city, with a growing roster of cultural attractions in the 1200-acre (490-hectare) Balboa Park and a revitalized Gaslamp Quarter with a hip shopping and nightlife scene. Active travellers love the city for its surfing, diving, and hang-gliding opportunities, and families come to explore SeaWorld, nearby Legoland, and the world-class San Diego Zoo.

Old Town

The six-block **Old Town** ❶ area (bounded by Juan, Twiggs, Congress, and Wallace streets) is where the town's original pueblo once stood. Now you'll find old adobes, restored Victorian homes, open-air stands, museums, and charming patio restaurants. Mariachi groups entertain in the Bazaar del Mundo, a Spanish-style plaza flanked by craft shops and Mexican restaurants.

Of special historical interest are the Thomas **Whaley House Museum** – possibly Southern California's first

two-story brick home and one of America's allegedly most haunted houses – and the **Robinson-Rose house.** The latter once housed law and railroad offices, and now serves as the Old Town State Historic Park Visitor Center (4002 Wallace Street; tel: 619-220-5422; www.parks.ca.gov). Stop in to pick up detailed maps including the neighborhood's historic attractions.

Presidio Hill

Up the hill from Old Town's historic center, **Presidio Hill** and its

Main Attractions
Old Town
SeaWorld
Balboa Park
Timken Museum of Art
San Diego Zoo
Hotel del Coronado
La Jolla

San Diego has numerous surf schools.

Mission San Diego de Alcalá.

sprawling park are an historic oasis in a sea of traffic (Interstates 5 and 8 are just to the west and north). Here Father Junípero Serra conducted a mass on July 16, 1769, dedicating first the Mission San Diego de Alcalá and then the military settlement that surrounded and protected it.

In 1774, the mission was moved from the hill to its present site in Mission Valley (10818 San Diego Mission Road; tel: 619-281-8449; www.missionsandiego.com; daily; donations accepted), where you can view original records in Father Serra's handwriting.

Take the curving road east of the Old Town to see, on the hillside, the elegant Junípero **Serra Museum** (2727 Presidio Drive; tel: 619-297-3258; www.sandiegohistory.org; daily; charge), which displays documents of early

California life. It looks like a mission, but was actually built in 1929.

Mission Bay and SeaWorld

The 4,600-acre (1,900-hectare) **Mission Bay** area combines parkland, beaches and inner lagoons with extensive outdoor leisure activities. Located here is the 189-acre (76-hectare) **SeaWorld** Ⓑ (500 SeaWorld Drive; tel: 619-226-3901; daily, hours vary by season; charge), one of the world's largest marine parks, filled with aquariums, live-animal shows, and rides. The most famous animals in the park are the orca whales that perform in an elaborate synchronized show; for good seats, arrive a half-hour early. Other popular attractions are the bottlenose dolphin shows, sharks, polar bears, and 300 penguins. On a hot day the Shipwreck Rapids ride will cool you off.

South of the channel leading into Mission Bay is **Ocean Beach.** To the north of Mission Beach is **Pacific Beach**, where activities center around Crystal Pier and the area along Mission Boulevard and up Garnet Avenue, and where locals shop and dine. The

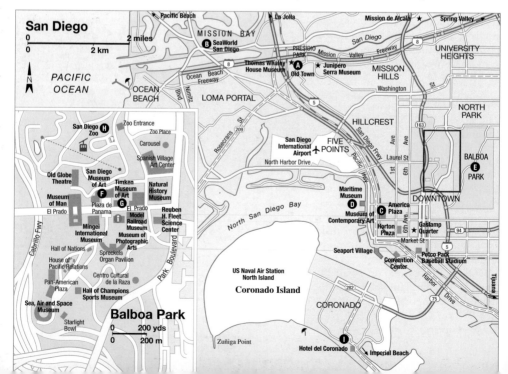

beaches are a great draw most of the year, but there are wonderful beaches along most of this coast – 25 miles (40km) of them in an unbroken line between Del Mar and Oceanside.

Downtown San Diego

Towards the top end of the vast bay discovered by Cabrillo is downtown San Diego. A complex adjoining what was formerly the Santa Fe railroad station now consists of the 34-story **One America Plaza** tower, a hotel, and the downtown branch of the **San Diego Museum of Contemporary Art**  (1001 Kettner Boulevard; tel: 619-234 1001; Tue–Sat 10am–5pm, Sun noon–5pm; charge). This a collection of world-class modern art, with rotating exhibitions and interesting programs. The museum's other branch has a delightful ocean-front setting at La Jolla (see page 322).

Along the Embarcadero just north of the station is the large **Maritime Museum** **D** (1492 North Harbor Drive; tel: 619-234-9153; www.sdmarine. org; daily 9am–5pm; charge), which encompasses six ships built prior to 1914. The *USS Midway* moored at Navy Pier in 2003 now serves as the **USS** *Midway* **Museum** (tel: 619-544-9600; www.midway.org; daily 10am–5pm; charge).

Much of the harbor is centered around attractive **Seaport Village**, with its cafés and live entertainment. Adjoining this carefully landscaped "village" is the spiffy-looking **Convention Center**, right opposite **Gaslamp Quarter**, a several-block area of brick-paved sidewalks flanked by restored Victorian buildings now occupied by galleries, trendy boutiques, and cafés. This refurbished section, with a demonstrable appeal to artists and young entrepreneurs, has also become the breeding ground of a flourishing theater movement, as well as a popular destination for nightlife and shopping.

Performing orca whales at SeaWorld.

Entering the city's Gaslamp Quarter.

Balboa Park

TIP

San Diego has always been a big naval town, and taking a harbor cruise will confirm that there is still plenty of activity on the water. In winter, whale-watching tours start from the harbor. Among the Maritime Musuem's ships is the 1863 Star of India, one of the last steel-hulled merchant sailing ships still afloat.

Located at the northeast edge of town, the 1,400-acre (570-hectare) **Balboa Park** Ⓔ is the largest urban cultural park in the country. Many people take pleasure in just strolling or picnicking in the park (though note, it is not a place to visit after dark), but Balboa Park is really an activity "city" all on its own. Many of the city's museums are housed here in Moorish- and Spanish-style buildings, several of which date back to international expositions held here in 1915 and 1935. Other attractions include a science center, an arts center, several theaters, and the city's famous zoo.

To learn about space and aviation history, visit the San Diego Air and Space Museum (2001 Pan American Plaza; tel: 619-234-8291; www.sandiegoairandspace.org; daily 10am–4pm; charge), which houses artifacts and aircrafts, including the actual Apollo 9 command module, a replica of *The Spirit of St Louis* in which Charles Lindbergh crossed the Atlantic, and the only real GPS satellite on display in the world.

The **San Diego Museum of Art** Ⓕ (1450 El Prado; tel: 619-232-7931; www.sdmart.org; Mon–Tue, Thur and Sat 10am–5pm, Sun noon–5pm; charge) is the region's largest and oldest art museum. In addition to 19th- and 20th- century American art, the collection features fine examples of European and Asian art and growing collections of contemporary and Latin American work.

Just next door is the white marble **Timken Museum of Art** Ⓖ (1500 El Prado; tel: 619-239-5548; www.timkenmuseum.org; Tue–Sat 10am–4.30pm, Sun 1.30–4.30pm; free). Considered one of the world's great small museums, its collection includes paintings by European old masters such as Rembrandt, Rubens, and Pieter Bruegel the Elder, as well as American paintings and Russian icons.

Other museums of note include the anthropology-focused Museum of Man; the Mingei International Museum (1439 El Prado; tel: 619-239-0003; www.mingei.org; charge), which showcases international folk art, craft, and design; and the Natural History

The Botanical Building in Balboa Park.

Museum (1788 El Prado; tel: 619-232-3821; www.sdnhm.org; Sun–Fri 10am–5pm, Sat 9am–5pm; charge).

Enthusaists of all ages will get a kick out of the large Model Railroad Museum (tel: 619-696-0199; www.sdrm.org; Tue–Fri 11am–4pm, Sat–Sun 11am–5pm; charge) and a ride on the park's 1910 carousel or its miniature train.

Visit the park's centrally located Visitors Center (tel: 619-239-0512) for more information on all museums and to buy a passport offering cost-effective admission to 13 of the park's museums.

San Diego Zoo

Giant pandas, Bornean sun bears, jaguars, California condors, and the largest colony of koalas outside Australia can all be found on the western side of Balboa Park in the famous **San Diego Zoo ❻** (tel: 619-234-3153; daily 9am–5pm; charge). One of the largest zoos in America, it houses over 4,000 rare and endangered animals representing more than 800 animal species. The zoo has a policy of eschewing cages in favor of moats wherever possible, in an attempt to recreate natural conditions.

Admission to the zoo includes a Children's Zoo – with more than 30 kid-friendly animal exhibits and activities – and a ride on Skyfari, an aerial tramway from which you can admire all the uncaged elephants, lions, tigers, giraffes, and bears in their canyon habitats.

Coronado

Coronado, with stately Victorian homes among the cottages and condos, is set on a peninsula and is the most popular and wealthiest of the string of communities surrounding the lower end of San Diego Bay. It is best known for the superlative **Hotel del Coronado ❶**, a perfect example of Victorian architecture (1888). A dozen presidents have stayed here since Thomas Edison personally installed the electric lighting; here Britain's future Edward VIII met his wife, the notorious Mrs Simpson, who lived

Sculpture at the outpost of the San Diego Museum of Contemporary Art, La Jolla.

Elephants in an uncaged enclosure in San Diego Zoo.

Around San Diego

0 — 5 miles
0 — 5 km

Hotel del Coronado.

Desirable houses in La Jolla.

in a bungalow on the grounds (the bungalow is still here); Charles Lindbergh dropped by for dinner before and after making the first trans-Atlantic flight; and author L. Frank Baum is said to have used it as an inspiration for *The Wizard of Oz*. Such milestones are memorialized in the **Museum of History and Art** (1100 Orange Avenue; tel: 619-437-8788; Mon–Fri 9am–5pm, Sat–Sun 10am–5pm) right **next door to the visitor center.**

La Jolla, Torrey Pines, and Del Mar

The wealthy, charming town of **La Jolla ❷** is the home of the San Diego campus of the University of California, the highly regarded **Salk Institute**, the cliff-top **Birch Aquarium at Scripps**, and an iconic outpost of the **San Diego Museum of Contemporary Art**. Overlooking the outdoor sculpture garden, with sweeping views of the Pacific ocean, this is the ideal setting for the strikingly modern building housing world-class contemporary art.

The San Diego-La Jolla Underwater Park Ecological Reserve is a popular destination for kayaking, diving, swimming, and snorkeling; snorkelers should head for the **La Jolla Caves**.

Heading up Interstate 5 toward Los Angeles, you can break up your journey from San Diego by stopping off for a walk through the groves of strangely twisted trees at **Torrey Pines State Reserve ❸** and watch daredevil hang-gliders soar off the 300ft (90-meter) cliffs.

Another detour is Del Mar, a beautiful spot with a sweeping hillside view of the Pacific. The San Diego County Fair is held here in June and July, and the Del Mar National Horse Show in the spring. The season begins in July, a week after the big fair ends, and continues to run until well into September.

LEGOLAND

Just a 30-minute drive north of San Diego, Legoland is one of the best amusement parks for children under 13 in Southern California. There are more than 60 rides, shows, and attractions to choose from, with areas themed on pirates, medieval times, dinosaurs, 1920s Egypt, and miniature American landmarks. Kids and parents will both be amazed by the more than 22,000 Lego models in the park – from a brontosaurus named Bronte to a tiny rabbit in a magician's hat – created from over 57 million Lego bricks. There are also plenty of restaurants and shops, with everything geared to families. Strollers and wheelchairs can be rented on a first-come, first-served basis. 1 Legoland Drive, Carlsbad; tel: 760-918-5346; www.legoland.com.

Tijuana, Mexico

Rancho Tía Juana (Aunt Jane's Ranch) became an international border town in the 1840s, following the Mexican–American War.

By the early 1900s, Tijuana was enticing countless North Americans with its diverse marketplaces, live bullfights, horse races, thermal baths, and other unique attractions. Today, Tijuana is fun, but can be dangerous, and visitors come as much for the nightclubs and duty-free bargains on jewelry, pottery, perfume, and fine art as they do for historic sites.

Heading "south of the border"

Crossing to and from San Diego is relatively easy, but time-consuming. Be sure that you have valid passports, proper health coverage, and Mexican auto insurance. As you drive into Tijuana or cross the footbridge, you'll soon enter the tourist zone of **Tijuana**, which stretches along Avenida Revolución. There are tourist information offices at the border but the main Tourist Assistance Office is in the **Viva Tijuana Shopping Center**, located on Calle Vía de la Juventud.

What to see

Avenida Revolución is lined with bars, nightclubs, crafts stores, and clothing and jewelry shops mixed up along with the traditional ponchos and leather sandals (for more shopping, visit the **Plaza Río Tijuana** shopping mall, the largest shopping center in northwestern Mexico). Behind the Plaza Revolución is the **Wax Museum,** whose eclectic subjects range from Madonna, Gandhi, Marilyn Monroe, and the Pope to Cortéz and an Aztec priest holding the bloody heart of a prostrate victim.

A few blocks down Revolución, past the former **Jai Alai Fronton** (an open-walled playing area for this sport that originated in Spain's Basque Country), turn left on 10th Street to head towards the river. The main street continues south, seguing

onto the Boulevard Agua Caliente and running past the city's old bullring, most of its best hotels, Hipódromo Caliente Racetrack, and the Sports Arena where concerts and the majority of big events take place.

The famous old **Hipódromo Caliente Racetrack** still has its marble floors, ornate decoration, mirrored elevators, and a lobby filled with sculptured cowboys, caged birds, and an incongruous pair of playful anteaters, but retains little of the glamour that once caused it to be regarded as the American Monte Carlo. In the days when the track's regular clientele included Charlie Chaplin, Jean Harlow, and heavyweight champion Jack Dempsey, fortunes were won and lost at dice, blackjack, and roulette.

Head eastwards along 10th Street, watching out for the giant globe (indicating a "world of culture") housing the concert hall and the 85ft (26-meter) -high **Omnitheater**. Adjoining is the ultra-modern **Tijuana Cultural Center**, whose historical survey embraces Olmec stone heads, Aztec charts showing the god of the hour, a meticulous model of the 16th-century Aztec capital, Tenochtitlan, plus skillfully embroidered Indian costumes, and is well worth a visit.

Traffic jams at the Tijuana border for those returning to California, with street vendors selling food.

Sunset over San Diego's beach.

Dune buggy on Pismo Beach.

Lake Siskyou in the High North.

Inside San Diego's lighthouse at Point Loma.

INSIGHT GUIDES TRAVEL TIPS

CALIFORNIA

TRANSPORTATION

GETTING THERE AND GETTING AROUND

GETTING THERE

By Air

San Francisco International Airport (SFO)
Tel: 650-821-8211 or 1-800-435-9736; www.flysfo.com.
The airport is 14 miles (23km) south of downtown San Francisco near the town of San Mateo. For public transportation to and from the city, Bay Area Rapid Transit (BART; www.bart.gov) provides a Metro rail service within the Bay Area and has a station at SFO and several within San Francisco. Take the SFO AirTrain to the Garage G/BART Station stop where you can buy your ticket and board. The one-way fare from SFO to downtown San Francisco is $8.10. SamTrans (tel: 800-660-4287; www.samtrans. com) operates a public bus service to San Mateo County. The taxi fare from SFO to downtown San Francisco is approximately $50. Several private shuttles, including BayPorter Express (tel: 415-467-1800; www.bayporter. com) can also be booked in advance or upon arrival.
Oakland International Airport
Tel: 510-563-3300; www.flyoakland. com.
Much smaller and less crowded than SFO, Oakland Airport is well-served by public transportation and much closer to East Bay destinations. Free shuttles link the airport with the BART system and SFO. As with SFO, private shuttles can also be booked.
Los Angeles International Airport (LAX)
Tel: 310-646-5252; www.lawa.org.
LAX is one of the world's busiest

Santa Fe train station in San Diego.

airports, handling the majority of the state's international, domestic, and regional air traffic. There are information booths just outside the terminal for MTA (Metropolitan Transportation Authority) buses (tel: 213-626 4455). A free, frequent shuttle bus connects LAX with METRO's Green Line Light Rail. The LAX FlyAway bus service provides frequent nonstop transportation between LAX and Van Nuys Bus Terminal, Union Station in downtown Los Angeles, and Westwood/UCLA. You can also arrange for door-to-door shuttle van service, rental cars, and taxicabs ($15.00 minimum fare for trips originating at LAX, a $46.50 flat fare for trips between LAX and Downtown, and a $4.00 surcharge for all trips originating at LAX).
Palm Springs International Airport
www.palmspringsairport.com.
San Diego International Airport (Lindbergh Field)
Tel: 619-231-2100; www.san.org.

Airlines
Numerous major airlines fly regularly into California, including:
Air France, www.airfrance.com
Alaska Airlines, www.alaskaair.com
American Airlines, www.aa.com
British Airways, www.britishair.com
Delta Airlines, www.delta.com
Southwest, www.southwest.com
United, www.united.com
US Airways, www.usairways.com
Virgin Atlantic, www.virginatlantic. com

Flights arrive from most major American cities. Transportation information: tel: 619-233 3004. In addition to the international airports listed above, there are smaller, regional airports in several locations throughout California, including Palmdale, Ontario, Burbank, Fresno, Sacramento, San Jose, Van Nuys, and Orange County. Shuttle flights are usually available at all of the larger air terminals.

By Rail
Amtrak
Tel: 1-800-872-7245; www.amtrak. com.
Amtrak is the major rail passenger carrier in the US. Though the system is little used by Californians, it can be a pleasant way to get around the state, provided you are not in a hurry. The California Zephyr is the main rail line into Northern California, stopping at Sacramento, Colfax, Davis, Martinez, and Truckee before reaching Emeryville station, where there is a free bus service to San Francisco.
Amtrak also offers several major rail lines in Southern California. The

Cable car in San Francisco.

Sunset Limited from New Orleans stops at North Palm Springs, Ontario, and Pomona before it reaches Los Angeles. The Pacific Surfliner links San Diego to Los Angeles and on to Santa Barbara and San Luis Obispo, while the San Joaquin runs between Sacramento and Bakersfield, with stops at Stockton, Modesto, Merced, and Fresno.

The state is tied together by the Coast Starlight, which travels north from Los Angeles all the way to Seattle, stopping at Van Nuys, Simi Valley, Oxnard, Santa Barbara, San Luis Obispo, Paso Robles, San Jose, Oakland (from here, there's a bus transfer to San Francisco before the route continues), Emeryville, Martinez, Davis, Sacramento, Chico, Redding, and across the Oregon border. Amtrak offers some local services also.

By Bus

Greyhound Lines
Tel: 800-231-2222; www.greyhound.com.
The national bus line, Greyhound Lines, as well as a number of smaller charter companies, provide an impressive network of ground travel throughout California, offering daily service to major towns and cities. Routes and schedules are subject to change; it is a good idea to check all arrangements with local stations, in advance. San Francisco, Oakland, Los Angeles, San Diego, and other

large towns all have municipal bus systems.

By Road

The principal **north–south** byways in California are listed below:
Interstate 5 (the Golden State and Santa Ana freeways), which covers the distance from Canada to Mexico via Seattle, Sacramento, Los Angeles, and San Diego.
Interstate 15, which transits San Bernardino and San Diego after a long passage from Montana's Canadian border, via Salt Lake City and Las Vegas.
US 101 (the Ventura and Hollywood freeways), which proceeds south down the Pacific coast from Washington state, crosses San Francisco's Golden Gate Bridge, and ends in downtown Los Angeles.
State Highway 1, which hugs the coast from south of Los Angeles to San Francisco and further north.
The principal **east–west** byways in California are:
Interstate 8, which departs from Interstate 10 at Casa Grande, Arizona, and ends in San Diego.
Interstate 10 (the San Bernardino and Santa Monica freeways), which begins on the east coast in Jacksonville, Florida, and continues through New Orleans, Houston, El Paso, Tucson, and Phoenix before cutting through Los Angeles, then ending at the coast in Santa Monica.

Interstate 40, which connects Knoxville, Tennessee, with Barstow, California, via Memphis, Oklahoma City, and Albuquerque.

GETTING AROUND

Public Transportation

San Francisco
San Francisco is served by an excellent public transportation system. The city's Muni network (tel: 415-673-6864; www.sfmuni.com; runs 6am–late, with some night service) of buses, street cars, and historic cable cars makes getting around a snap. Bus fare for adults is $2, which is paid in exact change upon boarding the front of the bus. Riders paying cash are given a transfer slip, and can ride other buses for several hours by just flashing this piece of paper to the bus driver. The "owl" late-night service runs every 30 minutes from 1–5am.

The Bay Area Rapid Transit (known locally as BART) subway system (tel: 415-989-2278; www.bart.gov; runs Mon–Fri 4am–midnight, Sat 6am–midnight and Sun 8am–midnight) connects San Francisco with the East Bay via a tunnel that goes under the bay. BART is one of the most efficient and modern rail lines in the United States and serves 43 stations in three counties, from San Francisco to Millbrae and throughout the East Bay. Its stations provide maps that clearly explain routes and fares, and nearby ticketing machines allow passengers to purchase tickets.

To save on transportation costs, consider purchasing a 1-day ($14), 3-day ($22), or 7-day ($28) Visitor Pass which covers unlimited bus, historic street car, and cable car rides.

Oakland and Berkeley are serviced by East Bay Transit (tel: 510-839-2882, www.actransit.org)

Caltrain (tel: 1-888-500-4636; www.caltrain.com) runs passengers between San Francisco and San Jose, with several stops along the peninsula. This rail service operates from the terminal at Fourth and King streets in San Francisco.

Many locals use ferries to get to and from work, but for visitors they provide a great scenic and environmental alternative to driving. Departing from Fisherman's Wharf or the Ferry Building, they travel to Angel Island and throughout the North and East Bay areas:

Blue and Gold Fleet, Pier 39 Marina Terminal, The Embarcadero at Beach St; tel: 415-705-8200; www.blueandgoldfleet.com.

Golden Gate Ferry, Ferry Building, The Embarcadeo at Market St; tel: 415-455-2000; www.goldengateferry.com.

Los Angeles

The main public transportation option in Los Angeles is the Los Angeles County Metropolitan Transportation Authority bus company (tel: 213-626-4455; www.mta.net), which everyone calls the Metro. The MTA oversees the city's surprisingly comprehensive bus system, as well as the newer Metro and light rail system.

The popular Red Line operates between Downtown, North Hollywood, and Universal City; the Purple line overlaps part of it. The Blue Line operates between Downtown and Long Beach. The Green Line runs all the way to Redondo Beach, crossing the Blue Line just north of Compton. The Gold Line, travels between Downtown and Pasadena, and the Expo Line goes out to Culver City.

A basic fare is $1.50, and a day pass (which is valid until 3am the next day) costs $5. Drivers do not have change, so carry the exact fare. A $20 seven-day pass for Metro bus and rail lines is also available – check sale locations at www.mta.net, where you can also plan your route with schedules and maps.

San Diego

The public transportation service here is the San Diego Metropolitan Transit System (tel: 619-231-1466; www.sdmts.com), which offers bus and trolley routes throughout the San Diego area, from Old Town to Mission Beach and Mission Valley. One-way bus tickets are $2.25, trolley tickets are $2.50; an all-day pass

for either is $5. Without the all-day pass, no transfers are allowed without purchasing a new ticket. Purchase your ticket before boarding the trolley from the ticket vending machines at each station.

The system also provides access to other towns in and around San Diego County, including Coronado, Del Mar, Escondido, Oceanside, Borrego Springs, and Tecate. For tickets, monthly passes, and general and route information, contact the Transit store (102 Broadway; tel: 619-234-1060).

A handy tool for public transportation in California is NextBus (www.nextbus.com). Also available as a mobile phone application, this service provides real-time arrival information for publication transportation so you can find out whether your bus is coming in 5 minutes or 35.

Private Transportation

Driver's License and Insurance

Drivers are required to carry a valid license at all times. California visitors may drive for up to 12 months with a non-California driver's license. Visitors can also obtain an International Driving Permit (IDP) from international automobile associations.

Be sure to keep these and a certificate proving you have liability insurance with you at all times because you will be required to show

The Napa and Sonoma Valleys are perfectly suited for scenic, day-long road trips.

Renting a Car

National car-rental companies are located at all airports and large towns. The best rates are usually available by booking in advance. In most cases, you must be at least 21 years old to rent a car (often 25), and you must have a valid driver's license and at least one major credit card. Foreign travelers may need to produce an international driver's license or a license from their home country. Be sure to take out collision and liability insurance, which may not always be included in the base price of the rental. It is also a good idea to inquire about an unlimited-mileage package, especially on a long trip, if not already included: given the vast area of California,

the extra mileage costs can add up quickly.
Alamo: Tel: 1-877-222-9075; www.alamo.com
Avis: Tel: 1-800-331-1212 in US, 1-800-331-1084 outside US; www.avis.com
Budget: Tel: 1-800-527-0700; www.budget.com
Dollar: Tel: 1-800-800-4000; www.dollar.com
Enterprise: Tel: 1-800-261-7331; www.enterprise.com
Hertz: Tel: 1-800-654-3131; www.hertz.com
National: Tel: 1-877-222-9058; www.nationalcar.com
Thrifty: Tel: 1-800-847-4389; www.thrifty.com

them to any law enforcement officers who stop your car. It is illegal to drive without these items.

Laws for Safety

Belts and child seats: California law requires that every passenger wear a seat belt. Youth or infant seats are required for babies and small children under 60lbs or 6 years of age.
Cell phones: It is illegal in California to talk on a cell phone while driving unless you are able to listen and talk hands-free.
Emergency vehicles: When a fire truck, ambulance, or police vehicle approaches from either direction with flashing lights and/or a siren, you must immediately pull over to the side of the road.
Helmets: State law requires all motorcycle riders to wear helmets.
Hitchhiking: Hitchhiking is illegal on all highways and Interstates and on many secondary roads as well. Because traffic is sparse in some regions, it can also be quite difficult. In California, as elsewhere in the United States, hitchhiking can be dangerous and unpredictable. However, if you do decide to hitch, it is best to do it from an exit ramp (if legal) or a highway rest stop, rather than on the road itself. For long distances, it is advisable to make a sign clearly stating your destination. To find the safest situations, try checking ride services and college campus bulletin boards for posted rideshares.
Roadside assistance: The Highway Patrol cruises the state's highways, not just monitoring speed limits but also looking for drivers in trouble. If you have any emergency that won't allow you to continue the trip, signal

your distress by raising the hood. Motorists are often advised that they are safer staying in the car with the doors locked until a patrol car stops to help, rather than leaving it and trying to hitchhike.

Motoring Advisories

If you plan on driving any distance, it's a good idea to join the American Automobile Association or one of its affiliate offices. Locations include those near the LA airport (tel: 310-390-9866; www.aaa-calif.com) and in San Francisco (tel: 415-565-2012; www.csaa.com). In addition to emergency road service, AAA offers maps, guidebooks, and insurance. There are reciprocal arrangements with many international AAA organizations, such as those in Great Britain, Germany, and Australia.

Parking

Parking meters accept coins, and sometimes credit cards. Parking meters do not need to be fed on Sundays or major holidays. When you're looking for a parking space, note the color of the curb, which corresponds to the following limitations:
No color: No specific limitations; follow guidelines on nearby signs or meters.
White: You may stop only long enough to pick up or drop off passengers.
Green: You may park for a limited time; look for a sign nearby with the time limit, or a time limit painted on the curb.
Yellow: Stop no longer than the time posted to load or unload passengers or freight; drivers of non-commercial vehicles usually must stay in the car.

Red: No stopping or parking.
Blue: Parking is permitted only for a disabled person who displays a special placard or license plate.

Rules of the Road

Some roads are for one-way traffic only and are identified by a black and white sign with an arrow pointing in the permitted direction of travel. At an intersection with a four-way red stop sign, motorists must completely stop and then proceed across the intersection following the order in which they arrived at the stop. If you arrive at the same time, the person to the right has the right of way, but usually one person just waves on another.

In California, it is legal to make a **right turn** on a red light after making a full stop, unless signs indicate otherwise.

Speed limits for roads and highways are posted on white signs to the right, as are all other **road signs**. Unless otherwise indicated, the speed limit is 65mph (105kmh) on freeways, 55mph (88kmh) on two-lane highways, 35mph (56kmh) on main city streets, and 25mph (40kmh) near schools and in residential or business districts.

Watch for white signs warning that you will be in a different "Speed Zone Ahead." Be prepared to slow to the lower speed you will soon see posted on upcoming white signs. Some very small towns are notorious for catching and fining drivers who have not slowed down quickly enough from the highway speed to the (much lower) in-town speed limit

Taxis

Taxis are an easy, though expensive, way to get about major cities. They hover around popular tourist or nightlife spots, but in out-of-the-way locations it's best to call a radio-dispatched taxi. Your fare will be displayed on the meter and will include a flag-drop charge plus a per-mile and/or a per-hour charge. Fares follow standard rules by city, listed below. A 10 percent tip, rounding up to the next dollar, is standard.

San Francisco

Standard charges are $3.50 for the first one-fifth mile or flag, $0.55 each additional one-fifth mile or fraction thereof, $0.55 each minute of waiting or traffic time delay, plus a $2 airport surcharge.
DeSoto Cab Company: Tel: 415-970-1370

TRANSPORTATION

ACCOMMODATIONS

EATING OUT

ACTIVITIES

A – Z

Sharing the road in Marin County.

Green Cab: Tel: 415-626-4733
Luxor Cab Company: Tel: 415-282-4141
Yellow Cab: Tel: 415-333-3333
All cabs authorized by the city (look for the metal "license plate" on the dashboard, and the driver's ID, visible from the back seat) Error! Hyperlink reference not valid.are obligated to let you pay by credit card, though they will often complain that their machine is "broken" as they prefer cash to avoid paying a surcharge to the credit card companies. For a list of these companies, see www.sfmta.com.

Los Angeles
Look for the Official City of Los Angeles Taxicab Seal before boarding – this means the taxi driver is insured, well trained, and authorized by the city to operate. Fare is $2.85 for the first 1/9 mile or flag, $0.30 for each additional 1/9 mile ($2.70 per mile), and 0.30 for each 37 seconds waiting ($29.19 per hour).
For taxi cab companies and

Tours via Car

Seagull signs in blue and white mark San Francisco's 49-Mile Scenic Drive, a name which says it all. A free map from the San Francisco Visitor Center at Powell and Market streets details the route.
Drivers who seek to explore old US Route 66 in the south of the state can get a free map from the LA Visitors Center (6801 Hollywood Blvd; tel: 323-467-6412) which charts 29 points of interest along 62 miles (100km) of the historic road.
The 17-Mile Drive in Pebble Beach is another beautiful ride (motorcycles prohibited).

the areas each serves, go to www.taxicabsla.org.

San Diego
Standard charges are $2.20 for the first 1/10 mile, $2.30 for each additional mile, and $19.00 per hour of waiting time.

Traveling in Deserts and Mountains
A word of caution for desert travelers: the single most important precaution you can take is to tell someone your destination, route, and expected time of arrival. Be sure to check tires carefully before setting out; heat builds pressure, so have tires at slightly below normal air pressure. The desert's arid climate makes carrying extra water – for passengers as well as for vehicles – essential. Carry at least 1 gallon (4 liters) per person. Keep an eye on the gas gauge; it's a good idea to have more than you think you need. Remember, if you should have car trouble or become lost, do not strike out on foot. A car, visible from the air and presumably on a road, is easier to spot than a person on their own, and it affords shelter from the weather. Just be patient and wait to be found.
Mountain drivers are advised to be equally vigilant. Winter storms in the Sierras occasionally close major roads, and at times chains are required for tires. For 24-hour information on road conditions throughout the state, call tel: 1-800-427-7623. Remember to phone ahead for road conditions before you depart.

Traveling to Mexico
Since March 1, 2010, all US citizens – including children – have been required to present a valid passport or passport card for travel into Mexico, as are all other nationalities (along with their Green Card, if they have one, for re-entry to the US.)
US citizens do not require a visa or a tourist card for tourist stays of 72 hours or less within the 12–19-mile (20–30km) "border zone". US citizens traveling as tourists beyond this zone, or entering Mexico by air, must pay a fee to obtain a tourist card, also known as an FMM, available from Mexican consulates, Mexican border crossing points, Mexican tourism offices, airports within the border zone, and most airlines serving Mexico. Proof of nationality must accompany the visa.
Mexican law requires that any non-Mexican citizen under the age of 18 departing Mexico must carry notarized written permission from any parent or guardian not traveling with the child to or from Mexico. This permission must include the name of the parent, the name of the child, the name of anyone traveling with the child, and the notarized signature(s) of the absent parent(s).
US insurance is not valid in Mexico and it is definitely a wise move to obtain short-term insurance, obtainable at innumerable sales offices just north of the border.
Crossing into Mexico can be relatively easy. There are three major crossings: at busy **San Ysidro**, 18 miles (29km) south of downtown San Diego, which is the gateway to Tijuana; at **Tecate** off State Highway 94, where there is rarely a wait, although the border does tend to close in early in the evening; and at **Mexicali** (which is also Baja's capital), a dreary industrial city situated opposite the California town of Calexico, about 90 miles (145km) to the east.
Because driving in Tijuana for those unfamiliar with the city (and the Spanish language) can be troublesome, many drivers park in San Diego's San Ysidro, crossing into Tijuana via the elevated pedestrian walkway. Avoid leaving your car in the parking places of merchants as it will be towed away by police.
There's an all-day secure lot off the "Last Exit US parking" ramp – turn right at the stop sign to the Tijuana side. Cheap taxis and buses are also available.
The return to California can be a bit more tense than the entry into Mexico, as US Border Patrol officers take far more interest in who's coming into the country (hence those passports and Green Cards). Waiting several hours to cross back into the US is not uncommon.

ACCOMMODATIONS

WHERE TO STAY

Hotels

California offers the complete spectrum of accommodations, from elegant European-style hotels to inexpensive motels that can be rented by the week.

In San Francisco, the most expensive hotels are generally located in Nob Hill, the Financial District, and Union Square. These grand hotels are particularly well suited to the international traveler, and many are attractive landmarks in their own right. In Los Angeles, the most expensive are situated Downtown and in Beverly Hills, with the best access to shopping and public transportation.

The concierge at most upscale hotels will arrange theater tickets, tours, limousines with bilingual drivers, and airline reservations.

There are also a large number of smaller hotels and hotel chains, which usually offer all of the essential comforts without the high prices of the grand hotels.

Motels

If you're traveling by car and don't plan on spending much time in your room, motels are the best solution. Whether located along busy Sunset Boulevard in Los Angeles or along the riverbank in a remote Northern California town, most motels provide parking space – at a premium in most of California – within just steps of your room.

Motel quality varies, but you can usually expect clean and simple accommodations. This is especially true for most of the national chains. A restaurant or coffee shop, swimming pool, and sauna are often found on the motel premises. Room facilities

Roosevelt Hotel, Hollywood.

generally include a telephone, television, and radio. Don't hesitate to ask the motel manager if you may inspect a room before agreeing to take it. Other than their accessibility by auto, the attraction of motels is price. Motels in California cities range from $75 to $150 per night, double occupancy. They are less expensive in the outlying areas.

Note: due to California's strict laws, most hotel and motel rooms are non-smoking. If smoking is important to you, check around before you book.

Bed and Breakfast Inns

B&Bs are extremely popular throughout the United States, and within California, especially in the north of the state. Most cluster in such scenic areas as the Wine Country, Gold Country, North Coast, and Monterey Peninsula. Situated in such beautiful rural settings, they do a thriving business with city dwellers

in search of a romantic or peaceful weekend retreat. In fact, intimate inns are even popping up in large cities to compete with hotels.

Converted from mansions and farmhouses with 5 to 15 rooms, these inns offer the traveler a highly individual experience; no two inns are alike, and, in most inns, no two rooms are alike. For those accustomed to the uniformity of hotels and motel chains, the inns provide a lovely alternative. However, many inns have shared bathrooms and only a few have televisions or telephones situated in the rooms. Most, though, do include breakfast with the price of the room, hence the name.

Prices vary greatly, but unlike in Europe, they tend to be fairly expensive. Call or email in advance – the inns are very popular on weekends and in summer.

For B&B information, contact the **California Association of Bed & Breakfast Inns** (CABBI; tel: 831-464 8159, 1-800-373-9251; www.cabbi. com).

Hostels

Some travelers may like to take advantage of California's chain of hostels. Hostels are clean, comfortable, and very inexpensive (as low as $10 per night). Although suitable for people of all ages, they are definitely geared toward the young at heart. Beds are provided in dormitory-like rooms, though some hostels also have single, double, triple, and quad private rooms. Hostelers bring their own gear (silverware, sleeping bag, towel) and are expected to help clean up and perform other communal tasks. Note: Hostels are closed 9.30am–4.30pm,

Motel Chains

Motel chains can be found all around California. Many chains have toll-free numbers available from other countries.
Best Western
Comfort Inn
Doubletree
Embassy
Holiday Inn
La Quinta
Marriott
Motel 6
Quality Inns
Ramada
Red Roof Inn
Super 8
Travelodge
Vagabond

so most guests fill their days with trips and nearby outdoor activities.

Northern California has a chain of more than 20 hostels up and down the Pacific coast, from Jedediah Smith Redwoods State Park at the Oregon border down to John Little State Beach. All the hostels are along the shoreline; some are located inside old lighthouses. Hosteling International has numerous hostels in California, including ones in Santa Cruz, Los Angeles, San Diego, and San Francisco, like the Adelaide Hostel (tel: 415-359-1915; www. adelaidehostel.com).

For a **complete directory** of hostels by region, go to: www.hostels.

Motor home camping in Yosemite National Park.

com/en/us.ca.html.
For lists of hostels area by area, try these numbers:
Central California Council, tel: 831-899-1252; www.westernhostels.org
Golden Gate Council, tel: 415-863-1444; www.norcalhostels.org
Los Angeles Council, tel: 310-393-3413; www.lahostels.org
San Diego Council, tel: 619-338-9981; www.sandiegohostels.org

Campgrounds

Public and private campgrounds are located in or near state and national parks. Most public campgrounds offer primitive facilities – a place to park, restrooms, and outdoor cooking. Private campgrounds are usually a little more expensive and offer additional facilities such as hook-ups, coin laundries, pools, and even restaurants. Most are busy from mid-June to September and are allotted on a first-come-first-served basis. If possible, make reservations. Campgrounds in popular destinations like Yosemite are reserved months in advance, so plan ahead.
California Department of Parks and Recreation, tel: 916-653 6995; www. parks.ca.gov
National Park Service Reservation Center, tel: 518-885-3639, 1-877-444-6777 (toll-free); www.recreation. gov
USDA Forest Service, Pacific Southwest Regional Office, tel: 707-562-8737; www.fs.fed.us

For information on specific campgrounds contact:
Buckhorn Campground, Angeles National Forest, above Cooper Canyon Falls. Sites for 38 small RVs and tents. Tel: 818-899-1900.
Gaviota State Park, between beach and mountains on the coast, 35 miles (56km) west of Santa Barbara. Tents and small RVs. Tel: 805-968-1033.
Palomar Mountain State Park, near Palomar Observatory and within easy reach of Lake Henshaw and the Anza-Borrego Desert State Park. Trail leads to Boucher Lookout with outstanding views. Tel: 1-800-444-7275.
Santa Catalina
The Santa Catalina Island Company operates the fully equipped campground **Hermit Gulch** about a mile (1.5km) from town (a shuttle bus operates), close to the Botanical Garden and hiking trails. Reservations are required (tel: 310-510-8368). Other campgrounds include Two Harbors, Parson's Landing, Blackjack, and Little Harbor.
Santa Rosa Island Campground, on one of the uninhabited Channel Islands reached after a three-hour boat ride from Ventura or Santa Barbara. Primitive facilities. No water or supplies available. Tel: 1-800-365-2267.
Serrano Campground, San Bernardino National Forest. Situated amid the tall pine trees along Big Bear Lake, the site has showers, toilets, a dump station, and full hookups for tents and RVs. Tel: 1-877-444 6777.

NORTHERN CALIFORNIA

San Francisco

Hotel reservations can be made directly with the hotel, or via third-party websites such as www.kayak.com, www.orbitz.com, or www.tripadvisor.com. The Convention and Visitors' Bureau (tel: 415-391-2000; www.sanfrancisco.travel.) can advise you regarding special needs or general information about their member hotels, motels, and inns. Hotel chains like Hilton, Hyatt, and Marriott offer toll-free telephone numbers for reservations.

Argonaut Hotel
495 Jefferson St
Tel: 415-563-0800
www.argonauthotel.com
Directly opposite the Wharf's Hyde Street Pier, this maritime-themed hotel boasts suites with sea views, tripod telescopes, and hot tubs. **$$$**

Chancellor Hotel
433 Powell St
Tel: 415-362 2004, 1-800-428-4748
www.chancellorhotel.com
First opened in 1914 and family-owned since 1917, this good-value hotel is a stone's throw from Union Square. With a palette of moss green and neutrals, rooms have a fresh, contemporary feel. **$–$$**

Clift Hotel
495 Geary St
Tel: 415-775-4700
www.clifthotel.com
A historic hotel redesigned by Philippe Starke, the Clift is a fusion of understated elegance and contemporary hipness. Dress smartly for cocktails at the Redwood Room bar, which is packed on weekends. **$$$**

Fairmont Hotel and Tower
950 Mason St
Tel: 415-772-5000, 1-866-540-4491
www.fairmont.com/sanfrancisco
The opulent Fairmont re-opened a

Fairmont Hotel, San Francisco.

year after the 1906 earthquake. You are greeted by a warm welcome, and an elegant atmosphere extends throughout, except perhaps at the tropical-themed Tonga Room & Hurricane Bar. Cozy rooms decorated in golden, cream, and royal blue hues afford sweeping city views. **$$$**

Four Seasons
757 Market St
Tel: 415-633-3000
www.fourseasons.com
With a giant health club and an ultra-convenient downtown location near high-end stores, this sleek highrise knows how to cater to its sophisticated and fairly exclusive clientele. **$$$**

Grand Hyatt
345 Stockton St
Tel: 415-398-1234, 1-800-233-1234
www.hyatt.com
With a lovely fountain in the garden, this central hotel towers 36 stories above Union Square. **$$$**

Hilton San Francisco Union Square
333 O'Farrell St
Tel: 415-771-1400, 1-800-445-8667
www.hilton.com
One of the largest hotels in the city, this conveniently located, three-towered hotel boasts a health club, indoor and outdoor pools, and the popular Urban Tavern restaurant serving gastro-pub cuisine. **$$**

Holiday Inns
Tel: 1-800-465-4329
www.holiday-inn.com
The city has four large Hiltons; amenities vary according to property but most have swimming pools. **$–$$**

Hotel Bohème
444 Columbus Ave
Tel: 415-433-9111
www.hotelboheme.com
Touches like fringed lamps, retro fabrics, and Jerry Stoll's black-and-

white photographs of the 1950s evoke the poetry of the Beatnik era in North Beach. All rooms have free Wi-fi. **$$**

Hotel Griffon
155 Steuart St
Tel: 415-495-2100, 1-800-321-2201
www.hotelgriffon.com
This charming brownstone offers attentive service and proximity to the Financial District and Ferry Building farmers' market. Some rooms have Bay views. **$$–$$$**

Hotel Rex
562 Sutter St
Tel: 415-433-4434, 1-800-433-4434
www.thehotelrex.com
Inspired by the art and literary salons of the 1920s and 1930s, the Rex is close to Union Square, and full of character. The lobby is a showpiece of period furnishings and fine antiquarian books, and the Library Bar features live jazz on Friday nights. **$$**

Hotel Triton
342 Grant St
Tel: 415-394-0500
www.hoteltriton.com
Steps from the Chinatown Gate, this trendy, eco-friendly hotel has a lobby with wild designs and furniture, and guestroom decor ranging from creamy whites to cherry red.

Huntington Hotel
1075 California St
Tel: 415-474-5400
www.huntingtonhotel.com
Overlooking Nob Hill's Huntington Square and a stone's throw from Grace Cathedral, the Huntington Hotel is one of the city's small luxury gems and the epitome of quiet, understated elegance, with 136 guestrooms and suites, outfitted in warm tones and plush decor. The on-site Nob Hill Spa is one of the city's best, and the clubby Big Four serves an excellent steak. **$$$**

Hyatt Regency
5 Embarcadero Center
Tel: 415-788-1234
www.sanfranciscoregency.hyatt.com
Conveniently located across from the Ferry Building in the Financial District, this waterfront hotel's triangular lobby atrium soars for 170ft (50 meters). The 802 rooms feature modern decor, granite bathrooms, and cherry wood desks. Unwind at the 24-hour gym, or

PRICE CATEGORIES

Prices are for a standard double room without breakfast:
$ = less than $150
$$ = $150–$225
$$$ = $225–$375
$$$$ = more than $375

with specialty cocktails in the lounge. **$$$**

InterContinental San Francisco
888 Howard St
Tel: 415-616-6500
www.intercontinentalsanfrancisco.com
This blue-glass tower is sexy, technologically sophisticated, and has earned the highest certification for green practices. A spa, Bar 888, and the Luce restaurant are also on the premises, and the Moscone West Convention Center is close by. **$$$**

King George Hotel
334 Mason St
Tel: 415-781-5050, 1-800-288-6005
www.kinggeorge.com
Offering small, traditional rooms with "European flair," this downtown hotel is also a member of the California Green Lodging program. **$$$**

Mandarin Oriental
222 Sansome St
415-276-9600
www.mandarinoriental.com
This Financial District luxury hotel features extraordinary views, some of which can be enjoyed from suites' private terraces and glass bathtubs positioned near the windows.

Mark Hopkins Intercontinental
1 Nob Hill
Tel: 415-392-3434, 1-800 327-0200
www.intercontinentalmarkhopkins.com
One of Nob Hill's most famous establishments, the Mark Hopkins offers panoramic views, neoclassical touches, lavish bathrooms, and the elegant "Top of the Mark" restaurant and bar, with its 100 Martinis menu. **$$$**

Monticello Inn
127 Ellis St
Tel: 415-392-8800, 1-866-778-6169
www.monticelloinn.com
Channeling the colonial style of Thomas Jefferson's gracious Virginia home, the Monticello Inn is a convenient boutique option near Union Square. Decor features bright blues, Wi-fi is free, and the hotel library has 100-plus books. **$**

The Palace Hotel
2 New Montgomery St
Tel: 415-512-1111
www.sfpalace.com
Home to lavish guestrooms and the magnificent Garden Court Restaurant, this opulent historical landmark – it was the city's first hotel – is one of San Francisco's premier luxury hotels. **$$$**

Petite Auberge
863 Bush St
Tel: 415-928-6000, 1-800 365-3004
www.jdvhotels.com
The gourmet breakfast buffet, cozy parlor, and French provincial details

make this value-for-money hotel appealing. Located near Union Square. **$$**

Phoenix Hotel
601 Eddy St
Tel: 415-776-1380, 1-800-248-9466
www.thephoenixhotel.com
Though the neighborhood is a bit dicey, this is where rock stars have been crashing since Bill Graham opened the Fillmore in the late Sixties. Chill out the day after by lounging poolside. **$**

Stanford Court Renaissance
905 California St
Tel: 415-989-3500, 1-800-468-3571
www.renaissancehotels.com
Two Tiffany-style glass doors grace the lobby of this luxury hotel, which is ideally situated where the cable cars cross on Nob Hill. After a $35 million dollar renovation, modern rooms feature caramel colors, geometric printed accents, and, often, great views. **$$–$$$**

Ritz-Carlton San Francisco
600 Stockton St
Tel: 415-296-7465, 1-800-241-3333
www.ritzcarlton.com
Oil paintings and crystal chandeliers were two of the innovations added when a major luxury hotel chain took over San Francisco's neoclassical Metropolitan Life Insurance Company building to create an "instant" landmark hotel. Enormous rooms mix dark woods and beiges and feature Italian marble bathrooms; elsewhere on site are a fine dining restaurant and fitness center. **$$$**

Royal Pacific Motor Inn
661 Broadway
Tel: 415-781-6661, 1-800-545-5574
www.royalpacificmotorinn.com
This no-frills motel is a budget option in a lively location between North Beach and Chinatown. **$**

San Francisco Fisherman's Wharf Marriott
1250 Columbus Ave
Tel: 415-775-7555
www.marriott.com
One of the best options in Fisherman's Wharf, the location of this hotel makes it a popular choice for families and business travelers. **$$**

San Remo Hotel
2237 Mason St
Tel: 415-776 8688, 1-800-352-7366
www.sanremohotel.com
Built in 1906 after the earthquake, the San Remo served as a boarding house for sailors, poets, and pensioners and a speakeasy during Prohibition. Today, it remains a bargain for lodgers who simply want a clean, bare-bones room to sleep in at night, with no need for telephone or TV. Some rooms share bathrooms. For couples, the rooftop

Liveried valets at the Sir Francis Drake.

penthouse is a real San Francisco treat. **$**

Sir Francis Drake
450 Powell St
Tel: 415-392-7755, 1-800-795-7129
www.sirfrancisdrake.com
Glide past the valets in Beefeater uniforms into the grand lobby of the 1928 landmark building. A $20-million renovation has recast guestrooms in a lovely sage green, cream, and plum color scheme. Scala's Bistro is located next door, and a lounge offers unparalleled city views. **$$–$$$**

Stanyan Park Hotel
750 Stanyan St
Tel: 415-751-1000
www.stanyanpark.com
Listed on the National Register of Historic Places, this early-20th-century boutique hotel in the Haight is ideal for those exploring neighborhoods west of downtown. Some rooms overlook Golden Gate Park, the large suites are good for families, and a continental breakfast is included. **$–$$**

Taj Campton Place
340 Stockton St
Tel: 415-781-5555
www.tajhotels.com
Housed in two early-20th-century buildings near Union Square, this sophisticated and intimate hotel is one of the city's most refined. The service is excellent, and the restaurant consistently wins high ratings. **$$$**

Washington Square Inn
1660 Stockton St
Tel: 415-981-4220, 1-800-388-0220
www.wsisf.com
A great place for an extended exploration of North Beach's cuisine and nightlife, this European-style B&B is right on one of San Francisco's

urban parks, and within walking distance of Fisherman's Wharf, Chinatown, and the Financial District. **$$**

Westin St Francis
335 Powell St
Tel: 415-397-7000, 1-800-917-7458
www.westinstfrancis.com
The location, across the street from Union Square, adds to the excitement of staying at this city landmark. If the historic aspects interest you, choose a room in the original 1904 building instead of the more modern tower. Rooms are rather dim and have small baths, but win with handsome chandeliers and reproductions. **$$$**

Greater San Francisco Bay Area

Cavallo Point
601 Murray Circle, Fort Baker, Sausalito
Tel: 415-339-4700, 1-888-651-2003
www.cavallopoint.com
At scenic Fort Baker, Cavallo Point is the first national park lodge in the Bay Area. With full spa amenities, it is a getaway in which to relax and explore the beautiful Marin headlands. **$$$–$$$$**

Claremont Resort and Spa
41 Tunnel Rd, Berkeley
Tel: 510-843-3000, 1-800-551-7266
www.claremontresort.com
Atop the Berkeley Hills in the East Bay, the Claremont is modern in services and amenities, but the setting is pure Gatsby and Garbo. An oasis of luxury, with a fabulous restaurant to boot and spa facilities are top-notch. **$$$$**

Inn Above Tide
30 El Portal, Sausalito
Tel: 415-332-9535, 800-893-8433
Proud to be the only Bay Area hotel actually on the water, this glamourous and elegant hotel's rooms all boast amazing views that include Angel Island, Alcatraz, and the San Francisco skyline. You can watch sailboats as you soak in an oversized hot tub, or use the binoculars in the room to spy on the sea lions. **$$$$**

Inn at Jack London Square
233 Broadway, Oakland
Tel: 510-452-4565, 1-800-633-5973
www.innatthesquare.com
Near the Amtrak station and only two blocks from the shops, movie theaters, and restaurants of Jack London Square, this is a convenient and affordable option for staying in the East Bay. Amenities include a pool, spacious and clean rooms, and free Wi-fi in most rooms. **$**

The Saint Claire
302 South Market St, San Jose
Tel: 408-295-2000
www.thesaintclaire.com

Doormen open brass-handled doors to the rich, hand-carved interior of the 170-room Sainte Claire, which is located downtown, near to all San Jose's cultural institutions. **$$$**

Wine Country

Auberge du Soleil
180 Rutherford Hill Rd, Rutherford
Tel: 707-963-1211
www.aubergedusoleil.com
The crème de la crème in Napa. Surrounded by vineyards and olive groves, this is often rated one of the world's finest hotels. Need we say more? **$$$$**

The Gaige House
13540 Arnold Dr, Glen Ellen
Tel: 707-935-0237, 1-800-935-0237
www.gaige.com
Delightful bed & breakfast inn located in an elegant restored 1890s property in the Valley of the Moon. **$$$**

Indian Springs
1712 Lincoln Ave, Calistoga
Tel: 707-942-4913
www.indianspringscalistoga.com
For more than a century, Calistoga drew visitors to take the waters. Stay in a cottage or the lodge but plan to spend much time in the geyser-fed mineral pool. **$$–$$$**

The Kenwood Inn & Spa
10400 Sonoma Highway, Kenwood
Tel: 707-833-1293
www.kenwoodinn.com
Surrounded by estate vineyards, the Kenwood Inn is the ultimate Wine Country retreat. The spa employs Kenwood's hooch with "vinotherapie" treatments using vine extracts. **$$$**

MacArthur Place
29 East MacArthur St, Sonoma
Tel: 707-938-2929, 1-800-722-1866
www.macarthurplace.com
MacArthur Place is a sprawling, impeccably landscaped spa for a truly special occasion. Robed guest stroll the gardens between spa services like Red Wine Grapeseed Baths. **$$$$**

La Residence
4066 Howard Lane, Napa
Tel: 707-253-0337, 1-800-253-9203
www.laresidence.com
This has been called one of Napa's most luxurious inns. Beautiful surroundings, a delightful pool, a wine-and-cheese reception every afternoon (free to guests), and in-room spa treatments are the perfect end to a hard day exploring the Napa Valley. **$$$**

Sonoma Hotel
10 West Spain Street, Sonoma
Tel: 707-966-2996, 1-800-468-6016
www.sonomahotel.com
A comfortable inn within easy reach of Sonoma's wineries and restaurants.

The Kenwood Inn and Spa.

Continental breakfast and evening wine tastings are included. Rooms are simple and attractive, and all have private bathrooms. **$–$$**

Monterey Penninsula and Big Sur Coast

Asilomar
800 Asilomar Blvd, Pacific Grove
Tel: 831-372-8016
www.vistasilomar.com
Peaceful and rustic, along the dunes of the Carmel coast, the historic rooms at this compound were designed by architect Julia Morgan in the Arts and Crafts style. Leave the phone behind and enjoy the serenity of lounging by the fireplace or walking along the beach. **$–$$**

Big Sur Lodge
47225 Highway 1, Big Sur
Tel: 831-667-3100, 1-800-424-4787
www.bigsurlodge.com
Big Sur architect Mickey Muennig used the sea and the mountains as a backdrop for this rustic lodge with 62 simple bungalows. **$$**

Costanoa Coastal Lodge and Camp
2001 Rossi Rd, Pescadero
Tel: 650-879-1100
www.costanoa.com
Close to Año Nuevo, the nation's largest northern elephant seal breeding colony, this coastal lodge and camp is surrounded by wilderness and secluded beaches. Accommodations

PRICE CATEGORIES

Prices are for a standard double room without breakfast:
$ = less than $150
$$ = $150–$225
$$$ = $225–$375
$$$$ = more than $375

range from no-frills campsites to cabins (with varying levels of luxury), to the lodge itself with full amenities. Spa services are also available. **$–$$**

Deetjen's Big Sur Inn
48865 Highway 1, Big Sur
Tel: 831-667-2378
www.deetjens.com
Cozy, wooden rooms and cottages with rustic stoves are tucked in among the lovely redwood groves of Castro Canyon. The inn, built in the 1930s by Norwegian Helmuth Deetjen, has attracted everyone from bohemian eccentrics and wayward itinerants to actors from Hollywood's golden era. **$–$$**

Olallieberry Inn
2476 Main St, Cambria
Tel: 1-888-927-3222
www.olallieberry.com
A stylish 1870s clapboard home, set in a pleasant garden with white picket fence, with charming rooms, gourmet breakfasts, and large sun deck. **$$**

Old Monterey Inn
500 Martin St, Monterey
Tel: 831-375-8284, 1-800-350-2344
www.oldmontereyinn.com
A stone pathway leads through the garden to an ivy-covered Tudor inn, where no expense has been spared to provide luxury accommodation: plush feather beds and down duvets, elegant furnishings, and wood-burning fireplaces. Massages and spa treatments are available if you need pampering, and horseback riding on the beach can be arranged if you need excitement. **$$$**

The Pine Inn
Ocean Ave bet.Lincoln St and Monte Verde St, Carmel
Tel: 831-624-3851, 1-800-228-3851
www.pine-inn.com
Situated in the heart of the village of Carmel, and just four blocks away from the city's lovely sandy beach, this elegant 1889 inn exudes the charm of a bygone age. Try and get a room with a view of the ocean. **$$**

Treebones Resort
71895 Highway 1, Big Sur
Tel: 1-877-424-4787
www.treebonesresort.com
A unique and memorable experience – yurts! Perched on the edge of the world in majestic Big Sur, 16 circular tents have views of mountains and ocean, redwoods and wildflowers. Hike in, relax at the pool and spa, and enjoy healthy home-cooked dinner and wine at the lodge. **$$**

Ventana Inn and Spa
48123 Highway 1, Big Sur
Tel: 831-667-2331
www.ventanainn.com
Nestled on a cliff overlooking the dramatic Pacific coastline, the unique

buildings offer premiere lodgings in a tranquil setting. Spa services and luxury suites are available. **$$$**

North Coast

Albion River Inn
3790 N. Highway 1, Albion
Tel: 707-937-1919, 1-800-479-7944
www.albionriverinn.com
One of the best inns on the West Coast, this casually elegant setting on the Mendocino coast (just south of Mendocino village) is ideal for a scenic, romantic retreat. The property's 10 acres (4 hectares) boast oceanfront gardens, headland bluffs, and breathtaking views to be admired from your room's private deck. **$$–$$$**

Brewery Gulch Inn
9401 North Highway 1, Mendocino
Tel: 1-800-578-4454
www.brewerygulchinn.com
Recently restored with salvaged redwood, this classic lodge overlooks the Pacific Ocean. The cozy parlor and friendly staff make for a relaxing, communal atmosphere. Guests are treated to afternoon wine and hors d'oeuvres. **$$–$$$$**

Carter House Inn
301 L St, Eureka
Tel: 1-800-404-1390
www.carterhouse.com
Actually four Victorian-era houses on the North Coast's Humboldt Bay, with marble fireplaces and jacuzzis in some rooms. Excellent restaurant and free afternoon wine (own label) and hors d'oeuvres. **$$–$$$**

The Gingerbread Mansion
400 Berding St, Ferndale
Tel: 707-786-4000, 1-800-952-4136
www.gingerbread-mansion.com
A lavish Queen Anne-style Victorian house with afternoon tea, manicured gardens, gourmet breakfasts, and

claw-foot bathtubs in many of the prettily decorated guest rooms. **$$–$$$**

Jenner Inn and Cottages
10400 Coast Route 1, Jenner
Tel: 707-865-2377, 1-800-732-2377
www.jennerinn.com
Rooms from small and affordable in the main lodge, to large and luxurious, overlooking the Russian River. Cottages have additional privacy, though many share hot tub and sauna facilities. Breakfast features fresh fruit, a light egg scramble, and bran muffins to die for. **$$**

MacCallum House
45020 Albion St, Mendocino
Tel: 707-937-0289, 1-800-609-0492
www.maccallumhouse.com
A beautiful compound of winding paths and lush gardens in the heart of downtown Mednocino, MacCallum House offers in-room saunas and private hot tubs. **$$**

Stanford Inn by the Sea
44850 Comptche–Ukiah Rd, Mendocino
Tel: 707-937-5615, 1-800-331-8884
www.stanfordinn.com
Located on a hilltop overlooking well-kept gardens and Mendocino Bay, the cozy, cabin-like rooms here have stunning views and invite total relaxation. Located on a working organic farm with a vegetarian restaurant. **$$$**

Central Valley

Citizen Hotel
926 J St, Sacramento
Tel: 916-447-2700
www.jdvhotels.com/hotels/sacramento/citizen/
Built in 1926 as the California Western States Life Insurance Building, the 14-story building is now one of the city's most chic boutique hotels, with 198 luxury rooms that retain an old-world character. **$$**

Stanford Inn by the Sea, Mendocino.

Dunbar House 1880
271 Jones Street, Murphys
Tel: 1-800-692-6006
www.dunbarhouse.com
This intimate 1880 Italianate home
offers five comfortable, elegant rooms
for a romantic Gold Country getaway.
Rooms are furnished with antiques
and plush linens; some rooms have
private porches and balconies.
Breakfasts, afternoon cookies, and
evening appetizers are included. **$$**

Inn at Parkside
2116 6th St, Sacramento
Tel: 916-658-1818
www.innatparkside.com
Built in 1936, this Mediterranean-style
mansion overlooking Southside Park
is a hotel offering the relaxed feel
of a spa resort (Spa Bloom is on the
premises). A complementary cheese
spread is served during a nightly social
hour. **$$–$$$**

Sterling Hotel
1300 H St, Sacramento
Tel: 916-448-1300
www.sterlinghotelsacramento.com
Located just three blocks from the
capitol building, this high-end inn feat-
ures 1890s architecture, contemporary
decor, a relaxing front porch, and 16
rooms with a Jacuzzi in each. **$–$$**

968 Park Hotel
968 Park Ave, South Lake Tahoe

Tel: 530-544-0968
www.968parkhotel.com
This stylish "rustic-zen" hotel is
conveniently located right across the
street from South Lake Tahoe's shops
and the Heavenly Gondola. **$$**

The Ahwahnee
Yosemite Valley, Yosemite National Park
Tel: 559-252-4848
www.yosemitepark.com
This spectacular, historic lodge
with equally spectacular views has
finely appointed rooms, parlors, and
cottages with massive stone hearths
and Native American artwork. Book up
to a year in advance. **$$$**

The Resort at Squaw Creek
400 Squaw Creek Rd,
Olympic Valley
Tel: 1-800-327-3353
www.squawcreek.com
One of the country's top resorts,
this is a luxury haven for outdoor
enthusiasts. The Squaw Valley slopes
are just outside, the on-site spa offers
a full menu of treatments, and a
Mountain Buddies Kids Camp program
offers daily counselor-led activities for
kids. **$$–$$$**

The Wuksachi Lodge
Tel: 1-888-252-5757
www.visitsequoia.com
This 102-room lodge sits at 7,200ft
(2,195 meters), in sight of Mount
Whitney. The rooms are set a short
distance away from the main lodge,
where facilities include a restaurant

with huge picture windows, a cocktail
lounge, and a couple of shops. **$$$**

Yosemite Lodge
Yosemite Valley
Tel: 559-252-4848
www.yosemitepark.com
Glass-and-wood detailing blend
harmoniously with rustic surroundings
at this lodge, the closest property to
Yosemite Falls. Book up to six months
in advance during summer, otherwise
try several weeks ahead. **$**

The Bidwell House
1 Main St, Chester
Tel: 530-258-3338
www.bidwellhouse.com
A charming B&B near Lassen Volcanic
National Park, this 1901-built retreat
on the southeastern slope of Mount
Lassen offers lovely views of Lake
Almanor, free Wi-fi ,and in-room TVs.
Half of the 14 rooms have a Jacuzzi,
and some have wood-burning stoves.
$

Bridge House Bed & Breakfast
1455 Riverside Drive, Redding
Tel: 530-247-7177
www.reddingbridgehouse.com
The best B&B in downtown Redding,
this cottage-style home with four
spacious rooms offers private baths,
a workout room, a buffet breakfast,
complementary Wi-fi, and views of the
Sacramento river from the upstairs
rooms. **$**

SOUTHERN CALIFORNIA

The 1880 Union Hotel
362 Bell St, Box 616, Los Alamos
Tel: 805-344-2744
www.unionhotelvictmansion.com
Unique theme rooms in an elegant
Victorian structure; well worth the trip.
$$–$$$

The Ballard Inn & Restaurant
2436 Baseline Ave, Ballard
Tel: 805-688-7770, 1-800-638-2466
www.ballardinn.com
This comfy inn comes decorated with
a mix of antiques and reproductions,
and country touches like handmade
rugs. The cozy restaurant features
a globally inspired menu, and full
breakfast is included. You can also
rent bikes on site. **$$$**

El Encanto Hotel & Garden Villas
1900 Lasuen Rd, Santa Barbara
Tel: 805-687-5000
www.elencantohotel.com
Part of the Orient Express group,
this gorgeous in-town hotel has a
restaurant, pool, and tennis courts.

$$$

Fess Parker's Doubletree Resort
633 E. Cabrillo Blvd, Santa Barbara
Tel: 805-564-4333
www.fpdtr.com
Across from beach in extensive
grounds; pool, sauna, putting green.
$$$

The Franciscan Inn
109 Bath St, Santa Barbara
Tel: 805-963-8845
www.franciscaninn.com
At the beach; health club, pool,
complimentary breakfast. **$**

Harbor View Inn
28 W. Cabrillo Blvd, Santa Barbara
Tel: 805-963-0780
www.harborviewinnsb.com
On the beach opposite Stearns Wharf;
pool, whirlpool, adjacent restaurant.
$$–$$$

Hyatt Santa Barbara
1111 E. Cabrillo Blvd, Santa Barbara
Tel: 805-963-0744
www.hotelmarmonte.com
Across from beach; pool, whirlpool,

health club. **$$**

Inn of the Spanish Garden
915 Garden St, Santa Barbara
Tel: 805-564-4700
www.spanishgardeninn.com
Mediterranean-style complex with pool
and courtyard; 23 spacious, elegant
rooms, and covered parking. **$$**

The JUST Inn
Justin Vineyards & Winery, 11680 Chimney
Rock Rd, Paso Robles
Tel: 1-800-726-0049
www.justinwine.com
Ultimately romantic and far off the
beaten path, this inn consists of
four sumptuous suites secluded
among the vines of Justin Winery.
$$$

Madonna Inn
100 Madonna Rd, San Luis Obispo
Tel: 805-543-3000
www.madonnainn.com
Well known for its eccentricity and bizarre decor, the landmark Madonna Inn boasts rooms with Western, Cave Man, Safari, Hawaiian, and Jungle themes, just to name a few. One of its famous features is the rock waterfall urinal in the men's restroom, which was designed by Hollywood set designer Harvey Allen Warren. **$$**

Paso Robles Inn
1103 Spring St, Paso Robles
Tel: 805-238-2660
www.pasoroblesinn.com
The Paso Robles Inn is a fantastic getaway with mineral spa rooms, lush gardens, a historic ballroom, and a popular steakhouse. **$**

Quality Inn
230 Five Cities Dr, Pismo Beach
Tel: 805-773-1841
A no-frills bargain option just off US 101, this motel is close to the Prime Outlets shopping mall, the Oceano Dunes State Vehicular Area, and offers beach views, free Wi-fi, and a simple continental breakfast. **$**

Sandcastle Inn
100 Stimson Ave, Pismo Beach
Tel: 805-773-2422, 1-800-822-6606
www.sandcastleinn.com
Located on the beach, the Sandcastle Inn boasts a contemporary design, sundecks with great views of the pier, and a whirlpool for guests. **$$**

Sandpiper Lodge
3525 State St, Santa Barbara
Tel: 805-687-5326
www.sandpiperlodge.com
North end of Midtown; pool, jacuzzi, nearby coffee shop. **$**

San Ysidro Ranch
900 San Ysidro Lane, Santa Barbara
Tel: 805-969-5046
www.sanysidroranch.com
Luxury resort with a celebrated history: John F. Kennedy brought his bride Jackie here on their honeymoon. **$$$**

The Upham
1404 De La Vina St, Santa Barbara
Tel: 805-962-0058
www.uphamhotel.com
Last of the great, old Santa Barbara hotels (founded 1871), with all the charm and style you'd expect. Beautifully furnished garden bungalows. **$$$**

Los Angeles

Downtown
Figueroa Hotel
939 S. Figueroa St
Tel: 213-627-8971
www.figueroahotel.com
A welcome retreat from Downtown's corporate hotels, the great-value Figueroa is an exotic addition, with a Moroccan decor, a cactus garden, and atmospheric suites. There's also a pool, a jacuzzi, and restaurants. **$**

Millennium Biltmore Hotel
506 S. Grand Ave
Tel: 213-624 1011
www.millenniumhotels.com
A fabulous, luxurious historic landmark with restaurants, pool, and jacuzzi. Rooms are plush and comfortable. **$$**

Omni Los Angeles Hotel at California Plaza
251 S. Olive St
Tel: 213-617-3300
www.omnihotels.com
Located in the California Plaza atop Bunker Hill, this luxurious hotel overlooks a water court, adjoins the Museum of Contemporary Art, and offers a health club, heated pool, sauna, Japanese fusion restaurant, and a host of superb suites. **$$$**

The Standard Downtown LA
550 S. Flower St
Tel: 213-892-8080
www.standardhotel.com
Hotelier André Balazs, of Hollywood's Chateau Marmont fame, opened Downtown's first style palace in a converted 12-story office building. One of the hippest places is the poolside bar on the roof. **$$$**

Vagabond Inn
3101 S. Figueroa St
Tel: 213-746-1531, 1-800-522-1555;
www.vagabondinn.com
Just steps from USC's campus and the Shrine Auditorium (home of the Emmy Awards), this on-the-cheap hotel caters to business travelers and families with its free parking, high-speed internet access, heated pool, cable TV, and pet-friendly rooms. **$**

Westin Bonaventure Hotel & Suites
404 S. Figueroa St
Tel: 213-624-1000
www.westin.com
One of LA's most photographed buildings, the Bonaventure has a distinctive circular interior and exterior, a pool, and a rooftop restaurant. There is a Hollywood Poster Gallery along the walk from the parking garage, and guests can ride the glass elevators that have appeared in movies like In the Line of Fire and True Lies. **$$$**

Beverly Hills, West Hollywood, and the West Side
Avalon Beverly Hills
9400 W. Olympic Blvd, Beverly Hills
Tel: 310-277-5221, 1-800-535-4715
www.avalonbeverlyhills.com
Offering a selection of stylish rooms, suites, and penthouse studios in three unique buildings around a beautifully illuminated pool. There's a highly regarded restaurant on the premises, too. **$$$**

Chamberlain West Hollywood
1000 Westmount Dr, West Hollywood
Tel: 310-657-7400
www.chamberlainwesthollywood.com
A glamourous boutique hotel on a residential street offering spacious suites, a stunning rooftop pool, jacuzzi, sauna, laundromat, and even a tiny gym. **$$**

Farmer's Daughter Hotel
115 S. Fairfax Ave
Tel: 1-800-334-1658
Directly across the street from the Farmers Market, the Grove entertainment complex, and CBS Television City, Farmer's Daughter is a country-styled hotel with rocking chairs, rain showers, and plenty of down-home hospitality. **$$$**

Hollywood Roosevelt Hotel
7000 Hollywood Blvd,
Tel: 323-466-7000
www.hollywoodroosevelt.com
Legendary landmark hotel with lots of Art Deco trimmings, but its palm-shaded pool and sleek steakhouse make this a modern-day, happening scene. **$$$**

Hotel Bel Air
701 Stone Canyon Rd, Bel-Air
Tel: 310-472-1211
www.hotelbelair.com
Deluxe and seductive, this is a long-standing movie-star hideaway in landscaped grounds in a secluded canyon, complete with elegant suites decorated in a style that harks back to the golden age of Hollywood. **$$$**

The London West Hollywood
1020 N. San Vicente Blvd, West Hollywood
Tel: 310-854-1111
www.thelondonla.com
Formerly the deluxe Wyndham Bel Age, this incarnation is a sexy, sophisticated addition to the Sunset Strip, with innovative design, fine dining, a full service spa and expert concierge service. **$$$**

Maison 140
140 Lasky Dr, Beverly Hills
Tel: 310-281-4000, 1-800-432-5444
www.maison140beverlyhills.com
This richly decorated and very stylish hotel was once owned by Lillian Gish. It is a comfortable sanctuary from the outside world, just a short stroll from Rodeo Drive. **$$$**

Mondrian Los Angeles
8440 Sunset Blvd, West Hollywood
Tel: 323-650-8999
www.mondrianhotel.com
This chic, Philippe Starck-designed hotel is a popular rendezvous for people in the movie industry. Have a cocktail in the Skybar. **$$$**

The Mission Inn Hotel and Spa.

Coastal Los Angeles

The Cadillac Hotel
8 Dudley Ave, Venice
Tel: 310-399-8876
www.thecadillachotel.com
Art Deco spot on the boardwalk with a roof sundeck. **$$**

Fairmont Miramar Hotel and Bungalows
101 Wilshire Blvd, Santa Monica
Tel: 310-576-7777
www.fairmont.com
Lush retreat above the ocean, big with celebs. **$$$**

The Hotel California
1670 Ocean Ave, Santa Monica
Tel: 310-393-2363, 1-866-571-0000
www.hotelca.com
Dating from 1948, this small, vintage hotel has ocean views, tropical murals, and free internet access. **$$**

Hotel Shangri-La
1301 Ocean Ave, Santa Monica
Tel: 310-394-2791
www.shangrila-hotel.com
Art Deco landmark opposite Palisades Park; kitchenettes. **$$**

Loews Santa Monica Beach Hotel
1700 Ocean Ave, Santa Monica
Tel: 310-458-6700, 1-800-235-6397
www.loewshotels.com
Sleek hotel with terrific Pacific views. **$$$**

Malibu Beach Inn
22878 Pacific Coast Highway, Malibu
Tel: 310-456-6444
www.malibubeachinn.com
Near the pier; some rooms have fireplaces. **$$**

Shutters Hotel on the Beach
1 Pico Blvd, Santa Monica

Tel: 310-458-0030, 1-800-334-9000
www.shuttersonthebeach.com
Cozy, low-key retreat on the beach; classy and full of artworks. **$$$**

Viceroy Santa Monica
1819 Ocean Ave, Santa Monica
Tel: 310-260-7500, 1-800-670-6185
www.viceroysantamonica.com
Urban retreat on the beach with sauna, whirlpool. **$$**

Around Los Angeles

The Anabella Hotel
1030 West Katella Ave
Tel: 714-905-1050, Anaheim
www.anabellahotel.com
Situated on 7 lush acres (3 hectares) and conveniently located across from Disneyland's California Adventure Park and the Anaheim Convention Center Campus, this California Mission-style boutique hotel features granite bathrooms, an on-site restaurant, and a quiet atmosphere. **$**

Anaheim Jolly Roger Hotel
640 W. Katella Ave, Anaheim
Tel: 714-782-7500
www.jollyrogerhotel.com
A budget option across the street from the Disneyland resort, the Jolly Roger offers simple guestrooms designed with families in mind – Kids Suites include bunk beds, and there's a coin-operated guest laundry facility. For the grown-ups there's free Wi-Fi, a cocktail lounge, and close proximity to the Anaheim Convention Center. **$**

Anaheim Plaza Hotel
1700 S. Harbor Boulevard, Anaheim
Tel: 1-800-631-4144

www.anaheimplazahotel.com
Across from Disneyland's main gate, this 300-room hotel spread across several two-story buildings offers an Olympic-size swimming pool and affordable rates. Some rooms have a patio or balcony. **$**

Bella Maggiore Inn
67 S. California St, Ventura
Tel: 805-652-0277
Homey decor and a courtyard café set an intimate atmosphere at this 1925 landmark near the beach, which some say is haunted. **$**

Disneyland Hotel
1150 Magic Way, Anaheim
Tel: 714-778-6600
disneyland.disney.go.com/disneyland-hotel
With modern luxury rooms, pools, and waterslides, and themed dining, the Disneyland Hotel is a great option for families (you can really make your kid's day with a wake-up call from Mickey Mouse). Wireless and wired internet are included. **$$$**

Disney's Grand Californian Hotel and Spa
1600 South Disneyland Dr, Anaheim
Tel: 714-635-2300, 1-800-225-2024
This craftsman-style resort has a private entrance to the California Adventure Park, as well as three pools (including one with a waterslide and a

PRICE CATEGORIES

Prices are for a standard double room without breakfast:
$ = less than $150
$$ = $150–$225
$$$ = $225–$375
$$$$ = more than $375

Zane Grey Pueblo Hotel, Santa Catalina Island.

second with private cabanas), a spa, and restaurant. **$$$**

Disney's Paradise Pier Hotel
1717 S. Disneyland Dr, Anaheim
Tel: 714-956-6425
www.disneyland.com
A surfer-themed hotel across the street from Disney's California Adventure Park, this family-friendly hotel offers a water slide and family suites. **$$–$$$**

Hilton Los Angeles/Universal City
555 Universal Hollywood Dr, Universal City
Tel: 818-506-2500
www.hilton.com
Just a block from the entrance to Universal Studios, this 24-story Hollywood hills hotel employs a multilingual staff, has an outdoor pool and whirlpool, and an on-site restaurant serving California, Chinese, and Continental cuisine. **$$**

Knott's Berry Farm Resort Hotel
7675 Crescent Avenue, Buena Park
Tel: 1-866-752-2444
www.knottshotel.com
Within walking distance of Knott's Berry farm, this family-friendly hotel has an arcade, pool, and even Peanuts-themed rooms. **$$**

Sheraton Universal Hotel
333 Universal, Hollywood Dr, Universal City
Tel: 818-980-1212, 1-800-325-3535
www.sheratonuniversal.com
Actually located on the back lot of Universal Studios, this refuge features contemporary decor in a palate of blues, browns, and ivories, rich fabrics, bold artwork, Shine by Bliss bath products, and an outdoor heated pool. **$$$**

South Bay and Orange Coast

Blue Lantern Inn
34343 Street of the Blue Lantern, Dana Point

Tel: 1-800-950-1236
www.bluelanterninn.com
With a dramatic bluff-top location above the Dana Point Yacht Harbor, the elegant Blue Lantern is a lovely bed and breakfast option in Orange County. After a complimentary breakfast, borrow bikes to explore the coastline, or get pampered with on-site spa treatments. **$$**

Hotel Queen Mary
1126 Queen's Highway, Long Beach
Tel: 1-800-437-2934
www.queemary.com
A historic 1930s cruise ship docked in Long Beach, the grand Queen Mary is a one-of-a-kind experience, with historic state rooms, operable portholes, Art Deco art, and a great champagne brunch. **$–$$**

The Inn on Mt Ada
398 Wrigley Rd, Catalina Island
Tel: 310-510-2030
www.innonmtada.com
Undoubtedly the most luxurious lodgings in town, this inn with spectacular views was once the hilltop mansion of William Wrigley Jr. who bought Catalina Island in 1921. **$$$**

Montage Resort & Spa
30801 S. Coast Highway, Laguna Beach
Tel: 1-866-271-6953
www.montagelagunabeach.com
The elegant 250-room Montage is a splurge-worthy beach resort with sweeping ocean panoramas and Craftsman-style architecture on 30 lushly landscaped acres. **$$$$**

Ritz-Carlton Laguna Niguel
1 Ritz Carlton Drive, Dana Point
Tel: 1-800-241-3333
www.ritzcarlton.com
Perched atop a high bluff overlooking the Pacific Ocean, this Dana Point resort has luxe rooms featuring feather beds and Egyptian cotton sheets, and

restaurants with gorgeous ocean views and impeccable service. **$$$$**

Snug Harbor Inn
108 Sumner Ave, Catalina Island
Tel: 310-510-8400
www.snugharbor-inn.com
Six lovely and luxurious bay-view rooms are situated in the century-old former Hotel Monterey. **$$–$$$**

St Regis Monarch Beach Resort
1 Monarch Beach Rd, Dana Point
Tel: 1-800-722-1543
www.stregismb.com
Championship golf, private beach access, and the award-winning Spa Gaucin are just a few of the exclusive offerings this boldly modern hotel. Rooms feature private balconies, spacious bathrooms, and 300-thread-count linens. **$$$$**

Surf and Sand Resort
1555 S. Coast Highway, Laguna Beach
Tel: 1-888-869-7569
www.surfandsandresort.com
First opened in 1948, this luxurious hotel is located right on Laguna Beach's oceanfront, and features rooms with private balconies, the Aquaterra spa, and coastal dining at an on-site restaurant. **$$$–$$$$**

Zane Grey Pueblo Hotel
199 Chimes Tower Rd, Catalina Island
Tel: 310-510-0966
www.zanegreypueblohotel.com
This hilltop hotel was once the home of famed novelist Zane Grey and now has a heated pool, courtesy taxi service, and airy rooms. **$$**

The Deserts

The Mission Inn Hotel & Spa
3649 Mission Inn Ave, Riverside
Tel: 951-784-0300
www.missioninn.com
A historic hotel once popular with presidents and movie stars, the Mission Inn and Spa in Riverside is a unique pastiche of architectural styles, with old world luxury (rich woods, plush fabrics, opulent details) and modern amenities like high-speed internet and plasma televisions. **$$$**

La Quinta
49449 Hacienda Dr, La Quinta
Tel: 760-564-4111, 1-800-598-3828
www.laquintaresort.com
Twenty miles (32km) from Palm Springs, La Quinta rests at the foot of the Santa Rosa Mountains in the Coachella Valley. The stunning hacienda-style resort has ballooned since opening in 1926 and now encompasses nearly 800 guest rooms and villas and over 40 pools. **$$–$$$**

Riviera Resort & Spa
1600 N. Indian Canyon Dr, Palm Springs
Tel: 760-327-8311
www.psriviera.com

Located near the Palm Springs Aerial Tramway, the Riviera Resort & Spa boasts tennis courts, pools, and a supervised children's camp. **$$$**

Viceroy Palm Springs
415 S. Belardo Rd, Palm Springs
Tel: 760-320-4117
www.viceroypalmsprings.com
Outdoors at this luxury resort you'll find poolside pavilions, terraced villas, citrus trees, and manicured gardens. In rooms, decor is in a fresh, crisp palate of white, black, and lemon yellow. **$$**

Villa Royale Inn
1620 Indian Trail, Palm Springs
Tel: 760-327-2314
www.villaroyale.com
Located in a secluded and quiet neighborhood, this bed and breakfast with charming courtyards and a pool offers rooms in varied styles, many with fireplaces or sunny terraces. **$$**

San Diego

Andaz Hotel
600 F Street
Tel: 619-849-1234
A chic, modern boutique hotel in the Gaslamp District, the Andaz is one of the coolest hotels in San Diego. Rooms are fresh white, and the rooftop lounge is perfect for sipping cocktails. **$$$**

Bahia Resort Hotel
998 W. Mission Bay Dr
Tel: 858-488-0551
www.bahiahotel.com
This beachfront resort has over 300 rooms, water sports, pool, children's activities, and moonlight cruises on the Bahia Belle. **$$**

Balboa Park Inn
3402 Park Blvd
Tel: 619-298-0823
www.balboaparkinn.com
Conveniently located in Balboa Park near the San Diego Zoo, this inn consists of four Spanish-Colonial

buildings with 26 distinctive rooms, each with a private bathroom, refrigerator, and TV. A free Continental breakfast is included. **$**

Hotel del Coronado
1500 Orange Ave, Coronado
Tel: 619-435-6611
www.hoteldel.com
This world-famous Victorian-era landmark with its red roof and turrets is situated on its own beach. Sumptuous and grand, the Del has tennis courts, pools, and restaurants galore. The hotel even "starred" in the movie Some Like It Hot. **$$$**

The Lodge at Torrey Pines
11480 N. Torrey Pines Rd, La Jolla
Tel: 858-453-4420,
1-800-656-0087
www.lodgetorreypines.com
A Craftsman-type mansion on an ocean bluff, the meticulously furnished Lodge at Torrey Pines is close to the world-renowned Torrey Pines Golf Course. **$$$**

Manchester Grand Hyatt
Harbor Dr and Market Pl, San Diego
Tel: 619-232-1234, 1-800-233-1234
www.hyatt.com
The Machester Grand Hyatt offers spacious rooms in downtown San Diego, as well as a pool, sauna, tennis courts, and exercise room. **$$$**

Paradise Point Resort & Spa
1404 Vacation Rd, San Diego
Tel: 858-274-4630, 1-800-344-2626
www.paradisepoint.com
Come for bungalows in spacious landscaped grounds on Mission Bay, along with pools, tennis courts, and boat rentals. **$$**

San Diego Marriott Gaslamp Quarter
660 K St, San Diego
Tel: 619-696-0234
www.marriott.com
Adjacent to PETCO Park and two blocks from the San Diego Convention

Center, this luxury hotel boasts a sauna and whirlpool, sky lounge, Gilchrest and Soames bath amenities, and a concierge level with a special lounge. **$$–$$$**

Town and Country Resort
500 Hotel Circle N., San Diego
Tel: 619-291-7131
www.towncountry.com
A family-owned Mission Valley resort, Town and Country offers landscaped grounds, pools, several restaurants and an on-site bakery. **$**

US Grant Hotel
326 Broadway, San Diego
Tel: 619-232-3121
www.usgrant.net
Originally built by the son of Ulysses S. Grant, this historic Beaux Arts hotel is located downtown near shopping. French and Native American Indian art decorate rooms with lofty ceilings, cream walls, and beautiful molding. Bathrooms have glass-enclosed marble showers and Remede bath products. **$$**

The Westgate Hotel
1055 2nd Ave, San Diego
Tel: 619-238-1818
www.westgatehotel.com
A perfect picture of refinement in the Gaslamp Quarter, the Westgate welcomes guests into a lobby with Baccarat crystal chandeliers, antique furnishings, bronze sculptures, and a Steinway grand. Lovely furnishings continue in the rooms, where you'll find luxurious bedding and marble bathrooms. **$$**

The Westin Gaslamp Quarter
910 Broadway Circle, San Diego
Tel: 619-239-2200
www.starwoodhotels.com
The 450-room hotel has neutral and calming rooms with bay and city views, and tons of ways to stay active: choose from the pool, saunas, lighted tennis courts, health club, and next-door shopping mall. **$$**

The Westin San Diego
400 West Broadway, San Diego
Tel: 619-239-4500
www.starwoodhotels.com
The Westin is a stunning green cluster of geometric towers with spectacular views of San Diego Bay. Other perks include ergonomic work chairs, a fitness center, an outdoor pool, and upscale contemporary cuisine. **$$$**

Hotel del Coronado.

PRICE CATEGORIES

Prices are for a standard double room without breakfast:
$ = less than $150
$$ = $150–$225
$$$ = $225–$375
$$$$ = more than $375

EATING OUT

RECOMMENDED RESTAURANTS, CAFES AND BARS

Choosing a Restaurant

California is a food-lover's delight, and has the statistics to prove it. San Francisco alone has more than 3,000 restaurants and bars, said to be more per capita than anywhere else in the world. It's also been estimated that Southern Californians dine out on average two or three times a week. It's perhaps no surprise, then, that California has reputation for fine food.

There is an endless variety of cuisines to try, from classic American and "California Cuisine," to all manner of ethnic food. From Europe you'll find Italian trattorias, French bistros, German beer halls, and Mediterranean eateries with hookah lounges. From Asia you can taste curries from India, Vietnamese *pho*, Korean BBQ (especially in Los Angeles), sushi, and dim sum, plus Americanized fusion fare from several regions. From nearby Central America, California has whole-heartedly adopted Mexican dishes, including the now-ubiquitous burritos, quesadillas, and tacos *al pastor*, especially in San Diego and in San Francisco's Mission District. South America is represented in the state as well, from Brazilian steakhouses to Peruvian restaurants serving savory *lomo saltado* and fresh ceviche. In short, California offers one of the most diverse dinner menus in the world. Of course, the drink menu has the best local wine in the country, too.

Dining in California is largely a casual affair, with thousands of neighborhood eateries catering to their local fans. Locals slip into their favorite cafés on weekday mornings between 7 and 9am for a coffee and muffin to bring to work, while freelance workers spend entire days at cafés,

Restaurant in Angels Camp, gateway to Columbia State Historic Park.

sipping lattes and using the free Wi-fi to work on laptops. Lunch standbys are usually sandwiches and salads, although the prevalence of ethnic eateries means you could just as easily have a crepe, burrito, or Pad Thai. On weekends, breakfast and lunch combine into casual brunches from 10am to 2pm, where hearty American fare (omelets, oatmeal, pancakes, waffles) is served with California, French, or Southern flair. Unfortunately, reservations are rarely taken for brunch, meaning you may need to grab a to-go coffee from a nearby café to sip as you wait for a table. Come

dinner – which is served as early as 5–6pm and until 10–11pm – you can really take advantage of the diversity of restaurants. At popular restaurants in larger cities, reservations are usually needed. Dressing up for dinner is rarely required (only at the very finest restaurants are jackets required), but in major cities some trendy restaurants do have a see-and-be-seen vibe, in which you'll feel more comfortable if you've left your sneakers and shorts at the hotel.

The following list is a mere sampling of some of the notable restaurants across the state.

NORTHERN CALIFORNIA

San Francisco

A16
2355 Chestnut St
Tel: 415-771-2216
www.a16sf.com
With an open kitchen up front and a crowded bar, lively A16 dishes up wood-fired Neapolitan pizzas and other rustic fare inspired by southern Italy, particularly Campania. **$$**

Absinthe Brasserie and Bar
398 Hayes St
Tel: 415-551-1590
www.absinthe.com
Ideal for a romantic dinner before the symphony, ballet, or opera (or a refresher after exploring Civic Center and Hayes Valley), this upscale brasserie serves American-influenced French and Northern Italian dishes in a casually romantic atmosphere; think leather banquettes, antique mirrors, and period art. The soft garlic pretzels are a local favorite.

The Alembic
1725 Haight St
Tel 415-666-0822
www.alembicbar.com
If you're craving a superlative cocktail near Haight-Ashbury, sidle up to The Alembic's bar, where mixology is an art form. For dinner consider savory pork belly sliders, caramelized scallops with sweetbreads, or, for the adventurous, bone marrow with caper gremolata and garlic confit. **$$–$$$**

Barbacco
220 California St
Tel: 415-955-1919
www.barbaccosf.com
There's always a lively buzz at

this modern Italian trattoria in the Financial District. Exposed brick walls, small communal tables, and wine lists on iPads set a casually cool vibe, while the Italian fare is simple and delicious: house-cured salumi, a half dozen different bruschette, Sicilian meatballs with raisins and pinenuts, and even gelato. Its mature big sister next door, Perbacco, is more formal. Closed Sunday. **$$**

La Boulange
1909 Union St, Marina
Tel: 415-440-4450
www.laboulangebakery.com
With a dozen outposts in San Francisco, this Marina branch of the French bakery and cafe chain is a go-to for locals when they're craving croissants and decadent French pastries, open-faced sandwiches, or a simple brunch. **$**

Boulevard
1 Mission St
Tel: 415-543-6084
www.boulevardrestaurant.com
One of the top special-occasion destinations in the city, this Embarcadero landmark delivers exceptional American regional food in an elegant Belle Epoque-inspired setting. The wood-oven specialties, like the pork prime rib chop with crispy bacon and sauerkraut dumplings, are standouts. Reservations essential. **$$$**

Cha Cha Cha
1801 Haight St, 2327 Mission Street
Tel: 415-386-7670, 415-824-1502
www.cha3.com
If you're in the mood for a boisterous atmosphere, tasty tapas, and pitchers

of sangria, Cha Cha Cha's outposts in the Haight and Mission districts are the place to go. No reservations.

Cotogna
490 Pacific Ave
Tel: 415-775-8508
www.cotognasf.com
Next door to its fine dining sister restaurant, Quince, Cotogna is a more casual (and less expensive) alternative. The rustic Italian menu changes daily, and includes spit-roasted or grilled meats and fish, pizzas from the wood-fired oven, and house-made pastas.

DOSA on Fillmore
1700 Fillmore St
Tel: 415-441-3672
www.dosasf.com
In a lofty and chic 200-seat space, DOSA serves up authentic Southern Indian regional cuisine with an innovative spin. Dishes like Tamil lamb curry, mango prawns, and dahi vada (lentil dumplings) can be paired with international wines or a gin-based, "spice-driven" cocktail.

Frances
3870 17th St
Tel: 415-621-3870
www.frances-sf.com
Opened in 2010, this relaxed Castro newcomer became a fast favorite with local foodies. Chef-owner Melissa Perello's daily changing menu of modern-Cal cuisine offers dishes like Sonoma duck breast with butter-bean ragout, and caramelized scallops with toasted faro and wild mushrooms. Reservations recommended.

Fresca
2114 Fillmore St, 3945 24th St
Tel: 415-447-2668, 415-695-0549
www.frescasf.com
In a lively dining room with an open kitchen, hungry couples and groups dig into nouveau Peruvian cuisine, including delicious fresh ceviche and savory lomo saltado. **$$**

Greens
Fort Mason, Building A
Tel: 415-771-6222
www.greensrestaurant.com
In a one-time army warehouse with bay views, this airy, upscale vegetarian restaurant earns raves even from carnivores. The Saturday evening

In 'N' Out Burger, San Francisco.

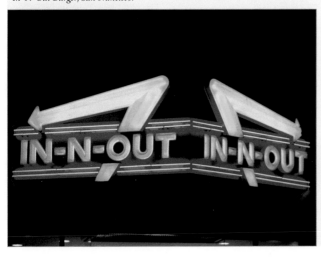

PRICE CATEGORIES

Prices are for a meal for two people, without wine.
$ = less than $30
$$ = $30–$60
$$$ = $60–$100
$$$$ = more than $100

prix-fixe is a relative bargain, and its takeout counter, Greens to Go, is open all day. Reservations recommended. Closed for Sunday dinner and Monday lunch. **$$**

In 'N Out Burger
333 Jefferson St
Tel: 1-800-786-1000
www.in-n-out.com
Founded in 1948, In 'N Out is possibly the most loved fast-food chain in California. In old-fashioned diner digs, this fisherman's outpost is an easy stop for a simple – and good – burger, fries, and milkshake. **$**

Kokkari
200 Jackson St
Tel: 415-981-0983
www.kokkari.com
The best place in the city for sophisticated Greek food, this inviting, upscale Greek taverna lures diners to the border of North Beach and the Financial District to feast (below its beamed ceilings and by its massive fireplace) on feta cheese filo pies, spiced and grilled lamb skewers, and of course walnut and honey baklava with vanilla-praline ice cream. **$$$**

Little Star Pizza
400 Valencia St (also 846 Divisadero St)
Tel: 415-551-7827
www.littlestarpizza.com
Local hipsters flock to this branch of Little Star for their deep-dish pizza with Chicago-style crust -- it's no wonder President Obama loves the recipe. Decor is simple, with exposed brick walls and wooden tables and chairs, but it hardly matters because everyone's focused on the pizza! The "Little Star" (spinach blended with ricotta and feta, mushrooms, onions, garlic) is a local fave. No reservations. **$**

Mama's
1701 Stockton St
Tel: 415-362-6421
Mama's delivers an excellent brunch in North Beach, but it's jammed on weekends, so try it during the week. If you're starving in line, grab some delicious fresh focaccia across the street at Liguria Bakery. Closed Monday. **$**

Molinari Delicatessen
373 Columbus Ave
Tel: 415-421-2337
www.molinarisalame.com
This classic Italian deli is a North Beach institution. In addition to deli sandwiches, you'll find imported cheese, cured meats, and canned goods, alaong with Molinari's own selection of sausage salamis and raviolis made in Hunters Point.

Osha Thai
696 Geary St

Tel: 415-278-9991
www.oshathai.com
There are five other outposts of this popular Thai restaurant, but this one stays open til 2am, making it a great pit-stop between bar-hops Downtown. **$**

Osome
3145 Fillmore St
Tel: 415-931-8898
This is an excellent sushi bar that also does the usual range of cooked Japanese food. Closed for lunch on weekends. **$$**

L'Osteria del Forno
519 Columbus Ave
Tel: 415-982-1124
For casual but satisfying Italian food, including antipasti, thin-crusted pizzas, and a fine roast pork loin, head to this crowd-pleaser that captures the spirit of North Beach. **$**

Park Chow
1240 9th Ave
Tel: 415-665-9912
www.chowfoodbar.com
South of Golden Gate Park, Park Chow is a family-friendly eatery serving simple comfort food -- pastas, sandwiches, salads, and pizzas – either downstairs by the fireplace or upstairs on the patio (don't worry, there are heat lamps!). **$**

Plouf
40 Belden Place
Tel: 415-986-6491
There are a number of good café-restaurants with outdoor seating on Belden Place, a narrow, European-style pedestrian alley in walking distance from Union Square. This seafood bistro with outdoor tables serves heavenly, heaped bowls of steamed mussels prepared eight different ways. **$$**

Rosamunde's Sausage Grill
2832 Mission St
Tel: 415-970-9015
www.rosamundesausagegrill.com
If you're feeling peckish in the Mission or the Lower Haight district, the perfect snack awaits you at Rosamunde's: over a dozen types of grilled sausage to choose from (like smoked pork, bacon-wrapped beef, duck and figs) and a hefty beer selection to pair it with. **$**

Sears Fine Food
439 Powell St
Tel: 415-986-0700
www.searsfinefood.com
At this old-school San Francisco institution (in business since 1938) you can have sourdough French toast and Swedish pancakes for breakfast, club sandwiches and Bay shrimp Louie for lunch, and prime rib or San Francisco cioppino (a fish stew) for dinner. **$$$**

Slanted Door
1 Ferry Building
Tel: 415-861-8032
www.slanteddoor.com
Chef Charles Phan's masterful take on Vietnamese cuisine wins over the foodies; so does the bay view, through the floor-to-ceiling windows. **$$–$$$**

Suppenkuche
525 Laguna St
Tel: 415-252-9289
www.suppenkuche.com
At one of the few German restaurants in the city, hearty portions of German classics – spaetzle, schnitzel, potato pancakes – are served to a loud and lively crowd seated at long communal tables. Around 30 beers (mostly German) are on tap.

La Taqueria
2889 Mission St
Tel: 415-285-7117
The epitome of the casual Mission district taqueria, this immensely popular spot is a perfect place to grab some carnitas (pulled pork) tacos or burritos. **$**

Wayfare Tavern
558 Sacramento St
Tel: 415-772-9060
www.wayfaretavern.com
The pre-meal popovers are so delicious at Tyler Florence's upscale tavern that it's hard not to have three. But restrain yourself, because the menu of American comfort food (with a turn-of-the-20th-century twist) includes gems like deviled eggs, organic fried chicken, and Scharffen Berger chocolate cream pie...and you'll want every last bite! **$$$**

Zuni
1658 Market St
Tel: 415-552 2522
www.zunicafe.com
Make reservations and elbow past the crowded copper bar for the best roasted chicken and bread salad (for two) imaginable. The daily changing menu is inspired by traditional Italian and French recipes. Closed Monday. **$$**

Greater San Francisco Bay Area

East Bay
À Côté
5478 College Ave, Oakland
Tel: 510-655-6469
www.acoterestaurant.com
Choose from cozy tables or larger communal ones at this 75-seat resto in the charming Rockridge district. The small-plates menu of seasonal Mediterranean dishes – like oven-roasted mussels with Pernod – are perfect for sharing family-style.

Bay Wolf
853 Piedmont Ave, Oakland

Tel: 510-655-6004
www.baywolf.com
A monthly changing Cal-Med menu maintains enviable quality, where seasonal delights are accompanied by a well-chosen wine list.
Breads of India
2448 Sacramento Ave, Berkeley
Te: 510-848-7684
High marks from students and foodies. **$**
Chez Panisse
1517 Shattuck Ave, Berkeley
Tel: 510-548-5525
www.chezpanisse.com
One of the most famous restaurants in the country, where "California Cuisine" is said to have started. The dinner-only downstairs restaurant (closed Sun) has only a set menu; the upstairs café is also open for lunch, and is cheaper. However both need reservations weeks in advance. **$$$$**
La Note
2377 Shattuck Ave, Berkeley
Tel: 510-843-1535
www.lanoterestaurant.com
Provençal-inspired bistro in downtown Berkeley, La Note is a brunch standby with locals, who come for lemon gingerbread pancakes, Emmenthal cheese omelets, baguette sandwiches, and salad Niçoise.
Yoshi's
510 Embarcadero West, Oakland
Tel: 510-238-9200
www.yoshis.com
This classy Japanese place on Jack London Square doubles as one of the Bay Area's best jazz venues. Superfresh sushi makes the perfect date night, but Sunday matinees are kid-friendly – as are the udon noodles. Call for reservations. **$$–$$$**
Zachary's Pizza
5801 College Ave, Oakland
Tel: 510-525-5950
www.zacharys.com
Be prepared to wait for a table at this loud and lively local standby that's been going since 1983. Don't worry, it's worth the wait for the hearty, buttery crust deep-dish pizzas piled with tomatoes and toppings.

North Bay
Fish
350 Harbor Dr, Sausalito
Tel: 415-331-3474
www.331fish.com
With a waterfront location, dedication to sustainability, and friendly atmosphere, there are plenty of reasons to visit this popular seafood restaurant. **$$**
Lark Creek Inn
234 Magnolia Ave, Larkspur
Tel: 415-924-7766

If you're spending time north of San Francisco, this is the tops. Inside a Victorian home, celebrity chef/restaurateur Bradley Ogden delivers seasonal fresh ingredients and American fare in a delightful setting. Enjoy a selection from the vast California-only wine list as you dine beneath the redwoods. **$$$–$$$$**
Murray Circle
601 Murray Circle, Sausalito
Tel: 415-339-4700
www.cavallopoint.com/dine
A relaxed but elegant dining room with fine art photography, restored ceilings, and Golden Gate Bridge views sets the scene for dining on refined California Cuisine like roasted rare California king salmon with caviar cream, and red wine braised Wagyu short rib with beer-battered onion rings. **$$$**
Sushi Ran
107 Caledonia St, Sausalito
Tel: 415-332-3620
www.sushiran.com
For the freshest fish in the Bay Area, head to this long-time Sausalito fixture, which delivers a creative fusion of traditional Japanese and Pacific cuisine, including sushi and sashimi and other entrees from land and sea like slow-cooked Pekin duck breast, miso-glazed black cod, and Vietnamese "shaking beef." **$$–$$$**

South Bay
Cafe Borrone
1010 El Camino Real, Menlo Park
Tel: 650-327-0830
Popular among students and entrepreneurs, Cafe Borrone has bistro fare and a large patio drenched in sun most days.
La Forêt
21747 Bertram Road, San Jose
Tel: 408-997-3458
On the site of the first adobe hotel in California (built in 1848), this charming old house is graced with tuxedo-clad waiters, French–Italian entrees, fresh mussels and clams, and tempting desserts. Dinner only Tue–Sun, plus Sunday brunch. **$$–$$$**
Henry's Hi-Life,
301 W. St John St, San Jose
Tel: 408-295-5414
Good barbecued food at reasonable prices. Open for lunch (Tue–Fri) and dinner. **$$**
Manresa
320 Village Lane, Los Gatos
Tel: 408-354-4330
Chef David Kinch's food is classic, with the adventuresome flair of haute cuisine. At Manresa, be prepared for a leisurely dining experience inspired by local ingredients. **$$$$**

Original Joe's
301 S. First St, San Jose
Tel: 408-292-7030
Home of the famous "Joe's Special" – a tasty sandwich of spinach, ground beef, mushrooms, onions, and scrambled eggs, this old-school Italian resto serves huge portions and is open til 1am. **$**
Rose and Crown English Food and Ale House
547 Emerson St, Palo Alto.
Tel: 650-327-7673
A little pub tucked next to posh University Avenue, offering a glimpse into Palo Alto before the days of the dot-com boom. A wide selection of beer, and the kitchen cooks up some of the best burgers around, complete with pungent Stilton, if that's what you desire. **$**
Tamarine
546 University Ave, Palo Alto
Tel: 650-325-8500
www.tamarinerestaurant.com
In an elegant dining room with Vietnamese fine art on the walls, Tamarine delivers delicious contemporary Vietnamese food. **$$$**

Wine Country
Auberge du Soleil
180 Rutherford Hill Rd, Rutherford
Tel: 707-963-1211
Sit on the small deck for beautiful views of vineyards, and enjoy impeccable Wine Country cuisine with Mediterranean influences, and an extensive wine list showcasing the best from nearby vineyards. **$$$$**
Bistro Jeanty
6510 Washington St, Yountville
Tel: 707-944-0130
Excellent flagship restaurant from chef/owner Philippe Jeanty, with a seasonal menu of homey dishes like coq au vin and cassoulet, served on the patio or in the attractive dining room. **$$**
Bottega
6525 Washington St, Yountville
Tel: 707-945-1050
www.botteganapavalley.com
Celebrity chef Michael Chiarello showcases micro-regional Italian cuisine and artisanal and housemade ingredients in a beautiful setting. **$$$$**
Brix
7377 St Helena Highway, Napa
Tel: 707-944-2749
www.brix.com

PRICE CATEGORIES

Prices are for a meal for two people, without wine.
$ = less than $30
$$ = $30–$60
$$$ = $60–$100
$$$$ = more than $100

A beautiful, quintessential Wine Country restaurant, Brix offers farm-to-table cuisine inspired by its extensive gardens and traditions of Southern France and Northern Italy. After filling up on ricotta gnocchi with spring vegetable ragout, wood-oven pizza, or sautéed scallops, you can stroll through their vegetable garden out back. **$$$$**

Café le Haye
140 E. Napa St
Tel: 707-935-5994
www.cafelahaye.com
Just off Sonoma's downtown square, Café le Haye delivers simply prepared food (think roast chicken with caramelized chicken jus, and grilled pork tenderloin with lemon-hazelnut drizzle) along with excellent service. **$$**

Calistoga Inn Restaurant and Brewery
1250 Lincoln Ave, Calistoga
Tel: 707-942-4101
Here in Calistoga's quaint Downtown, you'll find a popular and casual outdoor patio, friendly service, and large portions of American-style comfort food, like Dungeness crab cakes, baby back ribs, and peanut butter pie. **$$**

Farmstead
738 Main St, St Helena
Tel: 707-963-9101
www.longmeadowranch.com
In a former nursery barn with indoor and outdoor seating, this 110-seat restaurant balances comfort food with inventive accents, and organic ingredients at their most fresh. Wood-grilled Berkshire pork chop, chili-roasted local Dungeness crab, and strawberry shortcake are sample menu items. **$$$**

Fremont Diner
2698 Fremont Dr, Sonoma
Tel: 707-938-7370
www.thefreemontdiner.com
Look for the old, white wooden shack: here you can casually dine on burgers, bisuits, pulled pork sandwiches, onion rings, and the spicy Nashville Hot chicken. **$$**

The French Laundry
6640 Washington St, Yountville
Tel: 707-944-2380
A true Wine Country gem in a beautiful building serving award-winning, elegant cuisine. Call months in advance for reservations, and save money for months in order to sample the nine-course tasting menu. **$$$$**

The Girl and the Fig
110 W. Spain St, Sonoma
Tel: 707-938-3634
www.thegirlandthefig.com
Upscale with an informal vibe, this popular Sonoma square restaurant offers contemporary, French-influenced fare. There's croques monsieur with St George cheese, wild flounder meunière, duck confit, and profiteroles. There's wine, of course, but also great house cocktails, like a lavender mojito and honey gin sparkler. **$$$**

Harvest Moon Café
487 1st St W, Sonoma
Tel: 707-933-8160
www.harvestmooncafesonoma.com
The menu changes daily at this small family-run downtown café. In dishes like split pea soup with smoked ham and chives, grilled pork loin with crispy polenta and artichoke, and a Meyer lemon curd tartlet, the focus is highlighting the freshest and best local food. **$$**

Hydro Bar & Grill
1403 Lincoln Ave, Calistoga

Tel: 707-942 9777.
Over 20 microbrews and California Cuisine are served up in a breezy café atmosphere. **$$**

Kenwood Restaurant and Bar
9900 Highway 12, Kenwood
Tel: 707-833-6326
Good for dinner but even better for lunch on the patio, literally surrounded by vineyards and flowers. The menu is not daring, but uses fresh seasonal ingredients and pleases with duck, steak, and tasty seafood entrees. **$$$**

Pica Pica
Oxbow Public Market, 610 1st St, Napa
Tel: 707-251-3757
Corn (maize) plays the starring role at this casual eatery: with arepas (grilled cornflour cakes) stuffed with meat, cheese, and seasonal vegetables. Soups, salads, empanadas, and sangria round out the menu. **$**

Solbar
755 Silverado Trail, Calistoga
Tel: 707-226-0850
www.solagecalistoga.com
A spacious outdoor patio features a firepit and beautiful views of the surrounding mountains, while inside the warm atmosphere is rustic but chic. The California Cuisine menu with Southern influences is split between heartier dishes (roasted Hampshire double cut pork chops with sweet corn griddle cakes) and lighter fare (crispy panisse with pine nut chermoula). **$$$**

The Swiss Hotel
18 W. Spain St, Sonoma
Tel: 707-938-2884
Located on the beautiful and historic Sonoma Plaza, the cozy, low-ceilinged bar is a favorite among locals who also dig in to homemade pastas and wood-fired pizza (the house specialties), served on the garden patio or in the elegant dining room. **$$**

Zazu
3535 Guerneville Rd, Santa Rosa
Tel: 707-523 4814
www.zazurestaurant.com
A husband-and-wife chef team bring their individual styles to the table and the result is a refreshing mix of rustic Italian and American/Californian cuisine with an emphasis on seasonal fresh produce and creative combinations. **$$**

Monterey Peninsula and Big Sur

Casanova
Fifth Ave near San Carlos, Carmel
Tel: 831-625-0501
The emphasis here is on seafood served with light sauces, but there are also veal, lamb, and beef dishes. Open for breakfast, lunch, dinner, and Sunday brunch in a French cottage setting. **$$**

French-inspired cuisine at The Girl and the Fig, Sonoma.

Crow's Nest
2218 E. Cliff Dr, Santa Cruz
Tel: 831-476-4560
www.crowsnest-santacruz.com
Offering fresh seafood, chowder, and salads, with views over the harbor, Crow's Nest has something for everyone. There are different menus to choose from, and live nightly entertainment too. Happy Hour starts at 3pm. **$$**

Deetjen's Big Sur Inn
48865 Highway 1, Big Sur
Tel: 831-667-2377
Local ingredients inspire the menu here, whether for breakfast alfresco or a fireside dinner. A funky, rustic Big Sur legend. **$$$**

First Awakenings
125 Ocean View Blvd, Pacific Grove
Tel: 831-372-1125
www.firstawakenings.net
One of the best brunch spots in Monterey County, this no-frills café with friendly service offers fritatas, · crepes, raisin bread French toast, and a long list of sandwiches and salads. **$**

Hog's Breath Inn
San Carlos, Carmel
Tel: 831-625-1044
www.hogsbreathinn.net
This is a classic Carmel bar for locals, but tourists come for a glimpse of Clint Eastwood's digs and to enjoy a surf-turf-pasta-burger-salads kind of menu. **$$**

Monterey Fish House
2114 Del Monte Ave, Monterey
Tel: 831-373-4647
Make reservations and enjoy oak-grilled fish and oysters, hearty cioppino, and homemade linguini with seafood in a boisterous, informal atmosphere. **$$**

Nepenthe
State Highway 1, Big Sur
Tel: 831-667-2345
Enjoy spectacular views of waves crashing 800ft (250 meters) below, homemade soups, and enormous chef's salads. Tourists and locals mingle comfortably at this legendary café. **$$**

Pasta Moon
315 Main St #C, Half Moon Bay
Tel: 650-726-5125
www.pastamoon.com
The contemporary Italian food here gets rave reviews – especially the butternut squash ravioli, and porcinini mushroom pappardelle. Save room for butterscotch pudding! **$**

The Restaurant at Ventana
State Highway 1, Big Sur
Tel: 831-667 2331
At a luxurious resort set back in the woods, you can enjoy a rustic atmosphere (large wood pillars, a long

Café Beaujolais, Mendocino.

bar, and a cozy fireplace) and fresh California Cuisine, like spice-roasted duck breast with sweet potato and tarragon sauce, and Hawaiian coral cod with leek and corn risotto and Chardonnay-ginger butter. **$$$**

Sierra Mar
State Highway 1, Big Sur
Tel: 831-667-2800
The glass-walled restaurant overlooking the sea serves up some of the classiest cuisine around. **$$$**

North Coast

Albion River Inn
3790 N. State Highway 1, Albion
Tel: 707-937-1919
www.albionriverinn.com
Breathtaking views, a cozy fireplace, and piano tunes make for a beautiful setting to enjoy sea-inspired meat, poultry, pasta, and seafood dishes, as well as an award-winning wine list. Scotch tastings are available nightly. **$$$–$$$$**

Bovine Bakery
11315 State Highway 1, Point Reyes Station
Tel: 415-663-9420
The line often snakes out the door at this small Pt Reyes Station bakery, which serves morning buns, giant scones, and other pastries (including gluten-free options) as well as pizza and soup. It's a good stop going to or from Tomales Bay. There's another branch in Petaluma. **$**

Cafe Beaujolais
961 Ukiah St, Mendocino
Tel: 707-937-5614
This cozy California-French restaurant

in historic Mendocino offers beautifully prepared dishes with a focus on organic produce, local seafood, and free-range meats. **$$**

MacCallum House Restaurant
45020 Albion St, Mendocino
Tel: 1-800-609-0492
Local ingredients dominate the exquisite menu. Particular favorites include the Dungeness crab parfait and the seared duck breast served with a duck confit bread pudding and blood-orange port sauce. Superb at every level, this is a "must," regardless of whether you're staying at the inn.

Manka's Inverness Lodge
30 Callendar Way, Inverness
Tel: 415-669-1034
A cult favorite among coastal Bay Area foodies, Manka's serves seasonal cuisine featuring wild game in a rustic-chic former sportsman's lodge. **$$$$**

Marshalls
19225 State Highway 1, Marshall
Tel: 415-663-1339
www.themarshallstore.com
Perched on timber pylons with views of the bay, this roadside seafood shack serves up some of the freshest oysters you've ever tasted, served raw, Rockefeller (topped with spinach and cheese), or grilled with house-made barbeque sauce. **$**

PRICE CATEGORIES

Prices are for a meal for two people, without wine.
$ = less than $30
$$ = $30–$60
$$$ = $60–$100
$$$$ = more than $100

TRANSPORTATION

ACCOMMODATIONS

EATING OUT

ACTIVITIES

A – Z

Restaurant 301, Eureka.

Restaurant 301
301 L Street, Carter House Inn, Eureka
Tel: 707-444-8062
www.carterhouse.com
One of Northern California's best restaurants, Restaurant 301 offers a season-driven menu featuring produce from the inn's garden, fresh seafood specials, and a 3,400-bottle wine list. **$$$**

River's End
11048 Highway 1, Jenner
Tel: 707-865-2484
Great care and attention is paid to the food, wine, and experience of guests at this beautiful little restaurant stunningly perched over the mouth of the Russian River. Menu items not to be missed include the duck confit sandwich and the yellowfin tuna salad. **$$$$**

Samoa Cookhouse
Off US 101 across the Samoa Bridge
Tel: 707-442-1659
Breakfast includes orange juice, scrambled eggs, pancakes, sausages, hash browns, and coffee. Hefty lunches and dinners start with soup, salad, and plenty of bread, and end with apple pie. As they should. **$**

St Orres
36601 State Highway 1, Gualala
Tel: 707-884-3303
Just below Mendocino, this beautiful restaurant emphasizes North Coast cuisine in a Russian-style hotel. It also serves Sunday brunch. **$$$**

Station House Cafe
11180 Highway 1, Pt. Reyes Station
Tel: 415-663-1515
A perfect stop after a day's hiking on Point Reyes Peninsula, this café offers fresh, well-cooked food in a warm, busy atmosphere. **$–$$**

Table 128
State Highway 128, Boonville
Tel: 707-895-2210

California cooking to the core, the Boonville Hotel's restaurant serves family-style, prix-fixe menus of fresh, seasonally inspired food. Reservations required. **$$$$**

Vladimir's
12785 Sir Francis Drake Ave, Inverness
Tel: 415-669-1021.
Immense plates of rib-sticking Czech fare like chicken paprikash, red cabbage, and strudel have been served in this cozy European-style pub for more than 40 years. **$$**

Central Valley

Biba
2801 Capitol Ave, Sacramento
Tel: 916-455-2422
www.biba-restaurant.com
All white tablecloths and lemon walls, Biba's atmosphere is friendly and relaxed. Regional Italian fare includes house-made pastas, Milano-style breaded veal chop, and tiramisu. **$$**

La Bonne Soupe Café
920 8th St, Sacramento
Tel: 916-492-9506
A French eatery with charming red-and-yellow interior, this tiny soup and sandwich shop is a local favorite. **$**

Mulvaney's Building and Loan
1215 19th St, Sacramento
Tel: 916-441-6022
www.mulvaneysbl.com
For Sacramento fine dining, come here and enjoy daily changing, seasonally inspired new American cuisine such as roasted chestnut and cauliflower soup, griddled Mahi Mahi with sesame-orange butter sauce, and Pink Lady apple and persimmon bread pudding. **$$**

The Vintage Press
216 N. Willis, Visalia
Tel: 559-733-3033
There are four distinct dining rooms here, but the upscale food – wild mushroom puff pastries, filet mignon, warm pecan tart with cinnamon ice cream – is the same wherever you sit. **$$$**

The Waterboy
2000 Capitol Ave, Sacramento
Tel: 916-498-9891
www.waterboyrestaurant.com
This cozy Midtown resto delivers cuisine inspired by Southern France and Northern Italy, producing dishes like goat cheese bruschetta, grilled lamb with creamy cannellini beans, and a bittersweet chocolate-brioche bread pudding. **$$**

Zelda's
1415 21st St, Sacramento
Tel: 916-447-1400
There's often a wait, but there's a reason why locals queue for the deep-dish pizzas at this casual pizzeria. You

can call and order ahead; the pizzas take at least 30 minutes to arrive. **$**

Lake Tahoe, Sierra Nevada and Yosemite

Ahwahnee Dining Room
Yosemite National Park
Tel: 209-372-1489
The Grande Dame of hotels in breathtaking Yosemite Valley serves classy, healthy California Cuisine in its cathedral-like dining room. **$$$$**

Erna's Elderberry House
48688 Victoria Lane (State Highway 41), Oakhurst
Tel: 559-683-6800
Elegant French country inn hidden in the forest. Stunning interior design mingles with classic European cuisine, which is far from cheap but worth the trip. Reservations are recommended. **$$$$**

Mountain Room Restaurant
9010 Curry Village Dr, Yosemite National Park
Tel: 209-372-8333
www.yosemitepark.com
A lofty space with a relaxed atmosphere and views of the Yosemite Falls, the Mountain Room serves up steaks, pastas, and fresh seafood. **$$$**

Plumpjack Café
1920 Squaw Valley Rd, Squaw Valley
Tel: 530-583-1576
www.plumpjacksquawvalleyinn.com
One of the nicest Tahoe-area restaurants, Plumpjack serves seasonal delights like Alaskan halibut with artichoke and quinoa tabbouleh, Fulton Valley free-range chicken breast with smoked fingerling potatoes, squash blossom empanadas, and a vanilla crème brulée. **$$**

Rosie's Café
571 North Lake Blvd, Tahoe City
Tel: 530-583-8504
Breakfast, lunch, and dinner are served at this down-home restaurant that oozes charm. **$**

The Soule Domain
9983 Stateline Rd, Crystal Bay
Tel: 530-546-7529
Technically in Nevada, this place offers a creative, eclectic menu with American, French, and Asian influences served up in a romantic log-cabin setting. **$$**

Spindleshanks
6873 North Lake Blvd, Tahoe Vista
Tel: 530-546-2191
www.spindleshankstahoe.com
With a rustic mountain lodge feel, this laid-back bistro offers classic American fare, from fried calamari and Mac & Cheese, to a half-pound Angus cheeseburger and ice cream sundae. **$**

Wawona Hotel Dining Room
8308 Wawona Rd, Wawona
Tel: 209-375-6556

In a rustic Victorian ambiance, enjoy traditional favorites (think trout, pot roast, and grilled flat iron steak) and seasonal specials. **$$$**

The Far North

Good Harvest Café
575 US 101 S., Crescent City

Tel: 707-465-6028
Serving fresh-squeezed orange juice, a tasty Santa Fe scramble, large salads, and burgers, this casual resto with Native American art on the walls makes a good pit-stop. **$**

Seven Suns Coffee and Café
1011 S. Mt. Shasta Blvd,

Mt. Shasta
Tel: 530-926-0701
www.mtshastacoffee.com
This quaint converted old house is a popular and simple place for coffee, sandwiches, soups, salads, and wraps (including vegetarian options). **$**

SOUTHERN CALIFORNIA

Central Coast

Paula's Pancake Place
1531 Mission Dr, Solvang
Tel: 805-688-2867
There may be a wait, but it's worth it for the fluffy Danish pancakes, omelets, and friendly service. **$**

Playa Azul Café
914 Santa Barbara St, Santa Barbara
Tel: 805-966-2860
Come for happy hour margaritas, and chips and salsa, and stay for Mexican food in a lively atmosphere near the Presidio. **$$**

Root 246
420 Alisal Road, Solvang
Tel: 805-688-9003
If you're tired of Danish food in Solvang, the contemporary farm-to-table menu at Root 246 will be a welcome treat. Choose from an extensive selection of local wine or signature cocktails, then dine on heirloom tomato soup, plum-glazed pork chop, or seared Day Boat scallops with risotto, and finish with the likes of cinnamon-sugar donut puffs. **$$**

La Super-Rica
622 N. Milpitas St, Santa Barbara
Tel: 805-963-4940
A local institution, this unassuming shack dishes up tacos, tamales, horchata, and watermelon aqua fresca. Expect a bit of a line. **$**

Ventana Grill
2575 Price St, Pismo Beach
Tel: 805-773-0000
www.ventanagrill.com
Waves crash on the beach below as diners enjoy poblano-steamed clams, tequila lime chicken, and flat-iron Chimichurri steak, along with panoramic ocean views from a coastal bluff. A tapas menu is served daily 2–4.30pm. **$$$**

Wine Cask
813 Anacapa St, Santa Barbara
Tel: 805-966-9463
www.winecask.com
Located in the historic El Paseo complex, Wine Cask serves up delicious California Cuisine in a stylish setting. Sip cocktails and share plates on the patio, or settle in for a dinner of sesame-crusted hamachi, mushroom risotto, or grilled Wagyu New York strip in the main room, paired with

one of hundreds of wines sold in the adjoining wine shop. **$$$**

Zen Yai Thai Cuisine
425 State St, Santa Barbara
Tel: 805-957-1102
Some of the best Thai food in Santa Barbara – from pumpkin curry to Beef Pad See Ew – is served at this small eatery with attentive service and eclectic decor (including a huge portrait of John Lennon). **$**

Los Angeles

A.O.C. Wine Bar and Restaurant
8022 W. 3rd St
Tel: 323-653-6359
www.aocwinebar.com
Named after the French wine designation Appellation d'Origine Controlée, A.O.C. offers affordable wines, a delicious charcuterie and cheese bar, and bites like clams with sherry and garlic toast or brioche with prosciutto, gruyere, and egg cooked in the wood-burning oven. **$$$**

The Apple Pan
10801 W. Pico Blvd.,
Tel: 310-475-3585
Opened in 1947, this classic West Los Angeles diner with a single U-shaped counter serves hickory burgers, crispy fries, and apple pie a la mode. **$**

Barney's Beanery
8447 Santa Monica Blvd, West Hollywood
Tel: 323-654-2287
www.barneysbeanery.com
Barney's is casual, funky, and famous locally, with a newspaper-sized menu offering more different beer labels than you can shake a stick at, plus tables for a friendly game of pool. **$**

Bottega Louie
700 S. Grand Ave
Tel: 213-802-1470
www.bottegalouie.com
Chic and airy, Bottega draws a well-dressed crowd to dine on Kobe beef burgers, Portobello mushroom fries with basil aioli, several dozen upscale small-plates, and a rainbow of macaroons. **$$$**

Café Pinot
700 W. 5th St, Downtown
Tel: 213-239-6500
www.patinagroup.com
Adjoining LA's Central Library, Café Pinot offers an elegant dining room

with floor-to-ceiling windows, as well as a lovely garden patio. The contemporary California Cuisine includes daily rotisserie specials. **$$$**

Campanile
624 S. La Brea Ave
Tel: 323-938-1447
www.campanilerestaurant.com
Come for first-rate California-Mediterranean cooking with the fantastic bread from the bakery next door, and a classy atmosphere. Closed Sunday dinner. **$$$**

Canter's Delicatessen, Restaurant and Bakery
419 N. Fairfax Ave
Tel: 323-651-2030
www.cantersdeli.com
This famous, large, and lively deli with classic 1950s interior is open around the clock. **$**

Cicada
617 S. Olive St
Tel: 213-488-9488
A well-heeled crowd dines on fabulous Northern Italian food at this classy eatery in the plush surroundings of Downtown's Oviatt Building. **$$$**

Father's Office
3229 Helms Avenue
Tel: 310-736-2224
www.fathersoffice.com
An upscale pub serving craft-brewed beer and wine and food that is inspired by European bar food as well as the signature "Office burger." **$$$**

The Gumbo Pot
6333 W. 3rd St
Tel: 323-933-0358
www.thegumbopotla.com
Serving up seafood gumbo, jambalaya, and cornbread in the Farmers Market, the Gumbo Pot is open daily until 9pm; note, the market closes slightly earlier at weekends. **$**

Joe's Restaurant
1023 Abbot Kinney Blvd, Venice
Tel: 310-399-5811

PRICE CATEGORIES

Prices are for a meal for two people, without wine.
$ = less than $30
$$ = $30–$60
$$$ = $60–$100
$$$$ = more than $100

www.joesrestaurant.com
Venice's famous chef delivers mushroom ravioli in parmesan broth and other delicious Italian fare. **$$**

Kate Mantilini
9101 Wilshire Blvd, Beverly Hills
Tel: 310-278 3699
In a handsomely traditional setting, this popular spot serves an extensive menu of American classics (til 12.30am Fri–Sat). Open for breakfast, lunch, and dinner. **$$**

The Malibu Inn Bar & Restaurant
22969 Pacific Coast Highway, Malibu
Tel: 310-456-6060
www.malibu-inn.com
This unpretentious eating spot has long been familiar to Hollywood stars whose pictures line the walls. **$**

Michael's
1147 3rd St, Santa Monica
Tel: 310-451-0843
www.michaelssantamonica.com
The seasonal, contemporary cuisine – from Alaskan wild Red King salmon with pistachio pesto to rack of lamb with goat cheese polenta and rosemary jus – can be had either on the romantic outdoor garden patio or the lovely dining rooms decorated with modern art. Closed Sunday. **$$$**

Musso & Frank Grill
6667 Hollywood Blvd, Hollywood
Tel: 323-467 7788
www.mussoandfrank.com
A traditional American menu (steaks, sandwiches, and the "original Fettucine Alfredo") and classic cocktails are presented in an old-fashioned Hollywood hangout, where writers like Ernest Hemingway and Raymond Chandler used to dine. **$$$**

Nate 'n Al's
414 N. Beverly Dr, Beverly Hills
Tel: 310-274 0101
www.natenal.com
Sandwiches and other specialties are always superb at Beverly Hills' long-famous deli. **$**

The Original Pantry Café
877 S. Figueroa
Tel: 213-972 9279
www.pantrycafe.com
Always crowded, this inexpensive Downtown landmark has been around even longer than former mayor Richard Riordan, who bought the place to prevent its demolition. **$**

Philippe the Original
1001 N. Alameda St, Downtown
Tel: 213-628 3781
www.philippes.com
One block north of stylish Union Station, this busy, low-key eatery has been known since 1908 for its famous French dip sandwich. **$**

Pink's Hot Dogs
709 North La Brea Ave
Tel: 323-931-7594

www.pinkshollywood.com
Near the corner of Melrose and La Brea, look for a crowd of people and follow your nose to this famous hot dog stand, family-owned since 1939. If you're not in the mood for one of dozens of hot preparations, there's also burgers, chicken burritos, and nachos. **$**

Pizzeria Mozza
641 North Highland Ave
Tel: 323-297-0101
www.mozza-la.com
Courtesy of the all-star team of Nancy Silverton, Mario Batali, and Joe Bastianich, Pizzaria Mozza serves up scrumptius bruschette, panini, and two dozen different gourmet pizzas. **$$**

Reel Inn
18661 Pacific Coast Highway, Malibu
Tel: 310-456-8221
www.reelinnmalibu.com
Enjoy fresh seafood in a super-relaxed atmosphere. **$**

Señor Fish
422 E. 1st St, Downtown
Tel: 213-625-0566
www.senorfish.net
A low-key spot for authentic, flavorful Mexican food, from fish tacos to fresh ceviche. **$**

Sidewalk Café
1401 Ocean Front Walk, Venice
Tel: 310-399-5547
www.thesidewalkcafe.com
With red-and-white-checked tablecloths and simple American and Mexican fare, this is the best place on the Venice boardwalk for watching the non-stop action. **$**

Spago
176 N. Canon Dr, Beverly Hills
Tel: 310-385-0880
www.wolfgangpuck.com
The flagship of celebrity chef Wolfgang Puck's food empire, sophisticated Spago is among LA's most famous restaurants, serving imaginative California Cuisine with Italian and Asian influences. If you can, sit on the Tuscan-inspired garden patio. **$$$$**

Woody's Bar-B-Que
3446 W. Slauson Ave
Tel: 323-294-9443
This is the best in LA, according to some barbecue aficionados. **$**

Greater LA Area

Acapulco Mexican Restaurant
1535 W. Katella Ave, Orange
Tel: 714-639 9550
www.acapulcorestaurants.com
Not far from the Angel Stadium and Disneyland, Acapulco serves up generous portions of Mexican fare, from sizzling fajitas and fish tacos to enchiladas and burritos. **$$**

Bamboo Inn
14010 Ventura Blvd, Sherman Oaks

Tel: 818-788-0202
The friendly atmosphere and tasty Chinese and Asian fusion cuisine – from bamboo beef to orange chicken – makes this many locals' favorite Chinese food restaurant in the Valley. **$$**

Cafe Bizou
14016 Ventura Blvd., Sherman Oaks
Tel: 818-788-3536
Come to this cozy, romantic restaurant for stuffed mushrooms, lobster bisque, seafood pastas, and bread pudding. Bonus: there's only a $2 corkage fee. **$$**

The Castaway
1250 Harvard Rd, Burbank
Tel: 818-848 6691
www.castawayrestaurant.com
A Burbank landmark for over 40 years, this "Jewel on the Hill" seafood and steak restaurant offers breathtaking views of the city from its perch above the De Bell Golf Course. **$$$**

The Cellar
305 North Harbor Blvd, Fullerton
Tel: 714-525 5682
www.cellardining.com
You only have to go 4 miles (6.4km) from Disneyland to enjoy The Cellar's superb French cuisine (escargot, velvety lobster bisque, classic Chatteaubriand, chocolate and hazelnut souflée) and expansive wine cellar. **$$$**

Five Crowns
3801 East Coast Highway, Corona del Mar
Tel: 949-760-0331
ww.lawrysonline.com/five-crowns
Award-winning food is served in a beautiful two-story building modeled after Ye Olde Bell, an old English inn. Entrees range from Chamomile tea-smoked sturgeon with roasted beets, to filet mignon with blue cheese mashed potatoes. Signature sides include Moroccan-spiced sweet carrots and Stilcheddar Mac'n cheese. No tank tops, torn jeans, shorts, hats, or casual gym wear. **$$**

The Great Greek
13362 Ventura Blvd, Sherman Oaks
Tel: 818-905-5250
www.greatgreek.com
Authentic Greek fare is served in a boisterous setting with lively entertainment – think dancing waiters and plate-breaking. **$$**

Dr Hogly Wogly's Tyler Texas BBQ
8136 N. Sepulveda Blvd
(one block south of Roscoe Blvd), Van Nuys
Tel: 818-780-6701
www.hoglywogly.com
Here you'll find some of LA's most beloved briskets, as well as pork ribs, pulled pork, and chicken, all of which are smoked in an authentic brick pit oven using firewood. **$**

Karl Strauss Brewing Company
Universal CityWalk, Universal City
Tel: 818-753 brew
www.karlstrauss.com

After crispy calamari and sweet chilli lime fries to start, dive into burgers, steaks, and salads at this casual microbrewery. To drink, try the "featured flight", a taste of four different brews. **$$**

Mistral
13422 Ventura Blvd, Sherman Oaks
Tel: 818-981-6650
www.mistralrestaurant.com
Enjoy escargots a la Bourguignonne and grilled wild salmon or ahi tuna at this valley version of a French bistro. **$$**

National Sports Grill
450 N. State College Blvd, Orange
Tel: 714-935 0300
www.nationalsportsgrill.com
This branch of a national chain offers dozens of TV monitors, four giant screens, pool tables, 50 different beers, and an extensive menu. **$$**

Smoke House
4420 Lakeside Dr, Burbank
Tel: 818-845-3731
www.smokehouse1946.com
Ribs, chicken, and unforgettable garlic and cheese bread are favorites of the crowd from the nearby studios. **$$**

Tandoor Cuisine of India
1132 E. Katella Ave, Orange
Tel: 714-538 2234
There are 70 spiced and tasty dishes on the menu; many of the ingredients are made on the premises. **$$$**

South Bay and Orange Coast

21 Oceanfront Restaurant
2100 W. Oceanfront, Newport
Tel: 949-673-2100
www.21oceanfront.com
Across from the Newport Beach Pier, this opulent restaurant offers prime steaks and what some believe is the best seafood in Orange County. **$$$$**

Aimee's Bistro
800 S. Pacific Coast Highway, Redondo
Tel: 310-316-1081
www.aimeesbistro.com
Shrimp and salmon are local favorites at this French bistro, as well as the tasty desserts. **$$**

Belmont Brewing Co
25 39th Place, Long Beach
Tel: 562-433 3891
www.belmontbrewing.com
At the foot of Belmont Pier, gaze at the Queen Mary cruiseliner in a low-key brew-pub as you nosh on spinach artichoke dip, grilled shrimp salad, pizzas, seafood pastas, burgers, or short ribs. **$**

Chez Melange
Palos Verdes Inn
1716 Pacific Coast Highway, Redondo
Tel: 310-540-1222
www.chezmelange.com
Chez Melange offers a long menu of

diverse cuisines, including Italian, Chinese, and even Cajun. **$$**

The Crab Cooker
2200 Newport Blvd, Newport
Tel: 949-673-0100
www.crabcooker.com
A no-frills affair, the Crab Cooker serves up grilled seafood on paper plates at reasonable prices. **$$**

Duke's
317 Pacific Coast Highway, Huntington Beach
Tel: 714-374-6446
www.dukeshuntington.com
At the foot of Huntington Beach Pier, beachgoers sidle up to the barefoot bar for mai tais, or come inside for poke tacos, fish and chips, and grilled chicken sandwiches. **$**

L'Opera
101 Pine Ave, Long Beach
Tel: 562-491-0066
www.lopera.com
L'Opera is a romantic Italian spot with tasty veal and fettucine, and warm, attentive service. **$$**

Lou's Red Oak BBQ
21501 Brookhurst St #D, Huntington Beach
Tel: 714-965-5200
www.lousbbq.com
Hot soft pretzel bites are dished up while you decide on your order, and cookies to end the meal. In between, opt for tri tip (steak) with sweet potato fries or potato wedges. **$**

Sophy's
3240 E. Pacific Coast Highway, Long Beach
Tel: 562-494-1763
Here's the spot to discover Cambodian cuisine, from Chinese broccoli to crispy pork to Cambodian beef jerky. **$**

Sugar Shack
213 ½ Main St, Huntington Beach
Tel: 714-536-0355
Take a break from the beach on the patio of this family-owned breakfast and lunch spot, which has been satisfying locals since 1967. **$**

The Deserts

Las Casuelas Terraza
222 South Palm Canyon Dr, Palm Springs
Tel: 760-325-2794
www.lascasuelasterraza.com
Mexican-style cuisine on a pleasant outdoor patio. **$**

The Cheesecake Factory
The River at Rancho Mirage
71-800 Highway 111, Rancho Mirage, Palm Springs
Tel: 760-404 1400
www.thecheesecakefactory.com
The extensive menu ranges from avocado egg-rolls (spring rolls) and cajun jambalaya pasta to an assortment of luscious cheesecakes. **$$**

Elmer's
1030 East Palm Canyon Dr, Palm Springs

Tel: 760-327-8419
www.elmers-restaurants.com
Choose from 20 varieties of pancakes and waffles, plus fine steaks and seafood for dinner. Weekend mornings can be very crowded. **$**

Kobe Japanese Steak House
Highway 111 at Frank Sinatra Dr, Rancho Mirage, Palm Springs
Tel: 760-324-1717
www.koberanchomirage.com
Hibachi-style steak and chicken is served in a replica of a 300-year-old Japanese country inn. **$$$**

San Diego

Bali Hai Restaurant
2230 Shelter Island Dr
Tel: 619-222-1181
www.balihairestaurant.com
Opened in 1953, this lively joint was also the first Tiki temple erected on Shelter Island. It is all about Hawaiian and Polynesian cuisine. **$$**

Buca di Beppo San Diego
705 6th Ave
Tel: 619-233-7272
www.bucadibeppo.com
At this celebrated national chain, known for its kitschy decor, you'll enjoy family-sized portions and classic Italian cuisine. **$$**

Croce's Restaurant & Jazz Bar
802 Fifth Ave
Tel: 619-233-4355
www.croces.com
Dedicated to the late folk musician Jim Croce, this Gaslamp Quarter fixture combines inventive pasta, seafood, and poultry dishes with live music and memorabilia. **$$$**

The Marine Room
2000 Spindrift Dr, La Jolla
Tel: 858-459-7222
www.ljbtc.com
At high tide the waves crash dramatically just outside the windows at this fine-dining institution (open for 70 years), located in the beach and tennis club. **$$$**

The Oak Room
Pala Casino, Resort & Spa
35008 Pala Temecula Road, Pala
Tel: 760-510-5100
www.palacasino.com
A world-class steakhouse, The Oak Room is conveniently located not far from gaming tables, live entertainment, and a health spa. **$$$**

PRICE CATEGORIES

Prices are for a meal for two people, without wine.
$ = less than $30
$$ = $30–$60
$$$ = $60–$100
$$$$ = more than $100

ACTIVITIES

FESTIVALS AND EVENTS, THE ARTS, NIGHTLIFE, TOURS, SPORTS, AND SHOPPING

FESTIVALS AND EVENTS

Here are just a few of the most popular festivals and events in California.

January

Tournament of Roses Parade and Rose Bowl Football Game, Pasadena
Tel: 626-449-4100
www.tournamentofroses.com
Kick off New Year's Day alongside 100,000 happy spectators at this massive, float-filled parade in Pasadena.

February

AT&T Pebble Beach National Pro-Am Golf Tournament, Pebble Beach
www.attpb.golf.com

First hosted in 1937 by Bing Crosby in Santa Fe, the high-profile Pro-Am is now held in scenic Pebble Beach. There, celebrities and professional golfers team up on the links to raise money for hundreds of non-profits.

Chinese New Year
Fireworks, parades with dancing dragons, and Miss Chinatown pageants mark the start of the Chinese New Year. Especially large celebrations are held in San Francisco, Los Angeles, and San Diego. Visit each city's visitor center for more information.

Clam Chowder Cook-Off, Santa Cruz
Tel: 831-423-5590
www.beachboardwalk.com
A fundraiser for the City of Santa Cruz Parks and Recreation Department, this 30-year-old cook-off event draws individuals and restaurants – who whip up their best Boston- and Manhattan-style chowders – plus the public who gets to taste them!

Riverside County Fair & National Date Festival, Indio

Tel: 760-863-8247
www.datefest.org
Over 60 years old, this festival delights crowds with live music, hypnotist shows, sea lions, camel and ostrich races, and a nightly Arabian-themed pageant.

Sex Tour, San Francisco Zoo, San Francisco
Tel: 415-753-7080
www.sfzoo.org
If you're looking for something unique, the San Francisco Zoo heats up on Valentine's Day with a guided tour focused on animals' mating and courtship habits.

March

Academy Awards, Los Angeles
www.oscars.com
"And the Oscar goes to…" Before the rest of the country watches the Oscars on television, those in Los Angeles can brave the crowds and see the stars walk the red carpet live.

North Lake Tahoe Snow Festival, Tahoe
Tel: 530-583-7167
www.tahoesnowfestival.com
Held either in late February or early March, these 10 fun-filled days offer special on-snow events, parties, and parades.

Return of the Swallows, San Juan Capistrano
www.swallowsparade.com
Celebrate the mid-March return of the swallows to San Juan Capistrano on St Joseph's Day (March 19) with the Fiesta de las Golondrinas and Swallows' Day Parade, the country's biggest non-motorized parade.

Saint Patrick's Day
Don something green and drink to the luck of the Irish on March 17th. Parades and celebrations are held

Pebble Beach is home to the annual National Pro-Am Golf Tournament.

around the state, including in San Francisco, Los Angeles, and San Diego.

April

Cherry Blossom Festival,
San Francisco
Tel: 415-563-2313
A 45-year-old Japantown tradition, the Cherry Blossom Festival is a celebration of Japanese heritage and traditions – including martial arts, music, and dance – that draws 200,000 people each year.

Coachella Valley Music Festival,
Indio
Now one of the country's biggest music festivals, Coachella lures urbanites to the desert for three days of alternative rock, hip hop, and electronic music, plus large sculptural art.

Doo Dah Parade, Pasadena
Tel: 626-590-1134
www.pasadenadoodahparade.info
In the mood for a crazy frolic? This outrageous parade is full of off-beat floats and eccentric performers.

San Francisco International Film Festival, San Francisco
Tel: 415-561-5000
www.sffs.org
The country's longest-running film festival showcases more than 175 films from around the world.

May

Cinco de Mayo
With music and margaritas, Los Angeles, San Diego, Santa Barbara, and San Francisco all commemorate Mexico's May 5, 1863, victory over the French.

Jumping Frog Jubilee, Angels Camp
Tel: 209-736-2561
www.frogtown.org
Channel Mark Twain and watch amphibians hop to a prize, then have fun at the rodeo and county fair.

Kinetic Grand Championship, Arcata to Ferndale, Humboldt County
Tel: 707-733-3841
www.kineticgrandchampionship.com
Transportation meets art at this three-day race; participants ride human-powered sculptures over a 38-mile (61km) course.

Sacramento Music Festival, Sacramento
Tel: 916-444-2004
www.sacjazz.com
Once known as the Jazz Jubilee, this festival now features a full range of music: jazz, swing, blues, zydeco, rockabilly, bluegrass, Latin music, and more.

The Hollywood Bowl, a concert venue in Los Angeles.

Zazzle Bay to Breakers,
San Francisco
Tel: 415-864-3432
www.zazzlebaytobreakers.com
Thousands of costume-clad runners converge in San Francisco to for an entertaining 12km dash from Ferry Building to Ocean Beach.

June

Ojai Music Festival, Ojai
Tel: 805-646-2094
www.ojaifestival.org
Drawing an eclectic group of performers, this music celebration features everything from bluegrass and rockabilly to classical.

Playboy Jazz Festival, Los Angeles
Tel: 323-450-1173
www.playboyjazzfestival.com
At the Hollywood Bowl, this long-time jazz fest now features both classic styles (New Orleans, swing, bebop) and jazz-rock fusions.

San Francisco Pride
San Francisco
Tel: 415-864-5889
www.sfpride.org
Over 40 years old, this huge LGBT celebration includes a two-day festival culminating with a Sunday morning parade.

Temecula Valley Balloon and Wine Festival
Tel: 951-676-6713
www.tvbwf.com
Wine-tasting, live music, and balloon launches comprise this community affair, launched in 1983 by commercial air pilot and avid balloonist Walt Darren.

July

Comic-Con International, San Diego
Tel: 619-491-2475
www.comic-con.org
The largest comic book and popular

arts convention in the world.

Fourth of July
Fireworks explode throughout the state, celebrating America's Independence Day.

Gilroy Garlic Festival, Gilroy
Tel: 408-842-1625.
www.gilroygarlicfestival.com
Everything from traditional garlic fries to the more innovative garlic ice cream can be tasted at this celebration of Gilroy's major industry.

Pageant of the Masters, Laguna Beach
Tel: 949-497-6582
www.foapom.com
This long-standing festival wows audience with its tableaux vivants ("living pictures") – incredibly faithful live depictions of classical and contemporary artworks, complete with intricate sets.

August

California State Fair, Sacramento
Tel: 916-263-3247
www.bigfun.org
This 18-day state fair features competitions in livestock, wine and beer, and cheese; dozens of rides, and tons of food, music, and live entertainment.

Nisei Week, Little Tokyo, Los Angeles
Tel: 213-687-7193
www.niseiweek.org
One of the country's oldest Japanese-American festivals, Nisei Week includes a karate tournament, gyoza-eating competition, parade, and numerous other sport competitions.

Old Spanish Days Fiesta, Santa Barbara
Tel: 805-962-8101
www.oldspanishdays-fiesta.org
Take your pick from folk dancing, a market, a carnival, a rodeo, and a parade.

Try the goods at Gilroy Garlic Festival.

September

Monterey Jazz Festival, Monterey
Tel: 831-373-3366
www.montereyjazzfestival.org
Co-founded by Jimmy Lyons and
Ralph J. Gleason in 1958, this is the
world's longest-running jazz festival.
Among other renowned performers, it
has presented Louis Armstrong, Billie
Holiday, Dave Brubeck, Miles Davis,
Diana Krall, Wynton Marsalis, and
Terence Blanchard.
Sausalito Art Festival, Sausalito
Tel: 415-331-3757
www.sausalitoartfestival.org
Over 250 artists converge in Sausalito
on Labor Day weekend, showcasing
everything from ceramics and
sculpture to photography, watercolor,
glass, and mixed media.

October

Art and Pumpkin Festival, Half
Moon Bay
Tel: 650-726-9652
www.miramarevents.com/
pumpkinfest
At the World Pumpkin Capital you'll
find gigantic pumpkins, a Haunted
House, harvest-inspired crafts,
pie-eating and costume contests,
an enormous jack-o-lantern, and
pumpkin ale.
California Avocado Festival,
Carpinteria
Tel: 805-684-0038
www.avofest.com
Described as "three days of peace,
love, and guacamole," this eco-
friendly festival features music, recipe
contests, and the world's largest vat
of guacamole.
Fleet Week, San Diego and San
Francisco
Tel: 619-858-1545, 650-599-5057
www.fleetweeksandiego.org; fleetweek.
us

Contests, air shows, and ship tours
are all held in honor of the US military.

November

Death Valley '49ers Encampment,
Death Valley
www.deathvalley49ers.org
Fiddlers contest, art shows, and a trek
through the hot, hot valley.
Dia de los Muertos Festival, Los
Angeles
www.ladayofthedead.com
The Mexican Day of the Dead is
celebrated with processions, masks,
face-painting, and other rituals that
pay homage to the dearly departed.

December

Parade of Lights
Beautifully illuminated boats parade
through Southern California harbors,
including Newport Beach and San
Diego; call the local tourist bureaus
for information.

THE ARTS

Classical Music

San Francisco

The **San Francisco Opera** (301 Van
Ness Ave at Grove St; tel: 415-864-
3330; www.sfopera.com) features
internationally renowned stars of
the opera world. Having entered its
seventh decade of annual seasons,
around 10 operas are presented
each year in repertory. Standing-
room tickets can be purchased two
hours before the performance. Each
September, a free concert series is
held in Golden Gate Park.
The **San Francisco Symphony**

(Davies Symphony Hall, Van Ness Ave
at Grove St; tel: 415-864-6000; www.
sfsymphony.org) plays a summer pops
series, a Beethoven Festival, and the
Mostly Mozart Festival each year in
addition to its regular season.
For professional chamber
music, seek out the **San Francisco
Conservatory of Music** (50 Oak St;
tel: 415-864-7326 for a 24-hour
recording listing music activities,
415-503-6275 for box office; www.
sfcm.edu), which also hosts student
recitals. With graduates like Isaac
Stern to its credit, it is regarded as the
best West Coast music school.
Audium (1616 Bush St; tel: 415-
771-1616; www.audium.org) in the
Civic Center neighborhood experiments
with 169 speakers which move music
around you in a kind of sculpture.

Los Angeles

The Frank Gehry-designed **Walt
Disney Concert Hall,** home of the
Los Angeles Philharmonic (www.
laphil.com) is the premier concert
venue in the city. The nearby **Music
Center** complex also stages concerts.
Part of the this complex, the **Dorothy
Chandler Pavilion** (135 N. Grand Ave;
tel: 213-972-7211; www.musiccenter.
org) is richly appointed with marble
walls and chandeliers.
The June to September season
at the **Hollywood Bowl** (www.
hollywoodbowl.com) sees nightly
concerts: classical, but also jazz and
pop. There are also free morning
rehearsals on occasion.
LA also has regular concerts at the
Greek Theatre (tel: 323-665-5857;
www.greek_theatrela.com) in Griffith
Park and performances on summer
Sundays in Warner Center Park in
Woodland Hills. Call the Valley Cultural
Center (tel: 818-704-1358; www.
valleycultural.org) for schedules. Santa
Clarita's summer concerts take place
in **Old Orchard Park** (tel: 661-250-
3787); in Thousand Oaks, concerts
are held in **Conejo Community Park**
(tel: 805-495-2163).
The Los Angeles Opera Theater
and regular theatrical productions are
hosted at the **Wilshire Ebell Theatre**
(4401 W. Eighth St; tel: 323-939-
1128; www.ebellla.com), a Spanish-
designed venue built in 1924. The
Wiltern (3790 Wilshire Blvd and
Western Ave; tel: 213-388-1400),
built in 1930 and now a protected Art
Deco landmark, is also a refurbished
venue for musical events.

San Diego

Opened in 1929 as the fabulous Fox
Theatre, **Copley Symphony Hall**

(750 B St; tel: 619-235-0804; www.
sandiegosymphony.com) is now home
to both the San Diego Symphony and
the San Diego Youth Symphony.

Situated on a 12-acre (5-hectare)
campus in downtown Escondido,
adjacent to historic Grape Day Park,
the **California Center for the Arts**
(340 N. Escondido Blvd; tel: 760-839-
4138; www.artcenter.org) consists of
a 1,500-seat concert hall, a 400-seat
theater, a visual arts museum, as well
as art and dance studios. Since 1994,
the center has hosted classical and
holiday concerts, as well as opera
performances.

On Sunday afternoons, music
lovers flock to the outdoor **Spreckels
Organ Pavilion** (Balboa Park; tel:
619-702-8138; www.sosorgan.
com) for free organ concerts.
Meanwhile chamber music
ensembles, brass quintets, the San
Diego Master Chorale, and others
present their musical talents within
the **Neurosciences Institute's**
Performing Arts Auditorium (10640
John Jay Hopkins Dr, north of UC San
Diego in La Jolla; tel: 858-626-2000;
www.nsi.edu).

Besides theater and dance, the
**Poway Center for the Performing
Arts** (15498 Espola Rd, Poway; tel:
858-748-0505; www.powayarts.org)
hosts the San Diego Symphony
and other well-known musical acts.

Dance

San Francisco
After more than seven decades,
the **San Francisco Ballet** (tel: 415-
861-5600; www.sfballet.org) is still
delighting audiences. Well known
for traditional choreography and
consistently excellent productions,
the San Francisco Ballet was the
first in the country to perform the
Nutcracker Suite as a Christmas
event. Performances are held at the
San Francisco Opera House, Van
Ness and Grove in the Civic Center
area. Tickets may be purchased
through Bass or at the box office for
performances at the Opera house.

ODC Dance (tel: 415-863-6606;
www.odcdance.org) is known nationally
for its entrepreneurial savvy and
artistic innovation. ODC was the first
modern-dance company in America
to build its own resident facility. The
ever-popular company chalks up over
120 performances a year.

Los Angeles
The Music Center (135 N. Grand Ave;
tel: 213-972-7211; www.musiccenter.

org) is a key venue for traveling
ballet companies and modern-dance
troupes.

At the **UCLA Royce Hall** in
Westwood (tel: 310-825-2101),
famous ballet companies share
this center with modern-dance
performances.

The **Wiltern** (tel: 213-388-1400);
the **Veterans Wadsworth Theatre**
(tel: 310-479-3003); the **Pasadena
Civic Auditorium**; and **Glendale's
Alex Theatre** (tel: 818-243-2539;
www.alextheatre.org) also stage dance
concerts semi-regularly. For specific
listings, consult the Sunday Calendar
section of the *Los Angeles Times*.

San Diego
The 650-seat **Casa del Prado
Theater** (Balboa Park; tel: 619-239-
0512; www.balboapark.org) offers
diverse performances from San Diego
Civic Youth Ballet and San Diego Civic
Dance Arts. It also hosts to the annual
Celebrate Dance Festival.

At the **Mandell Weiss Center for
the Performing Arts** (9500 Gilman
Dr, University of California San
Diego, La Jolla; tel: 858-534-4574;
theatre.ucsd.edu), students present
innovative dance performances in
four spaces, shared with the La Jolla
Playhouse.

The **San Diego Civic Theatre**
(1100 Third Ave; tel: 619-570-
1100; www.sdcivic.org) hosts ballet
performances, Irish dancing, and
Broadway musicals.

Theater

You can choose from New York hits,
local experimental works, classic
revivals, and more in San Francisco
and Los Angeles, but be forewarned
that tickets can be expensive for the
big shows. An alternative to paying
full price is to attend a matinee
performance. In San Francisco, you
can purchase same-day tickets at half
price from TIX on Union Square. All
current offerings will be listed in the
local newspapers.

San Francisco
The Theatre District is bordered
by Taylor, Sutter, Market, and Post
streets, not far from Union Square.
Although safe while it's thronged
with theatre-goers, this district
borders the Tenderloin, so don't
wander around alone too much after
a show.

Close to Union Square is the
renowned American Conservatory
Theater (ACT) (415 Geary St; tel: 415-
749-2228; www.act-sfbay.org), as well

as the **Curran Theater** (445 Geary
St bet. Mason and Taylor; tel: 1-888-
746-1799; www.shnsf.com) and the
Orpheum Theater (1192 Market St
at 8th; tel: 1-888-746-1799), which
present big Broadway musicals that
have made their way to the West
Coast from New York.

The Actors' Theatre (855 Bush
Street; tel: 415-345-1287; www.
actorstheatresf.org) often presents
classics by such luminaries as
Tennessee Williams in an intimate,
fun setting.

The Magic Theatre (Fort Mason,
Building D; tel: 415-441-8822; www.
magictheatre.org) has a national
reputation for premiering new work
from both emerging and established
playwrights.

Other theaters include the Exit
Theater (156 Eddy; tel: 415-673-
3847; www.sffringe.org); Golden Gate
Theater (1 Taylor Street; tel: 1-888-
746-1799); Intersection for the Arts
(446 Valencia Street; tel: 415-626-
2787); and the **Yerba Buena Center
for the Arts** (701 Mission Street,
www.ybca.org).

Los Angeles
Repertory can be enjoyed at the
Theatre West (3333 Cahuenga Blvd
W., Hollywood; tel: 323-851-4839,
box office 323-851-7977; www.
theatrewest.org) or **Pantages** (6233
Hollywood Blvd; tel: 323-468-1770;
www.broadwayla.org).

Further afield are the **South Coast
Repertory** (655 Town Center Dr,
Costa Mesa; tel: 714-708-5555; www.
scr.org) and the **Pasadena Playhouse**
(39 S. El Molino Ave; tel: 626-356-
7529; www.pasadenaplayhouse.org).
In addition to dozens of tiny houses,
there are also the better-known **Mark
Taper Forum** (tel: 213-628-2772);
Ahmanson (135 N. Grand; tel: 213-
628-2772; www.musiccenter.org) in
the Music Center; and the **Geffen
Playhouse**, (10886 Le Conte Avenue;
tel: 310-208-5454; www.geffen_
playhouse.com).

Groundlings Theater (7307 Melrose
Ave; tel: 323-934-4747; www.
groundlings.com) is a long-established
improv venue. Improv, sketch, and
stand-up comdedy is also found at
ACME Comedy Theatre (135 N. La
Brea Ave; tel: 323-525-0202; www.
acmecomedy.com).

San Diego
Don Powell Theatre (5500
Campanile Dr, Performing Arts
Plaza, San Diego State University;
tel: 619-594-6884; theatre.sdsu.
edu), a 500-seat theater in SDSU's

School of Theatre, Television and Film, features zany musicals and modern adaptations. The nearby **Experimental Theatre** presents classic and contemporary plays, plus performances from the San Diego Asian American Repertory Theatre.

An award-winning regional theatre, **the La Jolla Playhouse** (2910 La Jolla Village Dr, La Jolla; tel: 858-550-1010; www.lajollaplayhouse.org) boasts three main venues and bold, eclectic programs.

Downtown, the **Lyceum Theatre** (79 Horton Plaza; tel: 619-544-1000; www.sdrep.org) has been home to the innovative San Diego Repertory Theatre since 1986, and has witnessed over 40 world premieres. The premises also house a two-level visual art gallery.

The Old Globe (1363 Old Globe Way, Balboa Park; tel: 619-234-5623; www.theoldglobe.org) hosts classic and contemporary productions on three stages: the 580-seat Old Globe Theatre, the 225-seat Cassius Carter Centre Stage, and the 612-seat outdoor Lowell Davies Festival Theatre.

Built in 1928, the **Stephen and Mary Birch North Park Theatre** (2891 University Ave, North Park; tel: 619-239-8836) is a vibrant 730-seat theater featuring performances by the Lyric Opera San Diego.

NIGHTLIFE

California's cities have a vibrant nightlife, with buzzing wine bars, laid-back brew pubs, trendy cocktail lounges, pulsing dance clubs, funky blues venues, and first-rate comedy clubs. Although most listed here are long-standing favorites, it's always advisable to consult up-to-date listings in local newspapers and magazines. Cover charges, dress codes, reservation policies, and show times vary from place to place, so always call ahead for details.

Clubs

San Francisco
DNA Lounge
374 11th Street
Tel: 415-626-1409
www.dnalounge.com
A dance emporium with a party almost every night – a rotating roster of shows includes goth/industrial, New Wave, and Brazilian.
The EndUp
401 6th Street
Tel: 415-646-0999
www.theendup.com
After-hours house music and dancing with a hard-partying and LGBT-friendly crowd.
Ruby Skye
420 Mason Street
Tel: 415-693-0777
www.rubyskye.com
Former theatre turned massive nightclub, this is likely the place you'll find international DJs spinning their grooves.

Los Angeles
Avalon
1735 Vine Street
Tel: 323-462-8900
A big-room nightclub experience with electronic dance music from top DJs like Paul Oakenfold and Markus Schultz, and a great stage for rock band concerts.
The Exchange
618 South Spring Street
Tel: 213-627-8700
www.exchangela.com
DJs like Skrillex, a solid sound system, and a breathtaking venue keep the crowds coming back to this popular dance club.
The Roxy Theatre
9009 Sunset Blvd
Tel: 310-278-9457
www.theroxyonsunset.com
Live music and famous neighboring clubs lure trendy shakers to this historic West Hollywood joint on the Strip, as legendary for its modern rock performances as for its celebrity guests, who have ranged from John Lennon to today's tabloid stars.

San Diego
The Bitter End
770 5th Ave
Tel: 619-338-9300
www.thebitterend.com
Situated in a historic Gaslamp Quarter building that dates back to 1874, this popular, sophisticated nightclub offers three levels of fun – a main bar with billiard tables, a dance hall, and an elegant VIP lounge. Famous for its signature "black martini."
Jimmy Love's
672 5th Ave
Tel: 619-595-0123
www.jimmyloves.com
Occupying two floors of the 125-year-old "Old City Hall" building in the Gaslamp, this restaurant and nightclub hosts live jazz, blues, dance, and disco bands every night of the week.
Stingaree
454 6th Ave
Tel: 619-544-9500
www.stingsandiego.com
Found in a historic warehouse in San Diego's former Red Light District, this popular tri-level Gaslamp hangout features a waterfall, a fire pit, and rooftop cabanas.

Comedy and Magic

San Francisco
Cobb's Comedy Club
915 Columbus Ave
Tel: 415-928-4320
www.cobbscomedyclub.com
Big-name bookings include familiar faces from the small screen.
Punch Line Comedy Club
444 Battery St (up the stairs)
Tel: 415-397-7573
www.punchlinecomedyclub.com
National and local talents crack up crowds every night of the week: alumni include Robin Williams, Ellen DeGeneres, and Chris Rock, so you never know when you might catch the next big thing.

Los Angeles
The Comedy & Magic Club
1018 Hermosa Ave, Hermosa Beach

Live music at Belly Up Tavern, San Diego.

Tel: 310-372-1193
www.comedyandmagicclub.com
Jay Leno, host of The Tonight Show, regularly tests out new material here.

The Comedy Store
8433 Sunset Blvd, West Hollywood
Tel: 323-650-6268
www.thecomedystore.com
Once the site of legendary nightclub Ciro's, this club has featured comic greats like Eddie Murphy, Richard Pryor, and George Carlin.

The Ice House Comedy Club
24 Mentor Ave, Pasadena
Tel: 626-577-1894
www.icehousecomedy.com
Since the 1970s, this comedy club has hosted famous stand-up comedians, from Lily Tomlin to Billy Crystal, as well as ambitious amateurs. The complex includes two showrooms, a restaurant, and an outdoor patio.

Improv Olympic West
6366 Hollywood Blvd, Hollywood
Tel: 323-962-7560
www.ioimprov.com
The West Coast branch of the famous Chicago venue offers improvisational shows and classes.

Laugh Factory
8001 Sunset Blvd, Hollywood
Tel: 323-656-1336
www.laughfactory.com
With branches in Long Beach and New York, too, this famous comedy club often surprises patrons with its all-star shows.

The Magic Castle
7001 Franklin Ave, Hollywood
Tel: 323-851-3313
www.magiccastle.com
Housed in a fanciful Victorian mansion, the world's most famous club for magicians showcases some of the globe's most legendary performers. it is a private club, but members, friends, and guests of the nearby Magic Castle Hotel are allowed inside.

Magicopolis
1418 4th St, Santa Monica
Tel: 310-451-2241
www.magicopolis.com
This classy venue presents shows that blend elements of magic, illusion, and laughter.

San Diego

The Comedy Store La Jolla
916 Pearl St, La Jolla
Tel: 858-454-9176
www.thecomedystore.com
A recent outpost of LA's famous comedy club.

National Comedy Theatre
3717 India St, Midtown
Tel: 619-295-4999

www.nationalcomedy.com
Appropriate for all ages, these 90-minute improvisational comedy shows pit two teams against each other, with the winner decided by the rowdy audience.

Music Venues

San Francisco

Boom Boom Room
1601 Fillmore Street
Tel: 415-673-8000
www.boomboomblues.com
Blues, blues, and more blues.

Café du Nord
2170 Market Street
Tel: 415-861-5016
www.cafedunord.com
Rich red walls and dark woods set an intimate mood at this funky nightclub and music venue, where everything from swing and jazz to spoken word can be heard.

The Fillmore
1805 Geary at Fillmore Street
Tel: 415-346-3000
www.thefillmore.com
Major headline acts – from Snoop Dog to Norah Jones – in a legendary 1960s venue that is part of SF's musical history.

Great American Music Hall
859 O'Farrell Street
Tel: 415-885-0750
www.slimpresents.com
A former Barbary Coast bordello now lures international performers, playing rock, blues, folk, and more.

The Independent
628 Divisadero
Tel: 415-771-1421
www.theindependentsf.com
Supplier of popular live rock, punk, hip-hop, and more.

Yoshi's
1330 Fillmore Street
415-655-5600
www.yoshis.com/sanfrancisco
With a sister venue in Oakland, this top-notch venue hosts the biggest touring acts in the jazz world.

Los Angeles

The Cowboy Palace Saloon
21635 Devonshire Street, Chatsworth
Tel: 818-341-0166
www.cowboypalace.com
For over 30 years, this honky-tonk has showcased live Country & Western music every night.

Harvelle's
1432 4th Street, Santa Monica
Tel: 310-395-1676
www.harvelles.com
Since 1931, this moody, sexy room has invited guests to drink, dance,

and listen to the hottest jazz, blues, and soul. Burlesque shows are also on the menu.

House of Blues Sunset Strip
8430 Sunset Blvd, West Hollywood
Tel: 323-848-5100
www.hob.com
The funky stage attracts famous rock and blues acts, and the gospel brunch lures the locals.

Troubadour
9081 Santa Monica Blvd, West Hollywood
Tel: 310-276-6168
www.troubadour.com
Live rock bands have been jamming at this legendary venue since 1957.

Whisky A Go-Go
8901 Sunset Blvd, West Hollywood
Tel: 310-652-4202
www.whiskyagogo.com
A famous history and rockin' bands continue to entice dancers to this LA landmark, opened in 1964.

San Diego

4th & B
345 B St, Downtown
Tel: 619-231-4343
www.4thandbevents.com
Managed by the House of Blues, one of San Diego's premier live music venues hosts everything from hip-hop dynamos to punk rock legends.

Belly Up Tavern
143 S. Cedros Ave, Solana Beach
Tel: 858-481-8140
www.bellyup.com
Consistently voted one of San Diego's best live music venues, this long-standing club entices a diverse selection of good musicians, from Stevie Wonder to Dr John.

The Casbah
2501 Kettner Blvd, Little Italy
Tel: 619-232-4355
www.casbahmusic.com
With an enclosed smoking patio, pool tables, and live bands at least six nights a week, this venue tempts music lovers of all varieties.

Humphrey's Backstage Music Club
2241 Shelter Island Dr, Shelter Island
Tel: 619-224-3577
www.humphreysbythebay.com
Overlooking the San Diego Bay, this outdoor venue lures jazz, soul, and rock legends to the stage behind Humphrey's restaurant.

SHOPPING

California has no shortage of distinct shopping districts,

each offering a different type of experience: large malls fills the San Fernando Valley, Rodeo Drive is packed with the ritziest of designers, small towns host art galleries and quirky craft shops, and the Wine Country and farmers markets brim with world-class vintages and artisan food products. For quick shopping trips, each city has its main shopping areas, but you'll also find local arts, vintage clothes, and designer fashions sprinkled in unassuming neighborhood streets.

Clothing Sizes

This table gives a comparison of American, Continental, and British clothing sizes. It is always advisable to try on any article before buying, however, as sizes may vary.

Women's Dresses/Suits

American	Continental	British
6	38/34N	8/30
8	40/36N	10/32
10	42/38N	12/34
12	44/40N	14/36
14	46/42N	16/38
16	48/44N	18/40

Women's Shoes

American	Continental	British
4.5	36	3
5.5	37	4
6.5	38	5
7.5	39	6
8.5	40	7
9.5	41	8
10.5	42	9

Men's Suits

American	Continental	British
34	44	34
–	46	36
38	48	38
–	50	40
42	52	42
–	54	44
46	56	46

Men's Shirts

American	Continental	British
14	36	14
14.5	37	14.5
15	38	15
15.5	39	15.5
16	40	16
16.5	41	16.5
17	42	17

Men's Shoes

American	Continental	British
6.5	39	6
7.5	40	7
8.5	41	8
9.5	42	9
10.5	43	10
11.5	44	11

What to Buy

Antiques

In San Francisco, the most concentrated source for old objects of desire is undoubtedly historic Jackson Square, where a variety of traders have outlets selling fine and decorative arts, from period textiles and silver to antique maps and French impressionist paintings from the 17th and 18th centuries.

Arts and Crafts

There is plenty of kitsch on the Santa Cruz Beach Boardwalk, but nearby **Capitola** is more boutique-friendly, with plenty of small jewelry and craft shops.

Because of its upscale nature, the shopping in Palm Springs, centered around **Palm Canyon Drive**, ranges from trendy art galleries and vintage furniture stores to wine emporiums and fine-jewelry boutiques.

Yet another era is evoked by San Diego's trendy **Gaslamp Quarter**, a 16-block district recommended for arts-and-crafts browsers.

Boutique Shopping

San Francisco's best streets for small boutique shopping are **Union Street** and **Chestnut Street** in the Marina, **Sacramento Street** in Presidio Heights (for high-end boutiques and consignment stores), **Hayes Street** between Laguna and Octavia, and Valencia in between 16th and 24th streets.

In the **East Bay**, visitors will find small neighborhoods of specialty shopping in Berkeley's famous "Gourmet Ghetto" along Shattuck Avenue and Oakland's Rockridge district along College Avenue. In Berkeley, 4th Street is one of the better shopping destinations in the East Bay.

Other locations in the Bay Area boasting boutiques, restaurants, and specialty stores include Solano Avenue in Albany, Piedmont Avenue and Jack London Square in Oakland, University Avenue in Palo Alto, Stanford's toned-down "Telegraph Avenue," and the entire business district of Sausalito.

In Los Angeles, trendy shopping streets include **La Brea Avenue** off Melrose and Santa Monica's **Montana Avenue**, and Venice's **Abbott Kinney Boulevard** (named after the visionary developer who created Venice at the turn of the 20th century), where palm trees set off art galleries, and vintage clothing and jewelry stores. The **Silver Lake**

Food and Wine

Farmers markets are a great place to stock up on California's gourmet food products, whether coffee or fruit preserves. California is also one of the best places to buy wine. Any of the wine country regions – Napa, Sonoma, Paso Robles, etc. – will have wineries begging you to buy, but you can also stock up on California vintages in urban wine shops, where the local offerings will be much broader than what visitors can find at home.

district – centered on Vermont Avenue and Sunset Boulevard – is also now full of fashion boutiques and street vendors.

In the Ferry Building on the Embarcadero, artisan food shops are interspersed with small stalls selling ceramics, gardening tools, and kitchen supplies.

Luxury Shopping and Big-Name Brands

For high-end shoppers, Southern California is right up there with the big guns like Paris, New York, and Hong Kong. Of course, the glitziest shopping street is Los Angeles' famous **Rodeo Drive**, home to outposts of luxury brands like Chanel, Armani, Cartier, Louis Vuitton, and Bottega Veneta. Admittedly, Rodeo has become something of a tourist trap, with more people window-shopping than buying. Rodeo Drive's luxurious amenities were increased by 40 percent with the addition **Two Rodeo** (or **Via Rodeo**), a curving, cobble-stoned walkway lined with top-name stores like Tiffany, Baracci, Versace, and Porsche, whose emporiums feature granite colonnades and copper-toned roofs.

In San Francisco, the best known shopping district is **Union Square**, where most of the large, prestigious department stores are located, including Neiman Marcus, Macy's, and Saks. A block away is **Maiden Lane**, a charming pedestrian street with high-end boutiques and outdoor cafés.

Mall Shopping and Outlets

For mall-lovers, Southern California is a shopper's Valhalla. The mind reels at the number of mega-malls dotted throughout the region: **Westfield, Century City, Beverly Center, Westfield Topanga, Westfield Fashion Square, Paseo Colorado,** and **Fashion Island** are just a few.

One of the Greater Los Angeles Area's most famous landmarks, the outstanding former Uniroyal tire plant beside the Santa Ana Freeway in the City of Commerce, is now the **Citadel Outlets** (www.citadeloutlets.com), an enticing shopping plaza whose 80 or so stores spread around a tree-flanked courtyard.

You might, however, want to concentrate your energies on the **South Coast Plaza** (www.southcoastplaza.com) in Costa Mesa (just a stone's throw from Newport in Orange County), a shopping tour-de-force. South Coast Plaza is huge and almost all the 300 stores are first-rate: Armani, a Metropolitan Museum of Art gift store, Christian Dior, Yves Saint-Laurent, Cartier, Chanel, Pottery, as well as a wide range of eateries in all price brackets.

In Santa Barbara, **El Paseo Mall** on State Street is host to gifts and clothes stores as well as galleries and restaurants. The city's biggest shopping mall is also on State Street, called **La Cumbre Plaza**. Two attractive, Spanish-style malls are **La Arcada Court** and **Paseo Nuevo**, the latter anchored by Nordstrom and Macy's.

The **Westfield San Francisco Centre,** on Market Street at Powell, is home to Nordstrom's and Bloomingdales, as well as over a hundred smaller stores, a movie theater, a spa, and an upscale food court downstairs.

In addition to San Diego's city's **Seaport Village** (www.seaportvillage.com) and the multi-level **Horton Plaza** is nearby **Mission Valley**, which has two shopping malls housing around 350 stores.

Souvenirs

In Los Angeles, it will be hard to escape Hollywood without mementos. For souvenirs in San Francisco, both **Fisherman's Wharf (with the Cannery,** the **Anchorage** and a host of street vendors) and Grant Street in **Chinatown** are filled with inexpensive

Tax

The sales tax in California is a minimum of 7.25 percent, but higher rates are common, for example San Francisco is 8.5 percent. The rate varies from city to city.

knick-knacks emblazoned with the Golden Gate Bridge. San Diego, meanwhile, is just a short distance away from the Mexican border town of **Tijuana**, offering souvenirs at super low prices, and of course the enticement of shopping for a day in a different country.

Thrift Shopping

San Francisco has a staggering array of thrift stores where you can rummage for almost anything to outfit your home, your children, or yourself at a fraction of the price of regular stores. The Mission and Haight-Asbury districts have the largest concentration. In the Mission, the place to be is Valencia and Mission streets between 16th and 24th. Thrift Town (2101 Mission Street, has a good selection of vintage clothes and musty books; and the Goodwill Superstore at 1580 Mission Street at Van Ness has the largest selection of clothes.) If you're on Haight Street, try Wasteland for fashions that take you back in time.

SPORTS AND OUTDOOR ACTIVITIES

Spectator Sports

Baseball

California possesses some of the finest teams in professional baseball;

the season runs from April to October. In Southern California, the Los Angeles Dodgers play at Dodger Stadium; the Anaheim Angels play at Angel Stadium; and the San Diego Padres play at Petco Park. In Northern California, the San Francisco Giants play at AT&T Park, and the Oakland Athletics (known as the As) play in Oakland-Alameda County Coliseum.

Basketball

The regular National Basketball Association (NBA) season runs from October through April, with championship play-offs continuing in June. The Los Angeles Lakers, who are almost always a league powerhouse, and the LA Clippers play at the popular Staples Center Downtown, and the Golden State Warriors play at Oracle Arena in Oakland. In Sacramento, the Kings play at Power Balance Pavilion Arena.

Football

The National Football League (NFL) season begins in September and ends in December, with pre-season games in August and post-season play-offs in January. San Diego's Chargers play at San Diego Qualcomm Stadium. The Rose Bowl is held annually on New Year's Day between the best team in the Pac-10 conference and the best team in the Big Ten. This popular event – with a great parade – is held at the Rose Bowl Stadium in Pasadena, which seats over 100,000 people, but it is still difficult to get seats. In Northern California, the San Francisco 49ers play at Monster Park, and the Oakland Raiders play at Oakland-Alameda County Coliseum.

Hockey

California has two professional hockey teams, the Los Angeles Kings, who play at the 19,000-seat Staples Center, Downtown, and the younger San Jose Sharks, who play at HP Pavilion. The hockey season runs October–April.

Soccer

Soccer has been steadily gaining interest in the US. From April to October, the Los Angeles Galaxy, starring David Beckham, faces other US teams in the Home Depot Center.

Participant Sports

Ballooning

Temecula in the Wine Country north of San Diego is one of the most popular

Los Angeles Fashion District

If you've never shopped in Los Angeles, the sprawling LA Fashion District is a great way to start. The 100-block downtown district is the hub of the city's $24.3 billion apparel industry, where wholesalers, designers, fashion students, stylists, and retail shoppers mix. Here you'll find about a thousand stores selling to the public at wholesale prices – that means bargains of 30–70 percent off normal retail prices. In general, stores are open 10am–5pm, except Sunday when

the majority are closed. On Sunday (or any other day) you can still head to Santee Alley, a festive alley between Santee Street and Maple Avenue, from Olympic Boulevard to 12th Street. The alley hosts about 150 stores and vendors selling everything from clothes and perfume to toys and gifts. Another Fashion District destination is the LA Flower Market, centered along Wall Street, between 7th Street and 8th Street, which is the largest flower market in the United States.

Hot-air ballooning over the Wine Country.

ballooning areas. **D&D Ballooning** (tel: 1-800-510-9000; www.hotairadventures.com) can show you the sights, or try **Lake Tahoe Balloons** (tel: 1-800-872-9294; www.laketahoeballoons.com) or **Balloons above the Valley** in Napa (tel: 1-800-464-6824; www.balloonrides.com).

Boats & Charters

Humboldt Bay
Humboldt Bay Harbor Cruise.
Tel: 707-445-1910; www.
humboldtbaymaritimemuseum.com
Hum Boats. Tel: 707-443-5157;
www.humboats.com

Lake Tahoe
Action Water Sports. Tel: 530-544-5387; www.action-watersports.com
Tahoe Adventure Company.
Tel: 1-866-830-6125; www.
tahoeadventurecompany.com
Tahoe City Marina.
Tel: 530-583-1039; www.
tahoecitymarina.com
Tahoe Sailing Charters. Tel: 530-583-6200; www.tahoesail.com
Zephyr Cove Marina. Tel: 1-800-238-2463; www.zephyrcove.com

Los Angeles
Free Spirit Sailing Adventures
(Marina del Rey). Tel: 424-217-9295
(Captain Larry's cellphone); www.
captlarry.com

Ojai
Lake Casitas Recreation Area
Boathouse. Tel: 805-649-2043

San Diego
Dennis Connor's America's Cup
Experience. Tel: 1-800-644-3454;
www.nextlevelsailing.com
Hornblower Cruises. Tel: 1-888-467-6256; www.hornblower.com

Mission Bay Sportcenter.
Tel: 858-488-1044; www.
missionbaysportcenter.com
San Diego Harbor Excursion. Tel:
1-800-442-7847; www.dhe.com
Seaforth Boat Rental. Tel: 1-888-834-2628; www.seaforthboatrental.
com

San Francisco
Cass' Marina (Sausalito). Tel:
1-800-472-4595; www.cassmarina.
com
Golden Gate Park Boat House. Tel:
415-752-0347

Santa Barbara
Santa Barbara Sailing Center. Tel:
1-800-350-9090; www.sbsail.com

Santa Cruz & Capitola
Capitola Boat & Bait. Tel: 831-462-2208; www.santacruzboatrentals.net

Cycling

Organized weekend and six-day bicycle adventures, which include accommodations, operate in the Napa and Sonoma valleys and other parts of the state from travel company Backroads (tel: 1-800 462 2848; www.backroads.com).

Mammoth Mountain Bike Park (tel: 1-800-626-6684) offers 90 miles (150km) of cycling trails and stunt tracks perfect for enthusiasts. Bike across San Francisco's Golden Gate Bridge by renting from one of Blazing Saddles' several locations near Fisherman's Wharf. Bike rentals include easy-to-follow maps. Tel: 415-202-8888; www.blanzingsaddles.com.

Golf Courses

San Francisco Area
Harding Park Golf Course, Harding Rd and Skyline Blvd, San Francisco; tel: 415-664-4690; www.harding-park.com
Lincoln Park Golf Course, 34th Ave and Clement St, San Francisco; tel: 415-221-9911; www.lincolnparkgc.com
Tilden Park Golf Course, Grizzly Peak Blvd and Shasta Rd, Berkeley; tel: 510-848-7373

Santa Cruz
Pasatiempo Golf Course, 20 Clubhouse Rd; tel: 831-459-9155; www.pasatiempo.com

Half Moon Bay
Half Moon Bay Golf Links, 2 Miramontes Point Rd; tel: 650-726-1800; www.halfmoonbaygolf.com

Monterey Peninsula
The Links at Spanish Bay, 2700 17-Mile Dr, Pebble Beach; tel: 1-800-654-9300; www.pebblebeach.com
Pacific Grove Municipal Golf Links, 77 Asilomar Blvd, Pacific Grove; tel: 831-648-5775; www.pggolflinks.com
Pebble Beach Golf Links, 17-Mile Dr, Pebble Beach; tel: 1-800-654-9300; www.pebblebeach.com
Poppy Hills Golf Course, 3200 Lopez Rd, Pebble Beach; tel: 831-625-4653; www.ncga.org
Spyglass Hill Golf Course, Stevenson Dr. and Spyglass Hill Rd,

Pebble Beach Golf Links has been named the country's best public golf course.

Pebble Beach; tel: 1-800 654 9300; www.pebblebeach.com

Greater Los Angeles Area
Brookside Golf Course, 1133 N. Rosemont Ave, Pasadena; tel: 626-585-3598.
Griffith Park Golf Courses, 4730 Crystal Springs Dr, Los Angeles; tel: 323-663-2255.
Industry Hills Golf Club, 1 Industry Hills Pkwy, Industry Hills; tel: 626-810-4653; www.ihgolfclub.com
Rancho Park Golf Course, 10460 W. Pico Blvd, Los Angeles; tel: 310-838-7373.

San Diego Area
Balboa Park Municipal Golf Course, 2600 Golf Course Dr, San Diego; tel: 619-858-0235
Mission Bay Golf Course, 2702 N. Mission Bay Dr, San Diego; tel: 858-581-7880
Pala Mesa Golf Resort, 2001 Old Highway 395, Fallbrook; tel: 760-728-5881; www.palamesa.com
Rancho Bernardo Inn Golf Resort and Spa, 17550 Bernardo Oaks Dr; tel: 1-877-517-9340; www.ranchobernardoinn.com

Santa Barbara Area
Alisal Golf Course, 1054 Alisal Rd, Solvang; tel: 805-688-6411; www.alisal.com
Ojai Valley Inn and Country Club, 905 Country Club Rd, Ojai; tel: 805-646-1111; www.ojairesort.com
La Purisima Golf Course, 3455 State Highway 246, Lompoc; tel: 805-735-8395; www.lapurisimagolf.com

Palm Springs Area
Indian Wells Golf Resort, 44–500 Indian Wells Lane, Indian Wells; tel: 760-346 4653; www.golfresortatindianwells.com
Mission Hills Country Club, 34–600 Mission Hills Dr, Rancho Mirage; tel: 760-459-7034
PGA West, 55–955 PGA Blvd, La Quinta; tel: 760-564-7111; www.pgawest.com
La Quinta Resort and Club, 49–499 Eisenhower Dr, La Quinta; tel: 760-564-4111; www.laquintaresort.com

Hang-gliding
There's more hang-gliding in California than in any other state because the good coastal winds are consistent. One of the best spots to watch or participate is the 200ft (60-meter) cliff at Fort Funston, just south of San Francisco, at the end of the Great Highway near Lake Merced. Recorded information about wind

Paragliding at Monterey Bay.

conditions is available at tel: 415-333-0100. The **San Francisco Hang-Gliding Center** (tel: 510-528-2300; www.sfhangglinding.com) specializes in tandem flights, launching from Mount Tamalpais.
In Southern California, the **Torrey Pines Gliderport** (2800 Torrey Pines Scenic Drive; tel: 858-452-9878; sandiegofreeflight.com) near San Diego is another great spot for hang-gliding, above Blacks Beach in La Jolla.

Kayaking
Angel Island Sea Trek. Tel: 415-488-1000. www.seatrekkayak.com
Channel Islands/Santa Barbara Aquasports. Tel: 1-800-733-2309; www.islandkayaking.com
Channel Islands/Santa Barbara Paddle Sports of Santa Barbara. Tel: 1-888-254-2094; www.kayaksb.com
Irvine. Southwind Kayak Center. Tel: 1-800-768-8494; www.southwindkayaks.com
Kern River Kern River Tours (tel: 1-800-844-7238; www.kernrivertours.com) operates out of Lake Isabella, three hours north of LA.
Monterey Monterey Bay Kayaks. Tel: 831-373-5357; www.montereybaykayaks.com
Point Reyes Blue Waters Kayaking. Tel: 415-669-2600; www.bwkayak.com
San Diego Aqua Adventures Kayak Center in San Diego and Paddle Power Inc (tel: 949-675-1215), of Newport Beach.
Sausalito Cass' Sailing School (tel: 415-332-6789); Sea Trek (tel: 415-332-8790; www.seatrek.com).

Kitesurfing
Kitesurfing is possible in many places along the California coast (Santa Cruz, Monterey, Pismo Beach), but in Northern California, the best place to learn is in Alameda. **Kite Wind Surf** (tel: 1-877-521-9463; www.kitewindsurf.

com) offers beginner lessons in the sheltered San Francisco Bay.
In Central California, San Simeon, Cayucos, Morro Bay, Pismo Beach, Oceano, and Jalama all offer good kitesurfing action.
In Southern California, Long Beach's Belmont Shores is a good spot for beginners. In the summer months, advanced kiters can use the dedicated launch spots on Sunset Beach and Seal Beach to kiteboard from 2pm to sundown.

River Rafting
Rafting expeditions are organized near Yosemite and Tahoe and throughout the Sierras by many companies, including:
Arta River Trips (tel: 1-800-323-2782)
Earthtrek Expeditions (tel: 1-800-229-8735)
Tributary White Water Tours (Grass Valley) tel: 1-800-672-3846; www.whitewatertours.com
White Water Connection (Coloma) tel: 1-800-336-7238; www.whitewaterconnection.com
Whitewater Voyages (tel: 1-800-400-7238)

Skiing

Lake Tahoe Area
Alpine Meadows, 2600 Alpine Meadows Rd off State 89 bet. Truckee and Tahoe City; tel: 1-800-403-0206; www.skialpine.com
Boreal, Castle Peak exit off Interstate 80 at Soda Springs; tel: 530-426-3666; www.borealski.com
Heavenly, Ski Run Blvd off US-50, South Lake Tahoe; tel: 775-586-7000; www.skiheavenly.com
Homewood, 5145 West Lake Blvd. State 89 (6 miles (10km) south of Tahoe City; tel: 530-525-2992; www.skihomewood.com

TRANSPORTATION

ACCOMMODATIONS

EATING OUT

ACTIVITIES

A – Z

Northstar-at-Tahoe, State 267 bet. Truckee and Kings Beach; tel: 530-562-1010; 1-800-466-6784; www.skinorthstar.com
Squaw Valley USA, Squaw Valley Rd off State 89, 5 miles (8km) north of Tahoe City; tel: 530-583-5585, 1-800-403-0206; www.squaw.com

Central Sierra
Badger Pass, Glacier Point Rd off State 41, Yosemite National Park; tel: 209-372-8430; www.yosemiterentals.com/badger.htm
Dodge Ridge, off State 108, 32 miles (50km) east of Sonora; tel: 209-965-3474; www.dodgeridge.com
Kirkwood, State 88 at Carson Pass, 35 miles (56km) south of South Lake Tahoe; tel: 209-258-6000; www.kirkwood.com
Mount Reba/Bear Valley, State 4 (52 miles (84km) east of Angels Camp); tel: 209-753-2301; www.bearvalley.com
Sierra Ski Ranch, off US 50, 12 miles (19km) west of South Lake Tahoe; tel: 530-659-7453; www.sierratahoe.com

Whale Watching
Spring and fall are the seasons for spotting whales. The **American Cetacean Society** (www.acsonline.org) is among the many groups that organize trips to see some of the thousands of magnificent 40-ton California gray whales on their 10,000-mile (16,000km) migration from Alaska to South America. Traveling 80–100 miles (130–160km) per day, some of these mammals can be seen from high spots along the coast – particularly from the Palos Verdes peninsula – and around the Channel Islands. Seals and sea lions are also plentiful in the islands, to which **Island Packers** (tel: 805-642-1393) trips and about which the **Channel Islands National Park** (tel: 805-658-5730) can provide a wealth of information. In addition, snowy plovers and cormorants are found on San Miguel; kestrels, larks, and owls on Santa Barbara; and brown pelicans, who nest between May and August, on Anacapa, the closest island to the mainland. For information about Santa Cruz, the largest island of the group, call the helpful **Nature Conservancy** (tel: 949-263-0933).
Another whale-watching option is Point Reyes Lighthouse at the Point Reyes National Seashore, north of San Francisco. Organized boat tours offered by whale-watching tour companies include:

Captain Don's Harbor Tours (Santa Barbara) tel: 805-969-5217; www.captdon.com
Condor (Santa Barbara) tel: 1-888-779-4253; www.condorcruise.com
Dana Wharf (Dana Point) tel: 1-800-979-3370; http://www.zerve.com/DanaWharf
Island Packers (Channel Islands) 805-642-1393; www.islandpackers.com
Redondo Sport Fishing (Redondo Beach) tel: 310-372-2111; www.redondosportfishing.com
San Diego Whale Watch (San Diego) tel: 619-839-0128; www.sdwhalewatch.com
SF Bay Whale Watching (San Francisco) tel: 415-331-6267; www.sfbaywhalewatching.com
Stagnaro Charter Boats (Santa Cruz) tel: 1-800-979-3370; www.santacruzwhalewatching.com

TOURS

Adventure Bus (tel: 1-888-737-5263; www.adventurebus.com) offers inexpensive transportation through much of California, departing from Salt Lake City and Las Vegas. Destinations include Yellowstone and the southwestern national parks, plus other trips, stopping at scenic spots en route.
Architours
Tel: 323-294-5821
www.architours.com
Various Los Angeles tours visit works by Frank Lloyd Wright and Richard Neutra, as well as restaurants and other facilities of architectural merit.
foot!
Tel: 415-793-5378
www.foottours.com
Fun, informative, interactive walking tours that allow for personal and memorable experiences. Guides are professional comedians who share their love and knowledge of San Francisco with you.
Mangia! North Beach – History, Food, and Culture Tours
e-mail: gaw@sbcglobal.net
Learn about the Italian heritage of the neighborhood, taste truffles and focaccia, and enjoy a three-course lunch with SF Chronicle food columnist GraceAnn Walden. Named one of the 100 best things about San Francisco by *Gourmet* magazine. Reservations necessary.
Old Town Trolley Tours
Tel: 1-888-910-8687
www.trolleytours.com
Vibrant green-and-orange trolleys,

For concerts, shows, festivals, and celebrations in Northern California, check out "Datebook" in the *San Francisco Chronicle* or the *SF Weekly*. Listings for more specialized events appear in smaller local papers. For Southern California, check the "Calendar" section of the *Los Angeles Times* or a current copy of *LA Weekly* or *Los Angeles Magazine*.

driven by spirited conductors, take visitors to San Diego's most popular sites, including Old Town, the San Diego Harbor Seaport Village, Petco Park, the Gaslamp Quarter, the Hotel del Coronado, the San Diego Zoo, and Balboa Park.
San Francisco City Guides
Tel: 415-557-4266
www.sfcityguides.org
Nearly 70 free architectural and history tours by trained volunteers are offered all year long. Tours cover topics from the murals of the Mission to the mansions of Pacific Heights, and everything in between.
Starline Tours
Tel: 1-800-959-3131
www.starlinetours.com
An assortment of LA sightseeing tours, from movie stars' homes to the delights of Disneyland.
Victorian Home Walk
Tel: 415-252-9485
www.victorianwalk.com
Go where buses can't. Learn about San Francisco architecture and history from long-time residents. Most days at 11am a tour leaves from the old lobby of the Westin St Francis on Powell and Geary in Union Square. No reservations required.
Warner Bros. Studios V.I.P. Tour
Tel: 1-877-492-8689
www.vipstudiotour.warnerbros.com
For two colorful hours, small groups of movie lovers can ride through this famous Burbank lot, visiting such classic sets as the Walton family home and Errol Flynn's Sherwood Forest as well as sound stages and post-production labs.
Wok Wiz Walking Tours
Tel: 650-355-9657
www.wokwiz.com
SF's Chinatown history, culture, and folklore are presented from an insider's view of the largest Chinatown outside of China. The daily tour includes a seven-course dim-sum lunch. Reservations required.

A – Z

A HANDY SUMMARY OF PRACTICAL INFORMATION

A

Admission Charges

Most large museums have reasonably moderate entrance fees – typically $7 to $15 for the first visit. Smaller art galleries tend to be free. Special exhibitions usually cost extra, but many museums have free general admission on certain days each month or once a week in the evenings. These free days are always indicated on the museum's website. Some attractions, like LA's Getty Center, are always free. Plays, concerts, and sporting events are often expensive, as are theme park tickets. You can sometimes get free tickets to live TV shows, especially sit-coms, if you call in advance.

Age Restrictions

In California, the legal age to consume alcohol is 21. The legal age for driving is 16.

B

Budgeting for your Trip

San Francisco and Los Angeles tend to be more expensive than other parts of California, although exclusive resorts for skiing or spa holidays are more expensive still. If you're looking for a hotel room with an acceptable minimum level of comfort, cleanliness, and facilities, a reasonable starting point for the price of a double room is $85 in budget-class hotels; upping your budget from there to at least $150 will make a significant difference in quality. For between $150 and $300 a whole range of hotels opens up, from bland but functional business traveler places to hip little boutique hotels. Beyond this, and certainly beyond $350, you're moving into deluxe territory; though you don't really arrive at "discreet hideaway for celebrities" status until $700 and above.

Food costs range from $3 to $10 for a perfectly acceptable hot dog, burrito or Asian delicacy, to $50 for a two- or three-course meal at a cute California-cuisine type restaurant. Expect to pay $100-plus at a fine restaurant. A glass of house wine is usually under $10, a beer around $5–6.

Getting around by public transportation can cost as little as $3–5 a day, with bus tickets $2 in San Francisco, $1.50 in Los Angeles, and $2.25 in San Diego. Car rentals cost $40 or more per day. A taxi to or from the airport can cost $50 in San Francisco and Los Angeles.

C

Children

Home to Disneyland, the San Diego Zoo, the Monterey Bay Aquarium and other kid-friendly attractions, the Golden State is a great place to bring kids, and a popular destination for family vacations. Playgrounds are plentiful, and children pay a reduced fee for admission to museums, other attractions, and on public transportation.

Children's menus are common (some restaurants even provide crayons), although young children rarely make an appearance at fancy restaurants. From beginning kids' ski lessons in Tahoe to nature walks in Yosemite, offering programs specifically for kids is the norm.

Childcare is not usually offered by hotels, but reputable baby-sitting services can be recommended by hotel concierges. It's best to call in advance to arrange this.

The official website of the California State Tourism Commission, www.visitcalifornia.com, has a separate link for families. Called "Fun Spots" (www.cafunspots.com), the pages include tips on traveling with youngsters, family discounts, and even games to play.

Climate

When to Visit

Northern California: San Francisco's climate is typical of the Northern California coast. Daytime temperatures average in the mid-50s Fahrenheit (12–14° C) and drop as much as 10°F (6°C) at night. Average temperatures are significantly higher in the South Bay and inland valleys. In fact, in the Sacramento and San Joaquin valleys, summer temperatures often reach the 90s°F (32–37°C). Summers tend to be warm and dry. Winters are generally rainy; temperatures rarely go below freezing along the coast.

Do note that San Francisco can be chilly and foggy during the summer

CLIMATE CHART
San Francisco

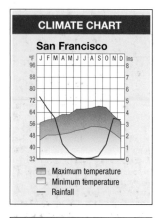

- Maximum temperature
- Minimum temperature
- Rainfall

CLIMATE CHART
Los Angeles

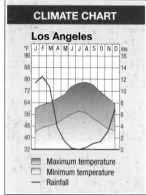

- Maximum temperature
- Minimum temperature
- Rainfall

CLIMATE CHART
Lake Tahoe

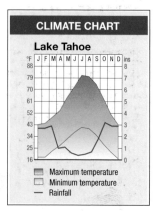

- Maximum temperature
- Minimum temperature
- Rainfall

months, even though the sun might be shining just over the bridge in the Bay Area. If you plan to visit the city itself, wait until the fall, when the weather is often perfect.

Southern California: This is one of the few places in the world where you can ski in the morning and surf in the afternoon. It is not uncommon for the temperature to vary by 30–40°F (17–22°C) as you travel from mountains

Ocean Beach, San Diego.

to deserts to the beach. The change of seasons is not as dramatic as it is elsewhere. The winters are mild, with a rainy season that lasts from January through March. In the summer months, the humidity is usually low, so discomfort is rare. The famous LA smog is at its worst in August and September.

What to Wear

Northern California: With the exception of the finer restaurants, jackets, ties, and formal dresses are unnecessary. San Francisco is famous for its fog and breezy hilltops, so bring along a sweater or jacket, even if it is warm when you first step out.

Southern California: Dress in Southern California is casual – designer jeans and handbags are quite common – and few restaurants require jackets and ties for men. Unless you are visiting the mountains, heavy clothing is unnecessary. Wool sweaters or lightweight overcoats are sufficient for winter evenings, and a light jacket is adequate for summer evenings. Expect rain in winter and springtime.

Crime and Safety

Like urban centers anywhere, California's cities have dangerous neighborhoods. Common sense is an effective weapon. Do not walk alone at night. Keep a careful eye on belongings. Lock valuable possessions in a safe. Never leave your car unlocked. Never leave children by themselves.

If you are driving, never pick up anyone you don't know. Always be wary of who is around you. If you have trouble on the road, stay in the car and lock the doors, turn on your hazard lights and leave the hood up in order to increase visibility and alert police cars.

Hotels usually warn that they do not guarantee the safety of belongings left in the rooms. If you have any valuables, you may want to lock them in the hotel safe.

Customs Regulations

Whether or not there is anything to declare, all people entering the country must fill out a US Customs form (usually provided on the airplane) and go through US Customs. This can be a time-consuming process, but, in order to speed things up, be prepared to open your luggage for inspection and try to keep the following restrictions in mind:

There is no limit to the amount of money you can bring in with you. If the amount exceeds $10,000, however, you must fill out a report.

Anything you have for your own personal use may be brought in duty- and tax-free.

Adults are allowed to bring in one quart (1 liter) of alcohol for personal use; 100 cigars (non-Cuban) or 3lbs of tobacco or 200 cigarettes; and $100 worth of gifts.

Agricultural items – including fruits, plants, and vegetables - may not be brought into the US.

Dogs, cats, and other animals may be brought into the country with certain restrictions. For details, contact the US consulate nearest you or write to the Department of Agriculture.

Automobiles may be driven into the US if they are for the personal use of the visitor, family, and guests.

For a full list of prohibited or restricted items, see: http://cbp.gov/xp/cgov/travel/vacation/kbyg/prohibited_restricted.xml

US Customs & Border Protection, 1300 Pennsylvania Avenue NW; Washington, DC 20229; tel: 202-344-1000; www.cbp.gov.

Disabled Travelers

California has legislation requiring public buildings and most public transportation to be accessible to the disabled. There are also some special concessions: Greyhound buses allow a disabled person plus a companion to travel for one fare plus a half-fare (tel: 1-800-752-4841) and the railway system, Amtrak, offers discounted tickets and accessible rooms. For more information, visit www.disabilityaccessinfo.ca.gov/transport.htm.

Electricity

The standard electric current in the United States is 110 volts, and outlets are generally for flat-blade, two-prong plugs. Foreign appliances usually require a converter and an adaptor plug. Many hotel bathrooms have plugs for electric shavers that work on either current.

Embassies and Consulates

Australia: 625 Market St, San Francisco. Tel: 415-536-1970
Also: 2049 Century Park E, Century City, Los Angeles. Tel: 310-229 4800
Canada: 555 Montgomery St, San Francisco. Tel: 415-834-3180
Also: 550 S. Hope St, Los Angeles. Tel: 213-346 2700
Great Britain: 1 Sansome St, San Francisco. Tel: 415-617-1300
Also: 11766 Wilshire Blvd, Los Angeles. Tel: 310-481 0031
Ireland: 100 Pine St, San Francisco. Tel: 415-392-4214
Also: 751 Seadrift Dr, Huntington Beach (Los Angeles). Tel: 714-658 9832
New Zealand: no SF address. Tel: 415-399-1255.
Also: 2425 Olympic Blvd, Santa Monica (Los Angeles). Tel: 310-566 6555
South Africa: 6300 Wilshire Blvd, Suite 600, Los Angeles. Tel: 323-651-0902

Emergency

In the case of an emergency, dial 911 from any telephone for the police, fire department, or ambulance service.

Gay and Lesbian Travelers

San Francisco is one of the world's most welcoming places for gay men and lesbians. The best sources for up-to-date information on new clubs, shows, films, events, and gay news are the free newspapers, notably the

Bay Times and the *Bay Area Reporter (BAR)* found in cafés or street-corner boxes. **The Center**, at 1800 Market Street, www.sf_center.org, has become a vital nexus for the LGBT community and has numerous flyers and listings for events. **The Women's Building**, www.womens_building.org, houses various non-profit organizations and you'll find newspapers, bulletin board postings, and information here too. Two free weekly newspapers, the *Bay Guardian* and *SF Weekly*, have useful listings and information as well.

In Los Angeles, **West Hollywood** contains Southern California's largest homosexual population, and sponsors LA's annual Gay Pride Parade. Visit www.visitwesthollywood.com for more information. Also check out the website www.oneinstitute.org for details about the **ONE National Gay & Lesbian Archives** (909 W. Adams Boulevard; tel: 213-741-0094), the world's largest research library on lesbian, gay, bisexual, and transgendered issues.

Health and Medical Care

There is nothing cheap about being sick in the United States. It is essential to have adequate medical insurance and to carry an identification card or policy number at all times.

In the event that you need medical assistance, consult the local *Yellow Pages* for the physician or pharmacist nearest you. In large cities, there is usually a physician referral service number listed. If you need immediate attention, go to a hospital emergency room.

Some medicines that are available over the counter in your home country may require a prescription in the US. Walgreens drugstores (pharmacies) have 24-hour locations in major cities.

Hospitals

San Francisco: some of the larger hospitals with 24-hour emergency services are:
California Pacific Medical Center, with buildings at 3700 California St, 3898 California St, 2333 Buchanan St, and at Castro and Deboce streets); main telephone number and information, tel: 415-387-8700.
Saint Francis Memorial Hospital, 900

Police take a break at San Francisco's Golden Gate Park.

Hyde St (Downtown); tel: 415-353-6300.

San Francisco General Hospital, 1001 Potrero Ave; tel: 415-206-8000.

UCSF Medical Center, 505 Parnassus Ave (Richmond); tel: 415-476-1000.

Los Angeles: some of the most central hospitals are:

California Hospital Medical Center, 1401 S. Grand Avenue (Downtown); tel: 213-748-2411.

Cedars-Sinai Medical Center, 8700 Beverly Boulevard (Beverly Hills); tel: 310-423-3506.

LAC+USC Medical Center, 1200 N. State Street (East LA); tel: 323-442-2830.

Saint John's Health Center, 1328 22nd Street (Santa Monica); tel: 310-829-5511.

UCLA Medical Center, 10833 Le Conte Avenue (West LA); tel: 310-825-8611.

I

Internet

You should be able to find internet cafés in all major cities and larger towns, but they are not nearly as commonplace as in Europe. Most public libraries have free terminals, and **FedEx Office,** a national chain (www.fedexoffice.com), rents out space on terminals, scanners, and printers by the minute or by the hour. The company has many locations throughout the state.

If you've brought your own laptop computer, nearly all cafés in cities now offer free wireless connections.

Nearly all city cafés offer free Wi-fi.

Check out California locations on www.wififreespot.com/ca.html.

Some cafés will ask you to pay a minimal service fee for use of their wireless router.

Most hotels offer high-speed internet connections in their guestrooms and common areas, although it's not always free. Even modest hotels tend to have at least one computer for the use of guests.

L

Lost Luggage

File claims for damaged or missing luggage before leaving the airport. For queries and complaints, contact the Federal Aviation Administration Consumer Hotline (tel: 1-866-835-5322, www.faa.gov) or the Aviation Consumer Protection Division (tel: 202-366-2220; airconsumer.ost.dot. gov).

M

Maps

In San Francisco, if you find yourself confused and without a map, look for a Muni bus shelter, which often has a detailed map of the city, including a close-up map of Downtown. Visitor centers also provide free maps. Some corner shops and gas stations also sell maps.

Tourists can receive a variety of Los Angeles maps from **MTA** and

individual visitor bureaus. In addition, the **AAA** has various branches in the area, offering assorted street maps of LA plus maps of California and Mexico. It's worth joining if you plan to drive within Los Angeles, because the cost of being towed away once by traffic wardens could be less than the annual membership fee.

Insight Flexi Map: San Francisco and *Insight Flexi Map: Los Angeles* are laminated, easy-to-fold maps that combine detailed cartography with pictures and essential information.

Media

Television & Radio

Television and radio are invaluable sources of up-to-the-minute information about weather, road conditions, and current events. Television and radio listings are published in local newspapers. Sunday papers usually have a detailed weekly guide to events and activities.

Newspapers, Magazines, and Websites

San Francisco's major daily newspaper is the *San Francisco Chronicle* (www.sfgate.com). The weekend edition of the *Chronicle* includes special sections, such as "Datebook," which highlights the area's sports, entertainment, and cultural events. Other papers in Northern California include the *Sacramento Bee,* the *San Jose Mercury-News,* and the *San Francisco Bay Guardian.*

The websites www.7x7.com and www.sanfranmag.com keep up to date with events and activities.

The *Los Angeles Times* (www. latimes.com) is one of the most widely read papers in the country. There are several editions, and there is probably no better local entertainment section than the *Times'* Sunday "Calendar" section. Other large daily papers are San Fernando Valley's *The Daily News, The San Diego Union-Tribune,* and the *Orange County Register.*

Los Angeles Magazine, Palm Springs Life, San Diego, Santa Barbara, and *Orange Coast* are monthly regional magazines that carry feature articles on Southern California culture, as well as listings of restaurants and current events.

The website www.la.com describes area attractions, spas, hotels, eateries, clubs, and shops, and lists most local events.

Some of the free local weekly

newspapers, available in cafés and newspaper boxes on the street, are excellent sources of up-to-the-minute information on what's going on in a particular town. Check out the *LA Weekly* in Los Angeles, the *East Bay Express* in the East Bay, the *San Francisco Bay Guardian*, and *SF Weekly* in San Francisco.

Money

Cash: Most banks belong to a network of ATMs (automatic teller machines) which dispense cash 24 hours a day.

Credit cards: Not all credit cards are accepted at all places, but most places accept either **Visa**, **American Express** or **MasterCard**. Major credit cards can also be used to withdraw cash from atms. (Look for an ATM that uses one of the banking networks indicated on the back of your credit card, such as Plus, Cirrus, or Interlink.) Most likely there will be a charge.

Traveler's Checks: With the popularity of ATMs, credit cards, and debit cards, traveler's checks are becoming less and less common. Still, banks, stores, restaurants, and hotels generally accept US dollar-denominated traveler's checks. If yours are in foreign denominations, they must be changed to dollars. Banks readily cash large traveler's checks, although be sure to take along your passport. When lost or stolen, most traveler's checks can be replaced; record the checks' serial numbers in a separate place to facilitate refunds of lost or stolen checks.

O

Opening Hours

Standard business hours are 9am–5pm weekdays. Most department stores open at 10am and many stores, especially those in shopping malls, stay open until 9pm. San Francisco, Los Angeles, and San Diego have a number of 24-hour restaurants. A few supermarkets and convenience stores are also open around the clock. Bank hours usually run from 9am to 5pm, although some stay open until 6pm. Some branch offices keep Saturday morning hours. However, most banks are equipped with 24-hour automated tellers on the outside of their buildings, and, if you

have an ATM card, you can use these machines for simple transactions at your convenience. Be careful at night.

Keep in mind that, during public holidays, post offices, banks, government offices, and many private businesses are closed.

P

Postal Services

Post offices open between 7am and 9am and usually close at 5pm, Monday–Friday. Many are also open for a few hours on Saturday morning. Post offices are closed all day on Sunday. If you don't know where you will be staying in any particular town, you can receive mail by having it addressed to General Delivery at the main post office in that town. You must pick up General Delivery mail in person and show proper identification.

You can buy stamps in most convenience stores, although you may have to buy a book of stamps. You can also buy them at post offices.

Public Holidays

National US holidays are:
New Year's Day (January 1)
Martin Luther King Jr. Day (3rd Monday in January)
Presidents' Day (3rd Monday in February)
Memorial Day (Last Monday in May)
Independence Day (July 4)
Labor Day (1st Monday in September)
Columbus Day (2nd Monday in October)
Veteran's Day (November 11)
Thanksgiving (4th Thursday in November)
Christmas Day (December 25)

R

Religious Services

There is no official religion in the US or California. The majority of Americans identify themselves as Protestant or Catholic. Non-Christian religions (including Judaism, Islam, Buddhism, and Hinduism) collectively make up about 5 percent of the adult population. In keeping with the state's open-minded culture, Californians

are generally very tolerant of diverse religions.

S

Senior Travelers

Senior citizens (65 and older) are entitled to many benefits, including reduced rates on public transportation and for entrance to museums. Seniors who want to be students should contact Elderhostels (tel: 1-800-454-5768, www.roadscholar. org) for information on places that provide both accommodation and classes. The Bay Area has a number of Elderhostel locations.

Smoking

California's famed tolerance is not extended to smokers. State law bans smoking in bars, clubs, restaurants, within 25ft (7.5 meters) of playgrounds or sandboxes, and within 20ft (6 meters) of all public buildings.

In San Francisco, smoking is also prohibited in all city-owned parks, plazas, and public sports facilities. Even some public beaches in Southern California have made cigarettes illegal; look for signs on the sand to see if you can light up. You may find it difficult to reserve a smoking room in a hotel, so be sure to check at the time of booking, and be prepared to shop around.

Student Travelers

With a current school ID, a student traveler can take advantage of discounts at some museums, movie theaters, and public transportation. Check out colleges in the summer for dormitory accommodation.

T

Tax

Depending on which county you are in, the sales tax in California ranges from 7.25 to 9.5 percent (San Francisco enjoys the most expensive rate). This will be added to your bill at shops and restaurants. When calculating a tip at restaurants, calculate a tip on the pre-tax total.

In most California cities, there is a hotel room tax of anywhere from 8 to

Students at the University of California, Berkeley.

14 percent (with both San Francisco and Los Angeles at the 14 percent mark).

Telephones

Telephones: with the growing popularity of cell phones, coin-operated telephones are not as common as before, but can usually be found in hotels, gas stations, and often in lighted booths on street corners.

Local US phone numbers are seven-digit numbers. When you're placing a long-distance call, you must first dial "1" and then the three-digit area code of the place you are calling, and then the seven-digit local number. Make use of toll-free numbers when possible (toll-free telephone numbers within the US are indicated by 1-800, 855, 866, 877 or 888). When making personal calls, take advantage of lower long-distance rates after 7pm on weekdays and during weekends. Helpful dialing information:
US calls outside your area code: Dial 1 + area code + local number.
International Calls: Dial 011 + country code + number.
Directly inquiries: Dial 411 for information assistance, which can provide telephone listings.
Operator: If you are having problems, dial "0" for assistance with local calls; or 00 for international calls.
Cell phones: To use your GSM cellular phone in the US, contact your service provider before you leave to set up international roaming. Depending on the length of your stay, it may be cheaper to buy a US-issue phone or SIM card.
Fax machines: Although email and cell phones have replaced the need for many faxes, machines can be found in most hotels and motels, and at FedEx Office locations.

Time Zone

California is on Pacific Standard Time (PST), which is two hours earlier than Chicago, three hours earlier than New York and eight hours earlier than Greenwich Mean Time. During Daylight Savings time, which occurs from the second Sunday of March to the first Sunday of November, the clocks are rolled forward one hour and PST becomes only seven hours earlier than GMT.

Tipping

Just as in other parts of the country, service personnel in California rely on tips for a large part of their income. In most cases, 18–20 percent is the going rate for waiters and bartenders and 10–15 percent for taxi drivers. The accepted rate for baggage handlers at airports and

hotels is around $1 per bag. The rule of thumb is to leave a minimum tip of one or two dollars per night stayed in the room for housekeeping staff. A doorman expects to be tipped at least $1 for unloading your car or for other services.

Tourist Information

General information on visiting the Golden State is available from:
California Tourism,
PO Box 1499, Sacramento, CA 95812
Tel: 1-800-862-2543
www.visitcalifornia.com
Anaheim/Orange County Visitor and Convention Bureau
800 W. Katella Ave, Anaheim
Tel: 855-405-5020
www.anaheimoc.org
Berkeley Convention and Visitors Bureau
2015 Center St, Berkeley
Tel: 510-549-7040
www.visitberkeley.com
Beverly Hills Conference and Visitors Bureau
239 South Beverly Drive, Beverly Hills
Tel: 310-248-1015, 1-800-345-2210
www.beverlyhillsbehere.com
Buena Park Convention and Visitors Office
6601 Beach Blvd, Suite 200, Buena Park
Tel: 714-542-3953
www.visitbuenapark.com
Catalina Island Chamber of Commerce
1 Green Pier, Avalon
Tel: 310-510-1520
www.catalinachamber.com
Hollywood Visitor Information Center
6801 Hollywood Blvd at Hollywood and Highland
Tel: 323-467-6412
www.discoverlosangeles.com

San Francisco Convention and Visitors' Bureau.

Lake Tahoe Incline Village and
Crystal Bay Visitors' Bureau,
969 Tahoe Blvd, Incline Village, NV
89451
Tel: 1-800-468-2463
www.gotahoenorth.com

South Lake Tahoe Visitors Center
3066 Lake Tahoe Blvd, South Lake
Tahoe
Tel: 530-541-5255
www.tahoesouth.com

Long Beach Area Convention and
Visitors Bureau
301 East Ocean Blvd #1900, Long
Beach
Tel: 562-436-3645
www.visitlongbeach.com

Los Angeles Area Chamber of
Commerce,
350 South Bixel
Tel: 213-580-1462
www.lachamber.org

Los Angeles Convention and
Visitors Bureau
333 S. Hope Street
Tel: 213-624-7300
www.discoverlosangeles.com

Monterey County Convention and
Visitors' Bureau
765 Wave St, Monterey
Tel: 831-657-6400
www.seemonterey.com

Napa Valley Conference and
Visitors' Bureau
1310 Napa Town Center
Tel: 707-226-7459
www.napavalley.com

Palm Springs Desert Resort
Communities Convention and
Visitors Authority
70100 State Highway 111, #100,
Rancho Mirage
Tel: 760-770-9000, 1-800-967-9001
www.palmspringsusa.com

Sacramento Convention and
Visitors' Bureau
1608 I St, Sacramento
Tel: 1-800-292-2334
www.discovergold.org

San Diego International Visitor
Information Center
1140 West Broadway, San Diego
Tel: 619-236-1212
www.sandiego.com

San Francisco Convention and
Visitors' Bureau
900 Market St, San Francisco
Tel: 415-391-2000
www.sanfrancisco.travel

San Jose Convention and Visitors'
Bureau
408 Almaden Blvd, San Jose
Tel: 408-295-9600
www.sanjose.org

San Luis Obispo County Visitor and
Conference Bureau
811 E1 Capitan Way, Suite 200, San
Luis Obispo

Tel: 805-541-8000
www.sanluisobispocounty.com

Santa Barbara Conference and
Visitors Bureau
1601 Anacapa St, Santa Barbara
Tel: 805-966-9222,
www.santabarbaraca.com

Santa Cruz County Conference and
Visitors Council
303 Walter St, Santa Cruz
Tel: 831-425-1234
www.santacruzca.org

Sonoma County Tourism Bureau
3637 Westwind Blvd. Santa Rosa
Tel: 707-522-5800
www.sonomacounty.com

Sonoma Valley Vistors' Bureau
453 First St East, Sonoma
Tel: 707-996-1090
www.sonomavalley.com

Ventura Visitors and Convention
Bureau
101 South California St, Ventura
Tel: 805-648-2075
www.ventura-usa.com

Yosemite and Sierra Visitors' Bureau
40637 State Highway 41, Oakhurst
Tel: 559-683-4636
www.yosemitethisyear.com

U

Useful Addresses

California has 20 Welcome Centers
situated throughout the state to assist
visitors. The centers provide maps,
brochures, and helpful on-the-spot
advice. For more information and
precise driving directions, go to: www.
VisitCWC.com

Alpine, 5005 Willows Rd Ste 110. Tel:
619-445-0180.
Anderson (Shasta Cascade), 1699
Highway 273, south of Redding on I-5.
Tel: 530-365-1180.
Arcata (North Coast), 1635 Heindon
Rd. Tel: 707-822-3619.
Auburn (Gold Country), 13411
Lincoln Way. Tel: 530-887-2111.
Barstow (Deserts), 2796 Tanger
Way, Suite 100. Tel: 760-253-4782.
Buena Park, 6601 Beach Blvd. Tel:
1-800-541-3953.
El Dorado Hills, 2085 Vine St Ste
105. Tel: 916-358-3700.
Mammoth Lakes, 2510 Highway
203/Main Street. Tel: 760-924-5500.
Merced (Central Valley), 710 W.
16th St, Suite A. Tel: 209-384-2791.
Oceanside (San Diego), 928 North
Coast Highway. Tel: 760-721-1101.
Oxnard (Central Coast), 1000
Town Center Dr., Suite 135.
Tel: 805-385-7545.

Pismo Beach (Central Coast), 333
Five Cities Drive, Suite 100, in the
Prime Outlets. Tel: 805-773-7924.
Salinas, 1213 N Davis Rd. Tel: 831-
757-8687.
San Bernardino, 159 Hospitality
Lane. Tel: 1-800-867-8366.
San Francisco, Pier 39, Building P.
Tel: 415-981-1280.
San Mateo, 60 31st Ave Ste 161.
Tel: 650-578-8033.
Santa Rosa (North Coast), 9 Fourth
St, Downtown. Tel: 1-800-404-7673.
Truckee, 10065 Donner Pass Rd.
Tel: 530-587-2757.
Tulare, 4500 S Laspina St.
Tel: 559-688-6894.
Yucca Valley (Deserts), 56711
Twentynine Palms Highway.
Tel: 760-365-5464.

V

Visas and Passports

Foreign travelers to the US must
have a passport, and, depending
on where they are arriving from,
a visa or a health record. However,
in an effort to attract more tourists,
the US initiated the Visa Waiver
Program (VWP) for those coming
on vacation for a maximum of 90
days. With several dozen countries
participating, the program allows
travelers to enter the US with
only a machine-readable
passport.

The terrorist attacks of
September 11, 2001 have
caused an increase in security
measures taken by the Department
of Homeland Security. It now requires
all VWP participants to apply with
the Electronic System for Travel
Authorization (ESTA). Done online,
authorization does not take much
time and can be done at any time
before entry into the US; try to apply
as early as possible to minimize
complications.

To check your eligibility for
the Visa Waiver Program, and for
complete and up-to-date travel entry
requirements, visit the US State
Department website, http://travel.
state.gov/visa.

If a visitor loses their visa while
in the country, a new one may be
obtained from the embassy of the
visitor's home country. Extensions are
granted by various service centers
of the Bureau of Citizenship and
Immigration Services (tel: 1-800 870-
3676; www.uscis.gov).

TRANSPORTATION

ACCOMMODATIONS

EATING OUT

ACTIVITIES

A – Z

FURTHER READING

General

Back Roads to the California Coast: Scenic Byways and Highways to the Edge of the Golden State, by Earl Thollander and Herb McGrew. A guide for meandering through the state on 15 scenic back-road drives.

Cruel Justice: Three Strikes and the Politics of Crime in America's Golden State, by Joe Domanick. A deep look at how the "three strikes" law came to be, and its wide-ranging impact.

A Guide to Architecture in Los Angeles and Southern California, by Gebhard and Winter. Considered a must-have guide to Los Angeles architecture by scholars and enthusiasts alike.

Los Angeles A–Z: An Encyclopedia of City & Country, by Dale & Leonard Pitt. A one-volume encyclopedia packed with information on everything from native trees and who the Black Dahlia was to Engine House #18 and O.J. Simpson.

My California: Journeys by Great Writers. Several dozen great writers – including Pico Iyer, Michael Chabon, and Thomas Steinbeck – share stories to benefit the California Arts Council.

Tales of the City, by Armistead Maupin. Originally a serial in the San Francisco Chronicle, Maupin's novel stitches together the lives of residents of the fictitious Barbary Lane, told with delightful candor.

A Very Good Year: The Journey of a California Wine from Vine to Table, by Mike Weiss. Award-winning journalist spent nearly two years with a Sonoma County winemaker to vividly chronicle all that goes into the process of winemaking.

People and Places

Baseball in San Diego: From Padres to Petco, by Bill Swank. A look at San Diego's love affair with the Padres, from 1936 to the present.

Hollywood Interrupted: Insanity Chic in Babylon – The Case Against Celebrity, by Andrew Breitbart and Mark Ebner. A journey into the entertainment industry's underbelly, complete with medications, meltdowns, and how the media plays along.

The Los Angeles Watts Towers, by Bud and Arloa Goldstone. How Simon Rodia's creation came into being, plus the history of the Watts neighborhood. The Mayor of Castro Street: The Life and Times of Harvey Milk, by Randy Shilts. Quintessential biography of the first openly gay man elected to office in America, from his triumphant election and ground-breaking championing of gay rights, to his tragic assassination and the subsequent rioting upon the sentence

Send Us Your Thoughts

We do our best to ensure the information in our books is as accurate and up-to-date as possible. The books are updated on a regular basis using local contacts, who painstakingly add, amend and correct as required. However, some details (such as telephone numbers and opening times) are liable to change, and we are ultimately reliant on our readers to put us in the picture.

We welcome your feedback, especially your experience of using the book "on the road". Maybe we recommended a hotel that you liked (or another that you didn't), or you came across a great bar or new attraction we missed.

We will acknowledge all contributions, and we'll offer an Insight Guide to the best letters received.

Please write to us at:
Insight Guides
PO Box 7910
London SE1 1WE
Or email us at:
insight@apaguide.co.uk

of his killer.

Movie Star Homes: The Famous to the Forgotten, by Judy Artunian. Nearly 400 entries on homes of celebrities, from Gloria Swanson to Buster Keaton.

Stairway Walks of San Francisco, by Adah Bakalinksky. A delightful guide to 27 urban hikes up and down some of the city's 350 stairways.

Geography and Natural History

California Wildlife Reviewing Guide, by Jeanne L. Clarke. Explores 150 of the state's top sites for wildlife viewing, including maps, access information, and nearly 100 color photos.

Day Hiker's Guide to California State Parks, by John Mckinney. Over 150 day hikes in California, from Lake Tahoe to Anza-Borrego.

Introduction to Air in California, by David Carle. Part natural history guide, part intriguing assessment of how humans have changed California's air.

History

Agrarian Dreams: The Paradox of Organic Farming in California, by Julie Guthman. Guthman casts doubt on the success of organic farming.

The California Gold Rush and the Coming of the Civil War, by Leonard L. Richards. An award-winning historian reveals how the Gold Rush in California spurred contention between Northern industrialists and slave-owning Southerners.

The Golden Game: The Story of California Baseball, by Kevin Nelson. From the 1850s to recent times, how California baseball came to be, and its impact.

The Times We Had: Life with William Randolph Hearst, by Marion Davies. The mistress of one of America's richest men, Davies chronicles the glittering life she led at Hearst Castle and in Los Angeles.

CREDITS

Aijohn784/Dreamstime.com 36/37T
Abraham Nowitz/Apa Publications 122, 336/337T, 339L
AF archive/Alamy 83, 87
AFP 98MR
Better Late Images/Alamy 58
Bigstock.com 34R, 148, 159, 172, 181, 209, 217B, 226, 281
Collective91/Dreamstime.com 240B
Corbis 43, 52, 53, 64, 177ML
CTTC 321B
Daniella Nowitz/Apa Publications 6ML, 8ML, 31T, 74, 115, 116, 117, 118, 123, 125, 127B, 127T, 128, 129, 134BR, 134/135T, 136/137, 340
David Dunai/Apa Publications 1, 2/3, 4/5, 6B, 6B, 7ML, 7BL, 7TL, 7B, 8BR, 9ML, 9BR, 10TR, 10BL, 10TL, 11, 12/13, 14/15, 16/17, 18, 19T, 19B, 20, 21, 22, 23, 24, 25, 26/27, 28/29, 30T, 31B, 35, 36L, 37BR, 37BL, 37TR, 65, 66/67, 68/69, 70/71, 72, 73, 76BL, 76MR, 76/77T, 76BR, 77BR, 77TR, 77BR, 78, 79, 80, 81, 88, 92R, 92L, 93, 94, 97, 100/101, 102/103, 104/105, 109T, 109B, 138, 139, 141B, 141T, 142, 143, 150/151, 152, 153, 155, 156B, 156T, 157, 158T, 158B, 161, 162/163, 164, 165, 166/167, 168T, 168B, 169B, 169T, 170T, 173, 174/175, 180, 182/183, 184, 185T, 186T, 186B, 187, 188/189, 190, 191, 193T, 193B, 194, 195T, 195B, 196, 197, 198B, 198T, 199B, 199T, 200T, 200B, 201, 202T, 202B, 203, 204/205, 206, 207, 217T, 220, 221, 222, 223B, 223T, 224, 225T, 225B, 227, 228/229, 230/231, 232/233, 234, 235ML, 235MR, 236, 237, 238T, 238B, 240T, 241, 242T, 242B, 244/245, 248, 249, 250, 251, 252, 253T, 253B, 254T, 254B, 255, 257B, 257T, 258, 259, 261, 262, 263, 264, 265B, 265T, 266, 267, 268/269B, 268/269T, 269BR, 270/271, 272, 273, 275, 276, 277B, 277T, 278/279, 279T, 279B, 280B, 280T, 283, 284/285, 286, 287, 288, 289B, 289T, 290B, 290T, 291, 292T, 292/293B, 293, 294B, 294T, 295, 299, 301, 302, 302/303B, 303T, 304B, 304T, 310, 314/315, 316, 317, 318, 319T, 319B, 320, 321T, 322T, 322B, 324/325, 326/327, 328/329, 330, 332T, 332B, 334, 336, 336/337M, 344, 345L, 346, 347L, 348T, 348B, 352, 353L, 354, 358T, 358B, 359L, 360, 362, 366T, 366B, 367L, 368/369, 370
Djschreiber/Dreamstime.com 177BR
Dreamstime 7TR, 9T, 96, 170/171B, 177BL, 282T, 282B, 305,
Elswarro/Dreamstime.com 41
Everett Collection Historical/Alamy 57
Getty 32/33, 33, 34L, 40, 63, 84, 86, 98B, 98/99T, 99ML, 99BR, 99TR, 269TR, 269ML
Harold Chapman/TopFoto 62R
iStockphoto 90, 149, 178/179, 210B, 268BL, 323, 376
Jandirkhansen/Dreamstime.com 185B
Library of Congress 44, 45, 46, 51, 56, 59, 135BL, 176MR
Lordprice Collection/Alamy 38
Martyn Goddard/Apa Publications 6MR, 6ML, 7MR, 91, 95, 210T, 211B,

211T, 212, 213, 214B, 214T, 215T, 215B, 216B, 216T, 218/219, 235BL, 296/297, 298, 308/309, 309, 311, 312B, 312T, 313, 338
Melastmohican/Dreamstime.com 36R
Michele Burgess/Alamy 99BL
Michele Wassell/Superstock 243
Moviestore collection Ltd/Alamy 82
National Archives and Records Administration 47
Niday Picture Library/Alamy 54
North Wind Picture Archives/Alamy 50
Photo The Print Collector/Heritage-Images/Scala, Florence. 177TR
Pictorial Press Ltd/Alamy 48, 85, 89
Public Domain 39
Rahurlburt | Dreamstime.com 176/177T
Richard Nowitz/Apa Publications 8BL, 8MR, 75, 108, 112, 113, 114B, 114T, 119, 120, 126, 130, 131, 132/133, 134BL, 135TR, 135ML, 145, 146, 147, 306, 306/307, 333L, 341L, 342, 349L, 371L, 372, 374B, 374T
San Francisco Public Library/San Francisco History Center 135BR
Sonoma Tourism Bureau 160/161
Steve Hamblin/Alamy 239
SuperStock 268MR
The Print Collector /Alamy 61
Topfoto 62L
Topham Picturepoint 60
Universal Images Group (Lake County Discovery Museum)/Alamy 55
UPPA/Photoshot All Rights Reserved 49
Wanderfoot | Dreamstime.com 176BR
Wikimedia Commons 42

Insight Guide Credits

Project Editor
Sian Lezard

Series Manager
Carine Tracanelli

Art Editor
Ian Spick

Map Production
Original cartography Phoenix Mapping, updated by Apa Cartography Department

Production
Tynan Dean, Linton Donaldson and Rebeka Ellam

Distribution
UK
Dorling Kindersley Ltd
A Penguin Group company
80 Strand, London, WC2R 0RL
customerservice@dk.com

United States
Ingram Publisher Services
1 Ingram Boulevard, PO Box 3006, La Vergne, TN 37086-1986
customer.service@ingrampublisherservices.com

Australia
Universal Publishers
PO Box 307
St Leonards NSW 1590
sales@universalpublishers.com.au

New Zealand
Brown Knows Publications
11 Artesia Close, Shamrock Park
Auckland, New Zealand 2016
sales@brownknows.co.nz

Worldwide
Apa Publications GmbH & Co.
Verlag KG (Singapore branch)
7030 Ang Mo Kio Avenue 5
08-65 Northstar @ AMK
Singapore 569880
apasin@singnet.com.sg

Printing
CTPS-China

© 2013 Apa Publications (UK) Ltd
All Rights Reserved

First Edition 1984
Eighth Edition 2013

www.insightguides.com

INDEX

Main references are in bold type

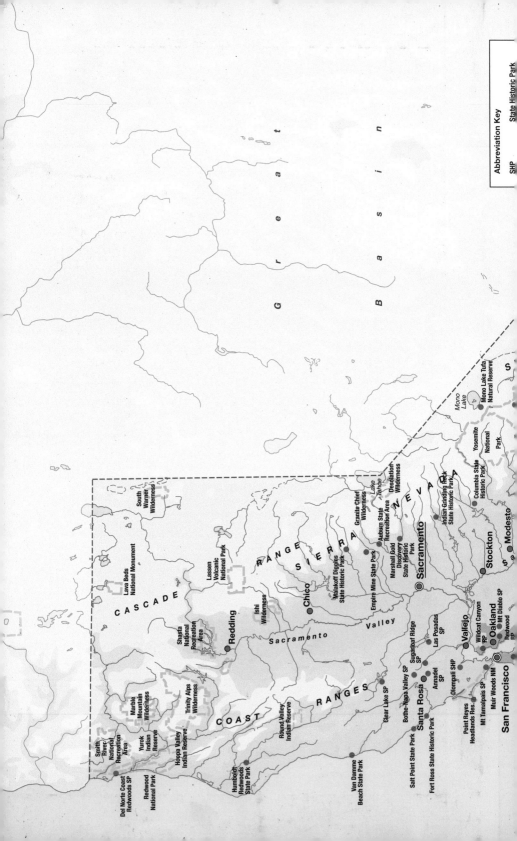

South Warner Wilderness

Lava Beds National Monument

CASCADE

Shasta National Recreation Area

Redding

Ishi Wilderness

Lassen Volcanic National Park

RANGE

SIERRA

Chico

Malakoff Diggins State Historic Park

Empire Mine State Park

Granite Chief Wilderness

Lake Tahoe

Desolation Wilderness

Auburn State Recreation Area

Marshall Gold Discovery State Historic Park

NEVADA

Sacramento

Indian Grinding Rock State Historic Park

Columbia State Historic Park

Yosemite National Park

Mono Lake

Mono Lake Tufa Natural Reserve

S

Stockton

Modesto

Sacramento

Valley

Marble Mountain Wilderness

Trinity Alps Wilderness

COAST

RANGES

Round Valley Indian Reserve

Clear Lake SP

Sugarloaf Ridge SP

Las Posadas SP

Mt Diablo SP

Wildcat Canyon RP

Vallejo

Oakland

Redwood RP

Bothe-Napa Valley SP

Santa Rosa

Annadel SP

Olompali SHP

San Francisco

Point Reyes Headlands Res.

Muir Woods NM

Mt Tamalpais SP

Smith River National Recreation Area

Yurok Indian Reserve

Hoopa Valley Indian Reserve

Del Norte Coast Redwoods SP

Redwood National Park

Humboldt Redwoods State Park

Van Damme Beach State Park

Salt Point State Park

Fort Ross State Historic Park

G   r   e   a   t

G   r   e   a   t   B   a   s   i   n